Charles S. Robinson

Songs for Christian Worship

in the chapel and family

Charles S. Robinson

Songs for Christian Worship
in the chapel and family

ISBN/EAN: 9783337291310

Printed in Europe, USA, Canada, Australia, Japan

Cover: Foto ©Lupo / pixelio.de

More available books at **www.hansebooks.com**

Songs for Christian Worship

IN THE

CHAPEL AND FAMILY:

SELECTED FROM THE

"SONGS OF THE CHURCH."

By REV. C. S. ROBINSON,

EDITOR OF THE "SONGS FOR THE SANCTUARY,"
AND
PASTOR OF THE AMERICAN CHAPEL IN PARIS.

New York and Chicago:
A. S. BARNES & COMPANY.
1869.

Entered, according to Act of Congress, in the year 1869, by
A. S. BARNES & CO.,
In the Clerk's Office of the District Court of the United States for the Southern District of New York.

Electrotyped by SMITH & McDOUGAL, 82 & 84 Beekman Street.
Printed by GEORGE W. WOOD, 2 Dutch Street.

TABLE OF CONTENTS.

II.—PUBLIC WORSHIP: PAGE
  1. Opening of Service.. 1
  2. General Praise.. 13
  3. Close of Service... 28
III.—THE SCRIPTURES.. 32
IV.—GOD: Being, Attributes, Providence... 36
V.—JESUS CHRIST:
  1. Advent.. 46
  2. Life and Character.. 48
  3. Sufferings and Death.. 52
  4. Resurrection and Ascension.. 55
  5. Adoration... 56
VI.—HOLY SPIRIT: Adoration, Invocation... 64
VII.—WAY OF SALVATION:
  1. Lost State of Man... 70
  2. Atonement and Pardon.. 76
  3. Invitation and Warning.. 78
  4. Repentance and Reception of Christ.. 92
VIII.—CHRISTIAN:
  1. Conflict with Sin... 106
  2. Encouragements.. 124
  3. Love for the Saviour.. 126
  4. Graces.. 160
  5. Privileges.. 170
  6. Duties.. 176
  7. Afflictions... 182
IX.—THE CHURCH:
  1. Institutions.. 192
  2. Ordinances.. 195
  3. Progress and Missions... 206
  4. Sabbath School.. 218
  5. Social Meetings... 227
X.—DEATH AND JUDGMENT... 244
XI.—HEAVEN.. 262

PREFATORY REMARKS.

The increasing interest in Congregational Singing is creating a demand for a book adapted for use in small Christian assemblies, at a reduced price! In view of this fact, the Publishers here present the *first part* of the "Songs of the Church," embracing a sufficient number of Hymns and Tunes, for all practical purposes in the Chapel, Lecture-Room, Prayer-Meeting, or Social Circle. The character of this selection is attested by the very extensive introduction of the "Songs of the Sanctuary" (from which book most of these pieces are taken) into numerous Presbyterian and Congregational Churches throughout the country.

PUBLISHERS.

SONGS FOR CHRISTIAN WORSHIP
IN THE
CHAPEL AND FAMILY.

SABBATH. 7s. 6 lines.   Dr. L. Mason.

1. Safe-ly through an-oth-er week, God has brought us on our way; Let us now a blessing seek, Waiting in his courts to-day: Day of all the week the best, Emblem of e-ter-nal rest, Day of all the week the best, Emblem of e-ter-nal rest.

1.

2 While we seek supplies of grace,
Through the dear Redeemer's name,
Show thy reconciling face—
Take away our sin and shame;
From our worldly cares set free,—
May we rest this day in thee.

3 Here we come thy name to praise;
Let us feel thy presence near:
May thy glory meet our eyes,
While we in thy house appear:
Here afford us, Lord, a taste
Of our everlasting rest.

4 May the gospel's joyful sound
Wake our minds to raptures new;
Let thy victories abound,—
Unrepenting souls subdue:
Thus let all our Sabbaths prove,
Till we rest in thee above.

PUBLIC WORSHIP.

SPOHR. L. M. *Arranged from Spohr.*

1. Thine earthly Sabbaths, Lord! we love; But there's a no - bler rest a - bove! To that our long-ing souls as - pire, With cheer-ful hope and strong de-sire.

2.

2 No more fatigue, no more distress,
Nor sin, nor death, shall reach the place;
No groans shall mingle with the songs
That warble from immortal tongues.

3 No rude alarms of raging foes;
No cares to break the long repose;
No midnight shade; no clouded sun;
But sacred, high, eternal noon.

4 Soon shall that glorious day begin,
Beyond this world of death and sin:—
Soon shall our voices join the song
Of the triumphant, holy throng.

3.

1 Another day has passed along,
And we are nearer to the tomb,
Nearer to join the heavenly song,
Or hear the last eternal doom.

2 Sweet is the light of Sabbath eve,
And soft the sunbeams lingering there;
For these blest hours, the world I leave,
Wafted on wings of faith and prayer.

3 The time how lovely and how still!
Peace shines and smiles on all below;
The plain, the stream, the wood, the hill,
All fair with evening's setting glow.

4 Season of rest! the tranquil soul
Feels the sweet calm, and melts to love—
And while these sacred moments roll,
Faith sees the smiling heaven above.

5 Nor will our days of toil be long.
Our pilgrimage will soon be trod;
And we shall join the ceaseless song—
The endless Sabbath of our God.

4.

1 My opening eyes with rapture see
The dawn of thy returning day;
My thoughts, O God, ascend to thee,
While thus my early vows I pay.

2 Oh, bid this trifling world retire,
And drive each earthly thought away;
Nor let me feel one vain desire—
One sinful thought through all the day.

3 Then, to thy courts when I repair,
My soul shall rise on joyful wing,
The wonders of thy love declare,
And join the strains which angels sing.

5.

1 Come, gracious Lord, descend and dwell,
By faith and love, in every breast;
Then shall we know, and taste, and feel
The joys that cannot be expressed.

2 Come, fill our hearts with inward strength,
Make our enlarged souls possess,
And learn the height, and breadth, and length
Of thine eternal love and grace.

3 Now to the God whose power can do
More than our thoughts and wishes know,
Be everlasting honors done,
By all the church, through Christ, his Son.

OPENING OF SERVICE.

MIGDOL. L. M.   Dr. L. Mason.

1. Sweet is the work, my God, my King, To praise thy name, give thanks, and sing, To show thy love by morning light, And talk of all thy truth at night.

6.

2 Sweet is the day of sacred rest;
No mortal care shall seize my breast;
Oh! may my heart in tune be found,
Like David's harp of solemn sound!

3 My heart shall triumph in my Lord,
And bless his works and bless his word;
Thy works of grace, how bright they shine!
How deep thy counsels! how divine!

4 Lord, I shall share a glorious part,
When grace hath well refined my heart,
And fresh supplies of joy are shed,
Like holy oil to cheer my head.

5 Then shall I see, and hear, and know
All I desired or wished below;
And every power find sweet employ,
In that eternal world of joy.

7.

1 How pleasant, how divinely fair,
O Lord of hosts, thy dwellings are!
With long desire my spirit faints,
To meet th' assemblies of thy saints.

2 My flesh would rest in thine abode,
My panting heart cries out for God;
My God, my King, why should I be
So far from all my joys and thee?

3 Blest are the saints who sit on high
Around thy throne of majesty;
Thy brightest glories shine above,
And all their work is praise and love.

4 Blest are the souls that find a place
Within the temple of thy grace;
There they behold thy gentler rays,
And seek thy face, and learn thy praise.

5 Blest are the men whose hearts are set
To find the way to Zion's gate;
God is their strength, and through the road
They lean upon their helper, God.

6 Cheerful they walk with growing strength,
Till all shall meet in heaven at length;
Till all before thy face appear,
And join in nobler worship there.

8.

1 Another six days' work is done,
Another Sabbath is begun;
Return, my soul! enjoy thy rest,
Improve the day thy God has blessed.

2 Oh! that our thoughts and thanks may rise,
As grateful incense to the skies;
And draw, from heaven, that sweet repose,
Which none, but he that feels it, knows.

3 This heavenly calm, within the breast,
Is the dear pledge of glorious rest,
Which for the church of God remains—
The end of cares, the end of pains.

4 In holy duties, let the day,
In holy pleasures, pass away;
How sweet a Sabbath thus to spend,
In hope of one that ne'er shall end.

PUBLIC WORSHIP.

MARLOW. C. M.   *Arranged by* Dr. L. Mason.

1. This is the day the Lord hath made; He calls the hours his own:
Let heaven re-joice, let earth be glad, And praise sur-round the throne.

9.

2 To-day he rose, and left the dead,
  And Satan's empire fell;
To-day the saints his triumph spread,
  And all his wonders tell.

3 Hosanna to th' anointed King,
  To David's holy Son:
Help us, O Lord! descend, and bring
  Salvation from thy throne.

4 Blest be the Lord who comes to men
  With messages of grace:
Who comes, in God his Father's name,
  To save our sinful race.

5 Hosanna in the highest strains
  The church on earth can raise;
The highest heavens, in which he reigns,
  Shall give him nobler praise.

10.

1 Blest morning! whose young dawning rays
  Beheld our rising God;
That saw him triumph o'er the dust,
  And leave his dark abode.

2 In the cold prison of a tomb
  The great Redeemer lay,
Till the revolving skies had brought
  The third, th' appointed day.

3 Hell and the grave combined their force
  To hold our God, in vain;
The sleeping conqueror arose,
  And burst their feeble chain.

4 To thy great name, almighty Lord,
  These sacred hours we pay,
And loud hosannas shall proclaim
  The triumph of the day.

5 Salvation and immortal praise
  To our victorious King!
Let heaven and earth, and rocks and seas,
  With glad hosannas ring.

11.

1 Early, my God, without delay,
  I haste to seek thy face;
My thirsty spirit faints away,
  Without thy cheering grace.

2 I've seen thy glory and thy power
  Through all thy temple shine;
My God, repeat that heavenly hour,
  That vision so divine.

3 Not all the blessings of a feast
  Can please my soul so well,
As when thy richer grace I taste,
  And in thy presence dwell.

4 Not life itself, with all its joys,
  Can my best passions move,
Or raise so high my cheerful voice,
  As thy forgiving love.

5 Thus, till my last expiring day,
  I'll bless my God and King;
Thus will I lift my hands to pray,
  And tune my lips to sing.

OPENING OF SERVICE. 5

CHURCH. C. M.   J. P. HOLBROOK.

1. My soul, how love-ly is the place, To which thy God re-sorts! 'Tis heaven to see his smil-ing face, Though in his earth-ly courts.

2
2 There the great Monarch of the skies
   His saving power displays;
   And light breaks in upon our eyes,
   With kind and quickening rays.

3 With his rich gifts, the heavenly Dove
   Descends and fills the place;
   While Christ reveals his wondrous love,
   And sheds abroad his grace.

4 There, mighty God! thy words declare
   The secrets of thy will;
   And still we seek thy mercy there,
   And sing thy praises still.

3
1 FAR from the world, O Lord, I flee,
   From strife and tumult far;
   From scenes where Satan wages still
   His most successful war.

2 The calm retreat, the silent shade,
   With prayer and praise agree;
   And seem by thy sweet bounty made
   For those who follow thee.

3 There, if thy Spirit touch the soul,
   And grace her mean abode,
   Oh! with what peace, and joy, and love,
   She communes with her God.

4 There, like the nightingale, she pours
   Her solitary lays;
   Nor asks a witness of her song,
   Nor thirsts for human praise.

5 Author and Guardian of my life!
   Sweet source of light divine,
   And—all harmonious names in one—
   My Saviour, thou art mine!

6 What thanks I owe thee, and what love,
   A boundless, endless store—
   Shall echo through the realms above,
   When time shall be no more.

4
1 FREQUENT the day of God returns
   To shed its quickening beams;
   And yet how slow devotion burns;
   How languid are its flames!

2 Accept our faint attempts to love,
   Our frailties, Lord, forgive;
   We would be like thy saints above,
   And praise thee while we live.

3 Increase, O Lord, our faith and hope,
   And fit us to ascend
   Where the assembly ne'er breaks up,
   The Sabbath ne'er shall end;—

4 Where we shall breathe in heavenly air,
   With heavenly lustre shine,
   Before the throne of God appear,
   And feast on love divine;—

5 Where we, in high seraphic strains,
   Shall all our powers employ;
   Delighted range th' ethereal plains,
   And take our fill of joy.

PUBLIC WORSHIP.

WARWICK. C. M. *Stanley.*

1. A-rise, O King of grace! a-rise, And en-ter to thy rest;
Lo! thy church waits with long-ing eyes, Thus to be owned and blest.

15.

2 Enter, with all thy glorious train,
　Thy Spirit and thy word;
　All that the ark did once contain,
　Could no such grace afford.

3 Here, mighty God! accept our vows,
　Here let thy praise be spread;
　Bless the provisions of thy house,
　And fill thy poor with bread.

4 Here let the Son of David reign,
　Let God's Anointed shine;
　Justice and truth his court maintain,
　With love and power divine.

5 Here let him hold a lasting throne;
　And as his kingdom grows,
　Fresh honors shall adorn his crown,
　And shame confound his foes.

16.

1 With joy we hail the sacred day
　Which God hath called his own;
　With joy the summons we obey
　To worship at his throne.

2 Thy chosen temple, Lord, how fair!
　Where willing votaries throng
　To breathe the humble, fervent prayer,
　And pour the choral song.

3 Spirit of grace! Oh, deign to dwell
　Within thy church below;
　Make her in holiness excel,
　With pure devotion glow.

4 Let peace within her walls be found;
　Let all her sons unite,
　To spread with grateful zeal around
　Her clear and shining light.

5 Great God, we hail the sacred day
　Which thou hast called thine own;
　With joy the summons we obey
　To worship at thy throne.

17.

1 Lord, in the morning thou shalt hear
　My voice ascending high;
　To thee will I direct my prayer,
　To thee lift up mine eye.

2 Up to the hills where Christ is gone,
　To plead for all his saints,
　Presenting at his Father's throne
　Our songs and our complaints.

3 Thou art a God before whose sight
　The wicked shall not stand;
　Sinners shall ne'er be thy delight,
　Nor dwell at thy right hand.

4 But to thy house will I resort
　To taste thy mercies there;
　I will frequent thy holy court,
　And worship in thy fear.

5 Oh, may thy Spirit guide my feet
　In ways of righteousness!
　Make every path of duty straight,
　And plain before my face.

OPENING OF SERVICE.

COLMAN. C. M.   Geo. Kingsley.

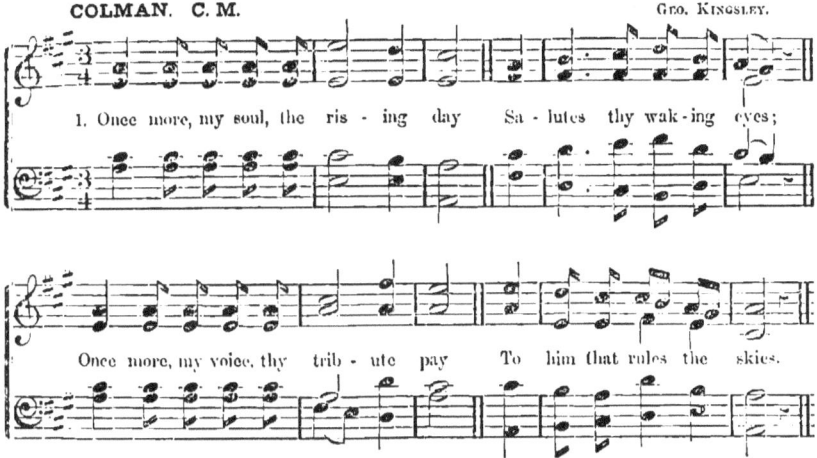

1. Once more, my soul, the rising day Salutes thy waking eyes;
Once more, my voice, thy tribute pay To him that rules the skies.

18.

1 Once more, my soul, the rising day
 Salutes thy waking eyes;
 Once more, my voice, thy tribute pay
 To him that rules the skies.
2 Night unto night his name repeats,
 The day renews the sound,
 Wide as the heaven on which he sits,
 To turn the seasons round.
3 'Tis he supports my mortal frame;
 My tongue shall speak his praise;
 My sins would rouse his wrath to flame,
 And yet his wrath delays.
4 Great God, let all my hours be thine,
 While I enjoy the light;
 Then shall my sun in smiles decline,
 And bring a pleasant night.

19.

1 How did my heart rejoice to hear
 My friends devoutly say:
 "In Zion let us all appear,
 And keep the solemn day."
2 I love her gates, I love the road;
 The church, adorned with grace,
 Stands like a palace built for God,
 To show his milder face.
3 Up to her courts, with joys unknown,
 The holy tribes repair;
 The Son of David holds his throne,
 And sits in judgment there.

4 He hears our praises and complaints;
 And, while his awful voice
 Divides the sinners from the saints,
 We tremble and rejoice.
5 Peace be within this sacred place,
 And joy a constant guest!
 With holy gifts and heavenly grace
 Be her attendants blest!
6 My soul shall pray for Zion still,
 While life or breath remains:
 There my best friends, my kindred dwell;
 There God, my Saviour, reigns.

20.

1 Come, ye that love the Saviour's name,
 And joy to make it known;
 The Sovereign of your hearts proclaim,
 And bow before his throne.
2 Behold your King, your Saviour, crowned
 With glories all divine;
 And tell the wondering nations round,
 How bright those glories shine.
3 When in his earthly courts we view
 The beauties of our King,
 We long to love as angels do,
 And with their voice to sing.
4 Oh, for the day—the glorious day!
 When heaven and earth shall raise
 With all their powers the raptured lay,
 To celebrate thy praise.

PUBLIC WORSHIP.

HYMN. C. M.   MODERN HARP.

1. Come, thou de-sire of all thy saints, Our hum-ble strains at-tend,
While, with our prais-es and com-plaints, Low at thy feet we bend.

21.

2 How should our songs, like those above,
   With warm devotion rise!
How should our souls, on wings of love,
   Mount upward to the skies!

3 O Lord, thy love alone can raise
   In us the heavenly flame;
Then shall our lips resound thy praise,
   Our hearts adore thy name.

4 Dear Saviour, let thy glory shine,
   And fill thy dwellings here,
Till life, and love, and joy divine
   A heaven on earth appear.

22.

1 BLEST day of God! most calm, most bright,
   The first and best of days;
The laborer's rest, the saint's delight,
   The day of prayer and praise.

2 My Saviour's face made thee to shine;
   His rising thee did raise;
And made thee heavenly and divine
   Beyond all other days.

3 The first-fruits oft a blessing prove
   To all the sheaves behind;
And they who do the Sabbath love,
   A happy week will find.

4 This day I must to God appear;
   For, Lord, the day is thine;
Help me to spend it in thy fear,
   And thus to make it mine.

23.

1 THE bird let loose in Eastern skies,
   Returning fondly home,
Ne'er stoops to earth her wing, nor flies
   Where idle warblers roam.

2 But high she shoots through air and light,
   Above all low delay,
Where nothing earthly bounds her flight,
   Nor shadow dims her way.

3 So grant me, Lord, from every snare
   Of sinful passion free,
Aloft through faith's serener air
   To hold my course to thee.

4 No sin to cloud, no lure to stay
   My soul, as home she springs;
Thy sunshine on her joyful way,
   Thy freedom in her wings.

24.

1 WEARIED with earthly toil and care,
   The day of rest how sweet!
To breathe the Sabbath's holy air,
   And sit at Jesus' feet.

2 Fain would I lay the burden down,
   That wounds me with its weight,
To gaze awhile at yonder crown,
   And press toward heaven's gate.

3 I ask a foretaste of the peace,
   The rest, the joy, the love,
Which, when their earthly Sabbaths cease,
   Await the saints above.

OPENING OF SERVICE.

BEMERTON. C. M. — Greatorex Coll.

1. Lord, when we bend be-fore thy throne, And our con-fes-sions pour, Oh, may we feel the sins we own, And late what we de-plore.

25.

2 Our contrite spirits pitying see;
  True penitence impart;
  And let a healing ray from thee
  Beam hope on every heart.

3 When we disclose our wants in prayer,
  May we our wills resign;
  Nor let a thought our bosom share,
  Which is not wholly thine.

4 Let faith each meek petition fill,
  And waft it to the skies;
  And teach our hearts 'tis goodness still
  That grants it or denies.

26.

1 SPIRIT of truth! on this thy day,
  To thee for help we cry,
  To guide us through the dreary way
  Of dark mortality.

2 We ask not, Lord, the cloven flame,
  Or tongues of various tone;
  But long thy praises to proclaim
  With fervor in our own.

3 No heavenly harpings soothe our ear,
  No mystic dreams we share;
  Yet hope to feel thy comfort near,
  And bless thee in our prayer.

4 When tongues shall cease, and power decay,
  And knowledge empty prove,
  Do thou thy trembling servants stay,
  With faith, and hope, and love.

27.

1 GOD of the sun-light hours, how sad
  Would evening shadows be,
  Or night, in deeper sable clad,—
  If aught were dark to thee!

2 How mournfully that golden gleam
  Would touch the thoughtful heart,
  If, with its soft, retiring beam,
  We saw thy love depart.

3 But, tho' the gathering gloom may hide
  Those gentle rays awhile,
  Yet they who in thy house abide,
  Shall ever share thy smile.

4 Then let creation's volume close
  Though every page be bright;
  On thine, still open, we repose
  With more intense delight.

28.

1 O GOD! by whom the seed is given,
  By whom the harvest blessed;
  Whose word, like manna showered from heaven,
  Is planted in our breast,—

2 Preserve it from the passing feet,
  And plunderers of the air,
  The sultry sun's intenser heat,
  And thorns of worldly care.

3 Though buried deep, or thinly strown,
  Do thou thy grace supply;
  The hope in earthly furrows sown,
  Shall ripen in the sky.

PUBLIC WORSHIP.

ST. THOMAS. S. M. — Williams.

1. Come, we who love the Lord! And let our joys be known: Join in a song of sweet ac-cord, And thus sur-round the throne.

29.

1 Come, we who love the Lord,
   And let our joys be known;
Join in a song of sweet accord,
   And thus surround the throne.

2 Let those refuse to sing
   Who never knew our God;
But children of the heavenly King
   May speak their joys abroad.

3 The men of grace have found
   Glory begun below;
Celestial fruits on earthly ground
   From faith and hope may grow.

4 The hill of Zion yields
   A thousand sacred sweets
Before we reach the heavenly fields
   Or walk the golden streets.

5 Then let our songs abound,
   And every tear be dry;
We're marching thro' Immanuel's ground
   To fairer worlds on high.

30.

1 Welcome, sweet day of rest,
   That saw the Lord arise!
Welcome to this reviving breast,
   And these rejoicing eyes!

2 The King himself comes near,
   And feasts his saints to-day;
Here may we sit, and see him here,
   And love, and praise, and pray.

3 One day, amid the place
   Where my dear Lord hath been,
Is sweeter than ten thousand days
   Within the tents of sin.

4 My willing soul would stay
   In such a frame as this,
And sit and sing herself away
   To everlasting bliss.

31.

1 Awake, and sing the song
   Of Moses and the Lamb;
Wake, every heart and every tongue
   To praise the Saviour's name.

2 Sing of his dying love;
   Sing of his rising power;
Sing—how he intercedes above
   For those whose sins he bore.

3 Ye pilgrims! on the road
   To Zion's city, sing!
Rejoice ye in the Lamb of God,—
   In Christ, th' eternal King.

4 Soon shall we hear him say,—
   "Ye blessed children! come;"
Soon will he call us hence away,
   And take his wanderers home.

5 There shall each raptured tongue
   His endless praise proclaim;
And sweeter voices tune the song
   Of Moses and the Lamb.

OPENING OF SERVICE.   11

WRIGHT. S. M.   J. P. HOLBROOK.

1. Sweet is the work, O Lord, Thy glorious name to sing;
To praise and pray— to hear thy word, And grateful offerings bring.

32.

2 Sweet, at the dawning light,
  Thy boundless love to tell;
And when approach the shades of night,
  Still on the theme to dwell.

3 Sweet, on this day of rest,
  To join, in heart and voice,
With those who love and serve thee best,
  And in thy name rejoice.

4 To songs of praise and joy
  Be every Sabbath given,
That such may be our blest employ
  Eternally in heaven.

33.

1 BEHOLD, the morning sun
  Begins his glorious way;
His beams through all the nations run,
  And light and life convey.

2 But where the Gospel comes,
  It spreads diviner light;
It calls dead sinners from their tombs,
  And gives the blind their sight.

3 How perfect is thy word!
  And all thy judgments just!
Forever sure thy promise, Lord,
  And we securely trust.

4 My gracious God, how plain
  Are thy directions given!
Oh, may I never read in vain,
  But find the path to heaven.

34.

1 O THOU above all praise,
  Above all blessing high,
Who would not fear thy holy name,
  And laud, and magnify!

2 Oh, for the living flame
  From thine own altar brought,
To touch our lips, our souls inspire,
  And wing to heaven our thought!

3 God is our strength and song,
  And his salvation ours;
Then be his love in Christ proclaimed
  With all our ransomed powers.

35.

1 How charming is the place
  Where my Redeemer, God,
Unvails the beauty of his face,
  And sheds his love abroad!

2 Not the fair palaces,
  To which the great resort,
Are once to be compared with this,
  Where Jesus holds his court.

3 Here, on the mercy-seat,
  With radiant glory crowned,
Our joyful eyes behold him sit
  And smile on all around.

4 Give me, O Lord, a place
  Within thy blest abode,
Among the children of thy grace,
  The servants of my God.

PUBLIC WORSHIP.

LISCHER. H. M.　　Arranged by Dr. L. Mason.

{ To God the Father's throne Your highest honors raise; }
{ Glo-ry to God the Son; To God the Spirit praise; } With all our powers, E-ter-nal King,
Thy name we sing, While faith adores—Thy name we sing, While faith a - dores.
Thy name we sing, While faith a - dores.

36.

1 Welcome, delightful morn,
　　Thou day of sacred rest!
　I hail thy kind return ;—
　　Lord, make these moments blest:
From the low train | I soar to reach
Of mortal toys, | Immortal joys.

2 Now may the King descend
　　And fill his throne of grace ;
　Thy sceptre, Lord, extend,
　　While saints address thy face :
Let sinners feel | And learn to know
Thy quickening word, | And fear the Lord.

3 Descend, celestial Dove,
　　With all thy quickening powers ;
　Disclose a Saviour's love,
　　And bless the sacred hours :
Then shall my soul | Nor Sabbaths be
New life obtain, | Enjoyed in vain.

37.

1 Awake, ye saints, awake !
　　And hail this sacred day ;
　In loftiest songs of praise
　　Your joyful homage pay :
Come bless the day that God hath blest,
The type of heaven's eternal rest.

2 On this auspicious morn
　　The Lord of life arose ;
　He burst the bars of death,
　　And vanquished all our foes ;
And now he pleads our cause above,
And reaps the fruit of all his love.

3 All hail, triumphant Lord !
　　Heaven with hosannas rings,
　And earth in humbler strains
　　Thy praise responsive sings :
Worthy the Lamb that once was slain,
Through endless years to live and reign !

38.

1 Upward I lift mine eyes,
　　From God is all my aid ;
　The God who built the skies,
　　And earth and nature made :
God is the tower | His grace is nigh
To which I fly; | In every hour.

2 My feet shall never slide,
　　Nor fall in fatal snares,
　Since God, my guard and guide,
　　Defends me from my fears :
Those wakeful eyes | Shall Israel keep
That never sleep, | When dangers rise.

3 No burning heats by day,
　　Nor blasts of evening air,
　Shall take my health away,
　　If God be with me there :
Thou art my sun, | To guard my head
And thou my shade, | By night or noon.

4 Hast thou not given thy word
　　To save my soul from death ?
　And I can trust my Lord
　　To keep my mortal breath :
I'll go and come, | Till from on high
Nor fear to die, | Thou call me home.

GENERAL PRAISE.   13

WARE. L. M. — KINGSLEY.

1. God of my life! thro' all my days, I'll tune the grateful notes of praise; The song shall wake with opening light, And warble to the silent night.

39.

2 When anxious cares would break my rest,
And griefs would tear my throbbing breast,
The notes of praise ascending high,
Shall check the murmur and the sigh.

3 When death o'er nature shall prevail,
And all the powers of language fail,
Joy thro' my swimming eyes shall break,
And mean the thanks I cannot speak.

4 But oh! when that last conflict's o'er,
And I am chained to earth no more,—
With what glad accents shall I rise
To join the music of the skies!

5 Then shall I learn th' exalted strains,
That echo through the heavenly plains,
And emulate, with joy unknown,
The glowing seraphs round thy throne.

40.

1 High in the heavens, eternal God!
Thy goodness in full glory shines;
Thy truth shall break through every cloud
That vails and darkens thy designs.

2 Forever firm thy justice stands,
As mountains their foundations keep:
Wise are the wonders of thy hands;
Thy judgments are a mighty deep.

3 My God, how excellent thy grace!
Whence all our hope and comfort springs;
The sons of Adam, in distress,
Fly to the shadow of thy wings.

4 From the provisions of thy house
We shall be fed with sweet repast;
There, mercy like a river flows,
And brings salvation to our taste.

5 Life, like a fountain rich and free,
Springs from the presence of my Lord;
And in thy light our souls shall see
The glories promised in thy word.

41.

1 Lord God of Hosts, by all adored!
Thy name we praise with one accord;
The earth and heavens are full of thee,
Thy light, thy love, thy majesty.

2 Loud hallelujahs to thy name
Angels and seraphim proclaim;
Eternal praise to thee is given
By all the powers and thrones in heaven.

3 Th' apostles join the glorious throng,
The prophets aid to swell the song,
The noble and triumphant host
Of martyrs make of thee their boast.

4 The holy church in every place
Throughout the world exalts thy praise;
Both heaven and earth do worship thee,
Thou Father of eternity!

5 From day to day, O Lord, do we
Highly exalt and honor thee;
Thy name we worship and adore,
World without end, forevermore.

PUBLIC WORSHIP.

OLD HUNDRED. L. M.

1. Be-fore Je-ho-vah's aw-ful throne, Ye na-tions, bow with sa-cred joy;
Know that the Lord is God a-lone, He can cre-ate, and he de-stroy.

42.

2 His sovereign power, without our aid,
Made us of clay, and formed us men;
And when, like wandering sheep, we strayed,
He brought us to his fold again.

3 We are his people, we his care,
Our souls, and all our mortal frame :
What lasting honors shall we rear,
Almighty Maker, to thy name!

4 We'll crowd thy gates with thankful songs;
High as the heavens our voices raise ;
And earth, with her ten thousand tongues,
Shall fill thy courts with sounding praise.

5 Wide as the world is thy command,
Vast as eternity thy love ;
Firm as a rock thy truth must stand,
When rolling years shall cease to move.

43.

1 Jehovah reigns; his throne is high ;
His robes are light and majesty ;
His glory shines with beams so bright,
No mortal can sustain the sight.

2 His terrors keep the world in awe;
His justice guards his holy law ;
Yet love reveals a smiling face ;
And truth and promise seal the grace.

3 Through all his works his wisdom shines,
And baffles Satan's deep designs;
His power is sovereign to fulfill
The noblest counsels of his will.

4 And will this glorious Lord descend
To be my Father and my Friend ?
Then let my songs with angels join ;
Heaven is secure, if God be mine.

44.

1 From all that dwell below the skies,
Let the Creator's praise arise :
Let the Redeemer's name be sung,
Through every land, by every tongue.

2 Eternal are thy mercies, Lord !
Eternal truth attends thy word :
Thy praise shall sound from shore to shore,
Till suns shall rise and set no more.

45.

1 All people that on earth do dwell,
Sing to the Lord with cheerful voice ;
Him serve with fear, his praise forth tell,
Come ye before him and rejoice.

2 The Lord, ye know, is God indeed,
Without our aid he did us make ;
We are his flock, he doth us feed,
And for his sheep he doth us take.

3 Oh, enter, then, his gates with praise;
Approach with joy his courts unto;
Praise, laud, and bless his name always,
For it is seemly so to do.

4 For why ? the Lord our God is good,
His mercy is for ever sure ;
His truth at all times firmly stood,
And shall from age to age endure.

GENERAL PRAISE. 15

LONG. L. M. — J. P. Holbrook.

1. Loud hallelujahs to the Lord, From distant worlds where creatures dwell! Let heaven begin the solemn word, And sound it dreadful down to hell, And sound it dreadful down to hell.

46.

1 LORD hallelujahs to the Lord,
From distant worlds where creatures dwell!
Let heaven begin the solemn word,
And sound it dreadful down to hell.

2 Wide as his vast dominion lies,
Make the Creator's name be known;
Loud as his thunder shout his praise,
And sound it lofty as his throne.

3 Jehovah—'t is a glorious word!
Oh, may it dwell on every tongue;
But saints who best have known the Lord,
Are bound to raise the noblest song.

4 Speak of the wonders of that love
Which Gabriel plays on every chord:
From all below, and all above,
Loud hallelujahs to the Lord!

47.

1 WHAT equal honors shall we bring
To thee, O Lord our God, the Lamb,
When all the notes that angels sing
Are far inferior to thy name?

2 Worthy is he who once was slain,
The Prince of Peace, who groaned and died;
Worthy to rise, and live, and reign
At his almighty Father's side.

3 Blessings forever on the Lamb,
Who bore the curse for wretched men:
Let angels sound his sacred name,
And every creature say, Amen!

48.

1 WITH glory clad, with strength arrayed,
The Lord, that o'er all nature reigns,
The world's foundation strongly laid,
And the vast fabric still sustains.

2 How sure established is thy throne!
Which shall no change or period see;
For thou, O Lord, and thou alone,
Art God from all eternity.

3 The floods, O Lord, lift up their voice,
And toss the troubled waves on high;
But God above can still their noise,
And make the angry sea comply.

49.

1 GIVE to the Lord, ye sons of fame,
Give to the Lord renown and power;
Ascribe due honors to his name,
And his eternal might adore.

2 The Lord proclaims his power aloud,
O'er all the ocean and the land;
His voice divides the watery cloud,
And lightnings blaze at his command.

3 The Lord sits Sovereign on the flood;
The Thunderer reigns forever King;
But makes his church his blest abode,
Where we his awful glories sing.

4 In gentler language, there the Lord
The counsels of his grace imparts:
Amid the raging storm, his word
Speaks peace and courage to our hearts.

PUBLIC WORSHIP.

EVENING HYMN. L. M. Th. Tallis.

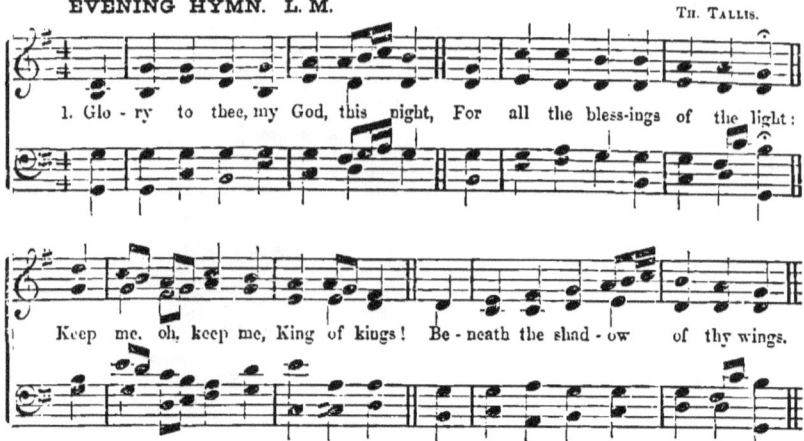

1. Glo - ry to thee, my God, this night, For all the bless-ings of the light: Keep me, oh, keep me, King of kings! Be - neath the shad - ow of thy wings.

50.

1 Glory to thee, my God, this night,
For all the blessings of the light:
Keep me, oh, keep me, King of kings!
Beneath the shadow of thy wings.

2 Forgive me, Lord! through thy dear Son,
The ill which I this day have done;
That with the world, myself, and thee,
I, ere I sleep, at peace may be.

3 Teach me to live, that I may dread
The grave as little as my bed;
Teach me to die, that so I may
Rise glorious at thy judgment day.

4 Be thou my guardian while I sleep,
Thy watchful station near me keep;
My heart with love celestial fill,
And guard me from th' approach of ill.

5 Lord, let my soul forever share
The bliss of thy paternal care!
'Tis heaven on earth, 't is heaven above,
To see thy face, and sing thy love.

6 Praise God, from whom all blessings flow;
Praise him, all creatures here below;
Praise him above, ye heavenly host;
Praise Father, Son, and Holy Ghost!

51.

1 The Lord is King! lift up thy voice,
O earth, and all ye heavens, rejoice!
From world to world the joy shall ring:
The Lord omnipotent is King!

2 The Lord is King! who then shall dare
Resist his will, distrust his care?
Holy and true are all his ways:
Let every creature speak his praise.

3 The Lord is King! exalt your strains,
Ye saints, your God, your Father reigns;
One Lord, one empire, all secures:
He reigns,—and life and death are yours.

4 Oh, when his wisdom can mistake,
His might decay, his love forsake,
Then may his children cease to sing,—
The Lord omnipotent is King!

52.

1 Now to the Lord a noble song!
Awake, my soul! awake, my tongue!
Hosanna to th' eternal name,
And all his boundless love proclaim.

2 See where it shines in Jesus' face,—
The brightest image of his grace!
God, in the person of his Son,
Hath all his mightiest works outdone.

3 Grace!—'tis a sweet, a charming theme:
My thoughts rejoice at Jesus' name:
Ye angels! dwell upon the sound:
Ye heavens! reflect it to the ground.

4 Oh! may I reach that happy place,
Where he unvails his lovely face,
Where all his beauties you behold,
And sing his name to harps of gold.

GENERAL PRAISE. 17

OCTAVIUS. L. M. — Root & Sweetser's Coll.

1. Praise ye the Lord—let praise em-ploy, In his own courts, your songs of joy; The spa-cious fir - ma-ment a - round Shall e - cho back the joy-ful sound.

53.

2 Recount his works in strains divine,
His wondrous works—how bright they shine!
Praise him for his almighty deeds,
Whose greatness all your praise exceeds.

3 Awake the trumpet's piercing sound,
To spread your sacred pleasures round;
In praise awake each tuneful string,
And to the solemn organ sing.

4 Let all, whom life and breath inspire,
Attend, and join the blissful choir;
But chiefly ye, who know his word,
Adore, and love, and praise the Lord!

54.

1 Awake, my tongue, thy tribute bring
To Him who gave thee power to sing:
Praise him, who is all praise above,
The source of wisdom and of love.

2 How vast his knowledge! how profound!
A depth where all our thoughts are drowned!
The stars he numbers, and their names
He gives to all those heavenly flames.

3 Through each bright world above, behold
Ten thousand thousand charms unfold;
Earth, air, and mighty seas combine,
To speak his wisdom all divine.

4 But in redemption, oh, what grace!
Its wonders, oh, what thought can trace!
Here wisdom shines forever bright:
Praise him, my soul, with sweet delight.

55.

1 Bless, O my soul, the living God;
Call home thy thoughts that rove abroad:
Let all the powers within me join
In work and worship so divine.

2 Bless, O my soul, the God of grace;
His favors claim thy highest praise:
Why should the wonders he hath wrought
Be lost in silence and forgot?

3 'T is he, my soul, that sent his Son
To die for crimes which thou hast done;
He owns the ransom, and forgives
The hourly follies of our lives.

4 Let every land his power confess;
Let all the earth adore his grace:
My heart and tongue with rapture join,
In work and worship so divine.

56.

1 The floods, O Lord, lift up their voice,
The mighty floods lift up their roar;
The floods in tumult loud rejoice,
And climb in foam the sounding shore.

2 But mightier than the mighty sea,
The Lord of glory reigns on high:
Far o'er its waves we look to thee,
And see their fury break and die.

3 Thy word is true, thy promise sure,
That ancient promise, sealed in love;
Here be thy temple ever pure,
As thy pure mansions shine above.

PUBLIC WORSHIP.

DOWNS. C. M. — Dr. L. Mason.

1. Come, ye that know and fear the Lord,
And raise your thoughts above;
Let ev-ery heart and voice accord,
To sing that "God is love."

57.

2 This precious truth his word declares,
   And all his mercies prove;
   Jesus, the gift of gifts, appears,
   To show that "God is love."

3 Behold his patience, bearing long
   With those who from him rove;
   Till mighty grace their hearts subdues,
   To teach them—"God is love."

4 Oh, may we all, while here below,
   This best of blessings prove;
   Till warmer hearts, in brighter worlds,
   Proclaim that "God is love."

58.

1 WHAT shall I render to my God,
   For all his kindness shown?
   My feet shall visit thine abode,
   My songs address thy throne.

2 Among the saints that fill thy house,
   My offering shall be paid;
   There shall my zeal perform the vows
   My soul in anguish made.

3 How much is mercy thy delight,
   Thou ever-blessed God!
   How dear thy servants in thy sight—
   How precious is their blood!

4 How happy all thy servants are!
   How great thy grace to me!
   My life, which thou hast made thy care,
   Lord! I devote to thee.

5 Now I am thine—for ever thine;
   Nor shall my purpose move;
   Thy hand hath loosed my bonds of pain,
   And bound me with thy love.

6 Here, in thy courts, I leave my vow,
   And thy rich grace record;
   Witness, ye saints! who hear me now,
   If I forsake the Lord.

59.

1 GLORY to God the Father be,
   Glory to God the Son,
   Glory to God the Holy Ghost—
   Glory to God alone!

2 My soul doth magnify the Lord,
   My spirit doth rejoice
   In God, my Saviour and my God;
   I hear his joyful voice.

3 I need not go abroad for joy,
   Who have a feast at home;
   My sighs are turned into songs,
   The Comforter is come!

4 Down from on high the blessed Dove
   Is come into my breast,
   To witness God's eternal love;
   This is my heavenly feast.

5 Glory to God the Father be,
   Glory to God the Son,
   Glory to God the Holy Ghost—
   Glory to God alone!

GENERAL PRAISE.

MANOAH. C. M. — GREATOREX COLL.

1. Begin, my tongue, some heaven-ly theme, And speak some bound-less thing: The might-y works, or might-ier name, Of our e-ter-nal King.

60.

1 Begin, my tongue, some heavenly theme,
   And speak some boundless thing :
   The mighty works, or mightier name,
   Of our eternal King.

2 Tell of his wondrous faithfulness,
   And sound his power abroad;
   Sing the sweet promise of his grace,
   And the performing God.

3 His very word of grace is strong,
   As that which built the skies;
   The voice that rolls the stars along
   Speaks all the promises.

4 Oh, might I hear thy heavenly tongue
   But whisper, "Thou art mine!"
   Those gentle words should raise my song
   To notes almost divine.

61.

1 Awake, my heart, arise my tongue,
   Prepare a tuneful voice ;
   In God, the life of all my joys,
   Aloud will I rejoice.

2 'Tis he adorned my naked soul,
   And made salvation mine ;
   Upon a poor polluted worm
   He makes his graces shine.

3 And, lest the shadow of a spot
   Should on my soul be found,
   He took the robe the Saviour wrought,
   And cast it all around.

4 How far this heavenly robe exceeds
   What earthly princes wear !
   These ornaments, how bright they shine!
   How white the garments are !

5 The Spirit wrought my faith, and love,
   And hope, and every grace ;
   But Jesus spent his life to work
   The robe of righteousness.

6 Strangely, my soul, art thou arrayed,
   By the great sacred Three !
   In sweetest harmony of praise,
   Let all thy powers agree.

62.

1 Come, shout aloud the Father's grace,
   And sing the Saviour's love ;
   Soon shall we join the glorious theme,
   In loftier strains above.

2 God, the eternal, mighty God,
   To dearer names descends ;
   Calls us his treasure and his joy,
   His children and his friends.

3 My Father, God ! and may these lips
   Pronounce a name so dear ?
   Not thus could heaven's sweet harmony
   Delight my listening ear.

4 Thanks to my God for every gift
   His bounteous hands bestow ;
   And thanks eternal for that love
   Whence all those comforts flow.

PUBLIC WORSHIP.

SILVER STREET. S. M.
I. Smith.

1. Come, sound his praise abroad, And hymns of glory sing: Jehovah is the sovereign God, The universal King.

63.

2 He formed the deeps unknown;
  He gave the seas their bound;
The watery worlds are all his own,
  And all the solid ground.

3 Come, worship at his throne,
  Come, bow before the Lord:
We are his work, and not our own,
  He formed us by his word.

4 To-day attend his voice,
  Nor dare provoke his rod;
Come, like the people of his choice,
  And own your gracious God.

64.

1 Raise your triumphant songs
  To an immortal tune;
Let the wide earth resound the deeds
  Celestial grace has done.

2 Sing—how eternal love
  Its chief beloved chose,
And bade him raise our ruined race
  From their abyss of woes.

3 His hand no thunder bears,
  No terror clothes his brow,
No bolts to drive our guilty souls
  To fiercer flames below.

4 'T was mercy filled the throne,
  And wrath stood silent by,
When Christ was sent, with pardons, down
  To rebels doomed to die.

5 Now, sinners! dry your tears;
  Let hopeless sorrow cease;
Bow to the sceptre of his love,
  And take the offered peace.

6 Lord! we obey thy call;
  We lay an humble claim
To the salvation thou hast brought,
  And love and praise thy name.

65.

1 To God the only wise,
  Our Saviour and our King,
Let all the saints below the skies
  Their humble praises bring.

2 'T is his almighty love,
  His counsel and his care,
Preserves us safe from sin and death,
  And every hurtful snare.

3 He will present our souls,
  Unblemished and complete,
Before the glory of his face,
  With joys divinely great.

4 Then all the chosen seed
  Shall meet around the throne,
Shall bless the conduct of his grace,
  And make his wonders known.

5 To our Redeemer God
  Wisdom and power belongs,
Immortal crowns of majesty,
  And everlasting songs.

GENERAL PRAISE. 21

STATE STREET. S. M.   Woodman.

1. Oh! bless the Lord, my soul! His grace to thee proclaim:
And all that is within me join To bless his holy name.

66.
2 Oh! bless the Lord, my soul!
His mercies bear in mind:
Forget not all his benefits:
The Lord to thee is kind.

3 He will not always chide;
He will with patience wait;
His wrath is ever slow to rise,
And ready to abate.

4 He pardons all thy sins,
Prolongs thy feeble breath;
He healeth thy infirmities,
And ransoms thee from death.

5 Then bless his holy name,
Whose grace hath made thee whole;
Whose loving-kindness crowns thy days;
Oh! bless the Lord, my soul!

67.
1 Now let our voices join
To raise a sacred song;
Ye pilgrims! in Jehovah's ways,
With music pass along.

2 See—flowers of paradise,
In rich profusion, spring;
The sun of glory gilds the path,
And dear companions sing.

3 See—Salem's golden spires,
In beauteous prospect, rise;
And brighter crowns than mortals wear,
Which sparkle through the skies.

4 All honor to his name,
Who marks the shining way,—
To him who leads the pilgrims on
To realms of endless day.

68.
1 Thy name, almighty Lord!
Shall sound through distant lands:
Great is thy grace, and sure thy word,
Thy truth forever stands.

2 Far be thine honor spread,
And long thy praise endure,
Till morning light and evening shade
Shall be exchanged no more.

69.
1 Lord, in this sacred hour
Within thy courts we bend,
And bless thy love, and own thy power,
Our Father and our Friend.

2 But thou art not alone
In courts by mortals trod;
Nor only is the day thine own
When man draws near to God.

3 Thy temple is the arch
Of yon unmeasured sky;
Thy Sabbath, the stupendous march
Of grand eternity.

4 Lord, may that holier day
Dawn on thy servants' sight;
And purer worship may we pay
In heaven's unclouded light.

22 PUBLIC WORSHIP.

BENEVENTO. 7s. Double. S. Webbe.

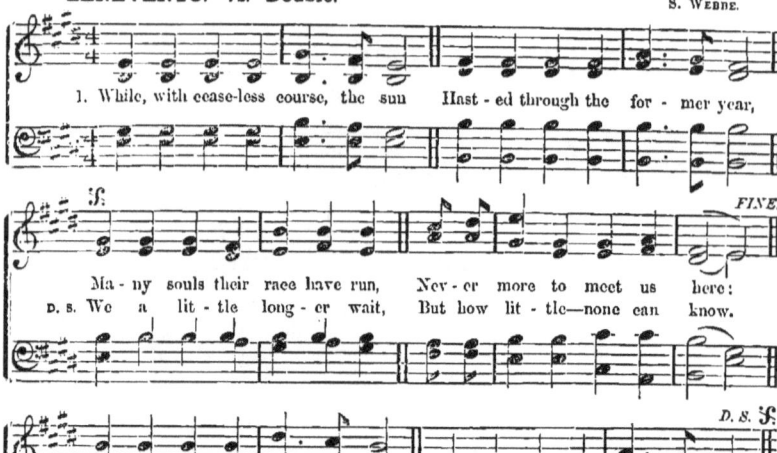

1. While, with ceaseless course, the sun
Hasted through the former year,
Many souls their race have run,
Never more to meet us here:
D. S. We a little longer wait,
But how little—none can know.
Fixed in an eternal state,
They have done with all below;

70.
New Year's Morning.

2 As the winged arrow flies
  Speedily the mark to find;
As the lightning from the skies
  Darts, and leaves no trace behind,—
Swiftly thus our fleeting days
  Bear us down life's rapid stream;
Upward, Lord, our spirits raise,
  All below is but a dream.

3 Spared to see another year,
  Let thy blessing meet us here;
Come, thy dying work revive,
  Bid thy drooping garden thrive:
Sun of Righteousness, arise!
  Warm our hearts and bless our eyes;
Let our prayer thy pity move,
  Make this year a time of love.

4 Thanks for mercies past receive,
  Pardon of our sins renew;
Teach us henceforth how to live,
  With eternity in view:
Bless thy word to old and young,
  Fill us with a Saviour's love;
When our life's short race is run,
  May we dwell with thee above.

71.

1 Let us with a joyful mind
  Praise the Lord, for he is kind,
For his mercies shall endure,
  Ever faithful, ever sure.
Let us sound his name abroad,
  For of gods he is the God
Who by wisdom did create
  Heaven's expanse and all its state;

2 Did the solid earth ordain
  How to rise above the main;
Who, by his commanding might,
  Filled the new-made world with light:
Caused the golden-tressèd sun
  All the day his course to run;
And the moon to shine by night,
  'Mid her spangled sisters bright.

3 All his creatures God doth feed,
  His full hand supplies their need;
Let us therefore warble forth
  His high majesty and worth.
He his mansion hath on high,
  'Bove the reach of mortal eye;
And his mercies shall endure,
  Ever faithful, ever sure.

GENERAL PRAISE. 23

ONIDO. 7s. Double. Arr. from PLEYEL. DR. L. MASON.

1. Lord of earth! thy forming hand Well this beauteous frame hath planned, Woods that wave, and hills that tower, Ocean rolling in his power; Yet a-mid this scene so fair, Should I cease thy smile to share, What were all its joys to me? Whom have I on earth but thee?

72.

2 Lord of heaven! beyond our sight
Shines a world of purer light;
There in love's unclouded reign
Parted hands shall meet again:
Oh, that world is passing fair!
Yet, if thou wert absent there,
What were all its joys to me?
Whom have I in heaven but thee?

3 Lord of earth and heaven! my breast
Seeks in thee its only rest:
I was lost; thy accents mild
Homeward lured thy wandering child.
Oh! should once thy smile divine
Cease upon my soul to shine,
What were earth or heaven to me?
Whom have I in each but thee?

73.

1 HOLY, holy, holy Lord
God of Hosts! when heaven and earth,
Out of darkness, at thy word
Issued into glorious birth,
All thy works before thee stood,
And thine eye beheld them good,
While they sung with sweet accord,
Holy, holy, holy Lord!

2 Holy, holy, holy! thee,
One Jehovah evermore,
Father, Son, and Spirit! we,
Dust and ashes, would adore:
Lightly by the world esteemed,
From that world by thee redeemed,
Sing we here with glad accord,
Holy, holy, holy Lord!

3 Holy, holy, holy! all
Heaven's triumphant choir shall sing,
While the ransomed nations fall
At the footstool of their King:
Then shall saints and seraphim,
Harps and voices, swell one hymn,
Blending in sublime accord,
Holy, holy, holy Lord!

PUBLIC WORSHIP.

LYONS. 10s & 11s. *Haydn.*

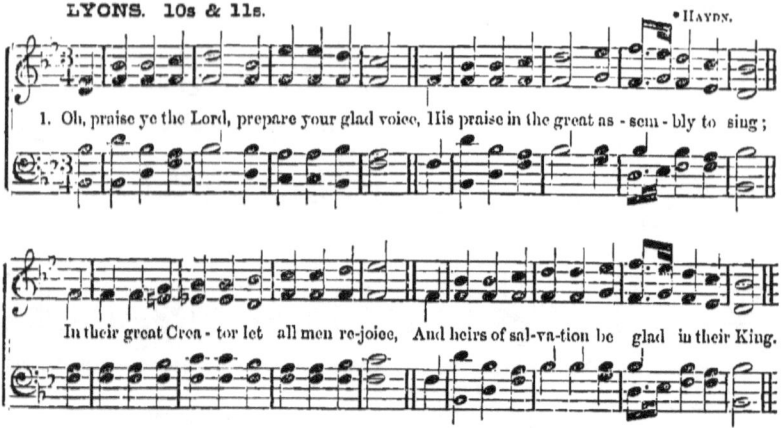

1. Oh, praise ye the Lord, prepare your glad voice, His praise in the great as-sem-bly to sing; In their great Crea-tor let all men re-joice, And heirs of sal-va-tion be glad in their King.

74.

2 Let them his great name devoutly adore ;
In loud-swelling strains his praises express,
Who graciously opens his bountiful store,
Their wants to relieve, and his children to bless.

3 With glory adorned, his people shall sing
To God, who defence and plenty supplies ;
Their loud acclamations to him, their great King,
Through earth shall be sounded, and reach to the skies.

75.

1 Oh, worship the King all-glorious above,
And gratefully sing his wonderful love ;
Our Shield and Defender, the Ancient of days,
Pavilioned in splendor, and girded with praise.

2 Oh, tell of his might, and sing of his grace,
Whose robe is the light, whose canopy space ;
His chariots of wrath the deep thunder-clouds form,
And dark is his path on the wings of the storm.

3 Thy bountiful care what tongue can recite ?
It breathes in the air, it shines in the light,

It streams from the hills, it descends to the plain,
And sweetly distills in the dew and the rain.

4 Frail children of dust, and feeble as frail,
In thee do we trust, nor find thee to fail ;
Thy mercies how tender ! how firm to the end !
Our Maker, Defender, Redeemer, and Friend.

76.

1 Ye servants of God ! your Master proclaim,
And publish abroad his wonderful name ;
The name all-victorious of Jesus extol ;
His kingdom is glorious, he rules over all.

2 Salvation to God, who sits on the throne,
Let all cry aloud, and honor the Son :
The praises of Jesus the angels proclaim,
Fall down on their faces, and worship the Lamb !

3 Then let us adore, and give him his right,
All glory and power, and wisdom and might ;
All honor and blessing, with angels above,
And thanks never ceasing, for infinite love.

GENERAL PRAISE. 25

WILMOT. 8s & 7s.   WEBER.

1. Praise the Lord! ye heavens, adore him; Praise him, angels in the height;
Sun and moon, rejoice before him; Praise him, all ye stars of light!

77.

2 Praise the Lord—for he hath spoken;
Worlds his mighty voice obeyed;
Laws which never shall be broken,
For their guidance he hath made.

3 Praise the Lord—for he is glorious;
Never shall his promise fail;
God hath made his saints victorious,
Sin and death shall not prevail.

4 Praise the God of our salvation,
Hosts on high his power proclaim;
Heaven and earth, and all creation,
Laud and magnify his name!

78.

1 Blest be thou, O God of Israel,
Thou, our Father, and our Lord!
Blest thy majesty forever!
Ever be thy name adored.

2 Thine, O Lord, are power and greatness,
Glory, victory, are thine own;
All is thine in earth and heaven,
Over all thy boundless throne.

3 Riches come of thee, and honor,
Power and might to thee belong;
Thine it is to make us prosper,
Only thine to make us strong.

4 Lord, to thee, thou God of mercy,
Hymns of gratitude we raise;
To thy name, forever glorious,
Ever we address our praise!

79.

1 May the grace of Christ, our Saviour,
And the Father's boundless love,
With the holy Spirit's favor,
Rest upon us from above.

2 Thus may we abide in union
With each other and the Lord,
And possess, in sweet communion,
Joys which earth can not afford.

80.

1 I would love thee, God and Father!
My Redeemer, and my King!
I would love thee; for, without thee,
Life is but a bitter thing.

2 I would love thee; every blessing
Flows to me from out thy throne:
I would love thee—he who loves thee
Never feels himself alone.

3 I would love thee; look upon me,
Ever guide me with thine eye:
I would love thee; if not nourished
By thy love, my soul would die.

4 I would love thee; may thy brightness
Dazzle my rejoicing eyes!
I would love thee; may thy goodness
Watch from heaven o'er all I prize.

5 I would love thee, I have vowed it;
On thy love my heart is set:
While I love thee, I can never
My Redeemer's blood forget.

26 PUBLIC WORSHIP.

RIGHINI. 6s & 4s.  *Arranged by Geo. Kingsley.*

1. Let us a-wake our joys; Strike up with cheer-ful voice; Each crea-ture, sing; Angels, begin the song; Mortals, the strain prolong, In accents sweet and strong, "Jesus is King."

81.

2 Proclaim abroad his name;
Tell of his matchless fame;
What wonders done;
Above, beneath, around,
Let all the earth resound,
'Till heaven's high arch rebound,
" Victory is won."

3 He vanquished sin and hell,
And our last foe will quell;
Mourners, rejoice:
His dying love adore;
Praise him, now raised in power;
Praise him for evermore,
With joyful voice.

4 All hail the glorious day,
When, through the heavenly way,
Lo, he shall come,
While they who pierced him wail;
His promise shall not fail;
Saints, see your King prevail:
Great Saviour, come!

82.

1 Sing, sing his lofty praise,
Whom angels can not raise,
But whom they sing;
Jesus, who reigns above,
Object of angels' love,
Jesus, whose grace we prove,
Jesus, our King.

2 Rich is the grace we sing,
Poor is the praise we bring,
Not as we ought;

But when we see his face,
In yonder glorious place,
Then shall we sing his grace,
Sing without fault.

83.

1 Come, thou almighty King,
Help us thy name to sing,
Help us to praise:
Father! all-glorious,
O'er all victorious,
Come, and reign over us,
Ancient of Days!

2 Come, thou incarnate Word!
Gird on thy mighty sword;
Our prayer attend.
Come, and thy people bless,
And give thy word success;
Spirit of holiness!
On us descend.

3 Come, holy Comforter!
Thy sacred witness bear,
In this glad hour:
Thou, who almighty art,
Now rule in every heart,
And ne'er from us depart,
Spirit of power!

4 To the great One in Three,
The highest praises be,
Hence evermore!
His sovereign majesty
May we in glory see,
And to eternity
Love and adore.

GENERAL PRAISE.   27

ITALIAN HYMN. 6s & 4s.   GIARDINI.

1. Praise ye Jo-ho-vah's name; Praise thro' his courts pro-claim; Rise and a-dore;
High o'er the heav'ns above, Sound his great acts of love, While his rich grace we prove, Vast as his power.

84.

1 PRAISE ye Jehovah's name;
Praise through his courts proclaim;
Rise and adore ;
High o'er the heavens above,
Sound his great acts of love,
While his rich grace we prove,
Vast as his power.

2 Now let the trumpet raise
Sounds of triumphant praise,
Wide as his fame ;
There let the harp be found ;
Organs, with solemn sound,
Roll your deep notes around,
Filled with his name.

3 While his high praise ye sing,
Shake every sounding string ;
Sweet the accord !
He vital breath bestows ;
Let every breath that flows,
His noblest fame disclose ;
Praise ye the Lord.

85.

1 GLORY to God on high !
Let heaven and earth reply ;
Praise ye his name ;
His love and grace adore,
Who all our sorrows bore ;
And sing forevermore,
" Worthy the Lamb."

2 Ye who surround the throne,
Cheerfully join in one,
Praising his name ;
Ye who have felt his blood
Sealing your peace with God,
Sound his dear name abroad :
" Worthy the Lamb."

3 Soon must we change our place ;
Yet will we never cease
Praising his name ;
To him our songs we'll bring,
Hail him our gracious King,
And through all ages sing,
" Worthy the Lamb."

86.

1 THOU ! whose almighty word
Chaos and darkness heard,
And took their flight,—
Hear us, we humbly pray,
And, where the gospel's day
Sheds not its glorious ray,
" Let there be light !"

2 Thou ! who didst come to bring
On thy redeeming wing,
Healing and sight,—
Health to the sick in mind,
Sight to the inly blind,—
Oh ! now to all mankind,
" Let there be light !"

3 Spirit of truth and love,
Life-giving holy Dove !
Speed forth thy flight :
Move on the waters' face,
Bearing the lamp of grace,
And, in earth's darkest place,
" Let there be light !"

PUBLIC WORSHIP.

HEBRON. L. M. Dr. L. Mason.

1. Dismiss us with thy blessing, Lord! Help us to feed upon thy word; All that has been a-miss, forgive, And let thy truth with-in us live.

87.

1 Dismiss us with thy blessing, Lord!
Help us to feed upon thy word;
All that has been amiss, forgive,
And let thy truth within us live.

2 Though we are guilty, thou art good;
Wash all our works in Jesus' blood;
Give every burdened soul release,
And bid us all depart in peace.

88.

1 Ere to the world again we go,
Its pleasures, cares, and idle show,
Thy grace, once more, O God, we crave,
From folly and from sin to save.

2 May the great truths we here have heard,
The lessons of thy holy word—
Dwell in our inmost bosoms deep,
And all our souls from error keep.

3 Oh! may the influence of this day
Long as our memory with us stay,
And as a constant guardian prove,
To guide us to our home above.

89.

1 Lord! may thy truth, upon the heart
Now fall, and dwell as heavenly dew,
And flowers of grace in freshness start
Where once the weeds of error grew.

2 May prayer now lift her sacred wings,
Contented with that aim alone
Which bears her to the King of kings,
And rests her at his sheltering throne.

90.

1 While now upon this Sabbath eve,
Thy house, Almighty God, we leave,
'T is sweet, as sinks the setting sun,
To think on all our duties done.

2 Oh! evermore may all our bliss
Be peaceful, pure, divine, like this;
And may each Sabbath, as it flies,
Fit us for joys beyond the skies.

91.

1 Lord, now we part in thy blest name,
In which we here together came;
Grant us our few remaining days
To work thy will, and spread thy praise!

2 Teach us in life and death to bless
Thee, Lord, our strength and righteousness;
And grant us all to meet above;
There shall we better sing thy love.

3 To God the Father, God the Son,
And God the Spirit, three in one,
Be honor, praise, and glory given,
By all on earth, and all in heaven.

CLOSE OF SERVICE.

WEBER. 7s.   *Arranged from* Weber.

1. Soft-ly fades the twi-light ray Of the ho-ly Sab-bath day; Gen-tly as life's set-ting sun, When the Chris-tian's course is run.

92.

2 Night her solemn mantle spreads
  O'er the earth as daylight fades;
  All things tell of calm repose
  At the holy Sabbath's close.

3 Peace is on the world abroad;
  'Tis the holy peace of God—
  Symbol of the peace within,
  When the spirit rests from sin.

4 Still the Spirit lingers near,
  Where the evening worshiper
  Seeks communion with the skies,
  Pressing onward to the prize.

5 Saviour! may our Sabbaths be
  Days of peace and joy in thee,
  Till in heaven our souls repose,
  Where the Sabbath ne'er shall close.

93.

1 For a season called to part,
  Let us now ourselves commend,
  To the gracious eye and heart
  Of our ever-present Friend.

2 Jesus! hear our humble prayer;
  Tender Shepherd of thy sheep!
  Let thy mercy and thy care
  All our souls in safety keep.

3 Then, if thou thy help afford,
  Joyful songs to thee shall rise,
  And our souls shall praise the Lord,
  Who regards our humble cries.

94.

1 Now may he who from the dead
  Brought the Shepherd of the sheep,
  Jesus Christ, our king and head,
  All our souls in safety keep.

2 May he teach us to fulfill
  What is pleasing in his sight;
  Make us perfect in his will,
  And preserve us day and night!

3 To that great Redeemer's praise,
  Who the covenant sealed with blood,
  Let our hearts and voices raise
  Loud thanksgivings to our God.

95.

1 For the mercies of the day,
  For this rest upon our way,
  Thanks to thee alone be given,
  Lord of earth and King of heaven!

2 Cold our services have been,
  Mingled every prayer with sin:
  But thou canst and wilt forgive;
  By thy grace alone we live.

3 While this thorny path we tread,
  May thy love our footsteps lead;
  When our journey here is past,
  May we rest with thee at last.

4 Let these earthly Sabbaths prove
  Foretastes of our joys above;
  While their steps thy children bend
  To the rest which knows no end.

PUBLIC WORSHIP.

GREENVILLE. 8s, 7s & 4s. — ROUSSEAU.

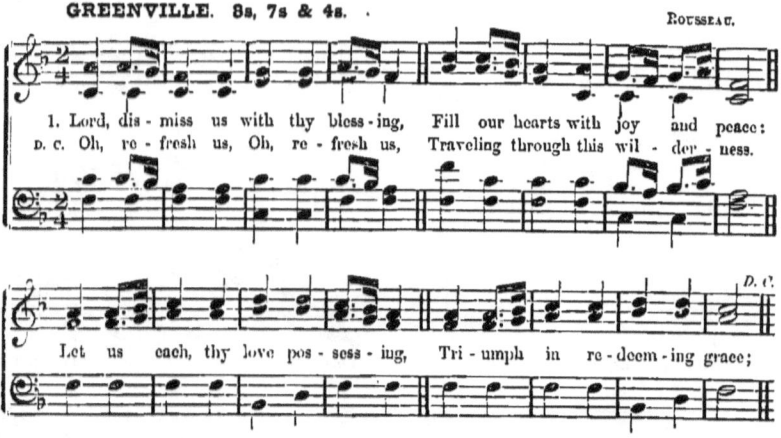

1. Lord, dismiss us with thy blessing, Fill our hearts with joy and peace:
D.C. Oh, refresh us, Oh, refresh us, Traveling through this wilderness.

Let us each, thy love possessing, Triumph in redeeming grace;

96.

1 LORD, dismiss us with thy blessing,
  Fill our hearts with joy and peace:
  Let us each, thy love possessing,
  Triumph in redeeming grace;
    Oh, refresh us,
  Traveling through this wilderness.

2 Thanks we give and adoration,
  For thy gospel's joyful sound;
  May the fruits of thy salvation
  In our hearts and lives abound;
    May thy presence,
  With us evermore be found.

3 So, whene'er the signal's given
  Us from earth to call away,
  Borne on angels' wings to heaven,
  Glad the summons to obey,
    May we ever
  Reign with Christ in endless day.

97.

1 COME, thou soul-transforming Spirit,
  Bless the sower and the seed:
  Let each heart thy grace inherit,
  Raise the weak, the hungry feed:
    From the gospel
  Now supply thy people's need.

2 Oh! may all enjoy the blessing,
  Which thy word's designed to give;
  Let us all, thy love possessing,
  Joyfully the truth receive;
    And forever
  To thy praise and glory live.

98.

1 GENTLY, Lord! oh, gently lead us,
  Through this lonely vale of tears;
  Through the changes thou'st decreed us,
  Till our last great change appears:
  When temptation's darts assail us,
  When in devious paths we stray,
  Let thy goodness never fail us,
  Lead us in thy perfect way.

2 In the hour of pain and anguish,
  In the hour when death draws near,
  Suffer not our hearts to languish,—
  Suffer not our souls to fear;
  And, when mortal life is ended
  Bid us on thy bosom rest,
  Till, by angel-bands attended,
  We awake among the blest.

99.

1 GOD of our salvation, hear us;
  Bless, Oh! bless us, ere we go;
  When we join the world, be near us,
  Lest we cold and careless grow:
    Saviour, keep us,
  Keep us safe from every foe.

2 As our steps are drawing nearer
  To our best and lasting home,
  May our view of heaven grow clearer;
  Hope more bright of joys to come;
    And when dying,
  May thy presence cheer the gloom.

THE SCRIPTURES.

UXBRIDGE. L. M.   Dr. L. Mason.

1. God, in the gos-pel of his Son, Makes his e-ter-nal coun-sels known, Where love in all its glo-ry shines, And truth is drawn in fair-est lines.

101.

1 God, in the gospel of his Son,
Makes his eternal counsels known,
Where love in all its glory shines,
And truth is drawn in fairest lines.

2 Here, sinners of an humble frame
May taste his grace, and learn his name;
May read, in characters of blood,
The wisdom, power and grace of God.

3 Here, faith reveals, to mortal eyes,
A brighter world beyond the skies;
Here, shines the light which guides our way
From earth to realms of endless day.

4 Oh! grant us grace, almighty Lord!
To read and mark thy holy word,
Its truths with meekness to receive,
And by its holy precepts live.

102.

1 The heavens declare thy glory, Lord!
In every star thy wisdom shines;
But when our eyes behold thy word,
We read thy name in fairer lines.

2 The rolling sun, the changing light,
And nights and days thy power confess,
But the blest volume thou hast writ,
Reveals thy justice and thy grace.

3 Sun, moon, and stars, convey thy praise
Round the whole earth, and never stand;
So, when thy truth began its race,
It touched and glanced on every land.

4 Nor shall thy spreading gospel rest,
Till through the world thy truth has run;
Till Christ has all the nations blessed
That see the light, or feel the sun.

5 Great Sun of righteousness, arise!
Bless the dark world with heavenly light:
Thy gospel makes the simple wise,
Thy laws are pure, thy judgments right.

6 Thy noblest wonders here we view,
In souls renewed, and sins forgiven;
Lord, cleanse my sins, my soul renew,
And make thy word my guide to heaven.

103.

1 The starry firmament on high,
And all the glories of the sky,
Yet shine not to thy praise, O Lord,
So brightly as thy written word.

2 The hopes that holy word supplies,
Its truths divine and precepts wise,
In each a heavenly beam I see,
And every beam conducts to thee.

3 Almighty Lord, the sun shall fail,
The moon forget her nightly tale,
And deepest silence hush on high
The radiant chorus of the sky;

4 But fixed for everlasting years,
Unmoved, amid the wreck of spheres,
Thy word shall shine in cloudless day,
When heaven and earth have passed away.

THE SCRIPTURES.

WILLINGTON. L. M.   Greatorex Coll.

1. I love the sacred Book of God! No other can its place supply; It points me to his own abode, It gives me wings, and bids me fly.

104.

1 I love the sacred Book of God!
No other can its place supply;
It points me to his own abode,
It gives me wings, and bids me fly.

2 Sweet Book! in thee my eyes discern
The very image of my Lord;
From thine instructive page I learn
The joys his presence will afford.

3 In thee I read my title clear
To mansions that will ne'er decay;—
Dear Lord, oh, when wilt thou appear,
And bear thy prisoner away!

4 While I am here, these leaves supply
His place, and tell me of his love;
I read with faith's discerning eye,
And gain a glimpse of joys above.

5 I know in them the Spirit breathes
To animate his people here;
Oh, may these truths prove life to all,
Till in his presence we appear!

105.

1 Now let my soul, eternal King,
To thee its grateful tribute bring;
My knee with humble homage bow,
My tongue perform its solemn vow.

2 All nature sings thy boundless love,
In worlds below, and worlds above;
But in thy blessed word I trace
Diviner wonders of thy grace.

3 Here what delightful truths I read!
Here I behold the Saviour bleed;
His name salutes my listening ear,
Revives my heart and checks my fear.

4 Here Jesus bids my sorrows cease,
And gives my laboring conscience peace;
Here lifts my grateful passions high,
And points to mansions in the sky.

5 For love like this, oh, let my song,
Through endless years, thy praise prolong;
Let distant climes thy name adore,
Till time and nature are no more.

106.

1 Upon the Gospel's sacred page
The gathered beams of ages shine;
And, as it hastens, every age
But makes its brightness more divine.

2 On mightier wing, in loftier flight,
From year to year does knowledge soar;
And, as it soars, the Gospel light
Adds to its influence more and more.

3 More glorious still as centuries roll,
New regions blessed, new powers unfurled,
Expanding with th' expanding soul,
Its waters shall o'erflow the world—

4 Flow to restore, but not destroy;
As when the cloudless lamp of day
Pours out its floods of light and joy,
And sweeps the lingering mist away.

THE SCRIPTURES.

KNOX. C. M.

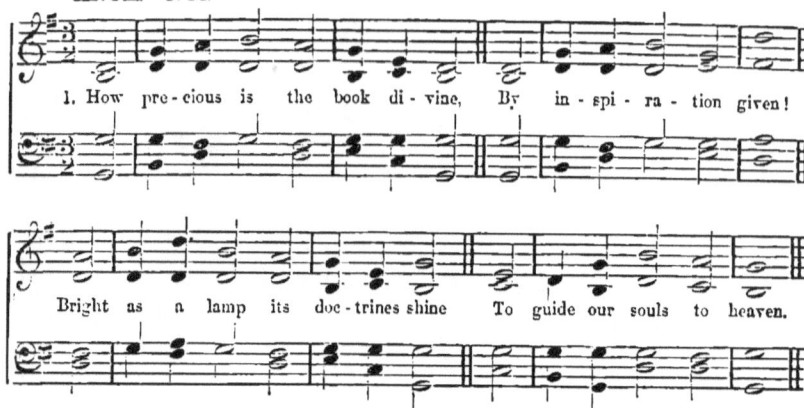

1. How pre-cious is the book di-vine, By in-spi-ra-tion given! Bright as a lamp its doc-trines shine To guide our souls to heaven.

107.

1 How precious is the book divine,
   By inspiration given!
   Bright as a lamp its doctrines shine
   To guide our souls to heaven.

2 O'er all the strait and narrow way
   Its radiant beams are cast;
   A light whose never-weary ray
   Grows brightest at the last.

3 It sweetly cheers our drooping hearts,
   In this dark vale of tears;
   Life, light, and joy, it still imparts,
   And quells our rising fears.

4 This lamp, through all the tedious night
   Of life, shall guide our way,
   Till we behold the clearer light
   Of an eternal day.

108.

1 Thou lovely Source of true delight,
   Whom I unseen adore!
   Unvail thy beauties to my sight,
   That I may love thee more.

2 Thy glory o'er creation shines;
   But in thy sacred word,
   I read in fairer, brighter lines,
   My bleeding, dying Lord.

3 'Tis here, whene'er my comforts droop,
   And sins and sorrows rise,
   Thy love with cheerful beams of hope,
   My fainting heart supplies.

4 Jesus, my Lord, my life, my light,
   Oh! come with blissful ray;
   Break radiant through the shades of night,
   And chase my fears away.

5 Then shall my soul with rapture trace
   The wonders of thy love;
   But the full glories of thy face
   Are only known above.

109.

1 How shall the young secure their hearts,
   And guard their lives from sin?
   Thy word the choicest rules imparts
   To keep the conscience clean.

2 When once it enters to the mind,
   It spreads such light abroad;
   The meanest souls instruction find,
   And raise their thoughts to God.

3 'Tis like the sun, a heavenly light,
   That guides us all the day;
   And, through the dangers of the night,
   A lamp to lead our way.

4 Thy precepts make me truly wise;
   I hate the sinner's road;
   I hate my own vain thoughts that rise,
   But love thy law, my God!

5 Thy word is everlasting truth;
   How pure is every page!
   That holy book shall guide our youth,
   And well support our age.

THE SCRIPTURES.

YORK. C. M.

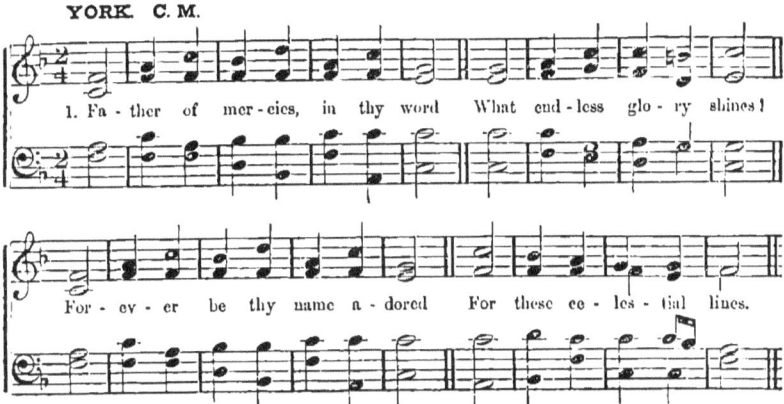

1. Fa-ther of mer-cies, in thy word What end-less glo-ry shines!
For-ev-er be thy name a-dored For these ce-les-tial lines.

110.

2 Here my Redeemer's welcome voice
  Spreads heavenly peace around;
  And life and everlasting joys
  Attend the blissful sound.

3 Oh, may these heavenly pages be
  My ever dear delight;
  And still new beauties may I see,
  And still increasing light!

4 Divine Instructor, gracious Lord!
  Be thou forever near;
  Teach me to love thy sacred word,
  And view my Saviour there.

111.

1 A GLORY gilds the sacred page,
  Majestic, like the sun;
  It gives a light to every age;—
  It gives, but borrows none.

2 The hand that gave it, still supplies
  The gracious light and heat;
  Its truths upon the nations rise,—
  They rise, but never set.

3 Let everlasting thanks be thine,
  For such a bright display,
  As makes a world of darkness shine
  With beams of heavenly day.

4 My soul rejoices to pursue
  The steps of him I love,
  Till glory breaks upon my view,
  In brighter worlds above.

112.

1 ALMIGHTY God! thy word is cast,
  Like seed into the ground;
  Let now the dew of heaven descend,
  And righteous fruits abound.

2 Let not the foe of Christ and man
  This holy seed remove;
  But give it root in every heart,
  To bring forth fruits of love.

3 Let not the world's deceitful cares
  The rising plant destroy;
  But let it yield, a hundredfold,
  The fruits of peace and joy.

4 Oft as the precious seed is sown,
  Thy quickening grace bestow,
  That all, whose souls the truth receive,
  Its saving power may know.

113.

1 BLEST are the souls that hear and know
  The gospel's joyful sound;
  Peace shall attend the path they go,
  And light their steps surround.

2 Their joy shall bear their spirits up
  Through their Redeemer's name;
  His righteousness exalts their hope,
  Nor Satan dares condemn.

3 The Lord, our glory and defence,
  Strength and salvation gives;
  Israel, thy King forever reigns,
  Thy God forever lives.

GOD.

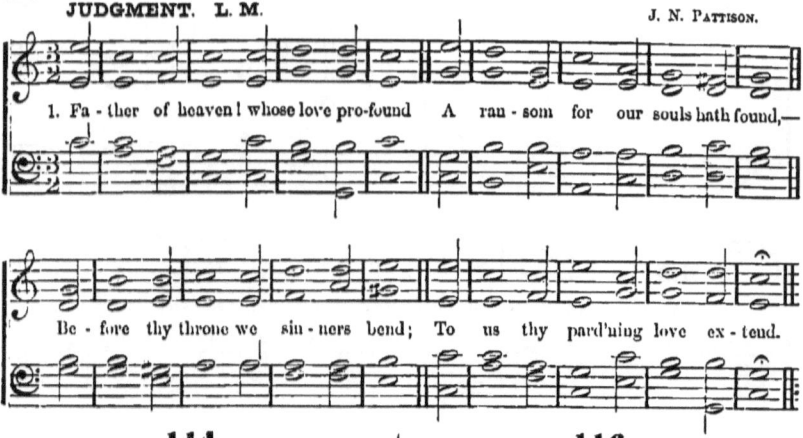

114.
Trinity.

2 Almighty Son—incarnate Word—
Our Prophet, Priest, Redeemer, Lord!
Before thy throne we sinners bend;
To us thy saving grace extend.

3 Eternal Spirit! by whose breath
The soul is raised from sin and death,—
Before thy throne we sinners bend;
To us thy quickening power extend.

4 Jehovah!—Father, Spirit, Son!—
Mysterious Godhead—Three in One!
Before thy throne we sinners bend;
Grace, pardon, life to us extend.

115.
Immensity.

1 With deepest reverence at thy throne,
Jehovah, peerless and unknown!
Our feeble spirits strive, in vain,
A glimpse of thee, great God! to gain.

2 Who, by the closest search, can find
Th' eternal, uncreated mind?
Nor men, nor angels can explore
Thy heights of love, thy depths of power.

3 We know thee not; but this we know,
Thou reign'st above, thou reign'st below:
And though thine essence is unknown,
To all the world thy power is shown.

4 That power we trace on every side;
Oh! may thy wisdom be our guide!
And while we live, and when we die,
May thine almighty love be nigh.

116.
Trinity.

1 O holy, holy, holy Lord!
Bright in thy deeds and in thy name,
Forever be thy name adored,
Thy glories let the world proclaim!

2 O Jesus! Lamb once crucified
To take our load of sins away,
Thine be the hymn that rolls its tide
Along the realms of upper day!

3 O Holy Spirit! from above,
In streams of light and glory given,
Thou source of ecstasy and love,
Thy praises ring through earth and heaven!

4 O God triune! to thee we owe
Our every thought, our every song;
And ever may thy praises flow
From saint and seraph's burning tongue!

117.
Being.

1 There is a God!—all nature speaks,
Through earth, and air, and seas, and skies;
See—from the clouds his glory breaks,
When the first beams of morning rise.

2 The rising sun, serenely bright,
O'er the wide world's extended frame,
Inscribes, in characters of light,
His mighty Maker's glorious name.

3 Ye curious minds, who roam abroad,
And trace creation's wonders o'er,
Confess the footsteps of your God;—
And bow before him—and adore.

GOD.   37

SEASONS. L. M.   PLEYEL.

1. What fi-nite power, with ceaseless toil, Can fath-om the e-ter-nal mind?
Or who th' al-might-y Three in One, By searching to per-fec-tion find?

118.
Infinity.

2 Angels and men in vain may raise,
Harmonious, their adoring songs;
The laboring thought sinks down oppressed,
And praises die upon their tongues.

3 Yet would I lift my trembling voice,
A portion of his ways to sing;
And mingling with his meanest works,
My humble, grateful tribute bring.

119.
Omniscience.

1 Lord, thou hast searched and seen me through:
Thine eye commands, with piercing view,
My rising and my resting hours,
My heart and flesh with all their powers.

2 My thoughts, before they are my own,
Are to my God distinctly known;
He knows the words I mean to speak,
Ere from my opening lips they break.

3 Within thy circling power I stand;
On every side I find thy hand:
Awake, asleep, at home, abroad,
I am surrounded still with God.

4 Amazing knowledge, vast and great!
What large extent! what lofty height!
My soul, with all the powers I boast,
Is in the boundless prospect lost.

5 Oh! may these thoughts possess my breast,
Where'er I rove, where'er I rest,
Nor let my weaker passions dare
Consent to sin, for God is there.

120.
Long-suffering.

1 God of my life, to thee belong,
The grateful heart, the joyful song;
Touched by thy love, each tuneful chord
Resounds the goodness of the Lord.

2 Yet why, dear Lord, this tender care?
Why does thy hand so kindly rear
A useless cumberer of the ground,
On which so little fruit is found?

3 Still let the barren fig-tree stand,
Upheld and fostered by thy hand;
And let its fruit and verdure be
A grateful tribute, Lord, to thee.

121.
Sovereignty.

1 May not the sovereign Lord on high
Dispense his favors as he will,
Choose some to life, while others die,
And yet be just and gracious still?

2 What if he means to show his grace
And his electing love employs
To mark out some of mortal race,
And form them fit for heavenly joys?

3 Shall man reply against the Lord,
And call his Maker's ways unjust,
The thunder of whose dreadful word
Can crush a thousand worlds to dust?

4 But, O my soul! if truth so bright
Should dazzle and confound thy sight,
Yet still his written will obey,
And wait the great decisive day.

ROCKINGHAM. L. M. GOD. Dr. L. Mason.

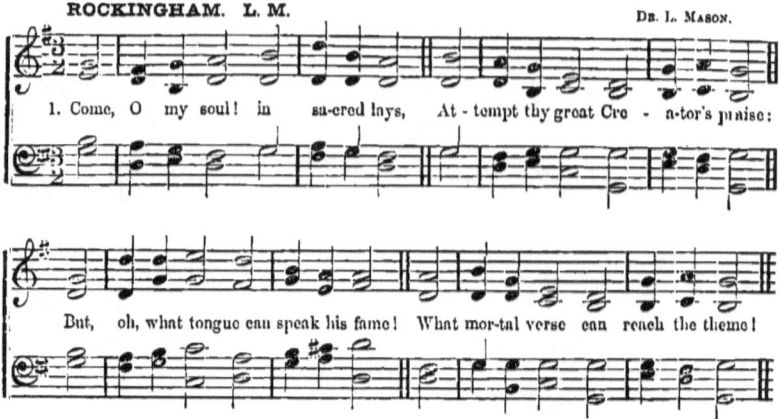

1. Come, O my soul! in sacred lays, Attempt thy great Creator's praise: But, oh, what tongue can speak his fame! What mortal verse can reach the theme!

122.
Perfections.

2 Enthroned amid the radiant spheres,
He glory, like a garment, wears;
To form a robe of light divine,
Ten thousand suns around him shine.

3 In all our Maker's grand designs,
Almighty power, with wisdom, shines;
His works, thro' all this wondrous frame,
Declare the glory of his name.

4 Raised on devotion's lofty wing,
Do thou, my soul, his glories sing;
And let his praise employ thy tongue,
Till listening worlds shall join the song!

123.
Omnipresence.

1 Thou, Lord, who rear'st the mountain's height,
And mak'st the cliffs with sunshine bright,
Oh grant that we may own thy hand
No less in every grain of sand!

2 With forests huge, of dateless time,
Thy will has hung each peak sublime;
But withered leaves beneath the tree
Have tongues that tell as loud of thee.

3 Teach us that not a leaf can grow
Till life from thee within it flow;
That not a grain of dust can be,
O Fount of being! save by thee;

4 That every human word and deed,
Each flash of feeling, will, or creed,
Hath solemn meaning from above,
Begun and ended all in love.

124.
Mystery.

1 Wait, O my soul! thy Maker's will;
Tumultuous passions, all be still!
Nor let a murmuring thought arise;
His ways are just, his counsels wise.

2 He in the thickest darkness dwells,
Performs his work, the cause conceals;
But, though his methods are unknown,
Judgment and truth support his throne.

3 In heaven, and earth, and air, and seas,
He executes his firm decrees;
And by his saints it stands confessed,
That what he does is ever best.

4 Wait, then, my soul! submissive wait,
Prostrate before his awful seat;
And, 'mid the terrors of his rod,
Trust in a wise and gracious God.

125.
Majesty.

1 Kingdoms and thrones to God belong;
Crown him ye nations, in your song;
His wondrous names and powers rehearse;
His honors shall enrich your verse.

2 He shakes the heavens with loud alarms;
How terrible is God in arms!
In Israel are his mercies known,
Israel is his peculiar throne.

3 Proclaim him King, pronounce him blest;
He's your defence, your joy, your rest;
When terrors rise, and nations faint,
God is the strength of every saint.

GOD. 39

LOUVAN. L. M. V. C. Taylor.

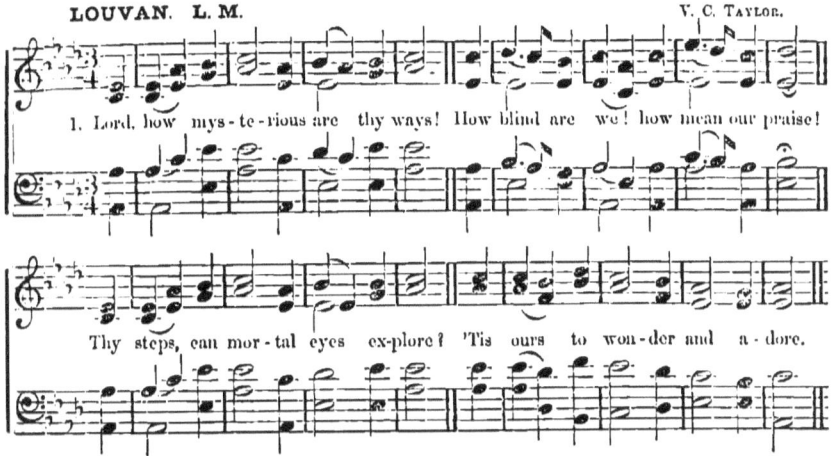

1. Lord, how mys-te-rious are thy ways! How blind are we! how mean our praise! Thy steps, can mor-tal eyes ex-plore? 'Tis ours to won-der and a-dore.

126.
Incomprehensible.

1 Lord, how mysterious are thy ways!
  How blind are we! how mean our praise!
  Thy steps, can mortal eyes explore?
  'Tis ours to wonder and adore.

2 Great God! I would not ask to see
  What in my coming life shall be;
  Enough for me if love divine,
  At length through every cloud shall shine.

3 Are darkness and distress my share?
  Then let me trust thy guardian care;
  If light and bliss attend my days,
  Then let my future hours be praise.

4 Yet this my soul desires to know,
  Be this my only wish below,
  That Christ be mine;—this great request
  Grant, bounteous God, and I am blest!

127.
Perfections.

1 The Lord! how wondrous are his ways!
  How firm his truth! how large his grace!
  He takes his mercy for his throne,
  And thence he makes his glories known.

2 Not half so high his power hath spread
  The starry heavens above our head,
  As his rich love exceeds our praise,
  Exceeds the highest hopes we raise.

3 Not half so far has nature placed
  The rising morning from the west,
  As his forgiving grace removes
  The daily guilt of those he loves.

4 How slowly doth his wrath arise!
  On swifter wings salvation flies:
  Or, if he lets his anger burn,
  How soon his frowns to pity turn!

5 His everlasting love is sure
  To all his saints, and shall endure;
  From age to age his truth shall reign,
  Nor children's children hope in vain.

128.
Omnipresence.

1 Lord of all being! throned afar,
  Thy glory flames from sun and star;
  Centre and soul of every sphere,
  Yet to each loving heart how near!

2 Sun of our life, thy quickening ray
  Sheds on our path the glow of day;
  Star of our hope, thy softened light
  Cheers the long watches of the night.

3 Our midnight is thy smile withdrawn;
  Our noontide is thy gracious dawn;
  Our rainbow arch thy mercy's sign;
  All, save the clouds of sin, are thine!

4 Lord of all life, below, above,
  Whose light is truth, whose warmth is love,
  Before thy ever-blazing throne
  We ask no lustre of our own.

5 Grant us thy truth to make us free,
  And kindling hearts that burn for thee,
  Till all thy living altars claim
  One holy light, one heavenly flame!

40   GOD.

BRATTLE STREET. C. M. Double.   PLEYEL.

1. { While thee I seek, pro-tect-ing Power! Be my vain wish-es stilled;
    And may this con-se-crat-ed hour — — — — — — With bet-ter hopes be filled. }
2. Thy love the power of thought bestowed! To thee my thoughts would soar; Thy mer-cy o'er my life has flowed; That mer-cy I a-dore.

129.
Providence.

3 In each event of life, how clear
  Thy ruling hand I see!
Each blessing to my soul more dear,
  Because conferred by thee.

4 In every joy that crowns my days,
  In every pain I bear,
My heart shall find delight in praise,
  Or seek relief in prayer.

5 When gladness wings my favored hour,
  Thy love my thoughts shall fill;
Resigned, when storms of sorrow lower,
  My soul shall meet thy will.

6 My lifted eye, without a tear,
  The gathering storm shall see;
My steadfast heart shall know no fear;
  That heart shall rest on thee.

130.
Providence.

1 When all thy mercies, O my God!
  My rising soul surveys,
Transported with the view, I'm lost
  In wonder, love, and praise.

2 Unnumbered comforts on my soul
  Thy tender care bestowed,
Before my infant heart conceived
  From whom those comforts flowed.

3 When in the slippery paths of youth
  With heedless steps I ran,
Thine arm, unseen, conveyed me safe,
  And led me up to man.

4 Ten thousand thousand precious gifts
  My daily thanks employ;
Nor is the least a cheerful heart,
  That tastes those gifts with joy.

5 Through every period of my life,
  Thy goodness I'll pursue;
And after death, in distant worlds,
  The glorious theme renew.

6 Through all eternity, to thee
  A joyful song I'll raise:
But oh! eternity's too short
  To utter all thy praise!

GOD.

131.
Beneficence.

1 When morning's first and hallowed ray
  Breaks, with its trembling light,
To chase the pearly dews away,
  Bright tear-drops of the night—
2 My heart, O Lord! forgets to rove,
  But rises gladly free,
On wings of everlasting love,
  And finds its home in thee.
3 When evening's silent shades descend,
  And nature sinks to rest,
Still, to my Father and my Friend,
  My wishes are addressed.
4 Though tears may dim my hours of joy,
  And bid my pleasures flee,
Thou reign'st where grief cannot annoy;
  I will be glad in thee.
5 And ev'n when midnight's solemn gloom
  Above, around is spread,
Sweet dreams of everlasting bloom
  Are hovering o'er my head.
6 I dream of that fair land, O Lord!
  Where all thy saints shall be;
I wake to lean upon thy word,
  And still delight in thee.

132.
"Our Father."

1 Father of mercies! God of love!
  My Father and my God!
I'll sing the honors of thy name,
  And spread thy praise abroad.
2 In every period of my life
  Thy thoughts of love appear;
Thy mercies gild each transient scene,
  And crown each passing year.
3 In all thy mercies, may my soul
  A Father's bounty see;
Nor let the gifts thy grace bestows
  Estrange my heart from thee.
4 Teach me, in times of deep distress,
  To own thy hand, O God!
And in submissive silence learn
  The lessons of thy rod.
5 Through every period of my life,
  Each bright, each clouded scene,
Give me a meek and humble mind,
  Still equal and serene.
6 Then may I close my eyes in death,
  Redeemed from anxious fear;
For death itself, my God, is life,
  If thou art with me there.

133.
Providence.

1 God, in the high and holy place,
  Looks down upon the spheres;
Yet in his providence and grace,
  To every eye appears.
2 He bows the heavens; the mountains stand
  A highway for our God;
He walks amid the desert land;
  'T is Eden where he trod.
3 The forests in his strength rejoice;
  Hark! on the evening breeze,
As once of old, Jehovah's voice
  Is heard among the trees.
4 In every stream his bounty flows,
  Diffusing joy and wealth;
In every breeze his Spirit blows,—
  The breath of life and health.
5 His blessings fall in plenteous showers
  Upon the lap of earth,
That teems with foliage, fruits, and flowers,
  And rings with infant mirth.
6 If God hath made this world so fair,
  Where sin and death abound;
How beautiful, beyond compare,
  Will Paradise be found!

134.
Watchful Care.

1 How are thy servants blest, O Lord!
  How sure is their defence!
Eternal wisdom is their guide,
  Their help, omnipotence.
2 In foreign realms, and lands remote,
  Supported by thy care,
Through burning climes they pass unhurt,
  And breathe in tainted air.
3 When by the dreadful tempest borne
  High on the broken wave,
They know thou art not slow to hear,
  Nor impotent to save.
4 The storm is laid, the winds retire,
  Obedient to thy will;
The sea, that roars at thy command,
  At thy command is still.
5 In midst of dangers, fears, and deaths,
  Thy goodness we'll adore;
We'll praise thee for thy mercies past,
  And humbly hope for more.
6 Our life, while thou preserv'st that life,
  Thy sacrifice shall be;
And death, when death shall be our lot,
  Shall join our souls to thee.

ST. ANN'S. C. M. GOD. Dr. Croft.

1. The Lord our God is full of might, The winds o-bey his will;
He speaks, and in his heaven-ly height, The roll-ing sun stands still.

135.
Power.

2 Rebel, ye waves, and o'er the land
With threatening aspect roar:
The Lord uplifts his awful hand,
And chains you to the shore.

3 Howl, winds of night, your force combine;
Without his high behest
Ye shall not, in the mountain-pine,
Disturb the sparrow's nest.

4 His voice sublime is heard afar,
In distant peals it dies;
He yokes the whirlwind to his car,
And sweeps the howling skies.

5 Ye nations, bend—in reverence bend;
Ye monarchs, wait his nod,
And bid the choral song ascend
To celebrate our God.

136.
Majesty.

1 O God! we praise thee, and confess
That thou the only Lord
And everlasting Father art,
By all the earth adored.

2 To thee, all angels cry aloud;
To thee the powers on high,
Both cherubim and seraphim,
Continually do cry:

3 O holy, holy, holy Lord,
Whom heavenly hosts obey,
The world is with the glory filled
Of thy majestic sway!

4 The apostles' glorious company,
And prophets crowned with light,
With all the martyrs' noble host
Thy constant praise recite.

5 The holy church throughout the world,
O Lord, confesses thee,
That thou th' eternal Father art,
Of boundless majesty.

137.
Providence.

1 Keep silence, all created things!
And wait your Maker's nod;
My soul stands trembling, while she sings
The honors of her God.

2 Life, death, and hell, and worlds unknown,
Hang on his firm decree;
He sits on no precarious throne,
Nor borrows leave to be.

3 His providence unfolds the book,
And makes his counsels shine;
Each opening leaf, and every stroke,
Fulfills some deep design.

4 My God! I would not long to see
My fate, with curious eyes—
What gloomy lines are writ for me,
Or what bright scenes may rise.

5 In thy fair book of life and grace,
Oh! may I find my name
Recorded in some humble place,
Beneath my Lord, the Lamb.

GOD. 43

THAXTED. C. M. — BEETHOVEN.

1. In all my vast con-cerns with thee, In vain my soul would try.... To shun thy pres-ence, Lord! or flee The no-tice of thine eye....

138.
Omniscience.

2 Thine all-surrounding sight surveys
  My rising and my rest,
  My public walks, my private ways,
  And secrets of my breast.

3 My thoughts lie open to the Lord,
  Before they're formed within;
  And, ere my lips pronounce the word,
  He knows the sense I mean.

4 Oh! wondrous knowledge, deep and high,
  Where can a creature hide?
  Within thy circling arms I lie,
  Enclosed on every side.

5 So let thy grace surround me still,
  And like a bulwark prove,
  To guard my soul from every ill,
  Secured by sovereign love.

139.
Providence.

1 God moves in a mysterious way
  His wonders to perform;
  He plants his footsteps in the sea,
  And rides upon the storm.

2 Deep in unfathomable mines
  Of never-failing skill,
  He treasures up his bright designs,
  And works his sovereign will.

3 Ye fearful saints, fresh courage take!
  The clouds ye so much dread
  Are big with mercy, and will break
  In blessings on your head.

4 Judge not the Lord by feeble sense,
  But trust him for his grace;
  Behind a frowning providence
  He hides a smiling face.

5 His purposes will ripen fast,
  Unfolding every hour;
  The bud may have a bitter taste,
  But sweet will be the flower.

6 Blind unbelief is sure to err,
  And scan his work in vain;
  God is his own interpreter,
  And he will make it plain.

140.
Lord of all.

1 The Lord our God is Lord of all;
  His station who can find?
  I hear him in the waterfall;
  I hear him in the wind.

2 If in the gloom of night I shroud,
  His face I cannot fly;
  I see him in the evening cloud,
  And in the morning sky.

3 He smiles, we live! he frowns, we die!
  We hang upon his word;
  He rears his mighty arm on high,
  We fall before his sword.

4 He bids his gales the fields deform;
  Then, when his thunders cease,
  He paints his rainbow on the storm,
  And lulls the winds to peace.

GOD.

DUNDEE. C. M.

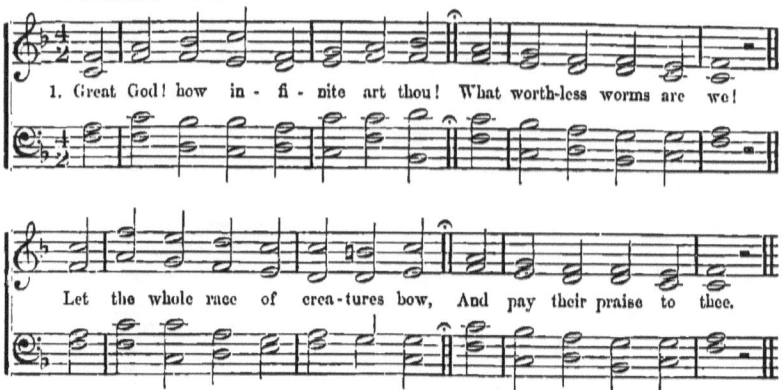

1. Great God! how in-fi-nite art thou! What worth-less worms are we! Let the whole race of crea-tures bow, And pay their praise to thee.

141.
Eternity.

2 Thy throne eternal ages stood,
  Ere seas or stars were made:
  Thou art the ever-living God,
  Were all the nations dead.

3 Eternity, with all its years,
  Stands present in thy view;
  To thee there's nothing old appears—
  Great God! there's nothing new.

4 Our lives thro' various scenes are drawn,
  And vexed with trifling cares;
  While thine eternal thought moves on
  Thine undisturbed affairs.

5 Great God! how infinite art thou!
  What worthless worms are we!
  Let the whole race of creatures bow,
  And pay their praise to thee.

142.
Perfections.

1 I sing th' almighty power of God,
  That made the mountains rise,
  That spread the flowing seas abroad,
  And built the lofty skies.

2 I sing the wisdom that ordained
  The sun to rule the day;
  The moon shines full at his command,
  And all the stars obey.

3 I sing the goodness of the Lord,
  That filled the earth with food;
  He formed the creatures with his word,
  And then pronounced them good.

4 Lord! how thy wonders are displayed
  Where'er I turn mine eye!
  If I survey the ground I tread,
  Or gaze upon the sky!

5 There's not a plant or flower below
  But makes thy glories known;
  And clouds arise, and tempests blow,
  By order from thy throne.

6 Creatures that borrow life from thee
  Are subject to thy care;
  There's not a place where we can flee
  But God is present there.

143.
Perfections.

1 ETERNAL Wisdom! thee we praise,
  Thee the creation sings;
  With thy loved name, rocks, hills, and seas,
  And heaven's high palace rings.

2 How wide thy hand hath spread the sky!
  How glorious to behold!
  Tinged with a blue of heavenly dye,
  And starred with sparkling gold.

3 Infinite strength, and equal skill,
  Shine through the worlds abroad,
  Our souls with vast amazement fill,
  And speak the builder, God.

4 But still the wonders of thy grace
  Our softer passions move;
  Pity divine in Jesus' face
  We see, adore, and love.

GOD. 45

CHESTERFIELD. C. M.   Dr. HAWEIS.

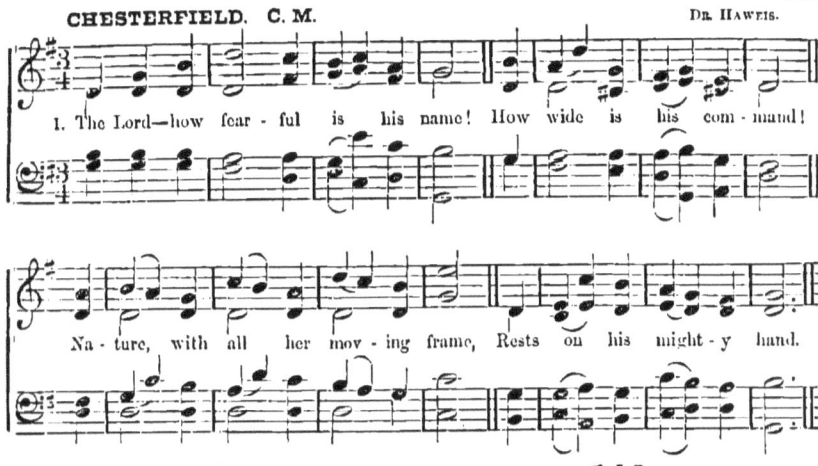

1. The Lord—how fear-ful is his name! How wide is his com-mand! Na-ture, with all her mov-ing frame, Rests on his might-y hand.

144.
Supremacy.

2 Immortal glory forms his throne,
  And light his awful robe;
While with a smile, or with a frown,
  He manages the globe.

3 A word of his almighty breath
  Can swell or sink the seas;
Build the vast empires of the earth,
  Or break them as he please.

4 On angels, with unvailèd face
  His glory beams above;
On men, he looks with softest grace,
  And takes his title, Love.

145.
Holiness.

1 Holy and reverend is the name
  Of our eternal King;
Thrice holy Lord! the angels cry;
  Thrice holy! let us sing.

2 The deepest reverence of the mind,
  Pay, O my soul! to God;
Lift with thy hands a holy heart
  To his sublime abode.

3 With sacred awe pronounce his name
  Whom words nor thoughts can reach;
A broken heart shall please him more
  Than the best forms of speech.

4 Thou holy God! preserve our souls
  From all pollution free;
The pure in heart are thy delight,
  And they thy face shall see.

146.
In nature.

1 Great Ruler of all nature's frame!
  We own thy power divine;
We hear thy breath in every storm,
  For all the winds are thine.

2 Wide as they sweep their sounding way,
  They work thy sovereign will;
And, awed by thy majestic voice,
  Confusion shall be still.

3 Thy mercy tempers every blast
  To them that seek thy face,
And mingles with the tempest's roar
  The whispers of thy grace.

4 Those gentle whispers let me hear,
  Till all the tumult cease;
And gales of paradise shall lull
  My weary soul to peace.

147.
Mystery.

1 Thy way, O Lord, is in the sea;
  Thy paths I cannot trace,
Nor comprehend the mystery
  Of thine unbounded grace.

2 'T is but in part I know thy will;
  I bless thee for the sight:
When will thy love the rest reveal,
  In glory's clearer light?

3 With rapture shall I then survey
  Thy providence and grace;
And spend an everlasting day
  In wonder, love, and praise.

46   CHRIST.

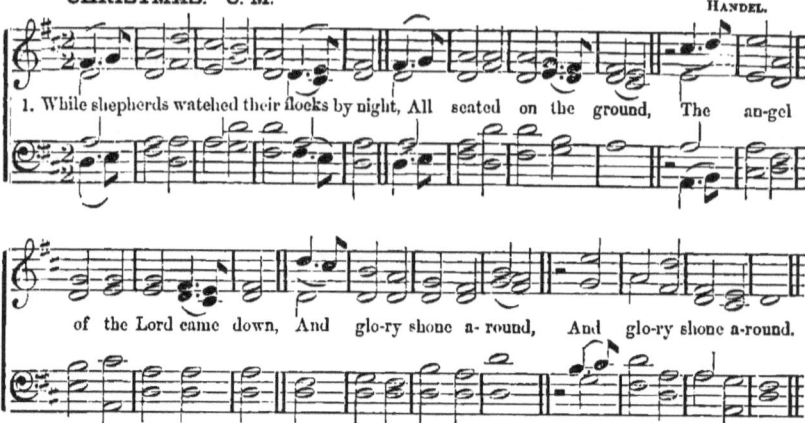

CHRISTMAS. C. M.   HANDEL.

1. While shepherds watched their flocks by night, All seated on the ground, The an-gel of the Lord came down, And glo-ry shone a-round, And glo-ry shone a-round.

148.

2 "Fear not," said he,—for mighty dread
   Had seized their troubled mind,—
"Glad tidings of great joy I bring,
   To you and all mankind.

3 "To you, in David's town, this day,
   Is born of David's line,
The Saviour, who is Christ, the Lord,
   And this shall be the sign;—

4 "The heavenly babe you there shall find
   To human view displayed,
All meanly wrapped in swathing bands,
   And in a manger laid."

5 Thus spake the seraph—and forthwith
   Appeared a shining throng
Of angels, praising God, who thus
   Addressed their joyful song:—

6 "All glory be to God on high,
   And to the earth be peace;
Good-will henceforth from heaven to men
   Begin, and never cease!

149.

1 Joy to the world! the Lord is come!
   Let earth receive her King;
Let every heart prepare him room,
   And heaven and nature sing.

2 Joy to the world! the Saviour reigns!
   Let men their songs employ;
While fields and floods, rocks, hills, and
      plains,
   Repeat the sounding joy.

3 No more let sin and sorrow grow,
   Nor thorns infest the ground:
He comes to make his blessings flow
   Far as the curse is found.

4 He rules the world with truth and grace,
   And makes the nations prove
The glories of his righteousness,
   And wonders of his love.

150.

1 AWAKE, awake the sacred song
   To our incarnate Lord!
Let every heart and every tongue
   Adore th' eternal Word.

2 That awful Word, that sovereign Power,
   By whom the worlds were made—
Oh happy morn! illustrious hour!—
   Was once in flesh arrayed!

3 Then shone almighty power and love,
   In all their glorious forms,
When Jesus left his throne above,
   To dwell with sinful worms.

4 Adoring angels tuned their songs
   To hail the joyful day;
With rapture then let mortal tongues
   Their grateful worship pay.

5 What glory, Lord, to thee is due!
   With wonder we adore;
But could we sing as angels do,
   Our highest praise were poor.

ADVENT.

NEWBOLD. C. M.   KINGSLEY.

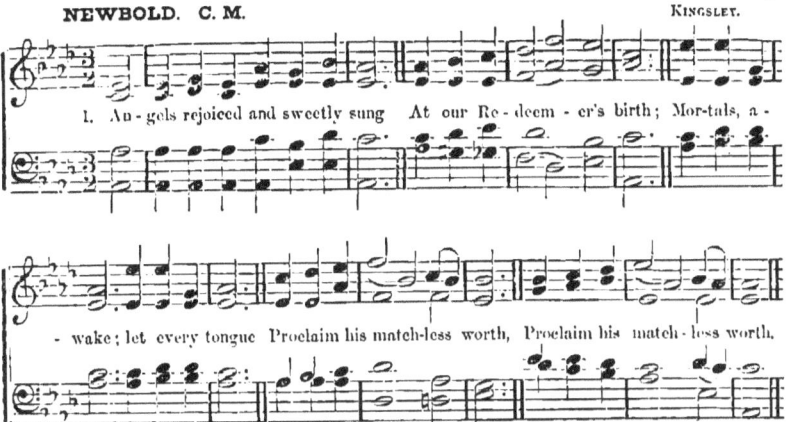

1. Angels rejoiced and sweetly sung At our Redeemer's birth; Mortals, a-wake; let every tongue Proclaim his match-less worth, Proclaim his match-less worth.

151.

1 Angels rejoiced and sweetly sung
    At our Redeemer's birth;
  Mortals! awake; let every tongue
    Proclaim his matchless worth.

2 Glory to God, who dwells on high,
    And sent his only Son
  To take a servant's form, and die,
    For evils we had done!

3 Good-will to men; ye fallen race!
    Arise, and shout for joy;
  He comes, with rich, abounding grace
    To save, and not destroy.

4 Lord! send the gracious tidings forth,
    And fill the world with light,
  That Jew and Gentile, through the earth,
    May know thy saving might.

152.

1 Hark, the glad sound! the Saviour comes,
    The Saviour promised long;
  Let every heart prepare a throne,
    And every voice a song.

2 He comes, the prisoner to release,
    In Satan's bondage held;
  The gates of brass before him burst,
    The iron fetters yield.

3 He comes, from thickest films of vice
    To clear the mental ray,
  And, on the eyes long closed in night,
    To pour celestial day.

4 He comes, the broken heart to bind,
    The bleeding soul to cure,
  And, with the treasures of his grace,
    Enrich the humble poor.

5 Our glad hosannas, Prince of Peace,
    Thy welcome shall proclaim,
  And heaven's eternal arches ring
    With thy beloved name.

153.

1 Calm on the listening ear of night,
    Come heaven's melodious strains,
  Where wild Judea stretches far
    Her silver-mantled plains.

2 Celestial choirs, from courts above,
    Shed sacred glories there,
  And angels, with their sparkling lyres,
    Make music on the air.

3 The answering hills of Palestine
    Send back the glad reply;
  And greet, from all their holy heights,
    The day-spring from on high.

4 O'er the blue depths of Galilee
    There comes a holier calm,
  And Sharon waves, in solemn praise,
    Her silent groves of palm.

5 "Glory to God!" the sounding skies
    Loud with their anthems ring —
  "Peace to the earth, good-will to men,
    From heaven's eternal King."

CHRIST.

TRENT. C. M.   Greatorex Coll.

1. Be-hold! where, in a mor-tal form, Ap-pears each grace di-vine: The vir-tues, all in Je-sus met, With mild-est ra-diance shine.

154.

2 To spread the rays of heavenly light,
To give the mourner joy,
To preach glad tidings to the poor,
Was his divine employ.

3 Mid keen reproach and cruel scorn,
He, meek and patient stood;
His foes, ungrateful, sought his life,
Who labored for their good.

4 In the last hour of deep distress,
Before his Father's throne,
With soul resigned he bowed, and said,—
"Thy will, not mine, be done!"

5 Be Christ our pattern, and our guide,
His image may we bear;
Oh! may we tread his holy steps,—
His joy and glory share.

155.

1 The Saviour! what a noble flame
Was kindled in his breast,
When hasting to Jerusalem,
He marched before the rest!

2 Good-will to men, and zeal for God,
His every thought engross;
He longs to be baptized with blood,
He pants to reach the cross.

3 With all his sufferings full in view,
And woes to us unknown,
Forth to the task his spirit flew;
'T was love that urged him on.

4 Lord, we return thee what we can;
Our hearts shall sound abroad;
Salvation to the dying man,
And to the rising God!

5 And while thy bleeding glories here
Engage our wondering eyes,
We learn our lighter cross to bear,
And hasten to the skies.

156.

1 What grace, O Lord, and beauty shone
Around thy steps below;
What patient love was seen in all
Thy life and death of woe.

2 For, ever on thy burdened heart
A weight of sorrow hung;
Yet no ungentle, murmuring word
Escaped thy silent tongue.

3 Thy foes might hate, despise, revile,
Thy friends unfaithful prove;
Unwearied in forgiveness still,
Thy heart could only love.

4 Oh, give us hearts to love like thee!
Like thee, O Lord, to grieve
Far more for others' sins than all
The wrongs that we receive.

5 One with thyself, may every eye,
In us, thy brethren, see
The gentleness and grace that spring
From union, Lord! with thee.

LIFE AND CHARACTER. 49

HELENA. C. M.   Wm. B. Bradbury.

1. Jesus! thy love shall we forget, And never bring to mind
The grace that paid our hopeless debt, And bade us pardon find?

157.

2 Shall we thy life of grief forget,
Thy fasting and thy prayer;
Thy locks with mountain vapors wet,
To save us from despair?

3 Gethsemane can we forget—
Thy struggling agony;
When night lay dark on Olivet,
And none to watch with thee?

4 Our sorrows and our sins were laid
On thee, alone on thee:
Thy precious blood our ransom paid—
Thine all the glory be!

5 Life's brightest joys we may forget—
Our kindred cease to love;
But he who paid our hopeless debt,
Our constancy shall prove.

158.

1 Lord, as to thy dear cross we flee,
And pray to be forgiven,
So let thy life our pattern be,
And form our souls for heaven.

2 Help us, through good report and ill,
Our daily cross to bear;
Like thee, to do our Father's will,
Our brother's griefs to share.

3 Let grace our selfishness expel,
Our earthliness refine;
And kindness in our bosoms dwell
As free and true as thine.

4 If joy shall at thy bidding fly,
And grief's dark day come on,
We, in our turn, would meekly cry,
"Father, thy will be done!"

5 Should friends misjudge, or foes defame,
Or brethren faithless prove,
Then, like thine own, be all our aim
To conquer them by love.

6 Kept peaceful in the midst of strife,
Forgiving and forgiven,
Oh, may we lead the pilgrim's life,
And follow thee to heaven!

159.

1 Thou art the Way: to thee alone
From sin and death we flee;
And he who would the Father seek,
Must seek him, Lord, by thee.

2 Thou art the Truth: thy word alone
True wisdom can impart;
Thou only canst instruct the mind,
And purify the heart.

3 Thou art the Life: the rending tomb
Proclaims thy conquering arm;
And those who put their trust in thee
Nor death nor hell shall harm.

4 Thou art the Way, the Truth, the Life:
Grant us to know that Way;
That Truth to keep, that Life to win,
Which leads to endless day.

50   CHRIST.
ROCKINGHAM. L. M.   Dr. L. Mason.

1. My dear Redeemer and my Lord! I read my duty in thy word; But in thy life the law appears, Drawn out in living characters.

160.

2 Such was thy truth, and such thy zeal,
Such deference to thy Father's will,
Thy love and meekness so divine,
I would transcribe and make them mine.

3 Cold mountains, and the midnight air,
Witnessed the fervor of thy prayer;
The desert thy temptations knew,
Thy conflict, and thy victory too.

4 Be thou my pattern; make me bear
More of thy gracious image here;
Then God, the Judge, shall own my name
Among the followers of the Lamb.

161.

1 How sweetly flowed the gospel sound
From lips of gentleness and grace,
When listening thousands gathered round,
And joy and gladness filled the place!

2 From heaven he came, of heaven he spoke,
To heaven he led his followers' way;
Dark clouds of gloomy night he broke,
Unvailing an immortal day.

3 "Come, wanderers, to my Father's home,
Come, all ye weary ones, and rest:"
Yes, sacred Teacher, we will come,
Obey thee, love thee, and be blest!

4 Decay, then, tenements of dust;
Pillars of earthly pride, decay:
A nobler mansion waits the just,
And Jesus has prepared the way.

162.

1 How beauteous were the marks divine,
That in thy meekness used to shine;
That lit thy lonely pathway, trod
In wondrous love, O Son of God!

2 Oh! who like Thee—so calm, so bright,
So pure, so made to live in light?
Oh! who like thee did ever go
So patient through a world of woe?

3 Oh! who like thee so humbly bore
The scorn, the scoffs of men, before?
So meek, forgiving, godlike, high,
So glorious in humility!

4 Oh! in thy light be mine to go,
Illuming all my way of woe;
And give me ever on the road
To trace thy footsteps, Son of God!

163.

1 Not to condemn the sons of men,
Did Christ, the Son of God, appear;
No weapons in his hands are seen,
No flaming sword, nor thunder there.

2 Such was the pity of our God,
He loved the race of man so well,
He sent his Son to bear our load
Of sins, and save our souls from hell.

3 Sinners, believe the Saviour's word;
Trust in his mighty name, and live:
A thousand joys his lips afford,
His hands a thousand blessings give.

LIFE AND CHARACTER. 51

BEETHOVEN. L. M.   HAYDN.

1. O'er the dark wave of Ga-li-lee The gloom of twi-light gath-ers fast, And on the wa-ters drear-i-ly De-scends the fit-ful evening blast.

164.

2 The weary bird hath left the air,
And sunk into his sheltered nest;
The wandering beast has sought his lair,
And laid him down to welcome rest.

3 Still near the lake, with weary tread,
Lingers a form of human kind;
And on his lone, unsheltered head,
Flows the chill night-damp of the wind.

4 Why seeks he not a home of rest?
Why seeks he not a pillowed bed?
Beasts have their dens, the bird its nest;
He hath not where to lay his head.

5 Such was the lot he freely chose,
To bless, to save the human race;
And through his poverty there flows
A rich, full stream of heavenly grace.

165.

1 THE morning dawns upon the place
Where Jesus spent the night in prayer;
Through yielding glooms behold his face!
Nor form, nor comeliness is there.

2 Brought forth to judgment, now he stands
Arraigned, condemned, at Pilate's bar;
Here, spurned by fierce prætorian bands,
There, mocked by Herod's men of war.

3 He bears their buffeting and scorn—
Mock-homage of the lip, the knee—
The purple robe, the crown of thorn—
The scourge, the nail, th' accursed tree.

4 No guile within his mouth is found;
He neither threatens, nor complains;
Meek as a lamb for slaughter bound,
Dumb, 'mid his murderers he remains.

5 But hark! he prays: 't is for his foes:
And speaks: 't is comfort to his friends;
Answers: and paradise bestows;
He bows his head: the conflict ends.

166.

1 WHEN, like a stranger on our sphere
The lowly Jesus wandered here,
Where'er he went, affliction fled,
And sickness reared her fainting head.

2 The eye that rolled in irksome night,
Beheld his face,—for God is light;
The opening ear, the loosened tongue,
His precepts heard, his praises sung.

3 With bounding steps, the halt and lame,
To hail their great deliverer came;
O'er the cold grave he bowed his head,
He spake the word, and raised the dead.

4 Despairing madness, dark and wild,
In his inspiring presence smiled;
The storm of horror ceased to roll,
And reason lightened through the soul.

5 Through paths of loving-kindness led,
Where Jesus triumphed we would tread;
To all, with willing hands, dispense
The gifts of our benevolence.

CHRIST.

HAMBURG. L. M — *Arranged by Dr. L. Mason.*

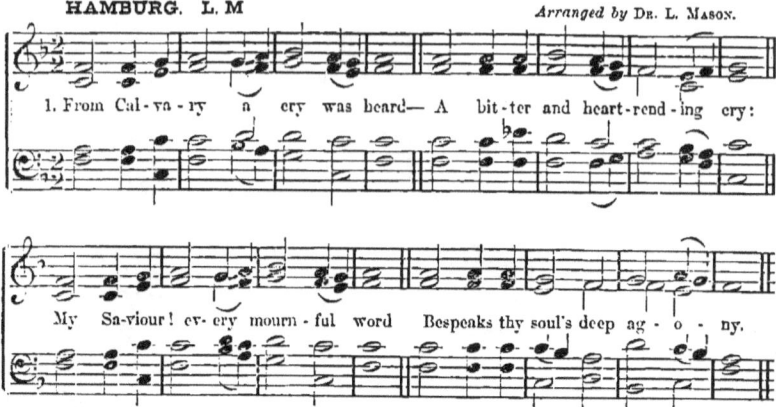

1. From Cal-va-ry a cry was heard— A bit-ter and heart-rend-ing cry: My Sa-viour! ev-ery mourn-ful word Bespeaks thy soul's deep ag-o-ny.

167.

2 A horror of great darkness fell
On thee, thou spotless, holy One!
And all the swarming hosts of hell
Conspired to tempt God's only Son.

3 The scourge, the thorns, the deep disgrace—
These thou could'st bear, nor once repine;
But when Jehovah vailed his face,
Unutterable pangs were thine.

4 Let the dumb world its silence break;
Let pealing anthems rend the sky;
Awake, my sluggish soul, awake!
He died, that we might never die.

5 Lord! on thy cross I fix mine eye,
If e'er I lose its strong control,
Oh! let that dying, piercing cry,
Melt and reclaim my wandering soul.

168.

1 Jesus, whom angel hosts adore,
Became a man of griefs for me;
In love, though rich, becoming poor,
That I through him enriched might be.

2 Though Lord of all, above, below,
He went to Olivet for me;
There drank my cup of wrath and woe,
When bleeding in Gethsemane.

3 The ever-blessed Son of God
Went up to Calvary for me;
There paid my debt, there bore my load,
In his own body on the tree.

4 Jesus, whose dwelling is the skies,
Went down into the grave for me;
There overcame my enemies,
There won the glorious victory.

5 'T is finished all: the vail is rent,
The welcome sure, the access free;—
Now then, we leave our banishment,
O Father, to return to thee!

169.

1 When I survey the wondrous cross,
On which the Prince of glory died,
My richest gain I count but loss,
And pour contempt on all my pride.

2 Forbid it, Lord! that I should boast,
Save in the death of Christ, my God;
All the vain things that charm me most,
I sacrifice them to his blood.

3 See, from his head, his hands, his feet,
Sorrow and love flow mingled down;
Did e'er such love and sorrow meet,
Or thorns compose so rich a crown?

4 His dying crimson, like a robe,
Spreads o'er his body on the tree;
Then I am dead to all the globe,
And all the globe is dead to me.

5 Were the whole realm of nature mine,
That were a present far too small;
Love so amazing, so divine,
Demands my soul, my life, my all.

SUFFERINGS AND DEATH. 53

SOLITUDE. L. M. V. C. Taylor.

1. 'Tis mid-night—and on O-live's brow The star is dimmed that lately shone;
'Tis mid-night—in the gar-den now The suf-fering Sa-viour prays a-lone.

170.

2 'T is midnight—and from all removed,
Immanuel wrestles lone with fears;
Ev'n the disciple that he loved,
Heeds not his Master's griefs and tears.

3 'T is midnight—and for others' guilt
The Man of sorrows weeps in blood;
Yet he that hath in anguish knelt,
Is not forsaken by his God.

4 'T is midnight—and from ether-plains
Is borne the song that angels know;
Unheard by mortals are the strains
That sweetly soothe the Saviour's woe.

171.

1 "'T is finished!"—so the Saviour cried,
And meekly bowed his head, and died:
'T is finished!—yes, the race is run,
The battle fought, the victory won.

2 'T is finished!—all that heaven foretold
By prophets in the days of old;
And truths are opened to our view,
That kings and prophets never knew.

3 'T is finished!—Son of God, thy power
Hath triumphed in this awful hour;
And yet, our eyes with sorrow see
That life to us was death to thee.

4 'T is finished!—let the joyful sound
Be heard through all the nations round;
'T is finished!—let the echo fly
Thro' heaven and hell, thro' earth and sky.

172.

1 Deep in our hearts let us record
The deeper sorrows of our Lord;
Behold the rising billows roll,
To overwhelm his holy soul!

2 Yet, gracious God, thy power and love
Have made the curse a blessing prove:
Those dreadful sufferings of thy Son
Atoned for crimes which we had done.

3 Oh, for his sake, our guilt forgive,
And let the mourning sinner live!
The Lord will hear us in his name,
Nor shall our hope be turned to shame.

173.

1 Stretched on the cross the Saviour dies!
Hark! his expiring groans arise:
See—from his hands, his feet, his side;
Fast flows the sacred, crimson tide!

2 But life attends the deathful sound,
And flows from every bleeding wound:
The vital stream,—how free it flows,
To save and cleanse his rebel foes.

3 Can I survey this scene of woe,
Where mingling grief and wonder flow,
And yet my heart unmoved remain,
Insensible to love or pain?

4 Come, dearest Lord! thy grace impart
To warm this cold, this stupid heart;
Till all its powers and passions move
In melting grief, and ardent love.

CHRIST.

AVON. C. M.   Scottish.

1. Alas! and did my Saviour bleed, And did my Sovereign die? Would he devote that sacred head For such a worm as I?

174.

1 Alas! and did my Saviour bleed,
   And did my Sovereign die?
   Would he devote that sacred head
   For such a worm as I?

2 Was it for crimes that I had done
   He groaned upon the tree?
   Amazing pity! grace unknown!
   And love beyond degree!

3 Well might the sun in darkness hide,
   And shut his glories in,
   When Christ, the great Creator, died
   For man, the creature's sin.

4 Thus might I hide my blushing face
   While his dear cross appears;
   Dissolve my heart in thankfulness,
   And melt my eyes to tears.

5 But drops of grief can ne'er repay
   The debt of love I owe;
   Here, Lord, I give myself away,
   'T is all that I can do.

175.

1 Behold the Saviour of mankind,
   Nailed to the shameful tree!
   How vast the love that him inclined
   To bleed and die for me!

2 Hark! how he groans, while nature shakes,
   And earth's strong pillars bend!
   The temple's vail asunder breaks,
   The solid marbles rend.

3 'T is finished! now the ransom's paid,
   "Receive my soul!" he cries:
   See—how he bows his sacred head!
   He bows his head and dies!

4 But soon he'll break death's iron chain,
   And in full glory shine;
   O Lamb of God! was ever pain—
   Was ever love like thine!

176.

1 Oh! if my soul were formed for woe,
   How would I vent my sighs!
   Repentance should like rivers flow
   From both my streaming eyes.

2 'T was for my sins my dearest Lord
   Hung on the cursed tree,
   And groaned away a dying life
   For thee, my soul! for thee.

3 Oh! how I hate these lusts of mine
   That crucified my Lord;
   Those sins that pierced and nailed his flesh
   Fast to the fatal wood!

4 Yes, my Redeemer—they shall die;
   My heart has so decreed;
   Nor will I spare the guilty things
   That made my Saviour bleed.

5 While with a melting, broken heart,
   My murdered Lord I view,
   I'll raise revenge against my sins,
   And slay the murderers too.

RESURRECTION AND ASCENSION.

LENOX. H. M. Edson.

1. Come, ev-ery pi-ous heart, That loves the Saviour's name! Your noblest powers exert To cel-e-brate his fame; Tell all a-bove, And Tell all a-bove, And all be-low, Tell all be-low, Tell all a-bove, And all be-low, The debt of love To him you owe.

177.

2 He left his starry crown,
  And laid his robes aside ;
On wings of love came down,
  And wept, and bled, and died :
What he endured, | To save our souls
No tongue can tell, | From death and hell.

3 From the dark grave he rose—
  The mansion of the dead ;
And thence his mighty foes
  In glorious triumph led ;
Up through the sky | And reigns on high,
The conqueror rode, | The Saviour-God.

4 From thence he 'll quickly come—
  His chariot will not stay—
And bear our spirits home
  To realms of endless day :
There shall we see | And ever be
His lovely face, | In his embrace.

178.

1 YES, the Redeemer rose ;
  The Saviour left the dead ;
And o'er our hellish foes
  High raised his conquering head,
In wild dismay, | Fall to the ground,
The guards around | And sink away.

2 Lo ! the angelic bands
  In full assembly meet,
To wait his high commands,
  And worship at his feet :
Joyful they come, | From realms of day,
And wing their way, | To Jesus' tomb.

3 Then back to heaven they fly,
  And the glad tidings bear :
Hark ! as they soar on high,
  What music fills the air !
Their anthems say : | Hath left the dead ;
"Jesus who bled | He rose to-day."

4 Ye mortals, catch the sound,
  Redeemed by him from hell ;
And send the echo round
  The globe on which you dwell :
Transported cry : | Hath left the dead,
"Jesus who bled | No more to die."

5 All hail, triumphant Lord,
  Who sav'st us with thy blood !
Wide be thy name adored,
  Thou rising, reigning God !
With thee we rise, | And empires gain
With thee we reign, | Beyond the skies.

BENNINGTON. L. M. Double.   CHRIST.   *Arranged from* PERCIVAL.

1. Our Lord is ris-en from the dead, Our Je-sus is gone up on high; The powers of hell are cap-tive led, Dragged to the portals of the sky. 2. There his triumphal chariot waits, And angels chant the sol-emn lay: "Lift up your heads, ye heav'nly gates, Ye everlasting doors! give way."

179.

3 Loose all your bars of massy light,
And wide unfold th' ethereal scene:
He claims these mansions as his right;
Receive the King of glory in.
4 Who is the King of glory—who?
The Lord who all our foes o'ercame;
Who sin, and death, and hell o'erthrew;
And Jesus is the conqueror's name.
5 Lo! his triumphal chariot waits,
And angels chant the solemn lay:—
"Lift up your heads, ye heavenly gates!
Ye everlasting doors! give way."
6 Who is the King of glory—who?
The Lord of boundless power possessed;
The King of saints and angels, too,
God over all, forever blessed.

180.

1 THE King of saints.—how fair his face!
Adorned with majesty and grace,
He comes, with blessings from above,
And wins the nations to his love.
2 At his right hand, our eyes behold
The queen, arrayed in purest gold;
The world admires her heavenly dress,
Her robe of joy and righteousness.

3 Oh! happy hour, when thou shalt rise
To his fair palace in the skies;
And all thy sons, a numerous train,
Each, like a prince, in glory reign.
4 Let endless honors crown his head;
Let every age his praises spread;
While we, with cheerful songs, approve
The condescension of his love.

181.

1 ETERNAL God, celestial King!
Exalted be thy glorious name;
Let hosts in heaven thy praises sing,
And saints on earth thy love proclaim.
2 My heart is fixed on thee, my God!
I rest my hope on thee alone;
I'll spread thy sacred truths abroad,
To all mankind thy love make known.
3 Awake, my tongue! awake, my lyre!
With morning's earliest dawn arise;
To songs of joy my soul inspire,
And swell your music to the skies.
4 With those who in thy grace abound,
To thee I'll raise my thankful voice;
While every land, the earth around,
Shall hear, and in thy name rejoice.

ADORATION. 57

DUKE STREET. L. M. J. HATTON.

1. Now to the Lord, who makes us know
The wonders of his dying love,
Be humble honors paid below,
And strains of nobler praise above.

182.

2 'T was he who cleansed our foulest sins,
And washed us in his precious blood;
'T is he who makes us priests and kings,
And brings us rebels near to God.

3 To Jesus, our atoning Priest,
To Jesus, our eternal King,
Be everlasting power confessed!
Let every tongue his glory sing.

4 Behold! on flying clouds he comes,
And every eye shall see him move;
Though with our sins we pierced him once,
He now displays his pardoning love.

5 The unbelieving world shall wail,
While we rejoice to see the day;
Come, Lord! nor let thy promise fail,
Nor let thy chariot long delay.

183.

1 COME, let us sing the song of songs—
The saints in heaven began the strain—
The homage which to Christ belongs:
" Worthy the Lamb, for he was slain!"

2 Slain to redeem us by his blood,
To cleanse from every sinful stain,
And make us kings and priests to God—
'" Worthy the Lamb, for he was slain!"

3 To him who suffered on the tree,
Our souls, at his soul's price, to gain,
Blessing, and praise, and glory be:
" Worthy the Lamb, for he was slain!"

4 To him, enthroned by filial right,
All power in heaven and earth proclaim,
Honor, and majesty, and might:
" Worthy the Lamb, for he was slain!"

5 Long as we live, and when we die,
And while in heaven with him we reign;
This song, our song of songs shall be:
" Worthy the Lamb, for he was slain;"

184.

1 BRIGHT King of Glory, dreadful God!
Our spirits bow before thy feet:
To thee we lift an humble thought,
And worship at thine awful seat.

2 A thousand seraphs strong and bright
Stand round the glorious Deity;
But who, among the sons of light,
Pretends comparison with thee?

3 Yet there is One of human frame,
Jesus, arrayed in flesh and blood,
Thinks it no robbery to claim
A full equality with God.

4 Their glory shines with equal beams:
Their essence is forever one,
Though they are known by different names,
The Father God, and God the Son.

5 Then let the name of Christ our King
With equal honors be adored;
His praise let every angel sing,
And all the nations own the Lord.

CHRIST.

HARWELL. 8s & 7s. Dr. L. Mason.

1. Hark! ten thousand harps and voices Sound the note of praise above: Jesus reigns, and heaven rejoices; Jesus reigns, the God of love: See, he sits on yonder throne; Jesus rules the world alone. Hal-le-lu-jah, hal-le-lu-jah, hal-le-lu-jah, A-men.

185.

2 Jesus! hail! whose glory brightens
All above, and gives it worth;
Lord of life! thy smile enlightens,
Cheers, and charms thy saints on earth:
When we think of love like thine,
Lord! we own it love divine.

3 King of glory! reign for ever—
Thine an everlasting crown;
Nothing, from thy love, shall sever
Those whom thou hast made thine own;—
Happy objects of thy grace,
Destined to behold thy face.

4 Saviour! hasten thine appearing;
Bring—oh, bring the glorious day,
When the awful summons hearing,
Heaven and earth shall pass away;—
Then, with golden harps, we'll sing,—
"Glory, glory to our King."

186.

1 Hail, thou once despiséd Jesus!
Crowned in mockery a king!
Thou didst suffer to release us;
Thou didst free salvation bring.
Hail, thou agonizing Saviour,
Bearer of our sin and shame!
By thy merits we find favor;
Life is given through thy name.

2 Jesus, hail! enthroned in glory,
There for ever to abide;
All the heavenly host adore thee,
Seated at thy Father's side:
There for sinners thou art pleading;
There thou dost our place prepare:
Ever for us interceding,
Till in glory we appear.

3 Worship, honor, power, and blessing
Thou art worthy to receive;
Loudest praises, without ceasing,
Meet it is for us to give.
Help, ye bright angelic spirits;
Bring your sweetest, noblest lays;
Help to sing our Saviour's merits;
Help to chant Immanuel's praise.

187.

1 Hail, my ever-blesséd Jesus!
Only thee I wish to sing;
To my soul thy name is precious,
Thou my Prophet, Priest, and King.
Oh! what mercy flows from heaven!
Oh! what joy and happiness!
Love I much? I'm much forgiven;
I'm a miracle of grace.

2 Once, with Adam's race in ruin,
Unconcerned in sin I lay,
Swift destruction still pursuing,
Till my Saviour passed that way.
Witness, all ye hosts of heaven,
My Redeemer's tenderness;
Love I much? I'm much forgiven;
I'm a miracle of grace.

ADORATION. 59

CARTHAGE. 8s & 7s.   Root & Sweetser's Coll.

1. Christ, a-bove all glo-ry seat-ed! King e-ter-nal, strong to save! To thee, Death by death de-feat-ed, Tri-umph high and glo-ry gave.

188.

2 Thou art gone, where now is given,
  What no mortal might could gain:
On the eternal throne of heaven,
  In thy Father's power to reign.

3 There thy kingdoms all adore thee,
  Heaven above and earth below,
While the depths of hell before thee,
  Trembling and defeated bow.

4 We, O Lord! with hearts adoring,
  Follow thee above the sky.
Hear our prayers thy grace imploring,
  Lift our souls to thee on high.

5 So when thou again in glory
  On the clouds of heaven shalt shine,
We thy flock may stand before thee,
  Owned forevermore as thine.

189.

1 Lo! Jehovah, we adore thee—
  Thee, our Saviour—thee, our God;
From thy throne let beams of glory
  Shine through all the world abroad.

2 Jesus! thee our Saviour hailing,
  Thee our God in praise we own;
Highest honors, never failing,
  Rise eternal round thy throne.

3 Now, ye saints, his power confessing,
  In your grateful strains adore;
For his mercy, never ceasing,
  Flows, and flows forevermore.

190.

1 One there is, above all others,
  Well deserves the name of Friend·
His is love beyond a brother's,
  Costly, free, and knows no end.

2 Which of all our friends, to save us,
  Could or would have shed his blood?
But our Jesus died to have us
  Reconciled in him to God.

3 When he lived on earth abased,
  Friend of sinners was his name;
Now above all glory raised,
  He rejoices in the same.

4 Oh! for grace our hearts to soften!
  Teach us, Lord, at length, to love;
We, alas! forget too often
  What a friend we have above.

191.

1 Jesus comes, his conflict over,
  Comes to claim his great reward;
Angels round the victor hover,
  Crowding to behold their Lord.

2 Yonder throne for him erected,
  Now becomes the victor's seat;
Lo, the man on earth rejected!
  Angels worship at his feet.

3 Day and night they cry before him,—
  "Holy, holy, holy Lord!"
All the powers of heaven adore him;
  All obey his sovereign word.

CHRIST.

MOZART. 7s. *Arranged from* MOZART.

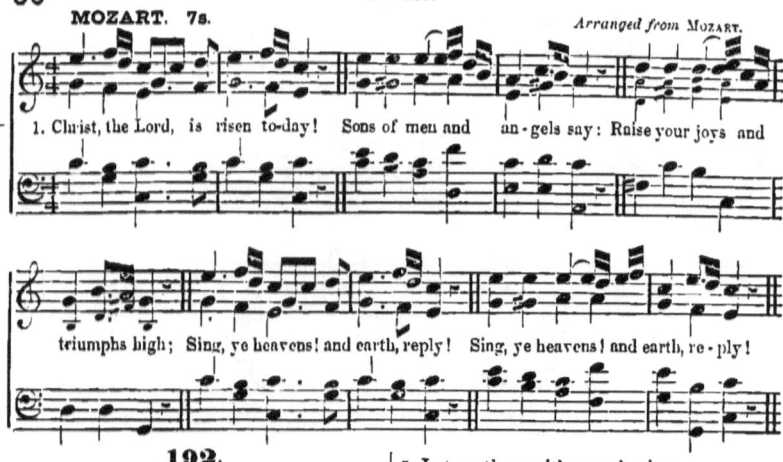

1. Christ, the Lord, is risen to-day! Sons of men and an-gels say: Raise your joys and triumphs high; Sing, ye heavens! and earth, reply! Sing, ye heavens! and earth, re-ply!

192.

2 Love's redeeming work is done,
Fought the fight, the battle won;
Lo! our sun's eclipse is o'er;
Lo! he sets in blood no more.

3 Vain the stone, the watch, the seal—
Christ hath burst the gates of hell:
Death in vain forbids his rise,
Christ hath opened paradise.

4 Lives again our glorious King!
Where, O Death, is now thy sting?
Once he died, our souls to save;
Where's thy victory, boasting Grave?

193.
Advent.

1 HARK! the herald angels sing,
"Glory to the new-born King!
Peace on earth, and mercy mild;
God and sinners reconciled."

2 Joyful, all ye nations, rise;
Join the triumphs of the skies;
With the angelic hosts proclaim,
"Christ is born in Bethlehem."

3 Mild he lays his glory by;
Born that man no more may die;
Born to raise the sons of earth;
Born to give them second birth.

4 Hail, the heaven-born Prince of Peace!
Hail, the Sun of Righteousness!
Light and life to all he brings,
Risen with healing in his wings.

5 Let us then with angels sing,
"Glory to the new-born King!—
Peace on earth and mercy mild,
God and sinners reconciled!"

194.

1 ANGELS! roll the rock away;
Death! yield up thy mighty prey;
See! the Saviour leaves the tomb,
Glowing with immortal bloom.

2 Hark! the wondering angels raise
Louder notes of joyful praise;
Let the earth's remotest bound
Echo with the blissful sound.

3 Now, ye saints, lift up your eyes,
See him high in glory rise!
Hosts of angels, on the road,
Hail him—the incarnate God.

4 Heaven unfolds its portals wide,
See the Conqueror through them ride!
King of glory! mount thy throne—
Boundless empire is thine own.

5 Praise him, ye celestial choirs!
Tune, and sweep your golden lyres;
Raise, O earth! your noblest songs,
From ten thousand thousand tongues.

6 Every note with wonder swell,
Sin o'erthrown, and captive hell!
Where, O death, is now thy sting?
Where thy terrors, vanquished king?

ADORATION. 61

CORONATION. C. M.   OLIVER HOLDEN.

1. All hail! the power of Jesus' name! Let angels prostrate fall! Bring forth the royal diadem, And crown him Lord of all, Bring forth the royal di-a-dem, And crown him Lord of all.

195.

2 Ye chosen seed of Israel's race,
  Ye ransomed from the fall;
  Hail him, who saves you by his grace,
  And crown him Lord of all.

3 Sinners, whose love can ne'er forget
  The wormwood and the gall;
  Go, spread your trophies at his feet,
  And crown him Lord of all.

4 Let every kindred, every tribe,
  On this terrestrial ball,
  To him all majesty ascribe,
  And crown him Lord of all.

5 Oh! that with yonder sacred throng,
  We at his feet may fall;
  We'll join the everlasting song,
  And crown him Lord of all.

196.

1 Behold the glories of the Lamb,
  Amid his Father's throne;
  Prepare new honors for his name,
  And songs before unknown.

2 Let elders worship at his feet,
  The church adore around,
  With vials full of odors sweet,
  And harps of sweeter sound.

3 Those are the prayers of all the saints,
  And these the hymns they raise:
  Jesus is kind to our complaints;
  He loves to hear our praise.

4 Now to the Lamb that once was slain,
  Be endless blessings paid!
  Salvation, glory, joy remain
  Forever on thy head!

5 Thou hast redeemed our souls with blood,
  Hast set the prisoners free,
  Hast made us kings and priests to God,
  And we shall reign with thee.

197.

1 Hosanna to the Prince of light,
  That clothed himself in clay;
  Entered the iron gates of death,
  And tore the bars away.

2 See how the Conqueror mounts aloft,
  And to his Father flies,
  With scars of honor in his flesh,
  And triumph in his eyes.

3 There our exalted Saviour reigns,
  And scatters blessings down,
  Our Jesus fills the middle seat,
  Of the celestial throne.

4 Raise your devotion, mortal tongues,
  To reach his blessed abode;
  Sweet be the accents of your songs
  To our incarnate God.

5 Bright angels! strike your loudest strings
  Your sweetest voices raise;
  Let heaven, and all created things,
  Sound our Immanuel's praise.

ORTONVILLE. C. M. — Dr. Hastings.

1. Majestic sweetness sits enthroned
On my Redeemer's brow;
His head with radiant glories crowned,
His lips with grace o'erflow.

198.

2 No mortal can with him compare
Among the sons of men;
Fairer he is than all the fair
That fill the heavenly train.

3 He saw me plunged in deep distress,
He flew to my relief;
For me he bore the shameful cross,
And carried all my grief.

4 To him I owe my life, and breath,
And all the joys I have:
He makes me triumph over death,
And saves me from the grave.

5 Since from his bounty I receive
Such proofs of love divine,
Had I a thousand hearts to give,
Lord, they should all be thine!

199.

1 The Saviour! oh! what endless charms
Dwell in the blissful sound!
Its influence every fear disarms,
And spreads sweet comfort round.

2 Here pardon, life and joys divine,
In rich effusion flow,
For guilty rebels lost in sin,
And doomed to endless woe.

3 The almighty Former of the skies
Stooped to our vile abode;
While angels viewed with wondering eyes
And hailed the incarnate God.

4 Oh! the rich depths of love divine!
Of bliss a boundless store!
Dear Saviour, let me call thee mine;
I cannot wish for more.

5 On thee alone my hope relies,
Beneath thy cross I fall;
My Lord, my Life, my Sacrifice,
My Saviour, and my All!

200.

1 Oh! for a thousand tongues to sing
My dear Redeemer's praise!
The glories of my God and King,
The triumphs of his grace!

2 My gracious Master and my God!
Assist me to proclaim,
To spread, through all the earth abroad,
The honors of thy name.

3 Jesus—the name that calms my fears,
That bids my sorrows cease;
'Tis music to my ravished ears;
'Tis life, and health, and peace.

4 He breaks the power of reigning sin,
He sets the prisoner free;
His blood can make the foulest clean;
His blood availed for me.

5 Let us obey, we then shall know,
Shall feel our sins forgiven;
Anticipate our heaven below,
And own, that love is heaven.

ADORATION.

BRADFORD. C. M.   HANDEL.

1. I know that my Redeemer lives, And ever prays for me: A token of his love he gives, A pledge of liberty.

201.

2 I find him lifting up my head;
He brings salvation near:
His presence makes me free indeed,
And he will soon appear.

3 He wills that I should holy be:
What can withstand his will?
The counsel of his grace in me
He surely shall fulfill.

4 Jesus, I hang upon thy word;
I steadfastly believe
Thou wilt return, and claim me, Lord,
And to thyself receive.

5 When God is mine, and I am his,
Of paradise possessed,
I taste unutterable bliss,
And everlasting rest.

202.

1 He, who on earth as man was known,
And bore our sins and pains,
Now, seated on th' eternal throne,
The God of glory reigns.

2 His hands the wheels of nature guide
With an unerring skill;
And countless worlds, extended wide,
Obey his sovereign will.

3 While harps unnumbered sound his praise
In yonder world above,
His saints on earth admire his ways,
And glory in his love.

4 When troubles, like a burning sun,
Beat heavy on their head;
To this almighty rock they run,
And find a pleasing shade.

5 How glorious he—how happy they,
In such a glorious friend!
Whose love secures them all the way,
And crowns them at the end.

203.

1 Come, let us join our songs of praise
To our ascended Priest;
He entered heaven, with all our names
Engraven on his breast.

2 Below he washed our guilt away,
By his atoning blood;
Now he appears before the throne,
And pleads our cause with God.

3 Clothed with our nature still, he knows
The weakness of our frame,
And how to shield us from the foes
Whom he himself o'ercame.

4 Nor time, nor distance, e'er shall quench
The fervor of his love;
For us he died in kindness here,
For us he lives above.

5 Oh! may we ne'er forget his grace,
Nor blush to bear his name;
Still may our hearts hold fast his faith—
Our lips his praise proclaim.

HOLY SPIRIT.

WIMBORNE. L. M.
Greatorex Coll.

1. E-ter-nal Spi-rit, we con-fess, And sing the won-ders of thy grace; Thy pow'r conveys our blessings down From God the Fa-ther and the Son.

204.

2 Enlightened by thy heavenly ray,
Our shades and darkness turn to day;
Thine inward teachings make us know
Our danger, and our refuge too.

3 Thy power and glory work within,
And break the chains of reigning sin;
All our imperious lusts subdue,
And form our wretched hearts anew.

4 The troubled conscience knows thy voice;
Thy cheering words awake our joys;
Thy words allay the stormy wind,
And calm the surges of the mind.

205.

1 Come, O Creator Spirit blest!
And in our souls take up thy rest;
Come, with thy grace and heavenly aid,
To fill the hearts which thou hast made.

2 Great Comforter! to thee we cry;
O highest gift of God most high!
O fount of life! O fire of love!
Send sweet anointing from above!

3 Kindle our senses from above,
And make our hearts o'erflow with love;
With patience firm, and virtue high,
The weakness of our flesh supply.

4 Far from us drive the foe we dread,
And grant us thy true peace instead;
So shall we not, with thee for guide,
Turn from the path of life aside.

206.

1 Come, blessed Spirit! source of light!
Whose power and grace are unconfined,
Dispel the gloomy shades of night,—
The thicker darkness of the mind.

2 To mine illumined eyes, display
The glorious truth thy word reveals;
Cause me to run the heavenly way,
Thy book unfold, and loose the seals.

3 Thine inward teachings make me know
The mysteries of redeeming love,
The vanity of things below,
And excellence of things above.

4 While through this dubious maze I stray,
Spread, like the sun, thy beams abroad,
To show the dangers of the way,
And guide my feeble steps to God.

207.

1 Come, Holy Spirit! calm my mind,
And fit me to approach my God;
Remove each vain, each worldly thought,
And lead me to thy blest abode.

2 Hast thou imparted to my soul
A living spark of holy fire?
Oh! kindle now the sacred flame;
Make me to burn with pure desire.

3 A brighter faith and hope impart,
And let me now my Saviour see;
Oh! soothe and cheer my burdened heart,
And bid my spirit rest in thee.

HOLY SPIRIT.

ZEPHYR. L. M.   Wm. B. Bradbury.

1. Sure, the blest Comforter is nigh,
'Tis he sustains my fainting heart;
Else would my hope forever die,
And every cheering ray depart.

208.

2 Whene'er, to call the Saviour mine,
With ardent wish my heart aspires,—
Can it be less than power divine,
That animates these strong desires?

3 And, when my cheerful hope can say,—
I love my God and taste his grace,—
Lord! is it not thy blissful ray,
That brings this dawn of sacred peace?

4 Let thy good Spirit in my heart
Forever dwell, O God of love!
And light and heavenly peace impart,—
Sweet earnest of the joys above.

209.

1 Stay, thou insulted Spirit! stay,
Though I have done thee such despite;
Cast not a sinner quite away,
Nor take thine everlasting flight.

2 Though I have most unfaithful been
Of all who e'er thy grace received;
Ten thousand times thy goodness seen,
Ten thousand times thy goodness grieved;—

3 Yet, oh! the chief of sinners spare,
In honor of my great High-Priest;
Nor, in thy righteous anger, swear
I shall not see thy people's rest.

4 My weary soul, O God! release,
Uphold me with thy gracious hand;
Guide me into thy perfect peace,
And bring me to the promised land.

210.

1 Come, gracious Spirit, heavenly Dove,
With light and comfort from above:
Be thou our guardian, thou our guide!
O'er every thought and step preside.

2 To us the light of truth display,
And make us know and choose thy way;
Plant holy fear in every heart,
That we from God may ne'er depart.

3 Lead us to holiness—the road
That we must take to dwell with God;
Lead us to Christ, the living way,
Nor let us from his precepts stray.

4 Lead us to God, our final rest,
To be with him forever blessed;
Lead us to heaven, its bliss to share,
And drink our fill of pleasure there.

211.

1 As when in silence, vernal showers
Descend, and cheer the fainting flowers,
So, in the secrecy of love,
Falls the sweet influence from above.

2 That heavenly influence let me find
In holy silence of the mind,
While every grace maintains its bloom,
Diffusing wide its rich perfume.

3 Nor let these blessings be confined
To me, but poured on all mankind,
Till earth's wild wastes in verdure rise,
And a young Eden bless our eyes.

66 HOLY SPIRIT.

STEPHENS. C. M. W. Jones.

1. Come, Holy Spirit, heavenly Dove! With all thy quickening powers, Kindle a flame of sacred love In these cold hearts of ours.

212.

2 Look! how we grovel here below,
Fond of these trifling toys!
Our souls can neither fly nor go
To reach eternal joys.

3 In vain we tune our formal songs;
In vain we strive to rise;
Hosannas languish on our tongues,
And our devotion dies.

4 Dear Lord, and shall we ever live
At this poor, dying rate—
Our love so faint, so cold to thee,
And thine to us so great?

5 Come, Holy Spirit, Heavenly Dove,
With all thy quickening powers,
Come, shed abroad a Saviour's love,
And that shall kindle ours.

213.

1 Spirit Divine! attend our prayer,
And make our hearts thy home;
Descend with all thy gracious power:
Come, Holy Spirit, come!

2 Come as the light: to us reveal
Our sinfulness and woe;
And lead us in those paths of life
Where all the righteous go.

3 Come as the fire, and purge our hearts,
Like sacrificial flame:
Let our whole soul an offering be
To our Redeemer's name.

4 Come as the dew, and sweetly bless
This consecrated hour;
May barrenness rejoice to own
Thy fertilizing power.

5 Come as the wind, with rushing sound,
With Pentecostal grace:
And make the great salvation known
Wide as the human race.

6 Spirit Divine, attend our prayer,
And make our hearts thy home;
Descend with all thy gracious power:
Come, Holy Spirit, come!

214.

1 Come, Holy Ghost, Creator, come,
Inspire these souls of thine;
Till every heart which thou hast made
Be filled with grace divine.

2 Thou art the Comforter, the gift
Of God, and fire of love;
The everlasting spring of joy,
And unction from above.

3 Enlighten our dark souls, till they
Thy sacred love embrace;
Assist our minds, by nature frail,
With thy celestial grace.

4 Teach us the Father to confess,
And Son, from death revived,
And thee, with both, O Holy Ghost,
Who art from both derived.

HOLY SPIRIT.

BOARDMAN. C. M. TEMPLI CARMINA.

1. Why should the chil-dren of a King Go mourn-ing all their days? Great Com-fort-er! de-scend, and bring Some to-kens of thy grace.

215.

1 Why should the children of a King
  Go mourning all their days?
  Great Comforter! descend, and bring
  Some tokens of thy grace.

2 Dost thou not dwell in all the saints,
  And seal the heirs of heaven?
  When wilt thou banish my complaints,
  And show my sins forgiven?

3 Assure my conscience of her part
  In the Redeemer's blood;
  And bear thy witness with my heart
  That I am born of God.

4 Thou art the earnest of his love,
  The pledge of joys to come;
  And thy soft wings, celestial Dove,
  Will safe convey me home.

216.

1 Enthroned on high, Almighty Lord!
  The Holy Ghost send down;
  Fulfill in us thy faithful word,
  And all thy mercies crown.

2 Though on our heads no tongues of fire
  Their wondrous powers impart,
  Grant, Saviour, what we more desire,
  Thy Spirit in our heart.

3 Spirit of life, and light, and love,
  Thy heavenly influence give;
  Quicken our souls, our guilt remove,
  That we in Christ may live.

4 To our benighted minds reveal
  The glories of his grace,
  And bring us where no clouds conceal
  The brightness of his face.

5 His love within us shed abroad,
  Life's ever-springing well;
  Till God in us, and we in God,
  In love eternal dwell.

217.

1 Spirit of power and might, behold
  A world by sin destroyed!
  Creator Spirit, as of old,
  Move on the formless void.

2 Give thou the word: that healing sound
  Shall quell the deadly strife,
  And earth again, like Eden crowned,
  Produce the tree of life.

3 If sang the morning stars for joy
  When nature rose to view,
  What strains will angel harps employ
  When thou shalt all renew!

4 And if the sons of God rejoice
  To hear a Saviour's name,
  How will the ransomed raise their voice,
  To whom that Saviour came!

5 Lo! every kindred, tongue, and tribe,
  Assembling round the throne,
  The new creation shall ascribe
  To sovereign love alone.

HOLY SPIRIT.

HAYDN. S. M. *Arranged from* HAYDN.

1. Come, Holy Spirit, come; Let thy bright beams arise; Dispel the sorrow from our minds, The darkness from our eyes.

218.

2 Convince us of our sin;
  Then lead to Jesus' blood,
And to our wondering view reveal
  The mercies of our God.

3 Revive our drooping faith,
  Our doubts and fears remove,
And kindle in our breasts the flame
  Of never-dying love.

4 'T is thine to cleanse the heart,
  To sanctify the soul,
To pour fresh life in every part,
  And new-create the whole.

5 Come, Holy Spirit, come;
  Our minds from bondage free;
Then shall we know, and praise, and love,
  The Father, Son, and thee.

219.

1 Lord God, the Holy Ghost!
  In this accepted hour,
As on the day of Pentecost
  Descend in all thy power!

2 We meet with one accord
  In our appointed place,
And wait the promise of our Lord,
  The Spirit of all grace.

3 Like mighty rushing wind
  Upon the waves beneath,
Move with one impulse every mind,
  One soul, one feeling breathe.

4 The young, the old inspire
  With wisdom from above;
And give us hearts and tongues of fire
  To pray, and praise, and love.

5 Spirit of light, explore,
  And chase our gloom away,
With lustre shining more and more
  Unto the perfect day.

6 Spirit of truth, be thou
  In life and death our guide;
O Spirit of adoption, now
  May we be sanctified.

220.

1 Blest Comforter divine!
  Let rays of heavenly love
Amid our gloom and darkness shine,
  And guide our souls above.

2 Turn us, with gentle voice,
  From every sinful way,
And bid the mourning saint rejoice,
  Though earthly joys decay.

3 By thine inspiring breath
  Make every cloud of care,
And ev'n the gloomy vale of death,
  A smile of glory wear.

4 Oh! fill thou every heart
  With love to all our race;
Great Comforter, to us impart
  These blessings of thy grace.

HOLY SPIRIT. 69

HORTON. 7s. German.

1. Gracious Spirit, Love divine! Let thy light within me shine; All my guilty fears remove, Fill me full of heaven and love.

221.

1 Gracious Spirit, Love divine!
Let thy light within me shine;
All my guilty fears remove,
Fill me full of heaven and love.

2 Speak thy pardoning grace to me,
Set the burdened sinner free;
Lead me to the Lamb of God,
Wash me in his precious blood.

3 Life and peace to me impart,
Seal salvation on my heart;
Breathe thyself into my breast,—
Earnest of immortal rest.

4 Let me never from thee stray,
Keep me in the narrow way;
Fill my soul with joy divine,
Keep me, Lord! forever thine.

222.

1 Holy Spirit! Lord of light!
From thy clear celestial height,
Come, thou Light of all that live!
Thy pure beaming radiance give!

2 Come, thou Father of the poor!
Come with treasures which endure;
Thou, of all consolers best,
Visiting the troubled breast.

3 Thou in toil art comfort sweet;
Pleasant coolness in the heat;
Solace in the midst of woe;
Dost refreshing peace bestow.

4 Light immortal! light divine!
Visit thou these hearts of thine;
If thou take thy grace away,
Nothing pure in man will stay.

5 Heal our wounds—our strength renew;
On our dryness pour thy dew;
Wash the stains of guilt away;
Guide the steps that go astray.

6 Give us comfort when we die;
Give us life with thee on high;
In thy sevenfold gifts descend;
Give us joys which never end.

223.

1 Holy Ghost! with light divine,
Shine upon this heart of mine;
Chase the shades of night away,
Turn my darkness into day.

2 Holy Ghost! with power divine,
Cleanse this guilty heart of mine;
Long hath sin, without control,
Held dominion o'er my soul.

3 Holy Ghost! with joy divine,
Cheer this saddened heart of mine;
Bid my many woes depart,
Heal my wounded, bleeding heart

4 Holy Spirit! all-divine,
Dwell within this heart of mine;
Cast down every idol-throne,
Reign supreme—and reign alone.

WAY OF SALVATION.

WINDHAM. L. M. DANIEL READ.

1. Shall the vile race of flesh and blood Con-tend with their Cre-a-tor, God? Shall mor-tal worms pre-sume to be More ho-ly, wise, or just, than he?

224.

2 Behold! he puts his trust in none
Of all the spirits round his throne;
Their natures, when compared with his,
Are neither holy, just, nor wise.

3 But how much meaner things are they
Who spring from dust, and dwell in clay;
Touched by the finger of thy wrath,
We faint and vanish like the moth.

4 From night to day, from day to night,
We die by thousands in thy sight;
Buried in dust whole nations lie,
Like a forgotten vanity.

5 Almighty Power, to thee we bow;
How frail are we! how glorious thou!
No more the sons of earth shall dare
With an eternal God compare.

225.

1 Lord, I am vile, conceived in sin,
And born unholy and unclean;
Sprung from the man, whose guilty fall
Corrupts the race, and taints us all.

2 Soon as we draw our infant breath,
The seeds of sin grow up for death:
Thy law demands a perfect heart—
But we're defiled in every part.

3 Great God! create my heart anew,
And form my spirit pure and true;
No outward rites can make me clean,—
The leprosy lies deep within.

4 No bleeding bird, nor bleeding beast,
Nor hyssop branch, nor sprinkling priest,
Nor running brook, nor flood, nor sea,
Can wash the dismal stain away.

5 Jesus, my God, thy blood alone,
Hath power sufficient to atone:
Thy blood can make me white as snow,
No Jewish types could cleanse me so.

6 While guilt disturbs and breaks my peace,
Nor flesh nor soul hath rest or ease;
Lord, let me hear thy pardoning voice,
And make my broken bones rejoice.

226.

1 Broad is the road that leads to death,
And thousands walk together there;
But wisdom shows a narrow path,
With here and there a traveler.

2 "Deny thyself and take thy cross,"—
Is the Redeemer's great command:
Nature must count her gold but dross,
If she would gain this heavenly land.

3 The fearful soul that tires and faints,
And walks the ways of God no more,
Is but esteemed almost a saint,
And makes his own destruction sure.

4 Lord! let not all my hopes be vain:
Create my heart entirely new:
Which hypocrites could ne'er attain,
Which false apostates never know.

LOST STATE OF MAN. 71

MALVERN. L. M. Dr. L. Mason.

1. Je-sus, en-grave it on my heart, That thou the one thing need-ful art;
I could from all things part-ed be, But nev-er, nev-er, Lord, from thee.

227.

2 Needful is thy most precious blood,
To reconcile my soul to God;
Needful is thy indulgent care;
Needful thy all-prevailing prayer.

3 Needful thy presence, dearest Lord,
True peace and comfort to afford;
Needful thy promise, to impart
Fresh life and vigor to my heart.

4 Needful art thou, my guide, my stay,
Through all life's dark and weary way;
Nor less in death thou 'lt needful be,
To bring my spirit home to thee.

5 Then needful still, my God, my King,
Thy name eternally I 'll sing!
Glory and praise be ever his,
The one thing needful Jesus is!

228.

1 How shall the sons of men appear,
Great God! before thine awful bar?
How may the guilty hope to find
Acceptance with th' eternal Mind?

2 Not vows, nor groans, nor broken cries,
Not the most costly sacrifice,
Not infant blood, profusely spilt,
Will expiate a sinner's guilt.

3 Thy blood, dear Jesus, thine alone,
Hath sovereign virtue to atone:
Here will we rest our only plea,
When we approach, Great God! to thee.

229.

1 What shall the dying sinner do,
That seeks relief for all his woe?
Where shall the guilty conscience find
Ease for the torment of the mind?

2 In vain we search, in vain we try,
Till Jesus brings his gospel nigh!
'T is there the power and glory dwell,
That save rebellious souls from hell.

3 This is the pillar of our hope,
That bears our fainting spirits up;
We read the grace, we trust the word,
And find salvation in the Lord.

230.

1 Like morning, when her early breeze
Breaks up the surface of the seas,
That, in their furrows, dark with night,
Her hand may sow the seeds of light,—

2 Thy grace can send its breathings o'er
The spirit dark and lost before;
And, freshening all its depths, prepare
For truth divine to enter there.

3 Till David touched his sacred lyre,
In silence lay the unbreathing wire;
But when he swept its chords along,
Then angels stooped to hear the song.

4 So sleeps the soul, till thou, O Lord,
Shalt deign to touch its lifeless chord;
Till, waked by thee, its breath shall rise
In music worthy of the skies.

WAY OF SALVATION.

MONSON. C. M. — BROWN.

1. How help-less guilt-y na-ture lies, Un-con-scious of its load!
The heart, un-changed, can nev-er rise To hap-pi-ness and God.

231.

1 How helpless guilty nature lies,
   Unconscious of its load!
   The heart, unchanged, can never rise
   To happiness and God.

2 Can aught, beneath a power divine,
   The stubborn will subdue?
   'T is thine, almighty Spirit! thine,
   To form the heart anew.

3 'T is thine, the passions to recall,
   And upward bid them rise;
   To make the scales of error fall,
   From reason's darkened eyes;—

4 To chase the shades of death away,
   And bid the sinner live;
   A beam of heaven, a vital ray,
   'T is thine alone to give.

5 Oh! change these wretched hearts of ours,
   And give them life divine;
   Then shall our passions and our powers,
   Almighty Lord, be thine.

232.

1 In vain we seek for peace with God
   By methods of our own:
   Nothing, O Saviour! but thy blood
   Can bring us near the throne.

2 The threatenings of the broken law
   Impress the soul with dread:
   If God his sword of vengeance draw,
   It strikes the spirit dead.

3 But thine illustrious sacrifice
   Hath answered these demands;
   And peace and pardon from the skies
   Are offered by thy hands.

4 'T is by thy death we live, O Lord!
   'T is on thy cross we rest:
   Forever be thy love adored,
   Thy name forever blessed.

233.

1 Lord, how secure my conscience was,
   And felt no inward dread!
   I was alive without the law,
   And thought my sins were dead.

2 My hopes of heaven were firm and bright;
   But since the precept came
   With a convincing power and light,
   I find how vile I am.

3 My guilt appeared but small before,
   Till terribly I saw
   How perfect, holy, just, and pure,
   Is thine eternal law.

4 Then felt my soul the heavy load;
   My sins revived again:
   I had provoked a dreadful God,
   And all my hopes were slain.

5 My God, I cry with every breath
   For some kind power to save,
   To break the yoke of sin and death,
   And thus redeem the slave.

LOST STATE OF MAN.

HUMMEL. C. M. — Zeuner.

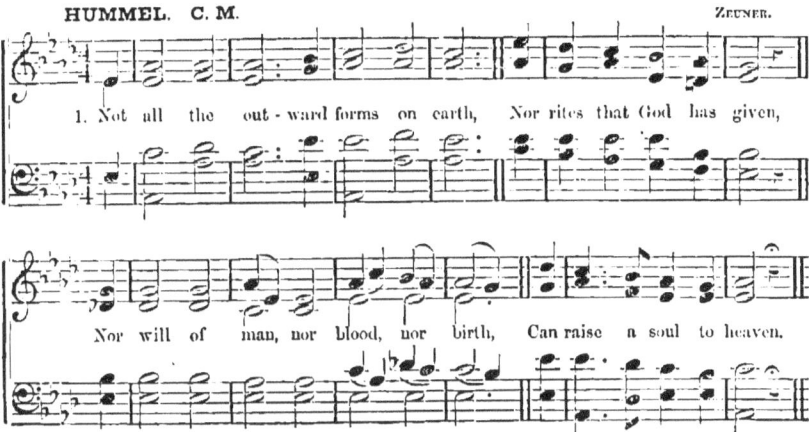

1. Not all the outward forms on earth,
Nor rites that God has given,
Nor will of man, nor blood, nor birth,
Can raise a soul to heaven.

234.

2 The sovereign will of God alone
Creates us heirs of grace;
Born in the image of his Son,
A new, peculiar race.

3 The Spirit, like some heavenly wind,
Breathes on the sons of flesh,
New-models all the carnal mind,
And forms the man afresh.

4 Our quickened souls awake and rise
From the long sleep of death;
On heavenly things we fix our eyes,
And praise employs our breath.

235.

1 How sad our state by nature is!
Our sin—how deep it stains!
And Satan holds our captive minds
Fast in his slavish chains.

2 But there's a voice of sovereign grace
Sounds from the sacred word:
"Ho! ye despairing sinners, come,
And trust a pardoning Lord."

3 My soul obeys th' almighty call,
And runs to this relief;
I would believe thy promise, Lord:
Oh, help my unbelief!

4 A guilty, weak, and helpless worm,
On thy kind arms I fall:
Be thou my Strength and Righteousness,
My Saviour and my All.

236.

1 Vain are the hopes, the sons of men
On their own works have built;—
Their hearts, by nature, all unclean,
And all their actions, guilt.

2 Let Jew and Gentile stop their mouths,
Without a murmuring word;
And the whole race of Adam stand
Guilty before the Lord.

3 In vain we ask God's righteous law
To justify us now;
Since to convince, and to condemn,
Is all the law can do.

4 Jesus! how glorious is thy grace;—
When in thy name we trust,
Our faith receives a righteousness,
That makes the sinner just.

237.

1 Strait is the way, the door is strait,
That leads to joys on high;
'Tis but a few that find the gate,
While crowds mistake and die.

2 Beloved self must be denied,
The mind and will renewed,
Passion suppressed, and patience tried,
And vain desires subdued.

3 Lord! can a feeble, helpless worm,
Fulfill a task so hard?
Thy grace must all my work perform,
And give the free reward.

74 WAY OF SALVATION.

SHAWMUT. S. M. Dr. L. Mason.

1. My former hopes are fled, My terror now begins; I feel, alas! that I am dead In trespasses and sins.

* The small notes are for the Organ.

238.

1 My former hopes are fled,
My terror now begins;
I feel, alas! that I am dead
In trespasses and sins.

2 Ah! whither shall I fly?
I hear the thunder roar;
The law proclaims destruction nigh,
And vengeance at the door.

3 When I review my ways,
I dread impending doom;
But sure a friendly whisper says—
"Flee from the wrath to come."

4 I see, or think I see,
A glimmering from afar;
A beam of day that shines for me
To save me from despair.

5 Forerunner of the sun,
It marks the pilgrim's way;
I'll gaze upon it while I run,
And watch the rising day.

239.

1 Ah! how shall fallen man
Be just before his God?
If he contend in righteousness,
We fall beneath his rod.

2 If he our ways should mark,
With strict inquiring eyes,
Could we, for one of thousand faults,
A just excuse devise?

3 All-seeing, powerful God!
Who can with thee contend?
Or who, that tries th' unequal strife,
Shall prosper in the end?

4 The mountains, in thy wrath,
Their ancient seats forsake;
The trembling earth deserts her place,
Her rooted pillars shake.

5 Ah! how shall guilty man
Contend with such a God?
None—none can meet him, and escape,
But through the Saviour's blood.

240.

1 Can sinners hope for heaven,
Who love this world so well?
Or dream of future happiness,
While on the road to hell?

2 Shall they hosannas sing,
With an unhallowed tongue?
Shall palms adorn the guilty hand
Which does its neighbor wrong?

3 Can sin's deceitful way
Conduct to Zion's hill?
Or those expect with God to reign
Who disregard his will?

4 Thy grace, O God, alone,
Good hope can e'er afford!
The pardoned and the pure shall see
The glory of the Lord.

LOST STATE OF MAN. 75

CAPELLO. S. M.   Cantica Laudis.

1. Did Christ o'er sin-ners weep, And shall our cheeks be dry? Let floods of pen-i-ten-tial grief Burst forth from ev-ery eye.

241.

2 The Son of God in tears,
   Angels with wonder see!
Be thou astonished, O my soul,
   He shed those tears for thee.

3 He wept that we might weep;
   Each sin demands a tear;
In heaven alone no sin is found,
   And there's no weeping there.

242.

1 How heavy is the night
   That hangs upon our eyes,
Till Christ with his reviving light
   Over our souls arise!

2 Our guilty spirits dread
   To meet the wrath of heaven;
But, in his righteousness arrayed,
   We see our sins forgiven.

3 Unholy and impure
   Are all our thoughts and ways:
His hands infected nature cure
   With sanctifying grace.

4 The powers of hell agree
   To hold our souls in vain;
He sets the sons of bondage free,
   And breaks the cursèd chain.

5 Lord, we adore thy ways
   To bring us near to God,
Thy sovereign power, thy healing grace,
   And thine atoning blood.

243.

1 Is this the kind return?
   Are these the thanks we owe?
Thus to abuse eternal love,
   Whence all our blessings flow!

2 To what a stubborn frame
   Hath sin reduced our mind!
What strange, rebellious wretches we,—
   And God as strangely kind!

3 Turn, turn us, mighty God!
   And mould our souls afresh;
Break, sovereign grace! these hearts of stone,
   And give us hearts of flesh.

244.

1 Astonished and distressed,
   I turn mine eyes within;
My heart with loads of guilt oppressed,
   The seat of every sin.

2 What crowds of evil thoughts,
   What vile affections there!
Distrust, presumption, artful guile,
   Pride, envy, slavish fear!

3 Almighty King of saints!
   These hateful sins subdue;
Dispel the darkness from my mind,
   And all my powers renew.

4 This done,—my cheerful voice
   Shall loud hosannas raise;
My soul shall glow with gratitude,—
   My lips pronounce thy praise.

WAY OF SALVATION.

COWPER. C. M.   Dr. L. Mason.

1. There is a foun-tain filled with blood, Drawn from Immanuel's veins; And sinners, plunged beneath that flood, Lose all their guilt-y stains, Lose all their guilt-y stains.

245.

2 The dying thief rejoiced to see
   That fountain in his day;
And there may I, as vile as he,
   Wash all my sins away.

3 Dear, dying Lamb, thy precious blood
   Shall never lose its power,
Till all the ransomed church of God
   Be saved, to sin no more.

4 E'er since, by faith, I saw the stream
   Thy flowing wounds supply,
Redeeming love has been my theme,
   And shall be, till I die.

5 Then in a nobler, sweeter song,
   I'll sing thy power to save,
When this poor, lisping, stammering tongue
   Lies silent in the grave.

246.

1 Come, happy souls, approach your God
   With new, melodious songs;
Come, render to almighty Grace
   The tribute of your tongues.

2 So strange, so boundless was the love
   That pitied dying men,
The Father sent his equal Son
   To give them life again.

3 Thy hands, dear Jesus, were not armed
   With a revenging rod;
No hard commission to perform
   The vengeance of a God.

4 But all was merciful and mild,
   And wrath forsook the throne,
When Christ on the kind errand came,
   And brought salvation down.

5 Here, sinners, come and heal your wounds;
   Come, wipe your sorrows dry:
Come, trust the mighty Saviour's name,
   And you shall never die.

6 See, dearest Lord, our willing souls
   Accept thine offered grace;
We bless the great Redeemer's love,
   And give the Father praise.

247.

1 O Lord, how infinite thy love!
   How wondrous are thy ways!
Let earth beneath, and heaven above,
   Combine to sing thy praise.

2 Man in immortal beauty shone,
   Thy noblest work below;
Too soon by sin made heir alone
   To death and endless woe.

3 Then, "Lo! I come," the Saviour said:
   Oh, be his name adored,
Who, with his blood, our ransom paid,
   And life and bliss restored!

4 O Lord, how infinite thy love!
   How wondrous are thy ways!
Let earth beneath, and heaven above,
   Combine to sing thy praise.

ATONEMENT AND PARDON.

GLASGOW. C. M.   Root & Sweetser's Coll.

1. Great God! when I ap-proach thy throne, And all thy glo-ry see, This is my stay, and this a-lone, That Je-sus died for me.

248.

2 How can a soul condemned to die
   Escape the just decree?
   Helpless and full of sin am I,
   But Jesus died for me.

3 Burdened with sin's oppressive chain,
   Oh! how can I get free?
   No peace can all my efforts gain,
   But Jesus died for me.

4 My anxious heart no joy could cheer,
   On life's tempestuous sea;
   Did not this truth relieve my fear,
   That Jesus died for me.

5 And, Lord, when I behold thy face,
   This must be all my plea;
   Save me by thine almighty grace,
   For Jesus died for me.

249.

1 Oh! what amazing words of grace
   Are in the Gospel found,
   Suited to every sinner's case
   Who hears the joyful sound!

2 Come, then, with all your wants and
      wounds,
   Your every burden bring;
   Here love, unchanging love, abounds—
   A deep, celestial spring.

3 This spring with living water flows,
   And heavenly joy imparts;
   Come, thirsty souls! your wants disclose,
   And drink, with thankful hearts.

250.

1 Salvation!—oh, the joyful sound!
   'T is pleasure to our ears;
   A sovereign balm for every wound,
   A cordial for our fears.

2 Buried in sorrow and in sin,
   At hell's dark door we lay;—
   But we arise by grace divine,
   To see a heavenly day.

3 Salvation!—let the echo fly
   The spacious earth around;
   While all the armies of the sky
   Conspire to raise the sound.

251.

1 Jesus,—and didst thou leave the sky,
   To bear our griefs and woes?
   And didst thou bleed and groan and die
   For thy rebellious foes?

2 Well might the heavens with wonder view
   A love so strange as thine!
   No thought of angels ever knew
   Compassion so divine!

3 Is there a heart that will not bend
   To thy divine control?
   Descend, O sovereign love, descend,
   And melt that stubborn soul.

4 Oh! may our willing hearts confess
   Thy sweet, thy gentle sway;
   Glad captives of thy matchless grace,
   Thy righteous rule obey.

WAY OF SALVATION.

BALERMA. C. M. *Scottish.*

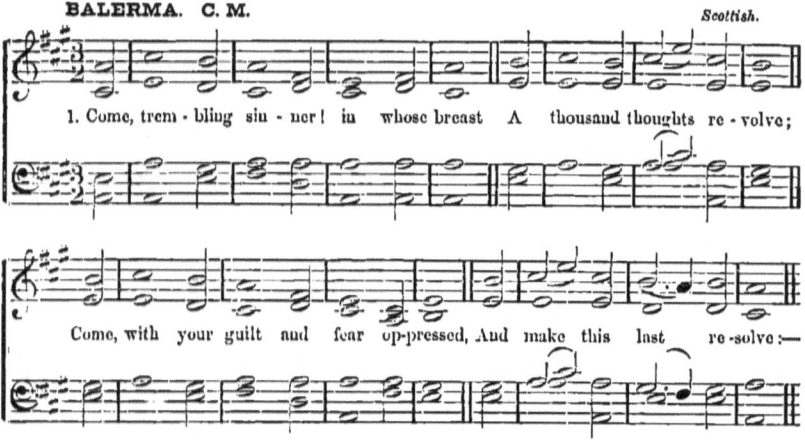

1. Come, trembling sinner! in whose breast A thousand thoughts revolve;
Come, with your guilt and fear oppressed, And make this last resolve:—

252.

2 "I'll go to Jesus, though my sins
Like mountains round me close;
I know his courts, I'll enter in,
Whatever may oppose.

3 "Prostrate I'll lie before his throne,
And there my guilt confess;
I'll tell him I'm a wretch undone,
Without his sovereign grace.

4 "Perhaps he will admit my plea,
Perhaps will hear my prayer;
But if I perish, I will pray,
And perish only there.

5 "I can but perish if I go;
I am resolved to try;
For if I stay away, I know
I must forever die."

253.

1 There is a line, by us unseen,
That crosses every path,
The hidden boundary between
God's patience and his wrath.

2 To pass that limit is to die,
To die as if by stealth;
It does not quench the beaming eye,
Nor pale the glow of health.

3 The conscience may be still at ease,
The spirit light and gay,
That which is pleasing still may please,
And care be thrust away.

4 Oh! where is this mysterious bourne
By which our path is crossed;
Beyond which God himself hath sworn
That he who goes is lost?

5 How far may we go on to sin?
How long will God forbear?
Where does hope end, and where begin
The confines of despair?

6 An answer from the skies is sent,—
"Ye that from God depart,
While it is called to-day, repent,
And harden not your heart."

254.

1 O sinner, bring not tears alone,
Or outward form of prayer,
But let it in thy heart be known
That penitence is there.

2 To smite the breast, the clothes to rend,
God asketh not of thee;
Thy secret soul he bids thee bend
In true humility.

3 Oh! let us, then, with heartfelt grief,
Draw near unto our God,
And pray to him to grant relief,
And stay the lifted rod.

4 O righteous Judge! if thou wilt deign
To grant us what we need,
We pray for time to turn again,
And grace to turn indeed.

WARNING AND INVITATION.

RETURN. C. M.   Dr. Hastings.

1. Re-turn, O wan-derer, to thy home, Thy Fa-ther calls for thee; No long-er now an ex-ile roam, In guilt and mis-e-ry. Re-turn, re-turn!

255.

2 Return, O wanderer, to thy home,
'T is Jesus calls for thee;
The Spirit and the Bride say—come;
Oh! now for refuge flee;
Return, return!

3 Return, O wanderer, to thy home,
'T is madness to delay;
There are no pardons in the tomb,
And brief is mercy's day:
Return, return!

256.

1 Return, O wanderer, now return,
And seek thy Father's face!
Those new desires, which in thee burn,
Were kindled by his grace.

2 Return, O wanderer, now return!
He hears thy humble sigh;
He sees thy softened spirit mourn,
When no one else is nigh.

3 Return, O wanderer, now return!
Thy Saviour bids thee live:
Go to his bleeding feet, and learn
How freely he'll forgive.

4 Return, O wanderer, now return,
And wipe the falling tear!
Thy Father calls—no longer mourn:
His love invites thee near.

257.

1 Come to the ark, come to the ark;
To Jesus come away:
The pestilence walks forth by night,
The arrow flies by day.

2 Come to the ark: the waters rise,
The seas their billows rear;
While darkness gathers o'er the skies,
Behold a refuge near!

3 Come to the ark, all, all that weep
Beneath the sense of sin:
Without, deep calleth unto deep,
But all is peace within.

4 Come to the ark, ere yet the flood
Your lingering steps oppose;
Come, for the door which open stood
Is now about to close.

258.

1 When rising from the bed of death
O'erwhelmed with guilt and fear,
I see my Maker face to face—
Oh! how shall I appear!

2 E'en now, while pardon may be found
And mercy may be sought,
My heart with inward horror shrinks,
And trembles at the thought.

3 When thou, O Lord! shalt stand disclosed
In majesty severe,
And sit in judgment on my soul,
Oh! how shall I appear!

WAY OF SALVATION.

BERA. L. M.   Root & Sweetser's Coll.

1. Why will ye waste on trifling cares That life which God's compassion spares? While, in the various range of thought, The one thing needful is forgot?

259.

1 Why will ye waste on trifling cares
That life which God's compassion spares?
While, in the various range of thought,
The one thing needful is forgot?

2 Shall God invite you from above?
Shall Jesus urge his dying love?
Shall troubled conscience give you pain?
And all these pleas unite in vain?

3 Not so your eyes will always view
Those objects which you now pursue:
Not so will heaven and hell appear,
When death's decisive hour is near.

4 Almighty God! thy grace impart;
Fix deep conviction on each heart;
Nor let us waste on trifling cares
That life which thy compassion spares.

260.

1 While life prolongs its precious light,
Mercy is found, and peace is given;
But soon, ah! soon, approaching night
Shall blot out every hope of heaven.

2 While God invites, how blest the day!
How sweet the gospel's charming sound!
Come, sinners, haste, oh, haste away,
While yet a pardoning God is found.

3 Soon, borne on time's most rapid wing,
Shall death command you to the grave,
Before his bar your spirits bring,
And none be found to hear or save.

4 In that lone land of deep despair
No Sabbath's heavenly light shall rise;
No God regard your bitter prayer,
Nor Saviour call you to the skies.

5 Now God invites—how blest the day!
How sweet the gospel's charming sound!
Come, sinners, haste, oh, haste away,
While yet a pardoning God is found.

261.

1 Say, sinner! hath a voice within
Oft whispered to thy secret soul,
Urged thee to leave the ways of sin,
And yield thy heart to God's control?

2 Sinner! it was a heavenly voice,—
It was the Spirit's gracious call;
It bade thee make the better choice,
And haste to seek in Christ thine all.

3 Spurn not the call to life and light;
Regard, in time, the warning kind;
That call thou may'st not always slight,
And yet the gate of mercy find.

4 God's Spirit will not always strive
With hardened, self-destroying man;
Ye who persist his love to grieve,
May never hear his voice again.

5 Sinner! perhaps, this very day,
Thy last accepted time may be:
Oh! shouldst thou grieve him now away,
Then hope may never beam on thee.

WARNING AND INVITATION.

DESIRE. L. M.

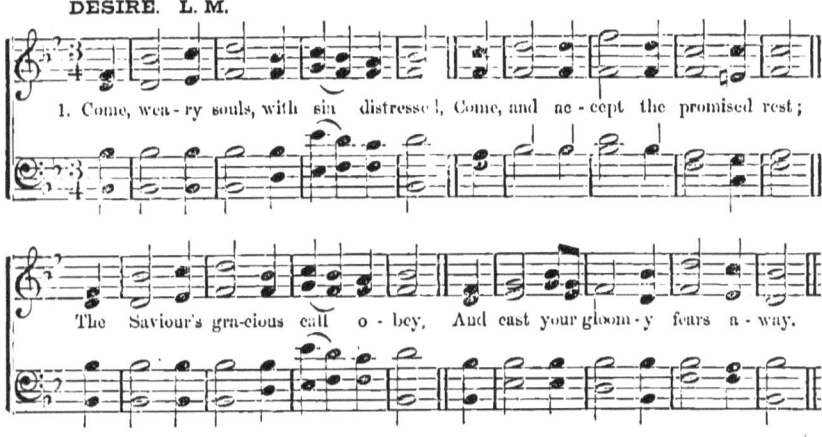

1. Come, weary souls, with sin distressed, Come, and accept the promised rest; The Saviour's gracious call obey, And cast your gloomy fears away.

262.

2 Oppressed with guilt,—a painful load,—
Oh, come and bow before your God!
Divine compassion, mighty love
Will all the painful load remove.

3 Here mercy's boundless ocean flows,
To cleanse your guilt and heal your woes;
Pardon, and life, and endless peace—
How rich the gift, how free the grace!

4 Dear Saviour! let thy powerful love
Confirm our faith, our fears remove;
Oh, sweetly reign in every breast,
And guide us to eternal rest.

263.

1 "Come hither, all ye weary souls;
Ye heavy-laden sinners, come!
I'll give you rest from all your toils,
And raise you to my heavenly home.

2 "They shall find rest who learn of me:
I'm of a meek and lowly mind;
But passion rages like the sea,
And pride is restless as the wind.

3 "Blest is the man whose shoulders take
My yoke, and bear it with delight:
My yoke is easy to his neck,
My grace shall make the burden light."

4 Jesus, we come at thy command;
With faith, and hope, and humble zeal;
Resign our spirits to thy hand,
To mould and guide us at thy will.

264.

1 Behold a Stranger at the door:
He gently knocks, has knocked before;
Has waited long, is waiting still:
You treat no other friend so ill.

2 Oh, lovely attitude! he stands
With melting heart and open hands:
Oh, matchless kindness!—and he shows
This matchless kindness to his foes!

3 Rise, touched with gratitude divine,
Turn out his enemy and thine;
Turn out thy soul-enslaving sin,
And let the heavenly stranger in.

4 Oh, welcome him, the Prince of Peace!
Now may his gentle reign increase!
Throw wide the door, each willing mind;
And be his empire all mankind.

265.

1 Ho! every one that thirsts! draw nigh;
'Tis God invites the fallen race;
Mercy and free salvation buy,
Buy wine, and milk, and gospel grace.

2 Ye nothing in exchange can give,—
Leave all ye have, and are, behind;
Freely the gift of God receive,
Pardon and peace in Jesus find.

3 Come to the living waters, come;
Sinners! obey your Maker's voice;
Return, ye weary wanderers! home,
And in redeeming love rejoice.

82. WAY OF SALVATION.

OLMUTZ. S. M. *Arranged by* Dr. L. Mason.

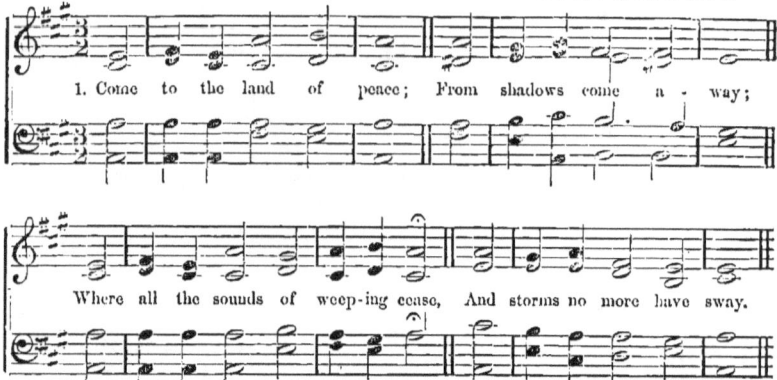

1. Come to the land of peace; From shadows come a-way;
Where all the sounds of weeping cease, And storms no more have sway.

266.

2 Fear hath no dwelling here;
But pure repose and love
Breathe through the bright celestial air
The spirit of the dove.

3 Come to the bright and blest,
Gathered from every land;
For here thy soul shall find its rest,
Amid the shining band.

4 In this divine abode
Change leaves no saddening trace;
Come, trusting spirit, to thy God,
Thy holy resting-place.

267.

1 The Spirit, in our hearts,
Is whispering, "Sinner, come;"
The bride, the church of Christ, proclaims
To all his children, "Come!"

2 Let him that heareth say
To all about him, "Come!"
Let him that thirsts for righteousness,
To Christ, the fountain, come!

3 Yes, whosoever will,
Oh! let him freely come,
And freely drink the stream of life;
'T is Jesus bids him come.

4 Lo! Jesus, who invites,
Declares, "I quickly come:"
Lord, even so! we wait thine hour;
O blest Redeemer, come!

268.

1 My Father bids me come,
Oh! why do I delay?
He calls the wandering spirit home,
And yet from him I stay.

2 Father, the hindrance show,
Which I have failed to see;
And let me now consent to know
What keeps me far from thee.

3 Searcher of hearts! in mine
Thy trying powers display;
Into its darkest corners shine—
Take every vail away.

4 In me the hindrance lies;
The fatal bar remove,
And let me see, in sweet surprise,
Thy full redeeming love.

269.

1 And canst thou, sinner! slight
The call of love divine?
Shall God, with tenderness invite,
And gain no thought of thine?

2 Wilt thou not cease to grieve
The Spirit from thy breast,
Till he thy wretched soul shall leave
With all thy sins oppressed?

3 To-day, a pardoning God
Will hear the suppliant pray;
To-day, a Saviour's cleansing blood
Will wash thy guilt away.

WARNING AND INVITATION.

WANDERER. S. M. J. P. HOLBROOK.

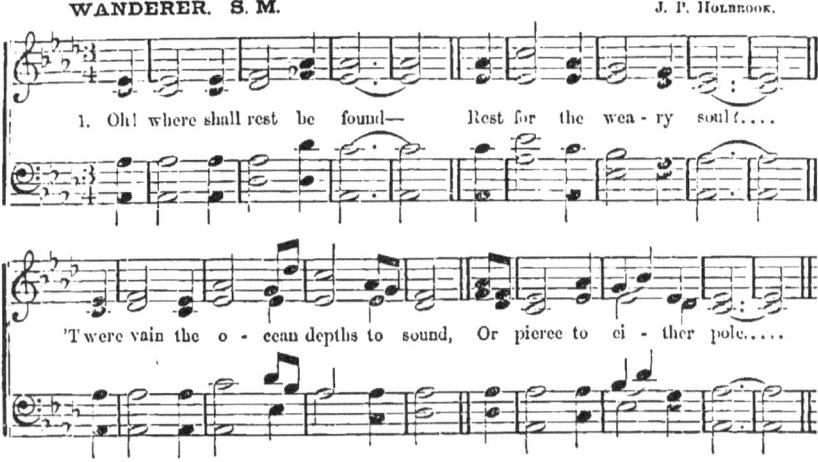

1. Oh! where shall rest be found— Rest for the wea-ry soul?.... 'T were vain the o-cean depths to sound, Or pierce to ei-ther pole.....

270.

1 Oh! where shall rest be found—
 Rest for the weary soul?
 'T were vain the ocean depths to sound,
 Or pierce to either pole.

2 The world can never give
 The bliss for which we sigh:
 'T is not the whole of life to live,
 Nor all of death to die.

3 Beyond this vale of tears
 There is a life above,
 Unmeasured by the flight of years;
 And all that life is love.

4 There is a death whose pang
 Outlasts the fleeting breath:
 Oh, what eternal horrors hang
 Around the second death!

5 Lord God of truth and grace!
 Teach us that death to shun;
 Lest we be banished from thy face,
 And evermore undone.

271.

1 Thou Judge of quick and dead,
 Before whose bar severe,
 With holy joy, or guilty dread,
 We all shall soon appear:—

2 Our cautioned souls prepare
 For that tremendous day;
 Oh! fill us now with watchful care,
 And stir us up to pray.

3 To damp our earthly joys,
 To wake our gracious fears,
 Forever let th' archangel's voice
 Be sounding in our ears.

4 The solemn, midnight cry—
 "Ye dead, the Judge is come!
 Arise, and meet him in the sky,
 And meet your instant doom!"

5 Oh! may we thus be found,
 Obedient to thy word;
 Attentive to the trumpet's sound,
 And looking for our Lord!

272.

1 Now is th' accepted time,
 Now is the day of grace;
 O sinners! come, without delay,
 And seek the Saviour's face.

2 Now is th' accepted time,
 The Saviour calls to-day;
 To-morrow it may be too late;—
 Then why should you delay?

3 Now is th' accepted time,
 The gospel bids you come;
 And every promise, in his word,
 Declares there yet is room.

4 Lord! draw reluctant souls,
 And melt them by thy love;
 Then will the angels speed their way,
 To bear the news above.

WAY OF SALVATION.

MARTYN. 7s. Double.　　　　　　　　　　　　　MARSH.

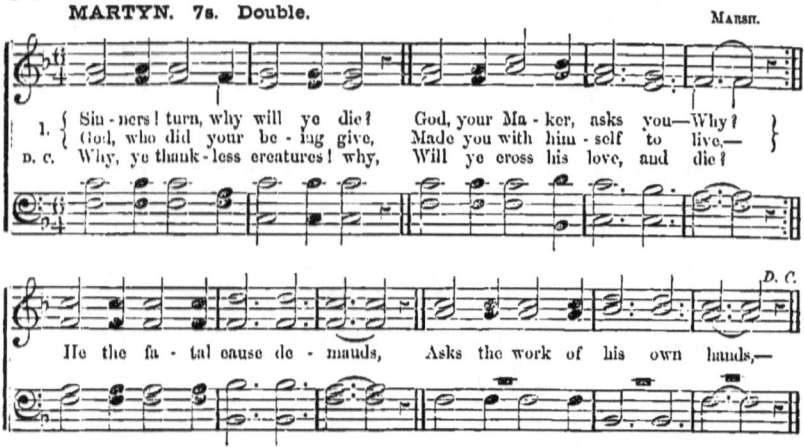

1. Sinners! turn, why will ye die?
   God, who did your being give,
   D.C. Why, ye thankless creatures! why,
   God, your Maker, asks you—Why?
   Made you with himself to live,—
   Will ye cross his love, and die?
   He the fatal cause demands,
   Asks the work of his own hands,—

273.

2 Sinners, turn, why will ye die?
　God, your Saviour, asks you—Why?
　He who did your souls retrieve,
　Died himself, that ye might live.
　Will ye let him die in vain?
　Crucify your Lord again?
　Why, ye ransomed sinners, why
　Will ye slight his grace, and die?

3 Sinners, turn, why will ye die?
　God, the Spirit, asks you—Why?
　He, who all your lives hath strove,
　Urged you to embrace his love:
　Will ye not his grace receive?
　Will ye still refuse to live?
　O ye dying sinners! why,
　Why will ye forever die?

274.

1 Pilgrim, burdened with thy sin,
　Come the way to Zion's gate;
　There, till mercy speaks within,
　Knock, and weep, and watch, and wait:
　Knock—he knows the sinner's cry;
　Weep—he loves the mourner's tears;
　Watch, for saving grace is nigh;
　Wait, till heavenly grace appears.

2 Hark! it is the Saviour's voice,
　"Welcome, pilgrim, to thy rest!"
　Now within the gate rejoice,
　Safe, and owned, and bought, and blest:
　Safe, from all the lures of vice;
　Owned, by joys the contrite know;
　Bought by love, and life the price;
　Blest, the mighty debt to owe.

3 Holy pilgrim! what for thee
　In a world like this remains?
　From thy guarded breast shall flee
　Fear, and shame, and doubts, and pains:
　Fear—the hope of heaven shall fly,
　Shame, from glory's view retire;
　Doubt, in full belief, shall die,
　Pain, in endless bliss, expire.

275.

1 Sinner, art thou still secure?
　Wilt thou still refuse to pray?
　Can thy heart or hands endure
　In the Lord's avenging day?
　See his mighty arm made bare!
　Awful terrors clothe his brow!
　For his judgment now prepare,
　Thou must either break or bow.

2 At his presence nature shakes,
　Earth affrighted hastes to flee;
　Solid mountains melt like wax,
　What will then become of thee?
　Who his coming may abide?
　You that glory in your shame,
　Will you find a place to hide
　When the world is wrapt in flame?

WARNING AND INVITATION. 85

HORTON. 7s. *German.*

1. Come! said Jesus' sacred voice; Come and make my paths your choice; I will guide you to your home, Weary wanderer! hither come.

276.

2 Thou, who homeless and forlorn,
Long hast borne the proud world's scorn,
Long hast roamed the barren waste,
Weary wanderer, hither haste.

3 Ye, who tossed on beds of pain
Seek for ease, but seek in vain;
Ye, by fiercer anguish torn,
In remorse for guilt who mourn:—

4 Hither come, for here is found
Balm that flows for every wound!
Peace, that ever shall endure,
Rest eternal, sacred, sure.

277.

1 Weary sinner! keep thine eyes
On th' atoning Sacrifice;
View him bleeding on the tree,
Pouring out his life for thee.

2 Surely Christ thy griefs hath borne;
Weeping soul, no longer mourn:
Now by faith the Son embrace,
Plead his promise, trust his grace.

3 Cast thy guilty soul on him;
Find him mighty to redeem:
At his feet thy burden lay;
Look thy doubts and care away.

4 Lord, come thou with power to heal;
Now thy mighty arm reveal:
At thy feet myself I lay;
Take, oh, take my sins away!

278.

1 Hasten, sinner! to be wise,
Stay not for the morrow's sun:
Wisdom, if you still despise,
Harder is it to be won.

2 Hasten mercy to implore,
Stay not for the morrow's sun,
Lest thy season should be o'er,
Ere this evening's stage be run.

3 Hasten, sinner! to return,
Stay not for the morrow's sun,
Lest thy lamp should cease to burn,
Ere salvation's work is done.

4 Hasten, sinner! to be blest,
Stay not for the morrow's sun,
Lest perdition thee arrest,
Ere the morrow is begun.

279.

1 Brother, hast thou wandered far
From thy Father's happy home,
With thyself and God at war?
Turn thee, brother; homeward come.

2 Hast thou wasted all the powers
God for noble uses gave?
Squandered life's most golden hours?
Turn thee, brother; God can save.

3 He can heal thy bitterest wound,
He thy gentlest prayer can hear:
Seek him, for he may be found;
Call upon him; he is near.

WAY OF SALVATION.

AVA. P. M.   DR. HASTINGS.

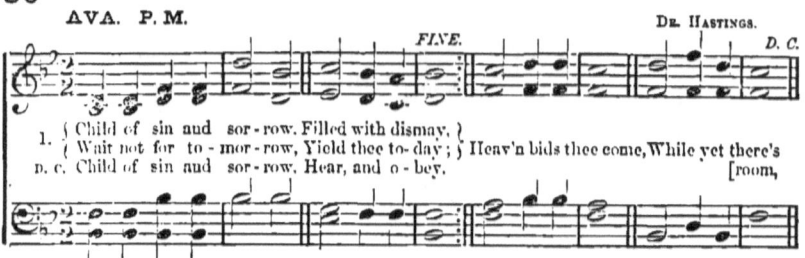

1. Child of sin and sor-row. Filled with dismay,
Wait not for to-mor-row, Yield thee to-day; Heav'n bids thee come, While yet there's
D. C. Child of sin and sor-row, Hear, and o-bey. [room,

280.

2 Child of sin and sorrow,
Why wilt thou die?
Come while thou canst borrow
Help from on high:
Grieve not that love
Which from above,
Child of sin and sorrow,
Would bring thee nigh.

3 Child of sin and sorrow,
Thy moments glide,
Like the flitting arrow,
Or the rushing tide;
Ere time is o'er,
Heaven's grace implore;
Child of sin and sorrow,
In Christ confide.

EXPOSTULATION. 11s.

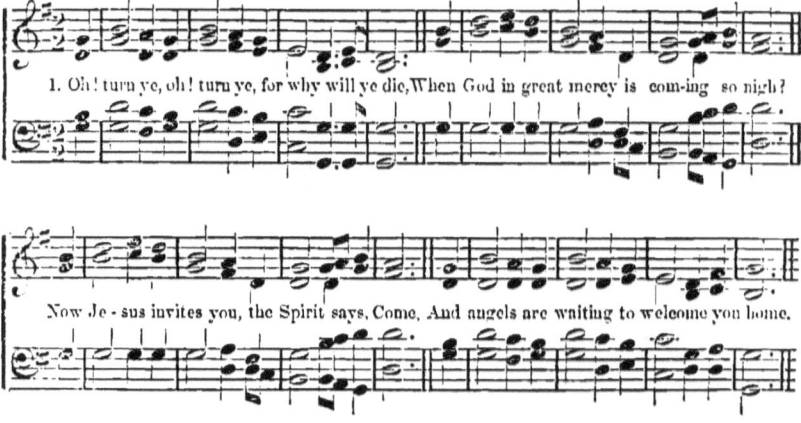

1. Oh! turn ye, oh! turn ye, for why will ye die, When God in great mercy is com-ing so nigh?
Now Je-sus invites you, the Spirit says, Come, And angels are waiting to welcome you home.

281.

2 How vain the delusion, that while you delay,
Your hearts may grow better by staying away;
Come wretched, come starving, come just as you are,
While streams of salvation are flowing so near.

3 And now Christ is ready your souls to receive,
Oh! how can you question if you will believe?
If sin is your burden, why will you not come?
'Tis you he bids welcome; he bids you come home.

WARNING AND INVITATION. 87

GOSHEN. 11s.

1. De-lay not, de-lay not, O sin-ner, draw near, The wa-ters of life are now flow-ing for thee; No price is de-mand-ed, the Sa-viour is here,
D. S. Re-demp-tion is purchased, sal-va-tion is free!

282.

2 Delay not, delay not, why longer abuse
  The love and compassion of Jesus thy God?
  A fountain is opened, how canst thou refuse
  To wash and be cleansed in his pardoning blood?

3 Delay not, delay not, O sinner, to come,
  For mercy still lingers, and calls thee to-day:

  Her voice is not heard in the vale of the tomb;
  Her message unheeded will soon pass away.

4 Delay not, delay not, the Spirit of Grace,
  Long grieved and resisted, may take its sad flight;
  And leave thee in darkness to finish thy race,
  To sink in the gloom of eternity's night.

SAY, BROTHERS. ANNIVERSARY HYMNS, S. S. U.

1. Say, brothers, will you meet us, Say, brothers, will you meet us,
Chorus. Glo-ry, glo-ry, hal-le-lu-jah, Glo-ry, glo-ry, hal-le-lu-jah,

Say, bro-thers, will you meet us, On Ca-naan's hap-py shore?
Glo-ry, glo-ry, hal-le-lu-jah, For ev-er, ev-er-more.

283.

2 By the grace of God we'll meet you,
  By the grace of God we'll meet you,
  By the grace of God we'll meet you,
  Where parting is no more.—*Chorus.*

3 Jesus lives and reigns for ever,
  Jesus lives and reigns for ever,
  Jesus lives and reigns for ever,
  On Canaan's happy shore.—*Chorus.*

WAY OF SALVATION.

COME, YE DISCONSOLATE. — WEBBE.

1. Come, ye dis-con-so-late, where'er ye languish; Come to the mer-cy-seat, fer-vent-ly kneel; Here bring your wound-ed hearts, here tell your an-guish, Earth has no sor-row that Heaven can-not heal.

284.

2 Joy of the comfortless, light of the straying,
Hope of the penitent, fadeless and pure;
Here speaks the Comforter, tenderly saying—
Earth has no sorrow that Heaven cannot cure.

3 Here see the Bread of Life; see waters flowing
Forth from the throne of God, pure from above;
Come to the feast prepared—come, ever knowing
Earth has no sorrow but Heaven can remove.

TO-DAY. 6s & 4s. — Dr. L. MASON.

1. To-day the Saviour calls; Ye wand'rers, come: Oh, ye benighted souls, Why longer roam?

285.

2 To-day the Saviour calls;
 Oh! hear him now;
Within these sacred walls
 To Jesus bow.

3 To-day the Saviour calls;
 For refuge fly;
The storm of justice falls,
 And death is nigh.

4 The Spirit calls to-day:
 Yield to his power;
Oh! grieve him not away:
 'Tis mercy's hour.

WARNING AND INVITATION.

WILL YOU GO? 8s & 3s.

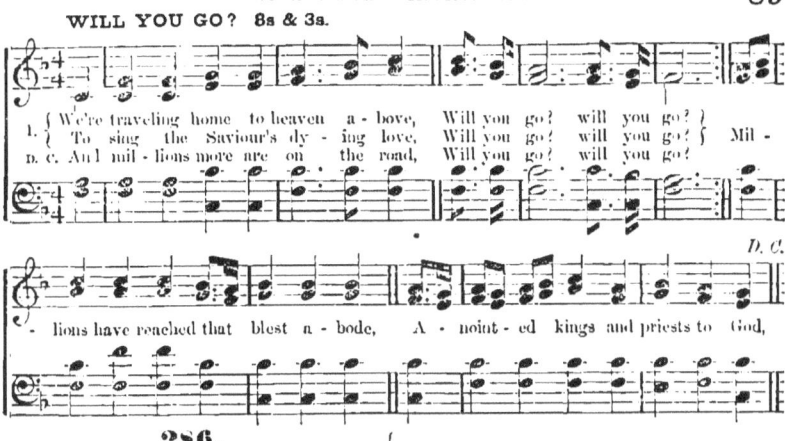

1. We're traveling home to heaven a-bove, Will you go? will you go?
   To sing the Saviour's dy-ing love, Will you go? will you go?
   D.C. And mil-lions more are on the road, Will you go? will you go?
   Mil-lions have reached that blest a-bode, A-noint-ed kings and priests to God,

286.

2 We're going to see the bleeding Lamb,
  Will you go?
 In rapturous strains to praise his name,
  Will you go?
 The crown of life we there shall wear,
 The conqueror's palms our hands shall bear,
 And all the joys of heaven we'll share,
  Will you go?

3 We're going to join the heavenly choir,
  Will you go?
 To raise our voice and tune the lyre,
  Will you go?
 There saints and angels gladly sing
 Hosanna to their God and King,
 And make the heavenly arches ring,
  Will you go?

PLEADING SAVIOUR. 8s & 7s.

1. Now the Sa-viour stand-eth plead-ing At the sin-ner's bolt-ed heart;
   Now in heaven he's in-ter-ced-ing, Tak-ing there the sin-ner's part:
   D.C. Once he died thro' your be-hav-ior, Now he calls you by his charms.

2. Sin-ner! can you hate this Sa-viour? Will you thrust him from your arms?

287.

3 Sinner! hear your God and Saviour,
  Hear his gracious voice to-day,
 Turn from all your vain behavior,
  Oh! repent, return and pray!

4 Now he's waiting to be gracious,
  Now he stands and looks on thee:
 See what kindness, love, and pity,
  Shine around on you and me.

288.

2 Haste, O sinner, to the Saviour!
  Seek his mercy while you may;
  Soon the day of grace is over;
  Soon your life will pass away:
    Haste, O sinner!
  You must perish if you stay.

289.

1 Sinners, will you scorn the message,
  Coming from the courts above?
  Mercy beams in every passage;
  Every line is full of love;
    Oh! believe it,
  Every line is full of love.

2 Now, the heralds of salvation,
  Joyful news from heaven proclaim:
  Sinners freed from condemnation,
  Through the all-atoning Lamb!
    Life receiving
  Through the all-atoning Lamb.

3 O ye angels, hovering round us,
  Waiting spirits, speed your way;
  Haste ye to the court of heaven,
  Tidings bear without delay:
    Rebel sinners
  Glad the message will obey.

290.

1 Come, ye sinners, poor and wretched,
  This is your accepted hour:
  Jesus ready stands to save you,
  Full of pity, love, and power:
    He is able,
  He is willing; doubt no more.

2 Agonizing in the garden,
  Lo! the Saviour prostrate lies;
  On the bloody tree behold him!
  Hear him cry before he dies,
    "It is finished!"
  Sinners, will not this suffice?

3 Lo! th' incarnate God ascended
  Pleads the merit of his blood;
  Venture on him, venture wholly,
  Let no other trust intrude:
    None but Jesus
  Can do helpless sinners good.

WARNING AND INVITATION.

NETTLETON. 8s & 7s.

291.

1 Come to Calvary's holy mountain,
    Sinners, ruined by the fall!
  Here a pure and healing fountain
    Flows to you, to me, to all,—
  In a full, perpetual tide,
    Opened when our Saviour died.

2 Come, in sorrow and contrition,
    Wounded, impotent, and blind!
  Here the guilty, free remission,
    Here the troubled, peace may find;
  Health this fountain will restore,
  He that drinks shall thirst no more—

3 He that drinks shall live forever;
    'T is a soul-renewing flood:
  God is faithful; God will never
    Break his covenant in blood,
  Signed when our Redeemer died,
  Sealed when he was glorified.

292.

1 When I view my Saviour bleeding,
    For my sins, upon the tree;
  Oh! how wondrous!—how exceeding
    Great his love appears to me!
  Floods of deep distress and anguish,
    To impede his labors, came;
  Yet they all could not extinguish
    Love's eternal, burning flame.

2 Now redemption is completed,
    Full salvation is procured:
  Death and Satan are defeated,
    By the sufferings he endured.
  Now the gracious Mediator,
    Risen to the courts of bliss,
  Claims for me, a sinful creature,
    Pardon, righteousness, and peace.

3 Sure such infinite affection
    Lays the highest claims to mine;
  All my powers, without exception,
    Should in fervent praises join.
  Jesus, fit me for thy service;
    Form me for thyself alone;
  I am thy most costly purchase;
    Take possession of thine own.

293.

1 Come, ye souls by sin afflicted,
    Bowed with fruitless sorrow down,
  By the perfect law convicted,
    Through the cross behold the crown;
      Look to Jesus;
    Mercy flows through him alone.

2 Take his easy yoke, and wear it;
    Love will make obedience sweet;
  Christ will give you strength to bear it,
    While his wisdom guides your feet
      Safe to glory,
    Where his ransomed captives meet.

3 Sweet as home to pilgrims weary,
    Light to newly-opened eyes;
  Or full springs in deserts dreary,
    Is the rest the cross supplies;
      All who taste it
    Shall to rest immortal rise.

WAY OF SALVATION.

WOODWORTH. L. M. — Wm. B. Bradbury.

1. Just as I am, with-out one plea, But that thy blood was shed for me, And that thou bid'st me come to thee, O Lamb of God, I come! I come!

294.

1 Just as I am, without one plea,
But that thy blood was shed for me,
And that thou bid'st me come to thee,
O Lamb of God, I come! I come!

2 Just as I am, and waiting not
To rid my soul of one dark blot,
To thee whose blood can cleanse each spot,
O Lamb of God, I come! I come!

3 Just as I am, though tossed about
With many a conflict, many a doubt,
Fightings within, and fears without,
O Lamb of God, I come! I come!

4 Just as I am—poor, wretched, blind;
Sight, riches, healing of the mind,
Yea, all I need, in thee to find,
O Lamb of God, I come! I come!

5 Just as I am—thou wilt receive,
Wilt welcome, pardon, cleanse, relieve;
Because thy promise I believe,
O Lamb of God, I come! I come!

6 Just as I am—thy love unknown
Hath broken every barrier down;
Now, to be thine, yea, thine alone,
O Lamb of God, I come! I come!

295.

1 With tearful eyes I look around;
Life seems a dark and stormy sea;
Yet, 'mid the gloom, I hear a sound,
A heavenly whisper, "Come to me."

2 It tells me of a place of rest;
It tells me where my soul may flee:
Oh, to the weary, faint, oppressed,
How sweet the bidding, "Come to me!"

3 "Come, for all else must fail and die;
Earth is no resting-place for thee;
To heaven direct thy weeping eye,
I am thy portion; Come to me."

4 O voice of mercy! voice of love!
In conflict, grief, and agony,
Support me, cheer me from above!
And gently whisper, "Come to me."

296.

1 God of my life! thy boundless grace,
Chose, pardoned, and adopted me;
My rest, my home, my dwelling-place;
Father! I come, I come to thee.

2 Jesus, my hope, my rock, my shield!
Whose precious blood was shed for me,
Into thy hands my soul I yield;
Saviour! I come, I come to thee.

3 Spirit of glory and of God!
Long hast thou deigned my guide to be;
Now be thy comfort sweet bestowed;
My God! I come, I come to thee.

4 I come to join that countless host
Who praise thy name unceasingly;
Blest Father, Son, and Holy Ghost!
My God! I come, I come to thee.

REPENTANCE AND RECEPTION OF CHRIST.

WARNER. L. M. *Templi Carmina.*

1. With bro-ken heart and con-trite sigh, A trembling sin-ner, Lord, I cry; Thy pardoning grace is rich and free: O God, be mer-ci-ful to me!

297.

2 I smite upon my troubled breast,
With deep and conscious guilt oppressed;
Christ and his cross my only plea:
O God, be merciful to me!

3 Far off I stand with tearful eyes,
Nor dare uplift them to the skies;
But thou dost all my anguish see:
O God, be merciful to me!

4 Nor alms, nor deeds that I have done
Can for a single sin atone;
To Calvary alone I flee:
O God, be merciful to me!

5 And when redeemed from sin and hell,
With all the ransomed throng I dwell,
My raptured song shall ever be,
God has been merciful to me!

298.

1 My sufferings all to thee are known,
Tempted in every point like me;
Regard my grief, regard thine own:
Jesus, remember Calvary!

2 For whom didst thou the cross endure?
Who nailed thy body to the tree?
Did not thy death my life procure?
Oh! let thy mercy answer me.

3 Art thou not touched with human woe?
Hath pity left the Son of Man?
Dost thou not all my sorrows know,
And claim a share in all my pain?

4 Thou wilt not break a bruised reed,
Or quench the smallest spark of grace,
Till through the soul thy power is spread,
Thy all-victorious righteousness.

5 The day of small and feeble things,
I know thou never wilt despise;
I know, with healing in his wings,
The Sun of Righteousness shall rise.

299.

1 Here at thy cross, my dying Lord!
I lay my soul beneath thy love,
Beneath the droppings of thy blood,
Jesus, nor shall it e'er remove.

2 Not all that tyrants think or say,
With rage and lightning in their eyes,
Nor hell shall fright my heart away,
Should hell with all its legions rise.

3 Should worlds conspire to drive me thence,
Moveless and firm this heart should lie;
Resolved, for that's my last defence,
If I must perish, there to die.

4 But speak, my Lord, and calm my fear;
Am I not safe beneath thy shade?
Thy vengeance will not strike me here,
Nor Satan dare my soul invade.

5 Yes, I'm secure beneath thy blood,
And all my foes shall lose their aim;
Hosanna to my dying Lord,
And my best honors to his name.

WAY OF SALVATION.

HAMBURG. L. M. *Arranged by* Dr. L. Mason.

1. Oh! for a glance of heaven-ly day, To take this stub-born heart a-way, And thaw, with beams of love di-vine, This heart, this fro-zen heart of mine.

300.

2 The rocks can rend ; the earth can quake ;
The seas can roar ; the mountains shake :
Of feeling, all things show some sign,
But this unfeeling heart of mine.

3 To hear the sorrows thou hast felt,
O Lord, an adamant would melt ;
But I can read each moving line,
And nothing moves this heart of mine.

4 Thy judgments, too, which devils fear—
Amazing thought—unmoved I hear ;
Goodness and wrath in vain combine
To stir this stupid heart of mine.

5 But Power Divine can do the deed ;
And, Lord, that power I greatly need ;
Thy Spirit can from dross refine,
And melt and change this heart of mine.

301.

1 Show pity, Lord ! O Lord, forgive ;
Let a repenting rebel live ;
Are not thy mercies large and free ?
May not a sinner trust in thee ?

2 My crimes are great, but ne'er surpass
The power and glory of thy grace :
Great God ! thy nature hath no bound,
So let thy pardoning love be found.

3 Oh, wash my soul from every sin,
And make my guilty conscience clean !
Here on my heart the burden lies,
And past offences pain mine eyes.

4 My lips with shame my sins confess,
Against thy law, against thy grace ;
Lord, should thy judgment grow severe,
I am condemned, but thou art clear.

5 Should sudden vengeance seize my breath
I must pronounce thee just in death ;
And if my soul were sent to hell,
Thy righteous law approves it well.

6 Yet save a trembling sinner, Lord !
Whose hope, still hovering round thy word,
Would light on some sweet promise there,
Some sure support against despair.

302.

1 No more, my God ! I boast no more,
Of all the duties I have done ;
I quit the hopes I held before,
To trust the merits of thy Son.

2 Now, for the love I bear his name,
What was my gain, I count my loss ;
My former pride I call my shame,
And nail my glory to his cross.

3 Yes,—and I must, and will esteem
All things but loss for Jesus' sake ;
Oh ! may my soul be found in him,
And of his righteousness partake.

4 The best obedience of my hands
Dares not appear before thy throne ;
But faith can answer thy demands,
By pleading what my Lord has done.

REPENTANCE AND RECEPTION OF CHRIST. 95

EASTON. L. M. — Mozart.

1. Oh! that my load of sin were gone! Oh! that I could at last submit At Jesus' feet to lay it down— To lay my soul at Jesus' feet!

303.

1 Oh! that my load of sin were gone!
  Oh! that I could at last submit
  At Jesus' feet to lay it down—
  To lay my soul at Jesus' feet!

2 Rest for my soul I long to find:
  Saviour of all, if mine thou art,
  Give me thy meek and lowly mind,
  And stamp thine image on my heart.

3 Break off the yoke of inbred sin,
  And fully set my spirit free:
  I cannot rest, till pure within—
  Till I am wholly lost in thee.

4 Fain would I learn of thee, my God;
  Thy light and easy burden prove,—
  The cross all stained with hallowed blood,
  The labor of thy dying love.

5 I would—but thou must give the power;
  My heart from every sin release;
  Bring near, bring near the joyful hour,
  And fill me with thy perfect peace!

304.

1 I send the joys of earth away;
  Away, ye tempters of the mind,
  False as the smooth, deceitful sea,
  And empty as the whistling wind.

2 Your streams were floating me along,
  Down to the gulf of dark despair;
  And while I listened to your song,
  Your streams had ev'n conveyed me there.

3 Lord, I adore thy matchless grace,
  Which warned me of that dark abyss,
  Which drew me from those treacherous seas,
  And bade me seek superior bliss.

4 Now to the shining realms above,
  I stretch my hands and glance my eyes;
  Oh! for the pinions of a dove,
  To bear me to the upper skies!

5 There, from the bosom of our God,
  Oceans of endless pleasure roll;
  There would I fix my last abode,
  And drown the sorrows of my soul.

305.

1 Jesus, the sinner's Friend, to thee,
  Lost and undone, for aid I flee;
  Weary of earth, myself, and sin,
  Open thine arms and take me in.

2 Pity and save my ruined soul;
  'T is thou alone canst make me whole;
  Dark, till in me thine image shine,
  And lost I am, till thou art mine.

3 At last I own it cannot be
  That I should fit myself for thee:
  Here, then, to thee I all resign;
  Thine is the work, and only thine.

4 What can I say thy grace to move?
  Lord, I am sin,—but thou art love:
  I give up every plea beside,
  Lord, I am lost,—but thou hast died!

WAY OF SALVATION.

MANOAH. C. M.   GREATOREX COLL.

1. I saw One hang-ing on a tree, In ag-o-ny and blood, Who fixed his lan-guid eyes on me, As near the cross I stood.

306.

2 Sure, never, till my latest breath,
Can I forget that look:
It seemed to charge me with his death,
Though not a word he spoke.

3 Alas! I knew not what I did,
But now my tears are vain;
Where shall my trembling soul be hid,
For I the Lord have slain!

4 A second look he gave, that said,
"I freely all forgive:
This blood is for thy ransom paid;
I die that thou may'st live."

5 Thus while his death my sin displays
In all its blackest hue,
Such is the mystery of grace,
It seals my pardon too!

307.

1 Approach, my soul! the mercy-seat,
Where Jesus answers prayer;
There humbly fall before his feet,
For none can perish there.

2 Thy promise is my only plea,
With this I venture nigh:
Thou callest burdened souls to thee,
And such, O Lord! am I.

3 Bowed down beneath a load of sin,
By Satan sorely pressed;
By wars without, and fears within,
I come to thee for rest.

4 Be thou my shield and hiding-place,
That, sheltered near thy side,
I may my fierce accuser face,
And tell him—thou hast died.

5 Oh! wondrous Love—to bleed and die,
To bear the cross and shame,
That guilty sinners, such as I,
Might plead thy gracious name!

308.

1 Lord! at thy feet we sinners lie,
And knock at mercy's door:
With heavy heart and downcast eye,
Thy favor we implore.

2 On us the vast extent display
Of thy forgiving love;
Take all our heinous guilt away;
This heavy load remove.

3 'T is mercy—mercy we implore;
We would thy pity move:
Thy grace is an exhaustless store,
And thou thyself art love.

4 Oh, for thine own, for Jesus' sake,
Our numerous sins forgive!
Thy grace our rocky hearts can break:
Heal us, and bid us live.

5 Thus melt us down, thus make us bend,
And thy dominion own;
Nor let a rival more pretend
To repossess thy throne.

REPENTANCE AND RECEPTION OF CHRIST.

AVON. C. M. — Scottish.

1. O Thou, whose tender mercy hears Contrition's humble sigh; Whose hand, indulgent, wipes the tears From sorrow's weeping eye,—

309.

2 See, low before thy throne of grace,
   A wretched wanderer mourn;
   Hast thou not bid me seek thy face?
   Hast thou not said—"Return?"

3 And shall my guilty fears prevail
   To drive me from thy feet?
   Oh! let not this dear refuge fail,
   This only safe retreat!

4 Oh! shine on this benighted heart,
   With beams of mercy shine!
   And let thy healing voice impart
   A taste of joys divine.

310.

1 O God of mercy! hear my call,
   My load of guilt remove;
   Break down this separating wall,
   That bars me from thy love.

2 Give me the presence of thy grace;
   Then my rejoicing tongue
   Shall speak aloud thy righteousness,
   And make thy praise my song.

3 No blood of goats, nor heifer slain,
   For sin could e'er atone:
   The death of Christ shall still remain
   Sufficient and alone.

4 A soul, oppressed with sin's desert,
   My God will ne'er despise;
   An humble groan, a broken heart,
   Is our best sacrifice.

311.

1 My God, accept my heart this day,
   And make it always thine;
   That I from thee no more may stray,
   No more from thee decline.

2 Before the cross of him who died,
   Behold, I prostrate fall;
   Let every sin be crucified,
   Let Christ be all in all.

3 May the dear blood, once shed for me,
   My blest atonement prove;
   That I, from first to last, may be
   The purchase of thy love.

4 Let every thought and work and word
   To thee be ever given;
   Then life shall be thy service, Lord,
   And death the gate of heaven!

312.

1 Welcome, O Saviour! to my heart;
   Possess thine humble throne;
   Bid every rival hence depart,
   And claim me for thine own.

2 The world and Satan I forsake—
   To thee, I all resign;
   My longing heart, O Jesus! take,
   And fill with love divine.

3 Oh! may I never turn aside,
   Nor from thy bosom flee;
   Let nothing here my heart divide—
   I give it all to thee.

WAY OF SALVATION.

ADRIAN. S. M.   J. E. GOULD.

1. Oh! cease, my wandering soul, On restless wing to roam; All this wide world, to either pole, Hath not for thee a home.

313.

1 Oh, cease, my wandering soul,
On restless wing to roam;
All this wide world, to either pole,
Hath not for thee a home.

2 Behold the ark of God!
Behold the open door!
Oh, haste to gain that dear abode,
And rove, my soul, no more.

3 There safe thou shalt abide,
There sweet shall be thy rest,
And every longing satisfied,
With full salvation blest.

314.

1 Ah! what avails my strife,
My wandering to and fro?
Thou hast the words of endless life;
Ah! whither should I go?

2 Thy condescending grace
To me did freely move;
It calls me still to seek thy face,
And stoops to ask my love.

3 My worthless heart to gain,
The God of all that breathe
Was found in fashion as a man,
And died a cursèd death.

4 And can I yet delay
My little all to give?
To tear my soul from earth away,
For Jesus to receive?

5 Ah! no: I all forsake,
My all to thee resign:
Gracious Redeemer, take, oh, take,
And seal me ever thine!

315.

1 Shall we go on to sin,
Because thy grace abounds?
Or crucify the Lord again,
And open all his wounds?

2 Forbid it, mighty God!
Nor let it e'er be said,
That we, whose sins are crucified,
Should raise them from the dead.

3 We will be slaves no more,
Since Christ has made us free,
Has nailed our tyrants to the cross,
And bought our liberty.

316.

1 Unto thine altar, Lord,
A broken heart I bring;
And wilt thou graciously accept
Of such a worthless thing?

2 To Christ, the bleeding Lamb,
My faith directs its eyes;
Thou mayst reject that worthless thing,
But not his sacrifice.

3 When he gave up the ghost,
The law was satisfied;
And now to its most rigorous claims
I answer, "Jesus died."

REPENTANCE AND RECEPTION OF CHRIST. 99

FERGUSON. S. M.   Geo. Kingsley.

1. Thou Lord of all a-bove, And all be-low the sky,
Pros-trate be-fore thy feet I fall, And for thy mer-cy cry.

317.

2 Forgive my follies past,
  The crimes which I have done;
  Oh! bid a contrite sinner live,
  Through thy incarnate Son.

3 Guilt, like a heavy load,
  Upon my conscience lies;
  To thee I make my sorrows known,
  And lift my weeping eyes.

4 The burden which I feel,
  Thou only canst remove;
  Display, O Lord! thy pardoning grace,
  And thy unbounded love.

5 One gracious look of thine
  Will ease my troubled breast;
  Oh! let me know my sins forgiven,
  And I shall then be blest.

318.

1 Jesus! I come to thee,
  A sinner doomed to die;
  My only refuge is thy cross,—
  Here at thy feet I lie.

2 Can mercy reach my case,
  And all my sins remove?
  Break, O my God! this heart of stone,
  And melt it by thy love.

3 Too long my soul has gone,
  Far from my God, astray;
  I've sported on the brink of hell,
  In sin's delusive way.

4 But, Lord! my heart is fixed,—
  I hope in thee alone;
  Break off the chains of sin and death,
  And bind me to thy throne.

5 Thy blood can cleanse my heart,
  Thy hand can wipe my tears;—
  Oh! send thy blessed Spirit down,
  To banish all my fears.

6 Then shall my soul arise,
  From sin and Satan free;
  Redeemed from hell and every foe,
  I'll trust alone in thee.

319.

1 Thou seest my feebleness,
  Jesus, be thou my power,—
  My help and refuge in distress,
  My fortress and my tower.

2 Give me to trust in thee;
  Be thou my sure abode:
  My horn, and rock, and buckler be,
  My Saviour and my God.

3 Myself I cannot save,
  Myself I cannot keep;
  But strength in thee I surely have,
  Whose eyelids never sleep.

4 My soul to thee alone,
  Now, therefore, I commend:
  Lord Jesus, love me as thine own,
  And love me to the end.

WAY OF SALVATION.

MERIBAH. L. C. M. Dr. L. Mason.

1. When thou, my righteous Judge, shalt come To bring thy ransomed people home, Shall I among them stand? Shall such a worthless worm as I, Who sometimes am afraid to die, Be found at thy right hand?

320.

2 I love to meet thy people now,
Before thy feet with them to bow,
Though vilest of them all;
But, can I bear the piercing thought,
What if my name should be left out,
When thou for them shalt call?

3 O Lord, prevent it by thy grace,
Be thou my only hiding-place,
In this the accepted day;
Thy pardoning voice, oh. let me hear,
To still my unbelieving fear,
Nor let me fall, I pray.

4 Among thy saints let me be found,
Whene'er the archangel's trump shall sound,
To see thy smiling face;
Then loudest of the throng I'll sing,
While heaven's resounding mansions ring
With shouts of sovereign grace.

321.

1 O thou who hear'st the prayer of faith,
Wilt thou not save a soul from death,
That casts itself on thee?
I have no refuge of my own,
But fly to what my Lord hath done,
And suffered once for me.

2 Slain in the guilty sinner's stead,
His spotless righteousness I plead,
And his availing blood;
Thy merit, Lord, my robe shall be;
Thy merit shall atone for me,
And bring me near to God.

3 Then save me from eternal death,
The spirit of adoption breathe,
His consolations send;
By him some word of life impart,
And sweetly whisper to my heart,
"Thy Maker is thy Friend."

4 The king of terrors then would be
A welcome messenger to me,
To bid me come away:
Unclogged by earth, or earthly things,
I'd mount, I'd fly with eager wings
To everlasting day!

322.

1 The mind was formed, to mount sublime,
Beyond the narrow bounds of time,
To everlasting things;
But earthly vapors dim her sight,
And hang, with cold oppressive weight,
Upon her drooping wings.

2 Bright scenes of bliss,—unclouded skies,
Invite my soul;—Oh! could I rise,
Nor leave a thought below,
I'd bid farewell to anxious care,
And say, to every tempting snare,—
Heaven calls, and I must go:—

3 Heaven calls,—and can I yet delay?
Can aught on earth engage my stay?
Ah! wretched lingering heart!
Come, Lord! with strength, and life, and light,
Assist and guide my upward flight,
And bid the world depart.

323.

1 Lord, thou hast won—at length I yield;
My heart, by mighty grace compelled,
　Surrenders all to thee:
Against thy terrors long I strove,
But who can stand against thy love?—
　Love conquers even me.

2 But since thou hast thy love revealed,
And shown my soul a pardon sealed,
　I can resist no more;
Couldst thou for such a sinner bleed?
Canst thou for such a rebel plead?
　I wonder and adore!

3 If thou hadst bid thy thunders roll,
And lightnings flash to blast my soul,
　I still had stubborn been;
But mercy has my heart subdued,
A bleeding Saviour I have viewed,
　And now, I hate my sin.

4 Now, Lord, I would be thine alone—
Come, take possession of thine own,
　For thou hast set me free;
Released from Satan's hard command,
See all my powers in waiting stand,
　To be employed by thee.

324.

1 Awaked by Sinai's awful sound,
My soul in bonds of guilt I found,
　And knew not where to go;
One simple truth increased my pain,
The sinner "must be born again,"
　Or sink to endless woe.

2 I heard the law its thunders roll,
While guilt lay heavy on my soul—
　A vast oppressive load;
All creature-aid I saw was vain;
The sinner "must be born again,"
　Or drink the wrath of God.

3 The saints I heard with rapture tell—
How Jesus conquered death and hell
　To bring salvation near;
Yet still I found this truth remain—
The sinner "must be born again,"
　Or sink in deep despair.

4 But while I thus in anguish lay,
The bleeding Saviour passed that way,
　My bondage to remove;
The sinner, once by justice slain,
Now by his grace is born again,
　And sings redeeming love.

325.

1 Lo! on a narrow neck of land,
'Twixt two unbounded seas, I stand,
　Secure! insensible!
A point of time, a moment's space,
Removes me to that heavenly place,
　Or shuts me up in hell.

2 O God! my inmost soul convert,
And deeply on my thoughtful heart
　Eternal things impress;
Give me to feel their solemn weight,
And save me ere it be too late;
　Wake me to righteousness.

3 Before me place, in bright array,
The pomp of that tremendous day,
　When thou with clouds shalt come
To judge the nations at thy bar;
And tell me, Lord! shall I be there
　To meet a joyful doom?

4 Be this my one great business here,—
With holy trembling, holy fear,
　To make my calling sure!
Thine utmost counsel to fulfill,
And suffer all thy righteous will,
　And to the end endure!

5 Then, Saviour, then my soul receive,
Transported from this earth, to live
　And reign with thee above;
Where faith is sweetly lost in sight,
And hope, in full, supreme delight,
　And everlasting love.

326.

1 No room for mirth or trifling here,
For worldly hope, or worldly fear,
　If life so soon is gone;
If now the Judge is at the door,
And all mankind must stand before
　The inexorable throne!

2 Nothing is worth a thought beneath,
But how I may escape the death
　That never, never dies!
How make mine own election sure;
And when I fail on earth, secure
　A mansion in the skies.

3 Jesus, vouchsafe a pitying ray;
Be thou my Guide, be thou my Way
　To glorious happiness!
Ah! write the pardon on my heart;
And whensoe'er I hence depart,
　Let me depart in peace.

WAY OF SALVATION.

ALETTA. 7s.   WM. B. BRADBURY.

1. Depth of mer-cy! can there be Mer-cy still re-served for me?
Can my God his wrath for-bear? Me, the chief of sin-ners, spare?

327.

2 I have long withstood his grace;
Long provoked him to his face;
Would not hearken to his calls;
Grieved him by a thousand falls.

3 Kindled his relentings are;
Me he now delights to spare;
Cries, How shall I give thee up?—
Lets the lifted thunder drop.

4 There for me the Saviour stands;
Shows his wounds and spreads his hands,
God is love! I know, I feel:
Jesus weeps, and loves me still.

328.

1 When on Sinai's top I see
God descend, in majesty,
To proclaim his holy law,
All my spirit sinks with awe.

2 When, in ecstacy sublime,
Tabor's glorious steep I climb;
At the too transporting light,
Darkness rushes o'er my sight.

3 When on Calvary I rest;
God in flesh made manifest,
Shines in my Redeemer's face,
Full of beauty, truth, and grace.

4 Here I would forever stay,
Weep and gaze my soul away;
Thou art heaven on earth to me,
Lovely, mournful Calvary!

329.

1 Jesus! full of truth and love,
We thy kindest word obey;
Faithful let thy mercies prove;
Take our load of guilt away.

2 Weary of this war within,
Weary of this endless strife,
Weary of ourselves and sin,
Weary of a wretched life;

3 Burdened with a world of grief,
Burdened with our sinful load,
Burdened with this unbelief,
Burdened with the wrath of God:

4 Lo! we come to thee for ease,
True and gracious as thou art:
Now our weary souls release;
Write forgiveness on each heart.

330.

1 Lord of mercy, just and kind!
Wilt thou ne'er my guilt forgive?
Never shall my troubled mind,
In thy kind remembrance, live?

2 Lord! how long shall Satan's art
Tempt my harassed soul to sin,
Triumph o'er my humbled heart,—
Fears without and guilt within?

3 Lord, my God! thine ear incline,
Bending to the prayer of faith;
Cheer my eyes with light divine
Lest I sleep the sleep of death.

REPENTANCE AND RECEPTION OF CHRIST. 103

ROSEFIELD. 7s. — Dr. Malan.

1. People of the living God, I have sought the world around,
Paths of sin and sorrow trod, Peace and comfort nowhere found.

331.

2 Now to you my spirit turns—
Turns, a fugitive unblest;
Brethren, where your altar burns,
Oh, receive me into rest!

3 Lonely I no longer roam,
Like the cloud, the wind, the wave:
Where you dwell shall be my home,
Where you die shall be my grave;

4 Mine the God whom you adore,
Your Redeemer shall be mine;
Earth can fill my soul no more,
Every idol I resign.

332.

1 Sovereign Ruler, Lord of all!
Prostrate at thy feet I fall!
Hear, oh, hear my earnest cry,
Frown not, lest I faint and die.

2 Vilest of the sons of men,—
Chief of sinners I have been;
Oft abused thee to thy face,
Trampled on thy richest grace.

3 Justly might thy righteous dart
Pierce this bleeding, broken heart;
Justly might thine angry breath
Blast me in eternal death.

4 But with thee there's mercy found,
Balm to heal my every wound:
Soothe, oh, soothe the troubled breast,
Give the weary wanderer rest.

333.

1 Jesus, save my dying soul;
Make the broken spirit whole:
Humble in the dust I lie:
Saviour, leave me not to die.

2 Jesus, full of every grace,
Now reveal thy smiling face;
Grant the joys of sin forgiven,
Foretaste of the bliss of heaven.

3 All my guilt to thee is known;
Thou art righteous, thou alone:
All my help is from thy cross;
All beside I count but loss.

4 Lord, in thee I now believe;
Wilt thou, wilt thou not forgive?
Helpless at thy feet I lie;
Saviour, leave me not to die.

334.

1 Jesus, all-atoning Lamb,
Thine, and only thine, I am:
Take my body, spirit, soul;
Only thou possess the whole.

2 Thou my one thing needful be;
Let me ever cleave to thee;
Let me choose the better part:
Let me give thee all my heart.

3 Whom have I on earth below?
Thee, and only Thee, I know:
Whom have I in heaven but thee?
Thou art all in all to me.

104   WAY OF SALVATION.

DORRNANCE. 8s & 7s.   I. B. Woodbury.

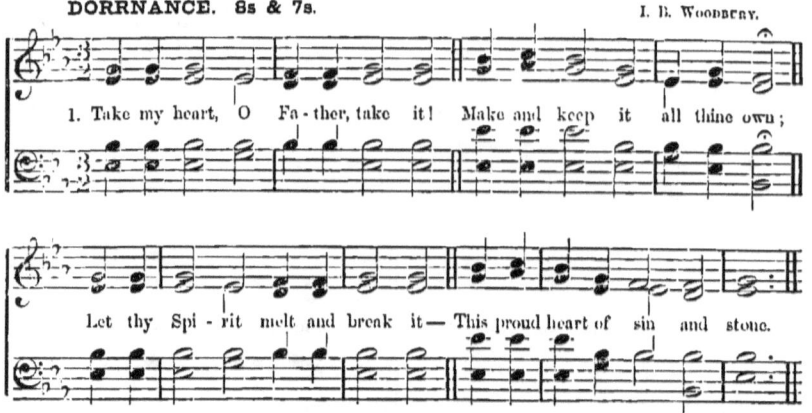

1. Take my heart, O Father, take it! Make and keep it all thine own; Let thy Spirit melt and break it— This proud heart of sin and stone.

335.

2 Father, make me pure and lowly,
  Fond of peace and far from strife ;
  Turning from the paths unholy
  Of this vain and sinful life.

3 Ever let thy grace surround me;
  Strengthen me with power divine ;
  Till thy cords of love have bound me :
  Make me to be wholly thine.

4 May the blood of Jesus heal me,
  And my sins be all forgiven ;
  Holy Spirit, take and seal me,
  Guide me in the path to heaven.

336.

1 SWEET the moments, rich in blessing,
  Which before the cross I spend ;
  Life, and health, and peace possessing,
  From the sinner's dying Friend.

2 Here I 'll sit, for ever viewing
  Mercy streaming in his blood ;
  Precious drops! my soul bedewing,
  Plead and claim my peace with God.

3 Truly blessed is this station,
  Low before the cross to lie ;
  While I see divine compassion
  Beaming in his gracious eye.

4 Here it is I find my heaven,
  While upon the cross I gaze ;
  Love I much? I 've much forgiven,
  I 'm a miracle of grace.

5 Love and grief my heart dividing,
  With my tears his feet I 'll bathe ;
  Constant still in faith abiding,
  Life deriving from his death.

6 Lord! in ceaseless contemplation,
  Fix my heart and eyes on thine,
  Till I taste thy whole salvation,
  Where, unvailed, thy glories shine.

337.

1 LABORING and heavy laden
  With my sins, O Lord, I roam,
  While I know thou hast invited
  All such wanderers to their home.

2 Make my stubborn spirit willing
  To obey thy gracious voice,
  At the cross to leave its burden,
  And departing to rejoice.

3 Thy sweet yoke I 'd take upon me,
  And would learn, O Lord, of thee ;
  Thou art meek in heart, and lowly,
  Teach me like thyself to be.

4 Rest my weary soul is seeking
  From its sins and all its woes ;
  In thy bosom I would place me,
  There to find a blest repose.

5 Laboring and heavy laden,
  Lord, no longer will I roam :
  Here I fix my habitation,
  In thy sheltering love at home.

REPENTANCE AND RECEPTION OF CHRIST. 105

RATHBUN. 8s & 7s. GREATOREX COLL.

1. In the cross of Christ I glory, Towering o'er the wrecks of time; All the light of sacred story Gathers round its head sublime.

338.

1 In the cross of Christ I glory,
  Towering o'er the wrecks of time;
  All the light of sacred story
  Gathers round its head sublime.
2 When the woes of life o'ertake me,
  Hopes deceive, and fears annoy,
  Never shall the cross forsake me:
  Lo! it glows with peace and joy.
3 When the sun of bliss is beaming
  Light and love upon my way,
  From the cross the radiance streaming,
  Adds new lustre to the day.
4 Bane and blessing, pain and pleasure,
  By the cross are sanctified;
  Peace is there, that knows no measure,
  Joys that through all time abide.
5 In the cross of Christ I glory,
  Towering o'er the wrecks of time;
  All the light of sacred story
  Gathers round its head sublime.

339.

1 Jesus, who on Calvary's mountain
  Poured thy precious blood for me,
  Wash me in its flowing fountain,
  That my soul may spotless be.
2 I have sinned, but oh, restore me!
  For unless thou smile on me,
  Dark is all the world before me,
  Darker yet eternity.
3 In thy word I hear thee saying,
  Come and I will give you rest;
  And the gracious call obeying,
  See, I hasten to thy breast.
4 Grant, oh, grant thy Spirit's teaching,
  That I may not go astray,
  Till the gate of heaven reaching,
  Earth and sin are passed away.

340.

1 Come, thou Fount of every blessing,
  Tune my heart to sing thy grace;
  Streams of mercy, never ceasing,
  Call for songs of loudest praise.
2 Teach me some melodious measure,
  Sung by flaming tongues above;
  Oh, the vast, the boundless treasure
  Of thy free, unchanging love!
3 Jesus sought me when a stranger,
  Wandering from the fold of God;
  He, to rescue me from danger,
  Interposed his precious blood.
4 Oh, to grace how great a debtor
  Daily I'm constrained to be!
  Let thy goodness, like a fetter,
  Bind my wandering heart to thee.
5 Prone to wander, Lord, I feel it;
  Prone to leave the God I love;
  Here's my heart; oh, take and seal it,—
  Seal it for thy courts above!

106   CHRISTIAN.

ROSE HILL. L. M.   Root & Sweetser's Coll.

1. O God, thou art my God a-lone: Ear-ly to thee my soul shall cry— A pil-grim in a land un-known, A thirsty land, whose springs are dry.

341.

2 Oh, that it were as it hath been,
When, praying in the holy place,
Thy power and glory I have seen,
And marked the footsteps of thy grace!
3 Yet, through this rough and thorny maze,
I follow hard on thee, my God:
Thy hand unseen upholds my ways;
I safely tread where thou hast trod.
4 Thee, in the watches of the night,
When I remember on my bed,
Thy presence makes the darkness light;
Thy guardian wings are round my head.
5 Better than life itself thy love,
Dearer than all beside to me;
For whom have I in heaven above,
Or what on earth, compared with thee?

342.

1 See a poor sinner, dearest Lord,
Whose soul, encouraged by thy word,
At mercy's footstool would remain,
And then would look,—and look again.
2 Ah! bring a wretched wanderer home,
Now to thy footstool let me come,
And tell thee all my grief and pain,
And wait and look,—and look again!
3 Take courage, then, my trembling soul;
One look from Christ will make thee
    whole:
Trust thou in him, 't is not in vain,
But wait and look,—and look again.

4 Look to the Lord, his word, his throne;
Look to his grace, and not your own;
There wait and look, and look again;
You shall not wait, nor look in vain.
5 Ere long that happy day will come,
When I shall reach my blissful home;
And when to glory I attain,
Oh, then I'll look,—and look again!

343.

1 I LEFT the God of truth and light;
I left the God who gave me breath,
To wander in the wilds of night,
And perish in the snares of death!
2 Sweet was his service, and his yoke
Was light and easy to be borne:
Through all his bonds of love I broke;
I cast away his gifts with scorn!
3 Heart-broken, friendless, poor, cast down,
Where shall the chief of sinners fly,
Almighty Vengeance! from thy frown,
Eternal Justice! from thine eye?
4 Lo! through the gloom of guilty fears,
My faith discerns a dawn of grace;
The Sun of Righteousness appears
In Jesus' reconciling face!
5 Prostrate before the mercy-seat,
I dare not, if I would, despair;
None ever perished at thy feet,
And I will lie forever there.

CONFLICT WITH SIN. 107

BLAKE. L. M. — J. P. Holbrook.

1. Thou only Sovereign of my heart, My Refuge, my almighty Friend— And can my soul from thee depart, On whom alone my hopes depend!

344.

1 Thou only Sovereign of my heart,
My Refuge, my almighty Friend—
And can my soul from thee depart
On whom alone my hopes depend!

2 Whither, ah! whither shall I go,
A wretched wanderer from my Lord?
Can this dark world of sin and woe
One glimpse of happiness afford?

3 Eternal life thy words impart;
On these my fainting spirit lives;
Here sweeter comforts cheer my heart,
Than all the round of nature gives.

4 Thy name my inmost powers adore;
Thou art my life, my joy, my care;
Depart from thee—'tis death—'tis more—
'Tis endless ruin, deep despair!

5 Low at thy feet my soul would lie;
Here safety dwells, and peace divine;
Still let me live beneath thine eye,
For life, eternal life, is thine.

345.

1 O thou, to whose all-searching sight
The darkness shineth as the light,
Search, prove my heart, it pants for thee;
Oh! burst these bonds, and set it free.

2 Wash out its stains, refine its dross;
Nail my affections to the cross;
Hallow each thought; let all within
Be clean, as thou, my Lord, art clean.

3 If in this darksome wild I stray,
Be thou my light, be thou my way:
No foes, no violence I fear,
No fraud, while thou, my God, art near.

4 When rising floods my soul o'erflow,
When sinks my heart in waves of woe—
Jesus, thy timely aid impart,
And raise my head, and cheer my heart.

5 Saviour, where'er thy steps I see,
Dauntless, untired, I follow thee;
Oh! let thy hand support me still,
And lead me to thy holy hill.

346.

1 Oh! where is now that glowing love
That marked our union with the Lord?
Our hearts were fixed on things above,
Nor could the world a joy afford.

2 Where is the zeal that led us then
To make our Saviour's glory known?
That freed us from the fear of men,
And kept our eye on him alone?

3 Where are the happy seasons spent
In fellowship with him we loved?
The sacred joy, the sweet content,
The blessedness that then we proved?

4 Behold, again we turn to thee;
Oh! cast us not away, though vile;
No peace we have, no joy we see,
O Lord our God, but in thy smile.

COOLING. C. M.   Abbey.

1. Sweet was the time when first I felt
The Saviour's pardoning blood
Applied to cleanse my soul from guilt,
And bring me home to God.

347.

2 Soon as the morn the light revealed,
  His praises tuned my tongue;
And, when the evening shade prevailed,
  His love was all my song.

3 In prayer, my soul drew near the Lord,
  And saw his glory shine;
And when I read his holy word,
  I called each promise mine.

4 Now, when the evening shade prevails,
  My soul in darkness mourns;
And, when the morn the light reveals,
  No light to me returns.

5 Rise, Saviour! help me to prevail,
  And make my soul thy care;
I know thy mercy cannot fail,
  Let me that mercy share.

348.

1 With tears of anguish I lament,
  Here, at thy feet, my God,
My passion, pride, and discontent,
  And vile ingratitude.

2 Sure there was ne'er a heart so base,
  So false as mine has been;
So faithless to its promises,
  So prone to every sin!

3 My reason tells me thy commands
  Are holy, just, and true;
Tells me whate'er my God demands
  Is his most righteous due.

4 Reason, I hear, her counsels weigh,
  And all her words approve;
But still I find it hard t' obey,
  And harder yet to love.

5 How long, dear Saviour, shall I feel
  These struggles in my breast?
When wilt thou bow my stubborn will,
  And give my conscience rest?

6 Break, sovereign grace, oh, break the charm,
  And set the captive free;
Reveal, almighty God, thine arm,
  And haste to rescue me.

349.

1 Oh! for that tenderness of heart,
  That bows before the Lord;
That owns how just and good thou art,
  And trembles at thy word.

2 Oh! for those humble, contrite tears,
  Which from repentance flow;
That sense of guilt, which, trembling, fears
  The long-suspended blow!

3 Saviour! to me, in pity give,
  For sin, the deep distress;
The pledge thou wilt, at last, receive,
  And bid me die in peace.

4 Oh! fill my soul with faith and love,
  And strength to do thy will;
Raise my desires and hopes above,—
  Thyself to me reveal.

CONFLICT WITH SIN.   109

EVAN. C. M.   HAVERGAL.

1. How oft, a - las! this wretch - ed heart Has wandered from the Lord!
How oft my rov - ing thoughts de - part, For - get - ful of his word!

350.

2 Yet sovereign mercy calls—"Return!"
Dear Lord, and may I come?
My vile ingratitude I mourn:
Oh, take the wanderer home!

3 And canst thou—wilt thou yet forgive,
And bid my crimes remove?
And shall a pardoned rebel live,
To speak thy wondrous love?

4 Almighty grace, thy healing power,
How glorious, how divine!
That can to life and bliss restore
A heart so vile as mine.

5 Thy pardoning love, so free, so sweet,
Dear Saviour, I adore;
Oh, keep me at thy sacred feet,
And let me rove no more!

351.

1 Searcher of Hearts!—from mine erase
All thoughts that should not be,
And in its deep recesses trace
My gratitude to thee!

2 Hearer of Prayer!—oh, guide aright
Each word and deed of mine;
Life's battle teach me how to fight,
And be the victory thine.

3 Giver of All!—for every good
That in the Saviour came—
For raiment, shelter and for food,
I thank thee in his name.

4 Father and Son and Holy Ghost!
Thou glorious Three in One!
Thou knowest best what I need most,
And let thy will be done.

352.

1 On! for a closer walk with God,
A calm and heavenly frame,—
A light to shine upon the road
That leads me to the Lamb!

2 Where is the blessedness I knew
When first I saw the Lord?
Where is the soul-refreshing view
Of Jesus and his word?

3 What peaceful hours I once enjoyed!
How sweet their memory still!
But they have left an aching void
The world can never fill.

4 Return, O holy Dove, return,
Sweet messenger of rest!
I hate the sins that made thee mourn,
And drove thee from my breast.

5 The dearest idol I have known,
Whate'er that idol be,
Help me to tear it from thy throne,
And worship only thee.

6 So shall my walk be close with God,
Calm and serene my frame;
So purer light shall mark the road
That leads me to the Lamb.

110   CHRISTIAN.

LITCHFIELD. C. M.   Dr. L. Mason.

1. Oh! that I knew the secret place Where I might find my God! I'd spread my wants before his face, And pour my woes abroad.

353.

2 I'd tell him how my sins arise,
   What sorrows I sustain;
How grace decays, and comfort dies,
   And leaves my heart in pain.

3 He knows what arguments I'd take
   To wrestle with my God:
I'd plead for his own mercy's sake—
   I'd plead my Saviour's blood.

4 My God will pity my complaints;
   And drive my foes away;
He knows the meaning of his saints
   When they in sorrow pray.

5 Arise, my soul! from deep distress,
   And banish every fear;
He calls thee to his throne of grace,
   To spread thy sorrows there.

354.

1 Alas! what hourly dangers rise!
   What snares beset my way!
To heaven, oh, let me lift mine eyes,
   And hourly watch and pray.

2 How oft my mournful thoughts complain,
   And melt in flowing tears!
My weak resistance, ah, how vain!
   How strong my foes and fears!

3 O gracious God! in whom I live,
   My feeble efforts aid;
Help me to watch, and pray, and strive,
   Though trembling and afraid.

4 Increase my faith, increase my hope,
   When foes and fears prevail;
And bear my fainting spirit up,
   Or soon my strength will fail.

5 Whene'er temptations fright my heart,
   Or lure my feet aside,
My God, thy powerful aid impart,
   My Guardian and my Guide.

6 Oh, keep me in thy heavenly way,
   And bid the tempter flee!
And let me never, never stray
   From happiness and thee.

355.

1 Oh! could I find, from day to day,
   A nearness to my God,
Then would my hours glide sweet away
   While leaning on his word.

2 Lord, I desire with thee to live
   Anew from day to day,
In joys the world can never give,
   Nor ever take away.

3 Blest Jesus, come and rule my heart,
   And make me wholly thine,
That I may never more depart,
   Nor grieve thy love divine.

4 Thus, till my last, expiring breath,
   Thy goodness I'll adore;
And when my frame dissolves in death,
   My soul shall love thee more.

CONFLICT WITH SIN.   **111**

CHESTERFIELD. C. M.   Dr. Haweis.

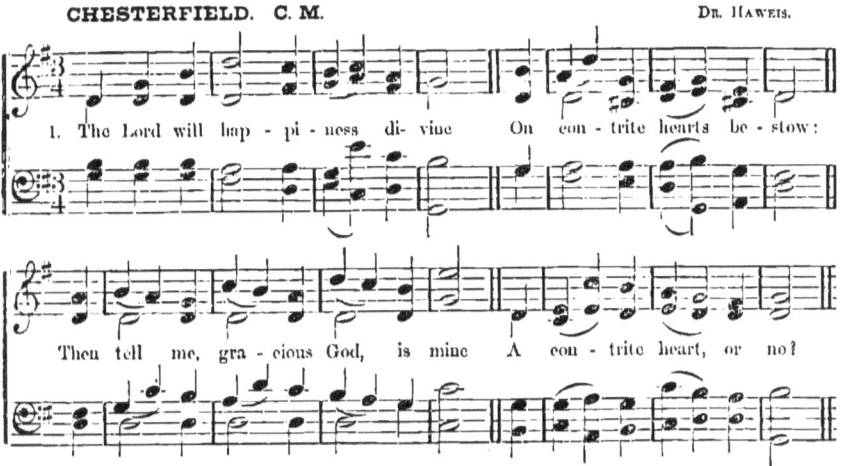

1. The Lord will happiness divine On contrite hearts bestow: Then tell me, gracious God, is mine A contrite heart, or no?

356.

2 I hear, but seem to hear in vain,
   Insensible as steel ;
   If aught is felt, 't is only pain
   To find I cannot feel.

3 My best desires are faint and few :
   Fain would I strive for more ;
   But, when I cry, " My strength renew,"
   Seem weaker than before.

4 Thy saints are comforted, I know,
   And love the house of prayer ;
   I therefore go where others go,
   But find no comfort there.

5 Oh! make this heart rejoice or ache ;
   Decide this doubt for me ;
   And if it be not broken, break—
   And heal it if it be.

357.

1 Why is my heart so far from thee,
   My God! my chief delight?
   Why are my thoughts no more, by day,—
   With thee, no more by night?

2 Why should my foolish passions rove ?
   Where can such sweetness be,
   As I have tasted in thy love,—
   As I have found in thee ?

3 When my forgetful soul renews
   The savor of thy grace,
   My heart presumes, I cannot lose
   The relish all my days.

4 But, ere one fleeting hour is past,
   The flattering world employs
   Some sensual bait, to seize my taste,
   And to pollute my joys.

5 Wretch that I am, to wander thus,
   In chase of false delight !
   Let me be fastened to thy cross,
   Rather than lose thy sight.

6 Make haste, my days ! to reach the goal,
   And bring my heart to rest
   On the dear centre of my soul,—
   My God, my Saviour's breast.

358.

1 I would be thine ; Oh ! take my heart,
   And fill it with thy love :
   Thy sacred image, Lord, impart,
   And seal it from above.

2 I would be thine ; but while I strive
   To give myself away,
   I feel rebellion still alive,
   And wander while I pray.

3 I would be thine ; but, Lord, I feel
   Evil still lurks within ;—
   Do thou thy majesty reveal,
   And overcome my sin.

4 I would be thine ; I would embrace
   The Saviour, and adore :
   Inspire with faith, infuse thy grace,
   And now my soul restore.

CHRISTIAN.

DETROIT. S. M. E. P. Hastings.

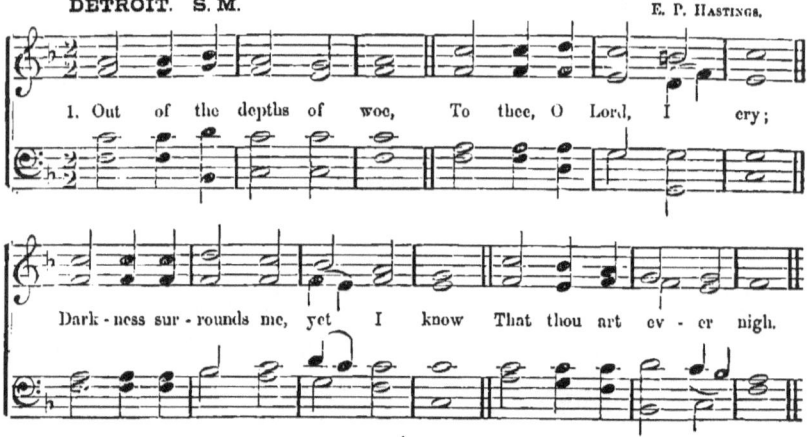

1. Out of the depths of woe, To thee, O Lord, I cry;
Darkness surrounds me, yet I know That thou art ever nigh.

359.

1 Out of the depths of woe,
  To thee, O Lord! I cry;
Darkness surrounds me, yet I know
  That thou art ever nigh.

2 I cast my hopes on thee;
  Thou canst, thou wilt forgive;
If thou shouldst mark iniquity,
  Who in thy sight could live?

3 I wait for thee; I wait,
  Confessing all my sin:
Lord! I am knocking at thy gate;
  Open, and take me in.

4 Glory to God above!
  The waters soon will cease;
For lo! the swift-returning dove
  Brings home the pledge of peace.

5 Though storms his face obscure,
  And dangers threaten loud,
Jehovah's covenant is sure,
  His bow is in the cloud.

360.

1 And shall I sit alone,
  Oppressed with grief and fear?
To God, my Father, make my moan,
  And he refuse to hear?

2 If he my Father be,
  His pity he will show;
From cruel bondage set me free,
  And inward peace bestow.

3 If still he silence keep,
  'T is but my faith to try;
He knows and feels whene'er I weep,
  And softens every sigh.

4 Then will I humbly wait,
  Nor once indulge despair:
My sins are great,—but not so great
  As his compassions are.

361.

1 I faint, my soul doth faint,
  My strength, a broken reed!
Would this so long be my complaint,
  Were I a saint indeed?

2 The sins I fancied quelled,
  Again in arms arise;
The promise that I thought I held,
  Refuses its supplies.

3 My bosom burns with shame,
  And yet is icy cold;
Even to breathe the Saviour's name
  Seems now to be too bold.

4 So oft my soul hath trod
  The same sad path astray,
How can I turn again to God?
  What venture now to say?

5 Thou, Saviour, only thou
  Canst meet my utter need,
And shouldst thou save the rebel now,
  It will be grace indeed!

CONFLICT WITH SIN.   113

362.

1 Where, O my soul, oh, where
  Thy image shall I view?
  In the light cloud that melts in air
  Or in the early dew.

2 This hour, with flowing tears,
  My follies I bewail:
  The next, my heart a waste appears,
  Where all the fountains fail.

3 To-day, her glimmering light
  Hope kindles in my breast;
  The morrow, with despair's black night,
  Has all my soul oppressed.

4 Oh! my unsteadfast mind,
  Tossed between good and ill!
  While brutes, with instinct sure though blind,
  Their Maker's law fulfill.

5 Oh! wavering, wretched state,
  Of hope by fear subdued!
  On thee, O Lord, for help I wait,—
  Fix, fix my soul in good.

363.

1 A charge to keep I have;
  A God to glorify;
  A never-dying soul to save,
  And fit it for the sky;

2 To serve the present age,
  My calling to fulfill;
  Oh! may it all my powers engage
  To do my Master's will.

3 Arm me with jealous care,
  As in thy sight to live;
  And oh! thy servant, Lord, prepare
  A strict account to give.

4 Help me to watch and pray,
  And on thyself rely;
  Assured if I my trust betray,
  I shall forever die.

364.

1 I lift my soul to God,
  My trust is in his name;
  Let not my foes that seek my blood
  Still triumph in my shame.

2 From the first dawning light
  Till the dark evening rise,
  For thy salvation, Lord! I wait
  With ever-longing eyes.

3 Remember all thy grace,
  And lead me in thy truth;
  Forgive the sins of riper days,
  And follies of my youth.

4 The Lord is just and kind,
  The meek shall learn his ways;
  And every humble sinner find
  The methods of his grace.

5 For his own goodness' sake
  He saves my soul from shame;
  He pardons, though my guilt be great,
  Through my Redeemer's name.

CHRISTIAN.

MARTYN. 7s.   MARSH.

1. Jesus, lover of my soul,
Let me to thy bosom fly,
While the billows near me roll,
While the tempest still is high:
Hide me, O my Saviour, hide,
Till the storm of life is past;
Safe into the haven guide:
Oh! receive my soul at last!

365.

2 Other refuge have I none;
Hangs my helpless soul on thee:
Leave, ah! leave me not alone,
Still support and comfort me:
All my trust on thee is stayed,
All my help from thee I bring;
Cover my defenceless head
With the shadow of thy wing.

3 Thou, O Christ, art all I want,
More than all in thee I find:
Raise the fallen, cheer the faint,
Heal the sick, and lead the blind:
Just and holy is thy name;
I am all unrighteousness:
False and full of sin I am;
Thou art full of truth and grace.

4 Plenteous grace with thee is found,
Grace to cover all my sin;
Let the healing streams abound,
Make and keep me pure within:
Thou of life the fountain art,
Freely let me take of thee;
Spring thou up within my heart;
Rise to all eternity.

366.

1 Jesus, merciful and mild,
Lead me as a helpless child:
On no other arm but thine
Would my weary soul recline;
Thou art ready to forgive,
Thou canst bid the sinner live—
Guide the wanderer, day by day,
In the strait and narrow way.

2 I am weakness, thou art might;
I am darkness, thou art light;
I am all defiled with sin,
Thou canst make me pure within;
Foes that threaten to devour,
In thy presence have no power;
Thou canst bid their rage be still,
And my heart with comfort fill.

3 Thou canst fit me by thy grace
For the heavenly dwelling-place;
All thy promises are sure,
Ever shall thy love endure;
Then what more could I desire,
How to greater bliss aspire?
All I need, in thee I see,
Thou art all in all to me.

4 Jesus, Saviour all divine,
Hast thou made me truly thine?
Hast thou bought me by thy blood?
Reconciled my heart to God?
Hearken to my tender prayer,
Let me thy own image bear;
Let me love thee more and more,
Till I reach heaven's blissful shore.

CONFLICT WITH SIN.

MESSIAH. 7s. Double. *Arranged by* Geo. Kingsley.

1. Brethren, while we sojourn here, Fight we must, but should not fear; Foes we have, but we've a Friend, One that loves us to the end. Forward, then, with courage go, Long we shall not dwell be-low: Soon the joy-ful news will come, "Child, your Father calls—come home!"

367.

2 In the way a thousand snares
Lie, to take us unawares;
Satan, with malicious art,
Watches each unguarded part:
But, from Satan's malice free,
Saints shall soon victorious be;
Soon the joyful news will come,
"Child, your Father calls—come home!"

3 But of all the foes we meet,
None so oft mislead our feet,
None betray us into sin
Like the foes that dwell within;
Yet let nothing spoil our peace,
Christ shall also conquer these;
Soon the joyful news will come,
"Child, your Father calls—come home!"

368.

1 Saviour, when in dust, to thee
Low we bow th' adoring knee;
When, repentant, to the skies
Scarce we lift our streaming eyes:
Oh! by all thy pains and woe,
Suffered once for man below,
Bending from thy throne on high,
Hear thy people when they cry.

2 By thy birth and early years,
By thy human griefs and fears,
By thy fasting and distress
In the lonely wilderness:
By thy victory in the hour
Of the subtle tempter's power;
Jesus, look with pitying eye;
Hear thy people when they cry.

3 By thine hour of dark despair,
By thine agony of prayer,
By the purple robe of scorn,
By thy wounds—thy crown of thorn;
By thy cross—thy pangs and cries;
By thy perfect sacrifice;
Jesus, look with pitying eye;
Hear thy people when they cry.

4 By thy deep expiring groan,
By the sealed sepulchral stone,
By thy triumph o'er the grave,
By thy power from death to save;
Mighty God, ascended Lord,
To thy throne in heaven restored,
Saviour, Prince, exalted high,
Hear thy people when they cry.

CHRISTIAN.

AUTUMN. 8s & 7s. Double. *Spanish.*

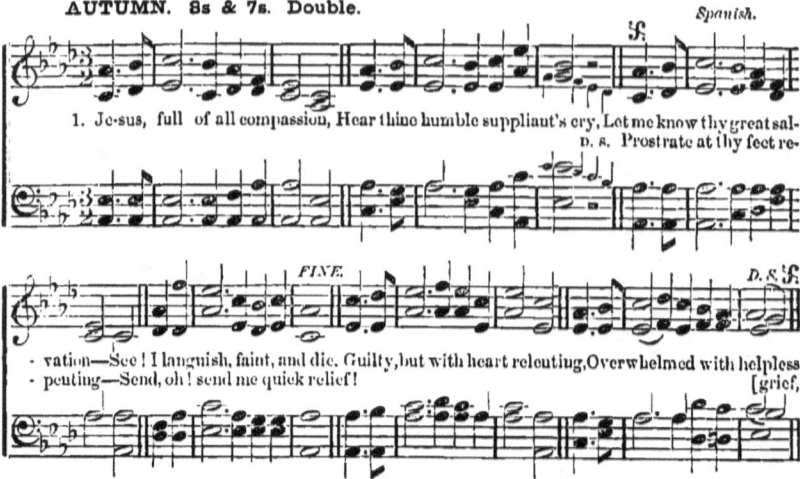

1. Je-sus, full of all compassion, Hear thine humble suppliant's cry, Let me know thy great sal-vation—See! I languish, faint, and die. Guilty, but with heart relenting, Overwhelmed with helpless
Prostrate at thy feet re-penting—Send, oh! send me quick relief! [grief,

369.

2 Whither should a wretch be flying,
But to him who comfort gives?
Whither, from the dread of dying,
But to him who ever lives?
While I view thee, wounded, grieving,
Breathless, on the cursèd tree,
Fain I'd feel my heart believing
Thou didst suffer thus for me.

3 In the world of endless ruin,
Let it never, Lord, be said,
"Here's a soul that perished, sueing
For the Saviour's boasted aid!"
Saved!—the deed shall spread new glory
Through the shining realms above;
Angels sing the pleasing story,
All enraptured with thy love.

370.

1 Jesus, I my cross have taken,
All to leave, and follow thee;
Naked, poor, despised, forsaken,
Thou, from hence, my all shalt be!
Perish, every fond ambition,
All I've sought, or hoped, or known;
Yet how rich is my condition,
God and heaven are still my own!

2 Let the world despise and leave me,
They have left my Saviour, too;
Human hearts and looks deceive me—
Thou art not, like them, untrue;

Oh! while thou dost smile upon me,
God of wisdom, love, and might,
Foes may hate, and friends disown me,
Show thy face, and all is bright.

3 Man may trouble and distress me,
'T will but drive me to thy breast,
Life with trials hard may press me,
Heaven will bring me sweeter rest!
Oh! 't is not in grief to harm me,
While thy love is left to me;
Oh! 't were not in joy to charm me,
Were that joy unmixed with thee.

371.

1 Lord, I hear of showers of blessing
Thou art scattering full and free;
Showers the thirsty soul refreshing;
Let some droppings fall on me!
Pass me not, O gracious Father!
Lost and sinful though I be;
Thou might'st curse me, but the rather
Let thy mercy light on me.

2 Have I long in sin been sleeping?
Long been slighting, grieving thee?
Has the world my heart been keeping?
Oh! forgive and rescue me!
Pass me not, O mighty Spirit!
Thou canst make the blind to see;
Testify of Jesus' merit,
Speak the word of power to me.

CONFLICT WITH SIN. 117

372.

1 Full of trembling expectation,
Feeling much, and fearing more,
Mighty God of my salvation!
I thy timely aid implore;
Suffering Son of Man! be near me,
All my sufferings to sustain,
By thy sorer griefs to cheer me,
By thy more than mortal pain.

2 Call to mind that unknown anguish,
In thy days of flesh below;
When thy troubled soul did languish
Under a whole world of woe;
When thou didst our curse inherit,
Groan beneath our guilty load,
Burdened with a wounded spirit,
Bruised by all the wrath of God.

3 By thy most severe temptation,
In that dark, satanic hour;
By thy last mysterious passion,
Screen me from the adverse power!
By thy fainting in the garden,
By thy bloody sweat, I pray,
Write upon my heart the pardon,
Take my sins and fears away.

373.

1 Saviour, visit thy plantation!
Grant us, Lord, a gracious rain:
All will come to desolation,
Unless thou return again.
Keep no longer at a distance,
Shine upon us from on high,
Lest, for want of thine assistance,
Every plant should droop and die.

2 Once, O Lord, thy garden flourished;
Every part looked gay and green;
Then thy word our spirits nourished:
Happy seasons we have seen.
But a drought has since succeeded,
And a sad decline we see:
Lord, thy help is greatly needed:
Help can only come from thee.

3 Let our mutual love be fervent:
Make us prevalent in prayers;
Let each one esteemed thy servant
Shun the world's bewitching snares,
Break the tempter's fatal power,
Turn the stony heart to flesh,
And begin from this good hour
To revive thy work afresh.

118   CHRISTIAN.

HOLLEY. 7s.   Geo. Hews.

1. Softly now the light of day
Fades upon my sight away;
Free from care, from labor free,
Lord, I would commune with thee!

374.

2 Thou, whose all-pervading eye
Naught escapes without, within,
Pardon each infirmity
Open fault, and secret sin.

3 Thou who, sinless, yet hast known
All of man's infirmity;
Now from thine eternal throne,
Jesus, look with pitying eye.

4 Soon, for me, the light of day
Shall forever pass away;
Then, from sin and sorrow free,
Take me, Lord, to dwell with thee!

375.

1 Prince of Peace, control my will;
Bid this struggling heart be still;
Bid my fears and doubtings cease;
Hush my spirit into peace.

2 Thou hast bought me with thy blood,
Opened wide the gate to God:
Peace I ask—but peace must be,
Lord, in being one with thee.

3 May thy will, not mine, be done;
May thy will and mine be one;
Chase these doubtings from my heart;
Now thy perfect peace impart.

4 Saviour! at thy feet I fall;
Thou my life, my God, my all!
Let thy happy servant be
One forevermore with thee!

376.

1 When, my Saviour, shall I be
Perfectly resigned to thee?
Poor and vile in mine own eyes,
Only in thy wisdom wise?

2 Only thee content to know,
Ignorant of all below?
Only guided by thy light,
Only mighty in thy might?

3 Fully in my life express
All the heights of holiness?
Sweetly let my spirit prove
All the depths of humble love.

377.

1 Gently, gently, lay the rod
On my sinful head, O God!
Stay thy wrath, in mercy stay,
Lest I sink beneath its sway.

2 Heal me, for my flesh is weak;
Heal me, for thy grace I seek;
This my only plea I make,—
Heal me for thy mercy's sake.

3 Who, within the silent grave,
Shall proclaim thy power to save?
Lord! my sinking soul reprieve;
Speak, and I shall rise and live.

4 Lo! he comes—he heeds my plea;
Lo! he comes—the shadows flee;
Glory round me dawns once more;
Rise, my spirit! and adore.

CONFLICT WITH SIN.

SEYMOUR. 7s. — *Arranged from* Weber.

1. God of mer-cy! God of love! Hear our sad, re-pent-ant song; Sor-row dwells on ev-ery face, Pen-i-tence on ev-ery tongue.

378.

2 Deep regret for follies past,
Talents wasted, time misspent;
Hearts debased by worldly cares,
Thankless for the blessings lent;

3 Foolish fears and fond desires,
Vain regrets for things as vain;
Lips too seldom taught to praise,
Oft to murmur and complain;

4 These, and every secret fault,
Filled with grief and shame we own;
Humbled at thy feet we lie,
Seeking pardon from thy throne.

5 God of mercy! God of grace!
Hear our sad, repentant songs;
Oh, restore thy suppliant race,
Thou to whom all praise belongs!

379.

1 Does the Gospel word proclaim
Rest for those that weary be?
Then, my soul, put in thy claim—
Sure that promise speaks to thee!

2 Marks of grace I cannot show,
All polluted is my best;
But I weary am, I know,
And the weary long for rest.

3 Burdened with a load of sin,
Harassed with tormenting doubt,
Hourly conflicts from within,
Hourly crosses from without;—

4 All my little strength is gone,
Sink I must without supply;
Sure upon the earth is none
Can more weary be than I.

5 In the ark the weary dove
Found a welcome resting-place;
Thus my spirit longs to prove
Rest in Christ, the Ark of grace.

6 Tempest-tossed I long have been,
And the flood increases fast;
Open, Lord, and take me in,
Till the storm be overpast!

380.

1 Wait, my soul, upon the Lord,
To his gracious promise flee,
Laying hold upon his word,
"As thy days thy strength shall be."

2 If the sorrows of thy case
Seem peculiar still to thee,
God has promised needful grace,
"As thy days thy strength shall be."

3 Days of trial, days of grief,
In succession thou may'st see;
This is still thy sweet relief,
"As thy days thy strength shall be."

4 Rock of Ages, I'm secure,
With thy promise full and free;
Faithful, positive, and sure—
"As thy days thy strength shall be."

120   CHRISTIAN.

MILNER. 7s. 6 lines.   HARP OF DAVID.

1. Hearken, Lord, to my complaints,
 For my soul within me faints;
 Thee, far off, I call to mind,
 In the land I left behind,
 Where the streams of Jordan flow,
 Where the heights of Hermon glow.

381.

2 Tempest-tossed, my failing bark
 Founders on the ocean dark;
 Deep to deep around me calls,
 With the rush of waterfalls,
 While I plunge to lower caves,
 Overwhelmed by all thy waves.

3 Once the morning's earliest light
 Brought thy mercy to my sight,
 And my wakeful song was heard
 Later than the evening bird;
 Hast thou all my prayers forgot?
 Dost thou scorn, or hear them not?

4 Why, my soul, art thou perplexed?
 Why with faithless troubles vexed?
 Hope in God, whose saving name
 Thou shalt joyfully proclaim,
 When his countenance shall shine
 Through the clouds that darken thine.

382.

1 Once I thought my mountain strong,
 Firmly fixed no more to move;
 Then my Saviour was my song,
 Then my soul was filled with love;
 Those were happy, golden days,
 Sweetly spent in prayer and praise.

2 Little then myself I knew,
 Little thought of Satan's power;
 Now I feel my sins anew;
 Now I feel the stormy hour!
 Sin has put my joys to flight;
 Sin has turned my day to night.

3 Saviour, shine and cheer my soul,
 Bid my dying hopes revive;
 Make my wounded spirit whole,
 Far away the tempter drive;
 Speak the word and set me free,
 Let me live alone to thee.

383.

1 Lord! I look for all to thee;
 Thou hast been a rock to me:
 Still thy wonted aid afford:
 Still be near, my shield, my sword!
 I my soul commit to thee,
 Lord! thy blood has ransomed me.

2 Faint and sinking on my road,
 Still I cling to thee, my God!
 Bending 'neath a weight of woes,
 Harassed by a thousand foes,
 Hope still chides my rising fears
 Joys still mingle with my tears.

3 On thy word I take my stand;
 All my times are in thy hand:
 Make thy face upon me shine;
 Take me 'neath thy wings divine;
 Lord! thy grace is all my trust;
 Save, oh! save thy trembling dust.

4 Oh! what mercies still attend
 Those who make the Lord their friend!
 Sweetly, safely shall they 'bide
 'Neath his eye, and at his side:
 Lord! may this my station be:
 Seek it, all ye saints! with me.

CONFLICT WITH SIN. 121

OLIVET. 6s & 4s. Dr. L. MASON.

1. My faith looks up to thee, Thou Lamb of Cal-va-ry. Sa-viour di-vine! Now hear me while I pray; Take all my guilt a-way; Oh, let me, from this day, Be whol-ly thine!

384.

2 May thy rich grace impart
Strength to my fainting heart;
  My zeal inspire;
As thou hast died for me,
Oh! may my love to thee
Pure, warm, and changeless be—
  A living fire.

3 While life's dark maze I tread,
And griefs around me spread,
  Be thou my Guide;
Bid darkness turn to day,
Wipe sorrow's tear away,
Nor let me ever stray
  From thee aside.

4 When ends life's transient dream,
When death's cold sullen stream
  Shall o'er me roll,
Blest Saviour! then in love,
Fear and distress remove;
Oh! bear me safe above,—
  A ransomed soul.

385.

1 SAVIOUR, I look to thee,
Be not thou far from me,
  'Mid storms that lower:
On me thy care bestow,
Thy loving kindness show,
Thine arms around me throw,
  This trying hour.

2 Saviour, I look to thee,
Feeble as infancy,
  Gird up my heart:
Author of life and light,
Thou hast an arm of might,
Thine is the sovereign right,
  Thy strength impart.

3 Saviour, I look to thee,
Let me thy fullness see,
  Save me from fear;
While at thy cross I kneel,
All my backslidings heal,
And a free pardon seal,
  My soul to cheer.

4 Saviour I look to thee,
Thine shall the glory be,
  Hearer of prayer:
Thou art my only aid,
On thee my soul is stayed,
Naught can my heart invade,
  While thou art near.

386.

1 PEACE, peace, I leave with you,
My peace I give to you,
  Trust to my care!
Thus the Redeemer said,
And bowed his sacred head,
Lone in the garden shade,
  Wrestling in prayer.

2 Peace, peace, I leave with you,
My peace I give to you,
  Perfect and pure;
Not as the world doth give,
Words that the soul deceive;
Ye who in me believe
  Shall rest secure.

3 Peace, peace, I leave with you,
My peace I give to you,
  Though foes invade;
All power is given to me,
I will your refuge be,
Now and eternally,
  Be not dismayed!

122 PENITENCE. 7s, 6s & 8s.

CHRISTIAN.

W. H. Oakley.

1. Jesus, let thy pitying eye Call back a wandering sheep; False to thee, like Peter, I Would fain like Peter weep! Turn, and look upon me, Lord! And break my heart of stone. Let me be by grace re-stored; On me be all long suffering shown;

387.

1 Jesus, let thy pitying eye
  Call back a wandering sheep;
 False to thee, like Peter, I
  Would fain like Peter weep!
 Let me be by grace restored,
  On me be all long-suffering shown,
 Turn, and look upon me, Lord!
  And break my heart of stone.

2 Saviour, Prince, enthroned above,
  Repentance to impart,
 Give me, through thy dying love,
  The humble, contrite heart:
 Give what I have long implored,
  A portion of thy grief unknown;
 Turn, and look upon me, Lord!
  And break my heart of stone.

3 For thine own compassion's sake,
  The gracious wonder show;
 Cast my sins behind thy back,
  And wash me white as snow:
 If thy mercies now are stirred,
  If now I do myself bemoan,
 Turn, and look upon me, Lord!
  And break my heart of stone.

388.

1 Vain, delusive world, adieu,
  With all of creature good!
 Only Jesus I pursue,
  Who bought me with his blood:
 All thy pleasures I forego;
  I trample on thy wealth and pride;
 Only Jesus will I know,
  And Jesus crucified.

2 Other knowledge I disdain;
  'Tis all but vanity:
 Christ, the Lamb of God, was slain,—
  He tasted death for me.
 Me to save from endless woe
  The sin-atoning Victim died:
 Only Jesus will I know,
  And Jesus crucified.

3 Him to know is life and peace,
  And pleasure without end;
 This is all my happiness,
  On Jesus to depend;
 Daily in his grace to grow,
  And ever in his faith abide;
 Only Jesus will I know,
  And Jesus crucified.

CONFLICT WITH SIN. 123

GERHARDT. 7s & 6s. J. P. HOLBROOK.

1. O sacred Head, now wounded, With grief and shame weighed down, Now scornfully surrounded With thorns, thy only crown; O sacred Head, what glory, What bliss till now was thine! Yet, tho' despised and gory, I joy to call thee mine.

389.

2 How art thou pale with anguish,
  With sore abuse and scorn !
  How does that visage languish,
  Which once was bright as morn !
  Thy grief, and thy compassion,
  Were all for sinners' gain ;
  Mine, mine was the transgression,
  But thine the deadly pain.

3 What language shall I borrow,
  To praise thee, heavenly Friend :
  For this, thy dying sorrow,
  Thy pity without end ?
  Lord, make me thine forever,
  Nor let me faithless prove :
  Oh ! let me never, never,
  Abuse such dying love.

4 Forbid that I should leave thee ;
  O Jesus, leave not me ;
  By faith I would receive thee ;
  Thy blood can make me free :
  When strength and comfort languish,
  And I must hence depart :
  Release me then from anguish,
  By thine own wounded heart.

5 Be near when I am dying,
  Oh ! show thy cross to me !
  And for my succor flying,
  Come, Lord, to set me free :
  These eyes new faith receiving,
  From Jesus shall not move ;
  For he who dies believing,
  Dies safely—through thy love.

390.

1 WHEN human hopes all wither,
  And friends no aid supply,
  Then whither, Lord, ah ! whither
  Can turn my straining eye ?
  'Mid storms of grief still rougher,
  'Midst darker, deadlier shade,
  That cross where thou didst suffer,
  On Calvary was displayed.

2 On that my gaze I fasten,
  My refuge that I make ;
  Though sorely thou may'st chasten,
  Thou never canst forsake :
  Thou, on that cross didst languish,
  Ere glory crowned thy head !
  And I, through death, and anguish,
  Must be to glory led.

124 CHRISTIAN.

PLEYEL'S HYMN. 7s.   PLEYEL.

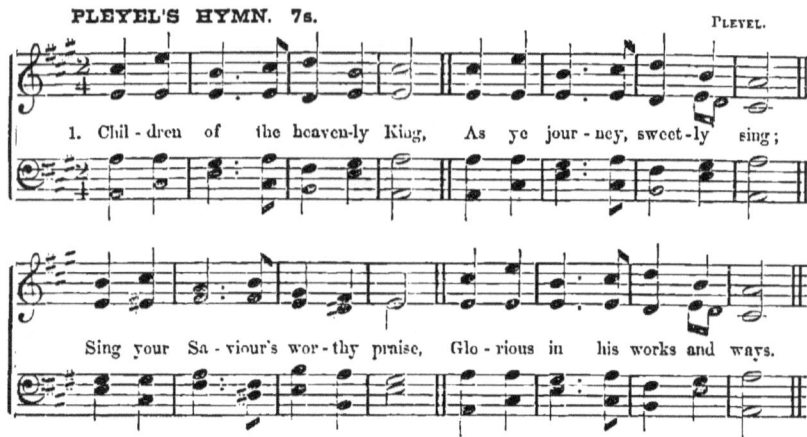

1. Chil-dren of the heaven-ly King, As ye jour-ney, sweet-ly sing; Sing your Sa-viour's wor-thy praise, Glo-rious in his works and ways.

391.

1 CHILDREN of the heavenly King,
As ye journey, sweetly sing;
Sing your Saviour's worthy praise,
Glorious in his works and ways.

2 Ye are traveling home to God,
In the way the fathers trod;
They are happy now—and ye
Soon their happiness shall see.

3 Shout, ye little flock, and blest;
You on Jesus' throne shall rest:
There your seat is now prepared—
There your kingdom and reward.

4 Fear not, brethren, joyful stand
On the borders of your land;
Jesus Christ, your Father's Son,
Bids you undismayed go on.

5 Lord! submissive make us go,
Gladly leaving all below;
Only thou our leader be,
And we still will follow thee.

392.

1 To thy pastures fair and large,
Heavenly Shepherd, lead thy charge,
And my couch, with tenderest care,
'Mid the springing grass prepare.

2 When I faint with summer's heat,
Thou shalt guide my weary feet,
To the streams that, still and slow,
Through the verdant meadows flow.

3 Safe the dreary vale I tread,
By the shades of death o'erspread,
With thy rod and staff supplied,
This my guard,—and that my guide.

4 Constant to my latest end,
Thou my footsteps shalt attend;
And shalt bid thy hallowed dome
Yield me an eternal home.

393.

1 FAINT not, Christian! though the road,
Leading to thy blest abode,
Darksome be, and dangerous too,
Christ thy Guide will bring thee through.

2 Faint not, Christian! though in rage
Satan would thy soul engage,
Gird on faith's anointed shield,
Bear it to the battle-field.

3 Faint not, Christian! though the world
Has its hostile flag unfurled;
Hold the cross of Jesus fast,
Thou shalt overcome at last.

4 Faint not, Christian! though within,
There's a heart so prone to sin;
Christ the Lord is over all,
He'll not suffer thee to fall.

5 Faint not, Christian! look on high,
See the harpers in the sky;
Patient wait, and thou wilt join—
Chant with them of love divine.

ENCOURAGEMENTS.

WILLIS. 7s. — R. Storrs Willis.

1. Now begin the heavenly theme, Sing aloud in Jesus' name! Ye, who his salvation prove, Triumph in redeeming love, Triumph in redeeming love.

394.

1 Now begin the heavenly theme,
Sing aloud in Jesus' name!
Ye, who his salvation prove,
Triumph in redeeming love.

2 Ye who see the Father's grace
Beaming in the Saviour's face,
As to Canaan on ye move,
Praise and bless redeeming love.

3 Mourning souls, dry up your tears;
Banish all your guilty fears;
See your guilt and curse remove,
Canceled by redeeming love.

4 Hither, then, your tribute bring,
Strike aloud each joyful string;
Saints below, and saints above,
Join to praise redeeming love.

395.

1 Hark! my soul! it is the Lord;
'T is thy Saviour—hear his word;
Jesus speaks, and speaks to thee,
"Say, poor sinner, lovest thou me?

2 "I delivered thee when bound,
And when bleeding, healed thy wound:
Sought thee wandering, set thee right,
Turned thy darkness into light.

3 "Can a woman's tender care
Cease toward the child she bare?
Yes, she may forgetful be,
Yet will I remember thee.

4 "Mine is an unchanging love,
Higher than the heights above;
Deeper than the depths beneath—
Free and faithful—strong as death.

5 "Thou shalt see my glory soon,
When the work of grace is done;
Partner of my throne shalt be!
Say, poor sinner! lovest thou me?"

6 Lord! it is my chief complaint,
That my love is weak and faint;
Yet I love thee, and adore;—
Oh! for grace to love thee more.

396.

1 Much in sorrow, oft in woe,
Onward, Christians, onward go;
Fight the fight; and worn with strife,
Steep with tears the bread of life.

2 Onward, Christians, onward go;
Join the war, and face the foe;
Faint not: much doth yet remain;
Dreary is the long campaign.

3 Shrink not, Christians—will ye yield?
Will ye quit the battle-field?
Fight till all the conflict 's o'er,
Nor your foes shall rally more.

3 But when loud the trumpet blown,
Speaks their forces overthrown,
Christ, your Captain, shall bestow
Crowns to grace the conqueror's brow.

CHRISTIAN.

MISSIONARY CHANT. L. M.   Ch. Zeuner.

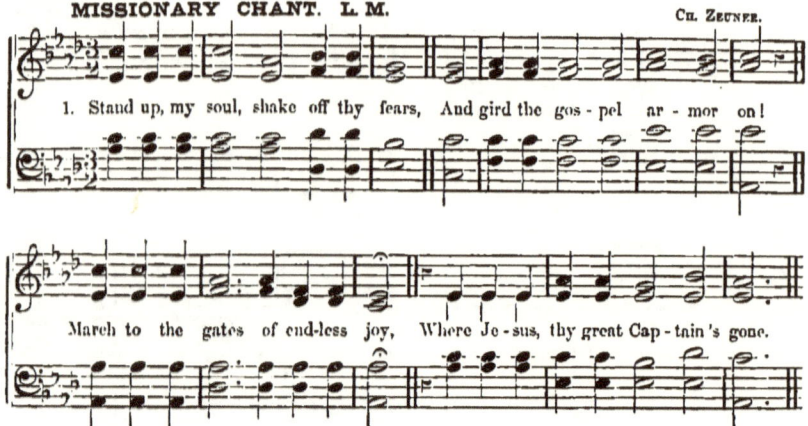

1. Stand up, my soul, shake off thy fears, And gird the gos-pel ar-mor on! March to the gates of end-less joy, Where Je-sus, thy great Cap-tain's gone.

397.

1 Stand up, my soul, shake off thy fears,
And gird the gospel armor on;
March to the gates of endless joy,
Where Jesus, thy great Captain's gone.

2 Hell and thy sins resist thy course;
But hell and sin are vanquished foes;
Thy Saviour nailed them to the cross,
And sung the triumph when he rose.

3 Then let my soul march boldly on,—
Press forward to the heavenly gate;
There peace and joy eternal reign,
And glittering robes for conquerors wait.

4 There shall I wear a starry crown,
And triumph in almighty grace,
While all the armies of the skies
Join in my glorious Leader's praise.

398.

1 Awake, our souls! away, our fears!
Let every trembling thought be gone;
Awake, and run the heavenly race,
And put a cheerful courage on!

2 True, 't is a strait and thorny road,
And mortal spirits tire and faint;
But they forget the mighty God,
Who feeds the strength of every saint—

3 The mighty God, whose matchless power
Is ever new and ever young,
And firm endures, while endless years
Their everlasting circles run.

4 From thee, the overflowing spring,
Our souls shall drink a fresh supply;
While such as trust their native strength,
Shall melt away, and droop, and die.

5 Swift as an eagle cuts the air,
We'll mount aloft to thine abode;
On wings of love our souls shall fly,
Nor tire amid the heavenly road!

399.

1 Awake, my soul! lift up thine eyes;
See where thy foes against thee rise,
In long array, a numerous host;
Awake, my soul! or thou art lost.

2 See where rebellious passions rage,
And fierce desires and lusts engage;
The meanest foe of all the train
Has thousands and ten thousands slain.

3 Thou treadest on enchanted ground;
Perils and snares beset thee round;
Beware of all, guard every part—
But most the traitor in thy heart.

4 The terror and the charm repel,
And powers of earth, and powers of hell;
The Man of Calvary triumphed here:
Why should his faithful followers fear?

5 Come then, my soul! now learn to wield
The weight of thine immortal shield;
Put on the armor, from above,
Of heavenly truth, and heavenly love.

ENCOURAGEMENTS.

CHRISTMAS. C. M. — HANDEL.

1. A-wake, my soul! stretch ev-ery nerve, And press with vigor on: A heaven-ly race demands thy zeal, A bright im-mor-tal crown, A bright im-mor-tal crown.

400.

2 A cloud of witnesses around
Hold thee in full survey:
Forget the steps already trod,
And onward urge thy way.

3 'T is God's all-animating voice,
That calls thee from on high;
'T is his own hand presents the prize
To thine aspiring eye,—

4 That prize with peerless glories bright,
Which shall new lustre boast,
When victor's wreaths and monarch's gems
Shall blend in common dust.

5 Blest Saviour, introduced by thee,
Have I my race begun;
And, crowned with victory, at thy feet
I'll lay my honors down.

401.

1 Am I a soldier of the cross,
A follower of the Lamb?
And shall I fear to own his cause,
Or blush to speak his name?

2 Must I be carried to the skies
On flowery beds of ease?
While others fought to win the prize,
And sailed through bloody seas?

3 Are there no foes for me to face?
Must I not stem the flood?
Is this vile world a friend to grace,
To help me on to God?

4 Sure I must fight, if I would reign;
Increase my courage, Lord!
I'll bear the toil, endure the pain,
Supported by thy word.

5 Thy saints, in all this glorious war,
Shall conquer, though they die;
They view the triumph from afar,
And seize it with their eye.

6 When that illustrious day shall rise,
And all thy armies shine
In robes of victory through the skies,
The glory shall be thine.

402.

1 I'm not ashamed to own my Lord,
Or to defend his cause;
Maintain the honor of his word,
The glory of his cross.

2 Jesus, my God!—I know his name—
His name is all my trust;
Nor will he put my soul to shame,
Nor let my hope be lost.

3 Firm as his throne his promise stands,
And he can well secure
What I've committed to his hands,
Till the decisive hour.

4 Then will he own my worthless name
Before his Father's face,
And in the New Jerusalem
Appoint my soul a place.

CHRISTIAN.

ARLINGTON. C. M.   Dr. Arne.

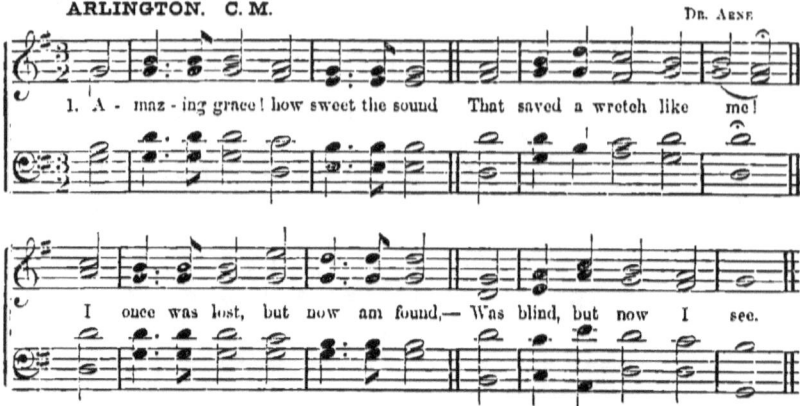

1. A-maz-ing grace! how sweet the sound That saved a wretch like me! I once was lost, but now am found,— Was blind, but now I see.

403.

1 Amazing grace! how sweet the sound
That saved a wretch like me!
I once was lost, but now am found—
Was blind, but now I see.

2 'T was grace that taught my heart to fear,
And grace my fears relieved;
How precious did that grace appear,
The hour I first believed!

3 Through many dangers, toils, and snares,
I have already come;
'T is grace hath brought me safe thus far,
And grace will lead me home.

4 Yea—when this flesh and heart shall fail,
And mortal life shall cease,
I shall possess, within the vail,
A life of joy and peace.

5 The earth shall soon dissolve like snow,
The sun forbear to shine;
But God, who called me here below,
Will be forever mine.

404.

1 Whence do our mournful thoughts arise,
And where 's our courage fled?
Has restless sin, or raging hell,
Struck all our comforts dead?

2 Have we forgot th' almighty Name
That formed the earth and sea?
And can an all-creating arm
Grow weary or decay?

3 Treasures of everlasting might
In our Jehovah dwell;
He gives the conquest to the weak,
And treads their foes to hell.

4 Mere mortal power shall fade and die,
And youthful vigor cease;
But we who wait upon the Lord
Shall feel our strength increase.

5 The saints shall mount on eagles' wings,
And taste the promised bliss,
Till their unwearied feet arrive
Where perfect pleasure is.

405.

1 How can I sink with such a prop
As my eternal God,
Who bears the earth's huge pillars up
And spreads the heavens abroad?

2 How can I die while Jesus lives,
Who rose and left the dead?
Pardon and grace my soul receives
From my exalted Head.

3 All that I am, and all I have,
Shall be forever thine;
Whate'er my duty bids me give,
My cheerful hands resign.

4 Yet, if I might make some reserve,
And duty did not call,
I love my God with zeal so great,
That I should give him all.

ENCOURAGEMENTS.   129

MOUNT AUBURN.   C. M.   GEO. KINGSLEY.

1. Chil-dren of God, who, faint and slow, Your pil-grim path pur - sue,
In strength and weak-ness, joy and woe, To God's high call - ing true!—

406.

2 Why move ye thus, with lingering tread,
A doubting mournful band?
Why faintly hangs the drooping head?
Why fails the feeble hand?

3 Oh! weak to know a Saviour's power,
To feel a father's care;
A moment's toil, a passing shower,
Is all the grief ye share.

4 The orb of light, though clouds awhile
May hide his noon-tide ray,
Shall soon in lovelier beauty smile
To gild the closing day,—

5 And, bursting through the dusky shroud
That dared his power invest,
Ride throned in light o'er every cloud,
Triumphant to his rest.

6 Then, Christian, dry the falling tear,
The faithless doubt remove;
Redeemed at last from guilt and fear,
Oh! wake thy heart to love.

407.

1 YE trembling souls! dismiss your fears,
Be mercy all your theme;—
Mercy,—which, like a river, flows,
In one perpetual stream.

2 Fear not the powers of earth and hell;—
Those powers will God restrain;
His arm shall all their rage repel,
And make their efforts vain.

3 Fear not the want of outward good;
For his he will provide,
Grant them supplies of daily food,
And all they need beside.

4 Fear not that he will e'er forsake,
Or leave his work undone;
He's faithful to his promises,
And faithful to his Son.

5 Fear not the terrors of the grave,
Nor death's tremendous sting;
He will, from endless wrath, preserve—
To endless glory bring.

408.

1 WHEN I can read my title clear
To mansions in the skies,
I bid farewell to every fear,
And wipe my weeping eyes.

2 Should earth against my soul engage,
And fiery darts be hurled,
Then I can smile at Satan's rage,
And face a frowning world.

3 Let cares like a wild deluge come,
And storms of sorrow fall;
May I but safely reach my home,
My God, my heaven, my all!

4 There shall I bathe my weary soul
In seas of heavenly rest;
And not a wave of trouble roll
Across my peaceful breast.

CHRISTIAN.

OLMUTZ. S. M.   *Arranged by* Dr. L. Mason.

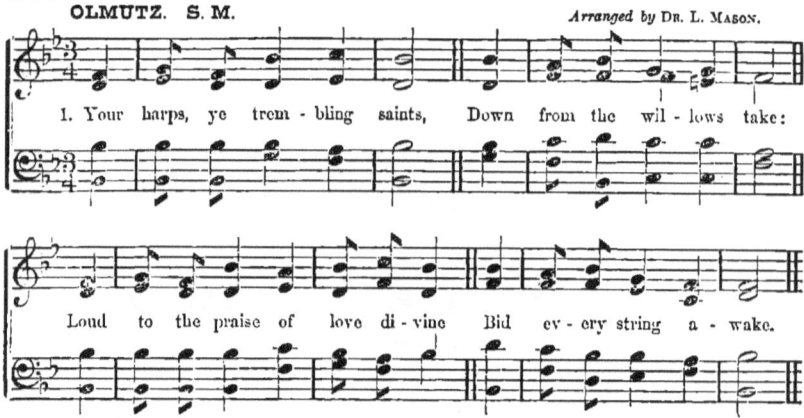

1. Your harps, ye trem-bling saints, Down from the wil-lows take: Loud to the praise of love di-vine Bid ev-ery string a-wake.

409.

2 Though in a foreign land,
  We are not far from home,
And nearer to our house above
  We every moment come.

3 His grace will to the end
  Stronger and brighter shine,
Nor present things, nor things to come,
  Shall quench the spark divine.

4 When we in darkness walk,
  Nor feel the heavenly flame,
Then is the time to trust our God,
  And rest upon his name.

5 Soon shall our doubts and fears
  Subside at his control;
His loving-kindness shall break through
  The midnight of the soul.

6 Blest is the man, O God,
  That stays himself on thee!
Who waits for thy salvation, Lord,
  Shall thy salvation see.

410.

1 Give to the winds thy fears,
  Hope, and be undismayed;
God hears thy sighs, and counts thy tears,
  God shall lift up thy head.

2 Through waves, and clouds, and storms,
  He gently clears the way;
Wait thou his time; so shall this night
  Soon end in joyous day.

3 Still heavy is thy heart?
  Still sink thy spirits down?
Cast off the weight, let fear depart,
  And every care be gone.

4 What though thou rulest not?
  Yet heaven, and earth, and hell
Proclaim God sitteth on the throne,
  And ruleth all things well.

5 Leave to his sovereign sway,
  To choose and to command;
So shalt thou, wondering, own his way
  How wise, how good his hand!

411.

1 The sun himself shall fade,
  The starry worlds shall fall;
Yet through a vast eternity,
  Shall God be all in all.

2 Though now his ways are dark,
  Concealed from mortal sight,
His counsels are divinely wise,
  And all his judgments right.

3 In God my trust shall stand,
  While waves of sorrow roll;
In life or death his name shall be
  The refuge of my soul.

4 Cease, cease my tears to flow,
  Cease, cease my heart to moan;
Betide what may to me, I'll say,
  His holy will be done!

ENCOURAGEMENTS. 131

DENNIS. S. M. NAGELI.

1. The Lord my Shepherd is, I shall be well supplied: Since he is mine, and I am his, What can I want beside?

412.

2 He leads me to the place,
  Where heavenly pasture grows,
  Where living waters gently pass,
  And full salvation flows.

3 If e'er I go astray,
  He doth my soul reclaim;
  And guides me in his own right way,
  For his most holy name.

4 While he affords his aid,
  I cannot yield to fear;
  Tho' I should walk thro' death's dark
      shade,
  My Shepherd's with me there.

5 In spite of all my foes,
  Thou dost my table spread;
  My cup with blessings overflows,
  And joy exalts my head.

6 The bounties of thy love
  Shall crown my future days;
  Nor from thy house will I remove,
  Nor cease to speak thy praise.

413.

1 THE harvest dawn is near,
  The year delays not long;
  And he who sows with many a tear,
  Shall reap with many a song.

2 Sad to his toil he goes,
  His seed with weeping leaves;
  But he shall come, at twilight's close,
  And bring his golden sheaves.

414.

1 How gentle God's commands!
  How kind his precepts are!
  Come, cast your burdens on the Lord,
  And trust his constant care.

2 Beneath his watchful eye
  His saints securely dwell;
  That hand which bears all nature up,
  Shall guard his children well.

3 Why should this anxious load
  Press down your weary mind?
  Haste to your heavenly Father's throne,
  And sweet refreshment find.

4 His goodness stands approved,
  Unchanged from day to day:
  I'll drop my burden at his feet,
  And bear a song away.

415.

1 I STAND on Zion's mount,
  And view my starry crown;
  No power on earth my hope can shake,
  Nor hell can thrust me down.

2 The lofty hills and towers,
  That lift their heads on high,
  Shall all be leveled low in dust—
  Their very names shall die.

3 The vaulted heavens shall fall,
  Built by Jehovah's hands;
  But firmer than the heavens, the Rock
  Of my salvation stands!

416.

1 Breathe, oh, breathe thy loving spirit
Into every troubled breast!
Let us all in thee inherit,
Let us find, thy promised rest:
Come, Almighty to deliver,
Let us all thy life receive!
Speedily return, and never,
Never more thy temples leave!

3 Finish then thy new creation,
Pure, unspotted may we be:
Let us see our whole salvation
Perfectly secured by thee!
Changed from glory into glory,
Till in heaven we take our place;
Till we cast our crowns before thee,
Lost in wonder, love, and praise.

417.

1 Know, my soul! thy full salvation;
Rise o'er sin, and fear, and care;
Joy to find, in every station,
Something still to do or bear:
Think what Spirit dwells within thee;
Think what Father's smiles are thine;
Think that Jesus died to win thee:
Child of heaven, canst thou repine?

2 Haste thee on from grace to glory,
Armed by faith, and winged by prayer!
Heaven's eternal day 's before thee,
God's own hand shall guide thee there:
Soon shall close thy earthly mission,
Soon shall pass thy pilgrim days,
Hope shall change to glad fruition,
Faith to sight, and prayer to praise.

418.

1 Hear what God, the Lord, hath spoken:
O my people, faint and few,
Comfortless, afflicted, broken,
Fair abodes I build for you;
Scenes of heartfelt tribulation
Shall no more perplex your ways;
You shall name your walls "Salvation,"
And your gates shall all be "Praise."

2 Ye no more your suns descending,
Waning moons no more shall see;
But your griefs forever ending,
Find eternal noon in me:
God shall rise, and, shining o'er you,
Change to day the gloom of night;
He, the Lord, shall be your Glory,
God your everlasting Light.

ENCOURAGEMENTS. 133

WESTMINSTER. 8s & 7s. J. P. Holbrook.

1. On-ward, Christian, though the re-gion Where thou art be drear and lone;
God has set a guar-dian le-gion Ve-ry near thee; press thou on.

419.

1 Onward, Christian, though the region
   Where thou art be drear and lone;
   God has set a guardian legion
   Very near thee; press thou on.

2 Listen, Christian; their hosanna
   Rolleth o'er thee: "God is love,"
   Write upon thy red-cross banner,
   "Upward ever; heaven's above."

3 By the thorn-road, and none other,
   Is the mount of vision won;
   Tread it without shrinking, brother;
   Jesus trod it; press thou on.

4 Be this world the wiser, stronger,
   For thy life of pain and peace;
   While it needs thee, oh! no longer
   Pray thou for thy quick release.

5 Pray thou, Christian, daily rather,
   That thou be a faithful son;
   By the prayer of Jesus, "Father,
   Not My will, but Thine, be done."

420.

1 Always with us, always with us—
   Words of cheer and words of love;
   Thus the risen Saviour whispers,
   From his dwelling-place above.

2 With us when we toil in sadness,
   Sowing much and reaping none,
   Telling us that in the future
   Golden harvests shall be won.

3 With us when the storm is sweeping
   O'er our pathway dark and drear,
   Waking hope within our bosoms,
   Stilling every anxious fear.

4 With us in the lonely valley,
   When we cross the chilling stream,
   Lighting up the steps to glory
   With salvation's radiant beam.

421.

1 Call Jehovah thy salvation,
   Rest beneath th' Almighty's shade;
   In his secret habitation
   Dwell, and never be dismayed!

2 There no tumult can alarm thee,
   Thou shalt dread no hidden snare;
   Guile nor violence can harm thee,
   In eternal safeguard there.

3 Thee, tho' winds and waves are swelling,
   God, thy Hope, shall bear through all;
   Plague shall not come nigh thy dwelling,
   Thee no evil shall befall.

4 He shall charge his angel legions
   Watch and ward o'er thee to keep,
   Though thou walk through hostile regions,
   Though in desert wilds thou sleep.

5 Since, with firm and pure affection,
   Thou on God hast set thy love,
   With the wings of his protection
   He shall shield thee from above.

134 CHRISTIAN.

PORTUGUESE HYMN. 11s.

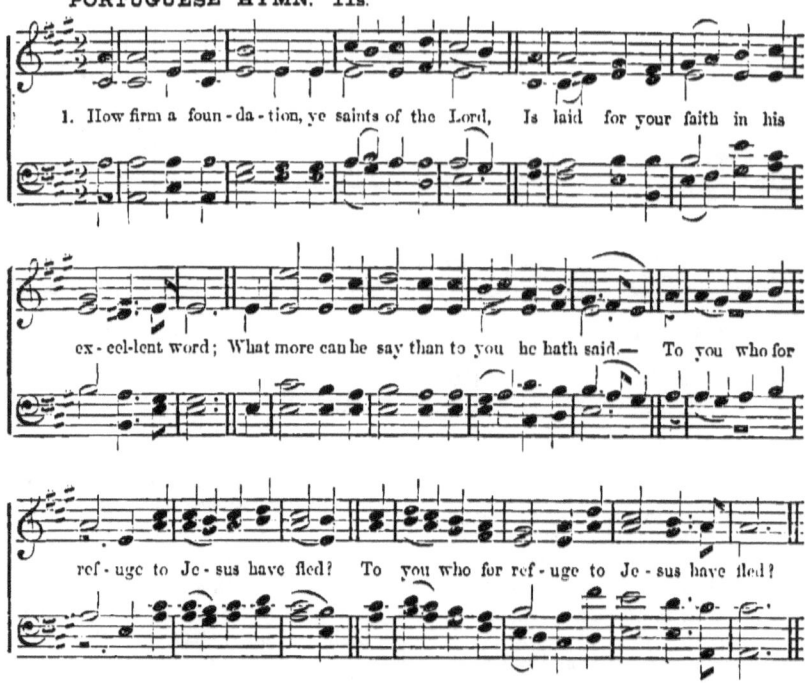

1. How firm a foun-da-tion, ye saints of the Lord, Is laid for your faith in his ex-cel-lent word; What more can he say than to you he hath said— To you who for ref-uge to Je-sus have fled? To you who for ref-uge to Je-sus have fled?

122.

2 "Fear not, I am with thee, oh, be not dismayed,
For I am thy God, I will still give thee aid;
I'll strengthen thee, help thee, and cause thee to stand,
Upheld by my righteous, omnipotent hand.

3 "When thro' the deep waters I call thee to go,
The rivers of sorrow shall not overflow;
For I will be with thee thy trials to bless,
And sanctify to thee thy deepest distress.

4 "When thro' fiery trials thy pathway shall lie,
My grace, all-sufficient, shall be thy supply;
The flame shall not hurt thee; I only design
Thy dross to consume, and thy gold to refine.

5 "Ev'n down to old age all my people shall prove
My sovereign, eternal, unchangeable love;
And then, when gray hairs shall their temples adorn,
Like lambs they shall still in my bosom be borne.

6 "The soul that on Jesus hath leaned for repose,
I will not—I will not desert to his foes;

That soul—though all hell should endeavor to shake,
I'll never—no never—no never forsake!"

423.

1 The Lord is my shepherd, no want shall I know,
I feed in green pastures, safe-folded I rest;
He leadeth my soul where the still waters flow,
Restores me when wandering, redeems when oppressed.

2 Thro' the valley and shadow of death, tho' I stray,
Since thou art my guardian, no evil I fear;
Thy rod shall defend me, thy staff be my stay;
No harm can befall, with my comforter near.

3 In the midst of affliction my table is spread;
With blessings unmeasured my cup runneth o'er;
With perfume and oil thou anointest my head;
Oh! what shall I ask of thy providence more?

4 Let goodness and mercy, my bountiful God!
Still follow my steps till I meet thee above;
I seek—by the path which my forefathers trod,
Thro' the land of their sojourn—thy kingdom of love.

424.

1 O Zion, afflicted with wave upon wave!
  Whom no man can comfort, whom no man can save;
  With darkness surrounded, by terrors dismayed,
  In toiling and rowing, thy strength is decayed.

2 Loud roaring, the billows now nigh overwhelm,
  But skillful 's the Pilot who sits at the helm;
  His wisdom conducts thee, his power defends;
  In safety and quiet thy warfare he ends.

3 "O fearful! O faithless!" in mercy he cries;
  "My promise, my truth, are they light in thine eyes?
  Still, still I am with thee, my promise shall stand;
  Thro' tempest and tossing I 'll bring thee to land.

4 "Forget thee I will not—I cannot; thy name,
  Engraved on my heart doth forever remain;
  The palms of my hands while I look on, I see
  The wounds that I suffered, when dying for thee.

5 "Then trust me, and fear not! thy life is secure,
  My wisdom is perfect, supreme is my power;
  In love I correct thee, thy soul to refine,
  To make thee at length in my likeness to shine."

425.

1 Tho' faint, yet pursuing, we go on our way;
  The Lord is our Leader, his word is our stay;
  Tho' suffering, and sorrow, and trial be near,
  The Lord is our refuge, and whom can we fear?

2 He raiseth the fallen, he cheereth the faint;
  The weak, and oppressed—he will hear their complaint;
  The way may be weary, and thorny the road,
  But how can we falter? our help is in God!

3 And to his green pastures our footsteps he leads;
  His flock in the desert how kindly he feeds!
  The lambs in his bosom he tenderly bears,
  And brings back the wanderers all safe from the snares.

4 Tho' clouds may surround us, our God is our light;
  Tho' storms rage around us, our God is our might;
  So faint, yet pursuing, still onward we come;
  The Lord is our Leader, and heaven is our home!

426.

1 O eyes that are weary, and hearts that are sore!
  Look off unto Jesus, now sorrow no more!
  The light of his countenance shineth so bright,
  That here, as in heaven, there need be no night.

2 While looking to Jesus, my heart cannot fear;
  I tremble no more when I see Jesus near;
  I know that his presence my safeguard will be,
  For, "Why are ye troubled?" he saith unto me.

3 Still looking to Jesus, oh, may I be found,
  When Jordan's dark waters encompass me round:
  They bear me away in his presence to be:
  I see him still nearer whom always I see.

4 Then, then shall I know the full beauty and grace
  Of Jesus, my Lord, when I stand face to face;
  Shall know how his love went before me each day,
  And wonder that ever my eyes turned away.

427.

1 I once was a stranger to grace and to God;
  I knew not my danger, and felt not my load;
  Tho' friends spoke in rapture of Christ on the tree,
  Jehovah, my Saviour, seemed nothing to me.

2 When free grace awoke me by light from on high,
  Then legal fears shook me; I trembled to die:
  No refuge, no safety, in self could I see;
  Jehovah, thou only my Saviour must be!

3 My terrors all vanished before his sweet name;
  My guilty fears banished, with boldness I came
  To drink at the fountain, so copious and free:
  Jehovah, my Saviour, is all things to me.

4 Jehovah, the Lord, is my treasure and boast;
  Jehovah my Saviour, I ne'er can be lost:
  In thee I shall conquer, by flood and by field,
  Jehovah my anchor, Jehovah my shield!

5 Ev'n treading the valley, the shadow of death,
  This watchword shall rally my faltering breath;
  For, while from life's fever my God sets me free,
  Jehovah, my Saviour, my death-song shall be!

428.

1 Oh that I could forever dwell,
Delighted at the Saviour's feet;
Behold the form I love so well,
And all his tender words repeat!

2 The world shut out from all my soul,
And heaven brought in with all its bliss,—
Oh! is there aught, from pole to pole,
One moment to compare with this?

3 This is the hidden life I prize—
A life of penitential love;
When most my follies I despise,
And raise my highest thoughts above;

4 When all I am I clearly see,
And freely own with deepest shame;
When the Redeemer's love to me
Kindles within a deathless flame.

5 Thus would I live till nature fail,
And all my former sins forsake;
Then rise to God within the vail,
And of eternal joys partake.

429.

1 Sun of my soul! thou Saviour dear,
It is not night if thou be near:
Oh, may no earth-born cloud arise
To hide thee from thy servant's eyes!

2 When soft the dews of kindly sleep
My wearied eyelids gently steep,
Be my last thought,—how sweet to rest
Forever on my Saviour's breast!

3 Abide with me from morn till eve,
For without thee I cannot live;
Abide with me when night is nigh,
For without thee I dare not die.

4 Be near to bless me when I wake,
Ere through the world my way I take;
Abide with me till in thy love
I lose myself in heaven above.

430.

1 Oh, sweetly breathe the lyres above,
When angels touch the quivering string,
And wake, to chant Immanuel's love,
Such strains as angel-lips can sing!

2 And sweet, on earth, the choral swell,
From mortal tongues, of gladsome lays;
When pardoned souls their raptures tell,
And, grateful, hymn Immanuel's praise.

3 Jesus, thy name our souls adore;
We own the bond that makes us thine;
And carnal joys, that charmed before,
For thy dear sake we now resign.

4 Our hearts, by dying love subdued,
Accept thine offered grace to-day:
Beneath the cross, with blood bedewed,
We bow, and give ourselves away.

5 In thee we trust,—on thee rely;
Though we are feeble, thou art strong;
Oh, keep us till our spirits fly
To join the bright, immortal throng!

LOVE FOR THE SAVIOUR. 137

PARK STREET. L. M.   VENUS.

1. Fountain of grace, rich, full, and free, What need I, that is not in thee? Full pardon, strength to meet the day, And peace which none can take away, And peace which none can take away.

431.

2 Doth sickness fill the heart with fear?
'T is sweet to know that thou art near;
Am I with dread of justice tried?
'T is sweet to feel that Christ hath died.

3 In life, thy promises of aid
Forbid my heart to be afraid;
In death, peace gently vails the eyes;
Christ rose, and I shall surely rise.

4 O all-sufficient Saviour! be
This all-sufficiency to me;
Nor pain, nor sin, nor death can harm
The weakest, shielded by thine arm.

432.

1 JESUS! and shall it ever be,
A mortal man ashamed of thee?
Ashamed of thee, whom angels praise,
Whose glories shine through endless days?

2 Ashamed of Jesus! sooner far
Let evening blush to own a star;
He sheds the beams of light divine
O'er this benighted soul of mine.

3 Ashamed of Jesus! that dear Friend
On whom my hopes of heaven depend!
No; when I blush—be this my shame,
That I no more revere his name.

4 Ashamed of Jesus! yes, I may,
When I've no guilt to wash away;
No tear to wipe, no good to crave,
No fears to quell, no soul to save.

5 Till then—nor is my boasting vain—
Till then I boast a Saviour slain!
And oh, may this my glory be,
That Christ is not ashamed of me!

433.

1 LIGHT of the soul! O Saviour blest!
Soon as thy presence fills the breast,
Darkness and guilt are put to flight,
And all is sweetness and delight.

2 Son of the Father! Lord most high!
How glad is he who feels thee nigh!
Come in thy hidden majesty;
Fill us with love, fill us with thee.

3 Jesus is from the proud concealed,
But evermore to babes revealed,
Through him, unto the Father be
Glory and praise eternally.

434.

1 NONE loves me, Saviour, with thy love,
None else can meet such needs as mine;
Oh, grant me, as thou shalt approve,
All that befits a child of thine!

2 Give me a faith shall never fail,
One that shall always work by love;
And then, whatever foes assail,
They shall but higher courage move.

3 A heart that, when my days are glad,
May never from thy way decline,
A heart that loves to trust in thee,
A patient heart, create in me!

138   CHRISTIAN.

CHURCH. C. M.   J. P. Holbrook.

1. Dear Ref-uge of my wea-ry soul, On thee, when sorrows rise— On thee, when waves of trouble roll, My faint-ing heart re-lies.

435.

2 To thee I tell each rising grief,
   For thou alone canst heal;
Thy word can bring a sweet relief
   For every pain I feel.

3 But oh! when gloomy doubts prevail,
   I fear to call thee mine;
The springs of comfort seem to fail,
   And all my hopes decline.

4 Yet, gracious God, where shall I flee?
   Thou art my only trust:
And still my soul would cleave to thee,
   Though prostrate in the dust.

5 Thy mercy-seat is open still,
   Here let my soul retreat,
With humble hope attend thy will,
   And wait beneath thy feet.

436.

1 Speak to me, Lord, thyself reveal,
   While here on earth I rove;
Speak to my heart, and let me feel
   The kindling of thy love.

2 With thee conversing, I forget
   All time and toil and care;
Labor is rest, and pain is sweet,
   If thou, my God, art here.

3 Here then, my God, be pleased to stay,
   And make my heart rejoice;
My bounding heart shall own thy sway,
   And echo to thy voice.

4 Thou callest me to seek thy face;
   Thy face, O God, I seek,—
Attend the whispers of thy grace,
   And hear thee inly speak.

5 Let this my every hour employ,
   Till I thy glory see,
Enter into my Master's joy,
   And find my heaven in thee.

437.

1 Dearest of all the names above,
   My Jesus and my God,
Who can resist thy heavenly love,
   Or trifle with thy blood?

2 'T is by the merits of thy death
   Thy Father smiles again;
'T is by thine interceding breath
   The Spirit dwells with men.

3 Till God in human flesh I see,
   My thoughts no comfort find:
The holy, just, and sacred Three
   Are terror to my mind.

4 But if Immanuel's face appear,
   My hope, my joy, begin:
His name forbids my slavish fear;
   His grace removes my sin.

5 While Jews on their own law rely,
   And Greeks of wisdom boast,
I love th' incarnate Mystery,
   And there I fix my trust.

LOVE FOR THE SAVIOUR. 139

HEBER. C. M.   KINGSLEY.

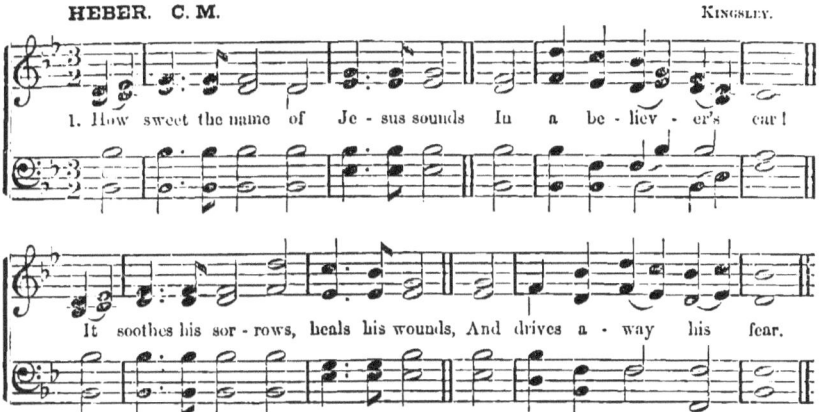

1. How sweet the name of Je-sus sounds In a be-liev-er's ear!
It soothes his sor-rows, heals his wounds, And drives a-way his fear.

438.

2 It makes the wounded spirit whole,
  And calms the troubled breast;
  'T is manna to the hungry soul,
  And to the weary, rest.

3 Jesus! my Shepherd, Guardian, Friend,
  My Prophet, Priest, and King;
  My Lord, my Life, my Way, my End,
  Accept the praise I bring!

4 Weak is the effort of my heart,
  And cold my warmest thought;
  But when I see thee as thou art,
  I'll praise thee as I ought.

5 Till then, I would thy love proclaim,
  With every fleeting breath;
  And may the music of thy name
  Refresh my soul in death.

439.

1 Jesus! I love thy charming name,
  'T is music to mine ear;
  Fain would I sound it out so loud,
  That earth and heaven should hear.

2 Yes!—thou art precious to my soul,
  My transport and my trust;
  Jewels, to thee, are gaudy toys,
  And gold is sordid dust.

3 All my capacious powers can wish,
  In thee doth richly meet;
  Not to mine eyes is light so dear,
  Nor friendship half so sweet.

4 Thy grace still dwells upon my heart,
  And sheds its fragrance there;—
  The noblest balm of all its wounds,
  The cordial of its care.

5 I'll speak the honors of thy name,
  With my last laboring breath;
  Then, speechless, clasp thee in mine arms,
  The antidote of death.

440.

1 Jesus, the very thought of thee,
  With sweetness fills my breast:
  But sweeter far thy face to see,
  And in thy presence rest.

2 Nor voice can sing, nor heart can frame,
  Nor can the memory find
  A sweeter sound than thy blest name,
  O Saviour of mankind!

3 O Hope of every contrite heart!
  O Joy of all the meek!
  To those who fall, how kind thou art!
  How good to those who seek!

4 But what to those who find? Ah! this,
  Nor tongue nor pen can show,
  The love of Jesus, what it is,
  None but his loved ones know.

5 Jesus, our only joy be thou,
  As thou our prize wilt be;
  Jesus, be thou our glory now,
  And through eternity.

140   CHRISTIAN.

TAPPAN. C. M.   KINGSLEY.

1. Go, tune thy voice to sacred song, Exert thy noblest powers, Go, mingle with the choral throng, The Saviour's praises to prolong, Amid life's fleeting hours.

441.

1 Go, tune thy voice to sacred song,
   Exert thy noblest powers,
Go, mingle with the choral throng,
The Saviour's praises to prolong,
   Amid life's fleeting hours.

2 Oh! hast thou felt a Saviour's love,
   That flame of heavenly birth?
Then let thy strains melodious prove,
With raptures soaring far above
   The trifling toys of earth.

3 Hast found the pearl of price unknown,
   That cost a Saviour's blood?
Heir of a bright celestial crown,
That sparkles near the eternal throne,
   Oh, sing the praise of God!

4 Sing of the Lamb that once was slain
   That man might be forgiven;
Sing how he broke death's bars in twain
Ascending high in bliss to reign,
   The God of earth and heaven!

442.

1 Wouldst thou eternal life obtain!
   Now to the cross repair;
There stand and gaze and weep and pray,
Where Jesus breathes his life away;
   Eternal life is there!

2 Go—'tis the Son of God expires!
   Approach the shameful tree;
See quivering there the mortal dart,
In the Redeemer's loving heart,
   O sinful soul, for thee!

3 Go—there from every streaming wound
   Flows rich atoning blood:
That blood can cleanse thy deepest stain,
Bid frowning justice smile again,
   And seal thy peace with God.

4 Go—at that cross thy heart subdued,
   With thankful love shall glow;
By wondrous grace thy soul set free,
Eternal life from Christ to thee
   A vital stream shall flow!

443.

1 O Saviour, lend a listening ear,
   And answer my request!
Forgive, and wipe the falling tear,
Now with thy love my spirit cheer,
   And set my heart at rest.

2 I mourn the hidings of thy face;
   The absence of that smile,
Which led me to a throne of grace,
And gave my soul a resting-place,
   From earthly care and toil.

3 'Tis sin that separates from thee
   This poor benighted soul;
My folly and my guilt I see,
And now upon the bended knee,
   I yield to thy control.

4 Up to the place of thine abode
   I lift my waiting eye;
To thee, O holy Lamb of God!
Whose blood for me so freely flowed,
   I raise my ardent cry.

LOVE FOR THE SAVIOUR. 141

BRIDGMAN. C. M. *Arranged from* BEETHOVEN.

1. Do not I love thee, O my Lord? Behold my heart and see;
And turn the dearest idol out That dares to rival thee.

444.

2 Do not I love thee from my soul?
  Then let me nothing love :
  Dead be my heart to every joy
  When Jesus cannot move.

3 Is not thy name melodious still
  To mine attentive ear?
  Doth not each pulse with pleasure bound,
  My Saviour's voice to hear?

4 Hast thou a lamb in all thy flock
  I would disdain to feed?
  Hast thou a foe before whose face
  I fear thy cause to plead?

5 Would not my heart pour forth its blood
  In honor of thy name?
  And challenge the cold hand of death
  To damp th' immortal flame?

6 Thou know'st I love thee, dearest Lord;
  But oh! I long to soar
  Far from the sphere of mortal joys,
  And learn to love thee more.

445.

1 Oh, see how Jesus trusts himself
  Unto our childish love!
  As though by his free ways with us
  Our earnestness to prove.

2 His sacred name a common word
  On earth he loves to hear;
  There is no majesty in him
  Which love may not come near.

3 The light of love is round his feet,
  His paths are never dim;
  And he comes nigh to us when we
  Dare not come nigh to him.

4 Let us be simple with him, then,
  Not backward, stiff, nor cold,
  As though our Bethlehem could be
  What Sinai was of old.

446.

1 JESUS! thou art the sinner's Friend;
  As such I look to thee;
  Now, in the fullness of thy love,
  O Lord! remember me.

2 Remember thy pure word of grace,—
  Remember Calvary;
  Remember all thy dying groans,
  And then remember me.

3 Thou wondrous Advocate with God!
  I yield myself to thee;
  While thou art sitting on thy throne,
  Dear Lord! remember me.

4 Lord! I am guilty—I am vile,
  But thy salvation's free;
  Then, in thine all-abounding grace,
  Dear Lord! remember me.

5 And, when I close my eyes in death,
  When creature-helps all flee,
  Then, O my dear Redeemer God!
  I pray, remember me.

142   CHRISTIAN.

DENFIELD. C. M.   *Arranged by Dr. L. Mason.*

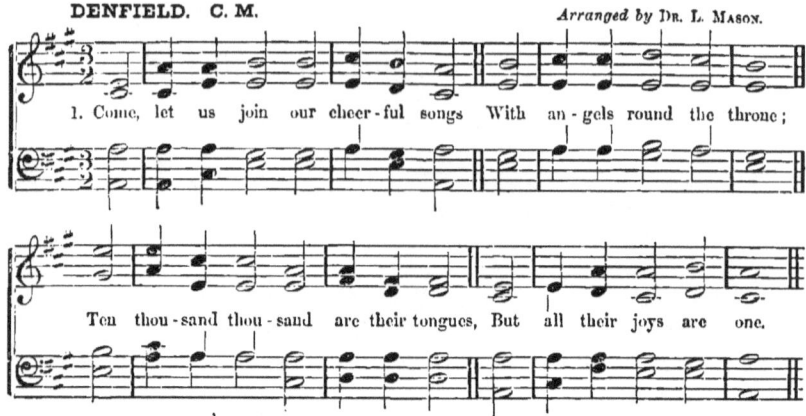

1. Come, let us join our cheerful songs With angels round the throne; Ten thousand thousand are their tongues, But all their joys are one.

447.

2 "Worthy the Lamb that died," they cry,
  "To be exalted thus!"
  "Worthy the Lamb!" our lips reply,
  "For he was slain for us."

3 Jesus is worthy to receive
  Honor and power divine;
  And blessings, more than we can give,
  Be, Lord, forever thine!

4 Let all that dwell above the sky
  And air, and earth, and seas,
  Conspire to lift thy glories high,
  And speak thine endless praise.

5 The whole creation join in one,
  To bless the sacred name
  Of him who sits upon the throne,
  And to adore the Lamb!

448.

1 My God! the spring of all my joys,
  The life of my delights,
  The glory of my brightest days,
  And comfort of my nights!

2 In darkest shades if he appear,
  My dawning is begun:
  He is my soul's sweet morning star,
  And he my rising sun.

3 The opening heavens around me shine
  With beams of sacred bliss,
  While Jesus shows his heart is mine,
  And whispers, I am his!

4 My soul would leave this heavy clay,
  At that transporting word;
  Run up with joy the shining way,
  T'embrace my dearest Lord!

5 Fearless of hell and ghastly death,
  I'd break through every foe;
  The wings of love and arms of faith
  Should bear me conqueror through.

449.

1 Blest Jesus! when my soaring thoughts
  O'er all thy graces rove,
  How is my soul in transport lost,—
  In wonder, joy, and love!

2 Not softest strains can charm my ears,
  Like thy beloved name;
  Nor aught beneath the skies inspire
  My heart with equal flame.

3 Where'er I look, my wondering eyes
  Unnumbered blessings see;
  But what is life, with all its bliss,
  If once compared with thee?

4 Hast thou a rival in my breast?
  Search, Lord, for thou canst tell
  If aught can raise my passions thus,
  Or please my soul so well.

5 No: thou art precious to my heart,
  My portion and my joy:
  Forever let thy boundless grace
  My sweetest thoughts employ.

LOVE FOR THE SAVIOUR. 143

GEER. C. M.   GREATOREX COLL.

1. To our Redeemer's glorious name, Awake the sacred song!
Oh! may his love—immortal flame—Tune every heart and tongue!

150.

1 To our Redeemer's glorious name,
  Awake the sacred song!
  Oh! may his love—immortal flame—
  Tune every heart and tongue!

2 His love, what mortal thought can reach?
  What mortal tongue display?
  Imagination's utmost stretch,
  In wonder, dies away.

3 Dear Lord! while we adoring pay
  Our humble thanks to thee,
  May every heart with rapture say,—
  "The Saviour died for me!"

4 Oh! may the sweet, the blissful theme,
  Fill every heart and tongue,
  Till strangers love thy charming name,
  And join the sacred song.

151.

1 Thou, O my Jesus, thou didst me
  Upon the cross embrace!
  For me didst bear the nails and spear,
  And manifold disgrace.

2 And griefs and torments numberless,
  And sweat of agony—
  Yea, death itself—and all for one
  That was thine enemy.

3 Then why, O blessed Jesus Christ,
  Should I not love thee well?
  Not for the hope of winning heaven,
  Nor of escaping hell!

4 Not with the hope of gaining aught
  Not seeking a reward;
  But as thyself hast loved me,
  O everlasting Lord!

5 Ev'n so I love thee, and will love,
  And in thy praise will sing,
  Solely because thou art my God,
  And my eternal King!

152.

1 Oh, speak that gracious word again,
  And cheer my broken heart!
  No voice but thine can soothe my pain,
  Or bid my fears depart.

2 And wilt thou still vouchsafe to own
  A worm so vile as I?
  And may I still approach thy throne,
  And "Abba, Father," cry?

3 Oh, then, let saints and angels join,
  And help me to proclaim
  The grace that healed a soul like mine,
  And put my foes to shame!

4 My Saviour, by his powerful word,
  Has turned my night to day;
  And all those heavenly joys restored,
  Which I had sinned away.

5 Dear Lord, I wonder and adore;
  Thy grace is all divine:
  Oh, keep me, that I sin no more
  Against such love as thine!

144   CHRISTIAN.

ARIEL. L. C. M.   Dr. L. Mason.

453.

1 Oh, could I speak the matchless worth,
  Oh, could I sound the glories forth,
    Which in my Saviour shine !
  I 'd soar, and touch the heavenly strings,
  And vie with Gabriel, while he sings
    In notes almost divine.

2 I 'd sing the precious blood he spilt,
  My ransom from the dreadful guilt
    Of sin and wrath divine !
  I 'd sing his glorious righteousness,
  In which all-perfect, heavenly dress
    My soul shall ever shine.

3 I 'd sing the characters he bears,
  And all the forms of love he wears,
    Exalted on his throne :
  In loftiest songs of sweetest praise,
  I would to everlasting days
    Make all his glories known.

4 Well—the delightful day will come,
  When my dear Lord will bring me home,
    And I shall see his face :
  Then with my Saviour, Brother, Friend,
  A blest eternity I 'll spend,
    Triumphant in his grace.

454.

1 Come join, ye saints, with heart and voice,
  Alone in Jesus to rejoice,
    And worship at his feet ;
  Come, take his praises on your tongues,
  And raise to him your thankful songs,
    " In him ye are complete !"

2 In him, who all our praise excels
  The fullness of the Godhead dwells,
    And all perfections meet ;
  The head of all celestial powers,
  Divinely theirs, divinely ours ;
    " In him ye are complete !"

3 Still onward urge your heavenly way,
  Dependent on him day by day,
    His presence still entreat ;
  His precious name forever bless,
  Your glory, strength and righteousness,
    " In him ye are complete !"

4 Nor fear to pass the vale of death ;
  In his dear arms resign your breath,
    He 'll make the passage sweet ;
  The gloom and fears of death shall flee,
  And your departing souls shall see
    " In him ye are complete !"

LOVE FOR THE SAVIOUR. 145

LOVING-KINDNESS. L. M.

1. Awake, my soul, to joyful lays, And sing thy great Redeemer's praise; He justly claims a song from me, His loving-kindness, O how free! Loving-kindness, Loving-kindness, His loving-kindness, O how free!

155.

2 He saw me ruined in the fall,
Yet loved me notwithstanding all;
He saved me from my lost estate;
His loving-kindness, oh! how great!

3 Though numerous hosts of mighty foes,
Though earth and hell my way oppose,
He safely leads my soul along;
His loving-kindness, oh! how strong!

4 When trouble, like a gloomy cloud,
Has gathered thick, and thundered loud,
He near my soul has always stood;
His loving-kindness, oh! how good!

5 Often I feel my sinful heart,
Prone from my Saviour to depart;
But though I oft have him forgot,
His loving-kindness changes not.

6 Soon shall I pass the gloomy vale,
Soon all my mortal powers must fail;
Oh! may my last expiring breath,
His loving-kindness sing in death.

CRUSADER'S HYMN. Hymn **156.** *Arranged by R. Storrs Willis.*

1. Fairest Lord Jesus! Ruler of all nature! O thou of God and man the Son! Thee will I cherish, Thee will I honor, Thou! my soul's glory, joy, and crown.
2. Fair are the meadows, Fairer still the woodlands! Robed in the blooming garb of spring; Jesus is fairer, Jesus is purer, Who makes the woeful heart to sing.
3. Fair is the sunshine, Fairer still the moonlight, And the twinkling starry host; Jesus shines brighter, Jesus shines purer Than all the angels heaven can boast.

146 CHRISTIAN.

BONAR. S. M. Double.   J. P. HOLBROOK.

1. I was a wandering sheep, I did not love the fold: I did not love my Shepherd's voice, I would not be con-trolled; I was a way-ward child, I did not love my home, I did not love my Shepherd's voice, I loved a-far to roam.

457.

2 The Shepherd sought his sheep,
   The Father sought his child;
He followed me o'er vale and hill,
   O'er deserts waste and wild;
He found me nigh to death,
   Famished, and faint, and lone;
He bound me with the bands of love,
   He saved the wandering one.

3 He spake in tender love,
   He raised my drooping head;
He gently closed my bleeding wounds,
   My fainting soul he fed;
He washed my filth away,
   He made me clean and fair;
He brought me to my home in peace,
   The long-sought wanderer.

4 Jesus my Shepherd is,
   'T was he that loved my soul.
'T was he that washed me in his blood,
   'T was he that made me whole:
'T was he that sought the lost,
   That found the wandering sheep,
'T was he that brought me to the fold—
   'T was he that still doth keep.

5 No more a wandering sheep,
   I love to be controlled,
I love my tender Shepherd's voice,
   I love the peaceful fold:
No more a wayward child,
   I seek no more to roam,
I love my heavenly Father's voice—
   I love, I love his home.

458.

1 For me to live is Christ,
   To die is endless gain,
For him I gladly bear the cross,
   And welcome grief and pain.
Faithful may I endure,
   And hear my Saviour say,
Thrice welcome home, beloved child,
   Inherit endless day!

2 A pilgrimage my lot,
   My home is in the skies,
I nightly pitch my tent below,
   And daily higher rise:
My journey soon will end,
   My scrip and staff laid down;
Oh! tempt me not with earthly toys,
   I go to wear a crown.

LOVE FOR THE SAVIOUR. 147
SHEPHERD. 11s & 10s. Spiritual Songs.

1. The Lord is my Shepherd, he makes me repose Where the pastures in beauty are growing; He leads me afar from the world and its woes, Where in peace the still waters are flowing.

459.
2 He strengthens my spirit, he shows me the path,
Where the arms of his love shall enfold me;
And when I walk through the dark valley of death,
His rod and his staff will uphold me!

460.
1 Oh, tell me, thou life and delight of my soul,
Where the flock of thy pasture are feeding;
I seek thy protection, I need thy control,
I would go where my Shepherd is leading.

2 Oh, tell me the place where thy flock are at rest,
Where the noontide will find them reposing;
The tempest now rages, my soul is distressed,
And the pathway of peace I am losing.

3 And why should I stray with the flocks of thy foes,
In the desert where now they are roving;
Where hunger and thirst, where contentions and woes,
And fierce conflicts their ruin are proving?

4 Ah, when shall my woes and my wandering cease,
And the follies that fill me with weeping?
O Shepherd of Israel, restore me that peace
Thou dost give to the flock thou art keeping!

5 A voice from the Shepherd now bids me return,
By the way where the foot-prints are lying;
No longer to wander, no longer to mourn:
And homeward my spirit is flying.

148   CHRISTIAN.
MADISON. 8s. Double.   *Arranged from* S. B. Pond.

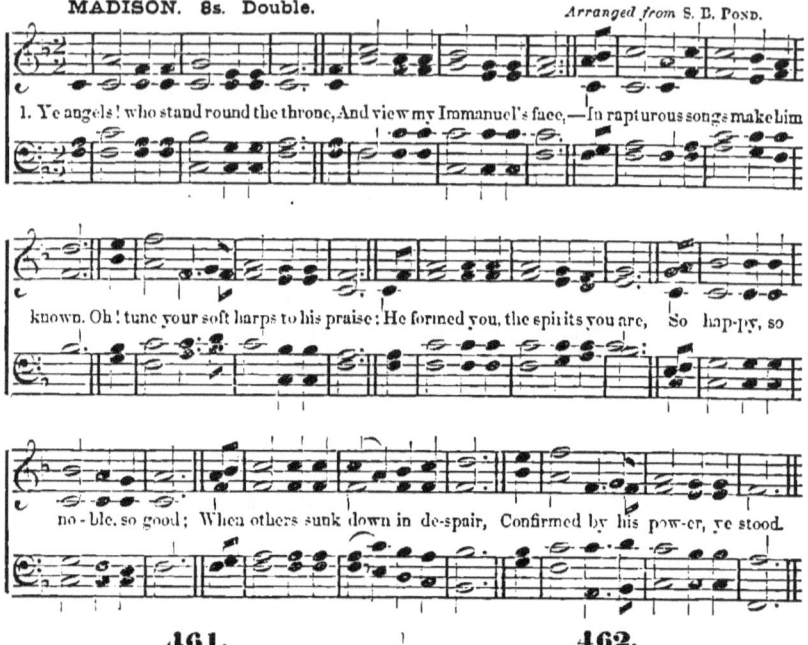

1. Ye angels! who stand round the throne, And view my Immanuel's face,—In rapturous songs make him known. Oh! tune your soft harps to his praise: He formed you, the spirits you are, So happy, so noble, so good; When others sunk down in despair, Confirmed by his power, ye stood.

461.

2 Ye saints! who stand nearer than they,
And cast your bright crowns at his feet,
His grace and his glory display,
And all his rich mercy repeat:
He snatched you from hell and the grave,
He ransomed from death and despair:
For you he was mighty to save,
Almighty to bring you safe there.

3 Oh! when will the period appear
When I shall unite in your song?
I'm weary of lingering here,
And I to your Saviour belong!
I'm fettered and chained up in clay;
I struggle and pant to be free;
I long to be soaring away,
My God and my Saviour to see!

4 I want to put on my attire,
Washed white in the blood of the Lamb;
I want to be one of your choir,
And tune my sweet harp to his name;
I want—oh! I want to be there,
Where sorrow and sin bid adieu—
Your joy and your friendship to share—
To wonder, and worship with you!

462.

1 My Saviour, whom absent I love,
Whom, not having seen, I adore,
Whose name is exalted above
All glory, dominion, and power,—
Dissolve thou those bands that detain
My soul from her portion in thee;
Ah! strike off this adamant chain,
And make me eternally free!

2 When that happy era begins,
When arrayed in thy glories I shine,
Nor grieve any more, by my sins,
The bosom on which I recline,
Oh! then shall the vail be removed,
And round me thy brightness be poured!
I shall meet him, whom absent I loved,
I shall see, whom unseen I adored.

3 And then, nevermore shall the fears,
The trials, temptations, and woes,
Which darken this valley of tears,
Intrude on my blissful repose:
To Jesus, the crown of my hope,
My soul is in haste to be gone;
Oh, bear me, ye cherubim, up,
And waft me away to his throne!

LOVE FOR THE SAVIOUR. 149

MANEPY. 8s.   Selah.

1. How te-dious and taste-less the hours, When Je-sus no long-er I see! The woodlands, the fields, and the flowers, Have lost all their sweet-ness to me.

463.

1 How tedious and tasteless the hours,
   When Jesus no longer I see!
   The woodlands, the fields, and the flowers
   Have lost all their sweetness to me.

2 His name yields the richest perfume,
   And softer than music his voice;
   His presence can banish my gloom,
   And bid all within me rejoice.

3 Dear Lord! if indeed thou art mine,
   And thou art my light and my song;
   Say, why do I languish and pine,
   And why are my winters so long?

4 Oh! drive these dark clouds from the sky,
   Thy soul-cheering presence restore;
   Or bid me soar upward on high,
   Where winter and storms are no more.

464.

1 INSPIRER and hearer of prayer,
   Thou Shepherd and Guardian of thine,
   My all to thy covenant care
   I sleeping or waking resign.

2 If thou art my shield and my sun,
   The night is no darkness to me;
   And, fast as my moments roll on,
   They bring me but nearer to thee.

3 Thy ministering spirits descend
   To watch while thy saints are asleep;
   By day and by night they attend,
   The heirs of salvation to keep.

4 Bright seraphs, despatched from the throne,
   Repair to their stations assigned;
   And angels elect are sent down,
   To guard the redeemed of mankind.

5 Thy worship no interval knows;
   Their fervor is still on the wing;
   And, while they protect my repose,
   They chant to the praise of my King.

6 I, too, at the season ordained,
   Their chorus forever shall join,
   And love and adore, without end,
   Their faithful Creator and mine.

465.

1 My gracious Redeemer I love,
   His praises aloud I'll proclaim:
   And join with the armies above,
   To shout his adorable name.

2 To gaze on his glories divine
   Shall be my eternal employ;
   To see them incessantly shine,
   My boundless, ineffable joy.

3 He freely redeemed, with his blood,
   My soul from the confines of hell,
   To live on the smiles of my God,
   And in his sweet presence to dwell:—

4 To shine with the angels in light,
   With saints and with seraphs to sing,
   To view, with eternal delight,
   My Jesus, my Saviour, my King!

CHRISTIAN.

TRUST. 7s. 6 lines. J. P. Holbrook.

1. Happy, Saviour, shall I be,
When I do but trust in thee;
Trust thy wisdom me to guide;
Trust thy goodness to provide;
Trust thy saving love and power;
Trust thee every day and hour:

466.

2 Trust thee as the only light
In the darkest hour of night;
Trust in sickness, trust in health;
Trust in poverty and wealth;
Trust in joy and trust in grief;
Trust thy promise for relief:

3 Trust thy blood to cleanse my soul;
Trust thy grace to make me whole;
Trust thee living, dying, too;
Trust thee all my journey through;
Trust thee till my feet shall be
Planted on the crystal sea.

467.

1 Chosen not for good in me,
Waked from coming wrath to flee,
Hidden in the Saviour's side,
By the Spirit sanctified—
Teach me, Lord, on earth to show,
By my love, how much I owe.

2 Oft I walk beneath the cloud,
Dark as midnight's gloomy shroud;
But, when fear is at the height,
Jesus comes, and all is light;
Blessed Jesus! bid me show
Doubting saints how much I owe.

3 Oft the nights of sorrow reign—
Weeping, sickness, sighing, pain;
But a night thine anger burns—
Morning comes, and joy returns:
God of comforts! bid me show
To thy poor how much I owe.

4 When in flowery paths I tread,
Oft by sin I'm captive led;
Oft I fall, but still arise—
Jesus comes—the tempter flies:
Blessèd Jesus! bid me show
Weary sinners all I owe.

468.

1 As the hart, with eager looks,
Panteth for the water-brooks,
So my soul, athirst for thee,
Pants the living God to see;
When, oh, when, with filial fear,
Lord, shall I to thee draw near?

2 Why art thou cast down, my soul?
God, thy God, shall make thee whole;
Why art thou disquieted?
God shall lift thy fallen head,
And his countenance benign
Be the saving health of thine.

LOVE FOR THE SAVIOUR. 151

HALLE. 7s. 6 lines. *Arranged by Dr. Hastings.*

1. Lord! before thy throne we bend;
   Servants, to our Master true,
   Now to thee our prayers ascend:
   Lo! we yield thee homage due.
   Children, to thy throne we fly,
   Abba—Father! hear our cry.

469.

2 Low before thee, Lord! we bow,
  We are weak—but mighty thou:
  Sore distressed, yet suppliant still,
  Here we wait thy holy will;
  Bound to earth and rooted here,
  Till our Saviour God appear.

3 Leave us not beneath the power
  Of temptation's darkest hour:
  Swift to seal their captives' doom,
  See our foes exulting come!
  Jesus, Saviour! yet be nigh,
  Lord of life and victory.

470.

1 O THOU God who hearest prayer
  Every hour and everywhere!
  For his sake, whose blood I plead,
  Hear me in my hour of need:
  Only hide not now thy face,
  God of all-sufficient grace!

2 Hear and save me, gracious Lord!
  For my trust is in thy word;
  Wash me from the stain of sin,
  That thy peace may rule within:
  May I know myself thy child,
  Ransomed, pardoned, reconciled.

3 Dearest Lord! may I so much
  As thy garment's hem but touch,
  Or but raise my languid eye,
  To the cross where thou didst die,
  It shall make my spirit whole,—
  It shall heal and save my soul.

4 Leave me not, my Strength, my Trust!
  Oh, remember I'm but dust!
  Leave me not again to stray;
  Leave me not the tempter's prey:
  Fix my heart on things above;
  Make me happy in thy love.

471.

1 WEARY, Lord, of struggling here
  With this constant doubt and fear,
  Burdened by the pains I bear,
  And the trials I must share—
  Help me, Lord, again to flee
  To the rest that's found in thee.

2 Weakened by the wayward will
  Which controls, yet cheats me still;
  Seeking something undefined
  With an earnest, darkened mind—
  Help me, Lord, again to flee
  To the light that breaks from thee.

3 Fettered by this earthly scope
  In the reach and aim of hope,
  Fixing thought in narrow bound
  Where no living truth is found—
  Help me, Lord, again to flee
  To the hope that's fixed in thee.

4 Fettered, burdened, wearied, weak,
  Lord, once more thy grace I seek;
  Turn, oh, turn me not away,
  Help me, Lord, to watch and pray—
  That I never more may flee
  From the rest that's found in thee.

CHRISTIAN.

GREENWOOD. S. M.   Root & Sweetser's Coll.

1. Not with our mortal eyes Have we beheld the Lord;
Yet we rejoice to hear his name, And love him in his word.

472.

2 On earth we want the sight
  Of our Redeemer's face ;
Yet, Lord, our inmost thoughts delight
  To dwell upon thy grace.

3 And when we taste thy love,
  Our joys divinely grow
Unspeakable, like those above,
  And heaven begins below.

473.

1 Since Jesus is my friend,
  And I to him belong,
It matters not what foes intend,
  However fierce and strong.

2 He whispers in my breast
  Sweet words of holy cheer,
How they who seek in God their rest
  Shall ever find him near ;

3 How God hath built above
  A city fair and new,
Where eye and heart shall see and prove
  What faith has counted true.

4 My heart for gladness springs;
  It cannot more be sad ;
For very joy it smiles and sings,—
  Sees naught but sunshine glad.

5 The sun that lights mine eyes,
  Is Christ, the Lord I love ;
I sing for joy of that which lies
  Stored up for me above.

474.

1 While my Redeemer's near,
  My shepherd and my guide,
I bid farewell to anxious fear :
  My wants are all supplied.

2 To ever fragrant meads,
  Where rich abundance grows,
His gracious hand indulgent leads,
  And guards my sweet repose.

3 Dear Shepherd, if I stray,
  My wandering feet restore ;
To thy fair pastures guide my way,
  And let me rove no more.

475.

1 My spirit on thy care,
  Blest Saviour, I recline,
Thou wilt not leave me to despair,
  For thou art love divine.

2 In thee I place my trust,
  On thee I calmly rest ;
I know thee good—I know thee just,
  And count thy choice the best.

3 Whate'er events betide,
  Thy will they all perform ;
Safe in thy breast my head I hide,
  Nor fear the coming storm.

4 Let good or ill befall,
  It must be good for me,—
Secure of having thee in all,
  Of having all in thee.

LOVE FOR THE SAVIOUR. 153

GOLDEN HILL. S. M.

1. Dear Saviour! we are thine, By ev-er-last-ing bands, Our hearts, our souls, we would re-sign En-tire-ly to thy hands.

476.

2 To thee we still would cleave
   With ever-growing zeal ;
   If millions tempt us Christ to leave,
   Oh, let them ne'er prevail !

3 Thy Spirit shall unite
   Our souls to thee, our Head ;
   Shall form in us thine image bright,
   And teach thy paths to tread.

4 Death may our souls divide
   From these abodes of clay ;
   But love shall keep us near thy side,
   Through all the gloomy way.

5 Since Christ and we are one,
   Why should we doubt or fear ?
   If he in heaven has fixed his throne,
   He 'll fix his members there.

477.

1 My God, my Life, my Love,
   To thee, to thee I call ;
   I cannot live, if thou remove,
   For thou art all in all.

2 To thee, and thee alone,
   The angels owe their bliss:
   They sit around thy gracious throne,
   And dwell where Jesus is.

3 Not all the harps above
   Can make a heavenly place,
   If God his residence remove,
   Or but conceal his face.

4 Nor earth, nor all the sky,
   Can one delight afford—
   No, not a drop of real joy
   Without thy presence, Lord.

5 Thou art the sea of love,
   Where all my pleasures roll ;
   The circle where my passions move,
   And centre of my soul.

478.

1 Not all the blood of beasts,
   On Jewish altars slain,
   Could give the guilty conscience peace,
   Or wash away the stain.

2 But Christ, the heavenly Lamb,
   Takes all our sins away—
   A sacrifice of nobler name,
   And richer blood than they.

3 My faith would lay her hand
   On that dear head of thine,
   While like a penitent I stand,
   And there confess my sin.

4 My soul looks back to see
   The burdens thou didst bear
   When hanging on the cursed tree,
   And hopes her guilt was there.

5 Believing, we rejoice
   To see the curse remove ;
   We bless the Lamb with cheerful voice,
   And sing his bleeding love.

154   CHRISTIAN.

YARMOUTH. 7s & 6s.   Dr. L. Mason.

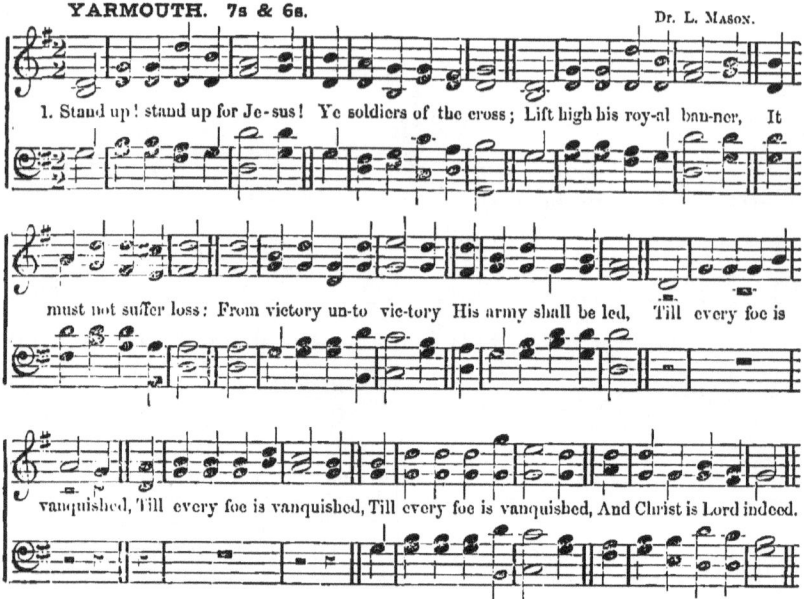

1. Stand up! stand up for Jesus! Ye soldiers of the cross; Lift high his royal banner, It must not suffer loss: From victory unto victory His army shall be led, Till every foe is vanquished, Till every foe is vanquished, Till every foe is vanquished, And Christ is Lord indeed.

479.

2 Stand up!—stand up for Jesus!
  The trumpet call obey;
Forth to the mighty conflict,
  In this his glorious day:
"Ye that are men, now serve him,"
  Against unnumbered foes;
Your courage rise with danger,
  And strength to strength oppose.

3 Stand up!—stand up for Jesus!
  Stand in his strength alone;
The arm of flesh will fail you—
  Ye dare not trust your own:
Put on the gospel armor,
  And, watching unto prayer,
Where duty calls or danger,
  Be never wanting there!

4 Stand up!—stand up for Jesus!
  The strife will not be long;
This day the noise of battle,
  The next the victor's song:
To him that overcometh,
  A crown of life shall be:
He with the King of Glory
  Shall reign eternally.

480.

1 In heavenly love abiding,
  No change my heart shall fear,
And safe is such confiding,
  For nothing changes here:
The storm may roar without me,
  My heart may low be laid,
But God is round about me,
  And can I be dismayed?

2 Wherever he may guide me,
  No want shall turn me back;
My Shepherd is beside me,
  And nothing can I lack:
His wisdom ever waketh,
  His sight is never dim:
He knows the way he taketh,
  And I will walk with him.

3 Green pastures are before me,
  Which yet I have not seen;
Bright skies will soon be o'er me,
  Where darkest clouds have been:
My hope I cannot measure;
  My path to life is free;
My Saviour has my treasure,
  And he will walk with me.

LOVE FOR THE SAVIOUR. 155

TULLY. 7s & 6s. Dr. L. Mason.

1. I lay my sins on Jesus, The spotless Lamb of God;
He bears them all, and frees us From the accursed load:
I bring my guilt to Jesus, To wash my crimson stains,
White in his blood most precious, Till not a stain remains.

481.

2 I lay my wants on Jesus;
   All fullness dwells in him;
He healeth my diseases,
   He doth my soul redeem:
I lay my griefs on Jesus,
   My burdens and my cares;
He from them all releases,
   He all my sorrow shares.

3 I rest my soul on Jesus,
   This weary soul of mine;
His right hand me embraces,
   I on his breast recline:
I love the name of Jesus,
   Immanuel, Christ, the Lord;
Like fragrance on the breezes,
   His name abroad is poured.

4 I long to be like Jesus,
   Meek, loving, lowly, mild;
I long to be like Jesus,
   The Father's holy child:
I long to be with Jesus
   Amid the heavenly throng,
To sing with saints his praises,
   And learn the angels' song.

482.

1 To thee, my God and Saviour!
   My heart exulting sings,
Rejoicing in thy favor,
   Almighty King of kings!
I'll celebrate thy glory,
   With all thy saints above,
And tell the joyful story
   Of thy redeeming love.

2 Soon as the morn, with roses,
   Bedecks the dewy east,
And when the sun reposes
   Upon the ocean's breast,
My voice, in supplication,
   Well-pleased the Lord shall hear:
Oh! grant me thy salvation,
   And to my soul draw near.

3 By thee, through life supported,
   I'll pass the dangerous road,
With heavenly hosts escorted,
   Up to thy bright abode;
Then cast my crown before thee,
   And, all my conflicts o'er,
Unceasingly adore thee:—
   What could an angel more?

156   CHRISTIAN.

ST. PETERSBURGH. L. M. 6 lines.   Bortniansky.

1. { As, pant-ing in the sul-try beam, The hart de-sires the cool-ing stream,
   So to thy pres-ence, Lord, I flee, So longs my soul, O God, for thee; }
   A-thirst to taste thy liv-ing grace, And see thy glo-ry face to face.

483.

2 High waves of sorrow o'er me roll,
   And troubles overwhelm my soul ;
   For many an evil voice is near,
   To chide my woe and mock my fear ;
   And silent memory weeps alone,
   O'er hours of peace and gladness flown.

3 For I have walked the happy round,
   That circles Zion's holy ground ;
   And gladly swelled the choral lays,
   That hymned my great Redeemer's praise,
   What time, the hallowed arch along,
   Responsive swelled the solemn song.

4 Ah, why by passing clouds oppressed,
   Should rising thoughts distract my breast!
   Turn, turn to him in every pain,
   Whom never suppliant sought in vain :
   Thy strength in joy's ecstatic day,
   Thy hope where joy has passed away.

484.

1 As oft with worn and weary feet,
   We tread earth's rugged valley o'er,
   The thought, how comforting and sweet,
   Christ trod this very path before ;
   Our wants and weaknesses he knows,
   From life's first dawning till its close.

2 Does sickness, feebleness, or pain,
   Or sorrow in our path appear ;
   The recollection will remain,
   More deeply did he suffer here,
   His life how truly sad and brief,
   Filled up with suffering and with grief.

3 If Satan tempt our hearts to stray,
   And whisper evil things within,
   So did he in the desert way,
   Assail our Lord with thoughts of sin ;
   When worn, and in a feeble hour,
   The tempter came with all his power.

4 Just such as I, this earth he trod,
   With every human ill but sin ;
   And, though indeed the very God,
   As I am now, so he has been :
   My God, my Saviour! look on me
   With pity, love, and sympathy.

485.

1 Why should I fear the darkest hour,
   Or tremble at the tempest's power?
   Jesus vouchsafes to be my tower.
   Though hot the fight, why quit the field?
   Why should I either flee or yield,
   Since Jesus is my mighty shield?

2 Though all the flocks and herds were dead,
   My soul a famine need not dread,
   For Jesus is my living bread.
   I know not what may soon betide,
   Or how my wants shall be supplied ;
   But Jesus knows and will provide.

3 Though sin would fill me with distress,
   The throne of grace I dare address,
   For Jesus is my righteousness.
   Against me earth and hell combine,
   But on my side is power divine :
   Jesus is all, and he is mine.

LOVE FOR THE SAVIOUR. 157

BROWNELL. L. M. 6 lines. HAYDN.

1. The Lord my pas-ture shall pre-pare, And feed me with a shepherd's care; His pres-ence shall my wants sup-ply, And guard me with a watch-ful eye: My noon-day walks he shall at-tend, And all my mid-night hours de-fend.

486.

2 When in the sultry glebe I faint,
Or on the thirsty mountain pant,
To fertile vales, and dewy meads,
My weary, wandering steps he leads;
Where peaceful rivers, soft and slow,
Amid the verdant landscape flow.

3 Though in the paths of death I tread,
With gloomy horrors overspread,
My steadfast heart shall fear no ill,
For thou, O Lord, art with me still:
Thy friendly rod shall give me aid,
And guide me through the dreadful shade.

4 Though in a bare and rugged way,
Through devious, lonely wilds I stray,
Thy presence shall my pains beguile:
The barren wilderness shall smile,
With sudden greens and herbage crowned;
And streams shall murmur all around.

487.

1 "PERFECT in love!"—Lord, can it be,
Amid this state of doubt and sin?
While foes so thick without, I see,
With weakness, pain, disease within;
Can perfect love inhabit here,
And, strong in faith, extinguish fear?

2 O Lord! amid this mental night,
Amid the clouds of dark dismay,
Arise! arise! shed forth thy light,
And kindle love's meridian day:
My Saviour God, to me appear,
So love shall triumph over fear.

488.

1 JESUS, thou source of calm repose,
All fullness dwells in thee divine;
Our strength, to quell the proudest foes;
Our light, in deepest gloom to shine;
Thou art our fortress, strength, and tower,
Our trust and portion, evermore.

2 Jesus, our Comforter thou art;
Our rest in toil, our ease in pain;
The balm to heal each broken heart,
In storms our peace, in loss our gain;
Our joy, beneath the worldling's frown;
In shame, our glory and our crown;—

3 In want, our plentiful supply;
In weakness, our almighty power;
In bonds, our perfect liberty;
Our refuge in temptation's hour;
Our comfort, amidst grief and thrall;
Our life in death; our all in all.

489.

1 Saviour! I follow on,
　Guided by thee,
Seeing not yet the hand
　That leadeth me;
Hushed be my heart and still,
Fear I no further ill,
Only to meet thy will
　My will shall be.

2 Riven the rock for me
　Thirst to relieve,
Manna from heaven falls
　Fresh every eve;
Never a want severe
Causeth my eye a tear,
But thou art whispering near,
　"Only believe!"

3 Often to Marah's brink
　Have I been brought;
Shrinking the cup to drink,
　Help I have sought;
And with the prayer's ascent,
Jesus the branch has rent;—
Quickly relief he sent,
　Sweetening the draught.

4 Saviour! I long to walk
　Closer with thee;
Led by thy guiding hand,
　Ever to be;
Constantly near thy side,
Quickened and purified,
Living for him who died
　Freely for me!

490.

1 Fade, fade, each earthly joy;
　Jesus is mine!
Break, every tender tie;
　Jesus is mine.
Dark is the wilderness;
Earth has no resting-place;
Jesus alone can bless;
　Jesus is mine.

2 Tempt not my soul away;
　Jesus is mine:
Here would I ever stay;
　Jesus is mine:
Perishing things of clay
Born but for one brief day,
Pass from my heart away;
　Jesus is mine.

3 Farewell, ye dreams of night,
　Jesus is mine:
Lost in this dawning bright,
　Jesus is mine:
All that my soul has tried
Left but a dismal void;
Jesus has satisfied;
　Jesus is mine.

4 Farewell, mortality;
　Jesus is mine:
Welcome, eternity;
　Jesus is mine:
Welcome, O loved and blest!
Welcome, sweet scenes of rest;
Welcome, my Saviour's breast;
　Jesus is mine!

LOVE FOR THE SAVIOUR. 159

ELY. 6s & 4s.   J. P. HOLBROOK.

1. Near-er, my God, to thee, Near-er to thee: Ev'n tho' it be a cross That raiseth me, Still all my song shall be, Near - er, my God, to thee, Near - er to thee.

491.

2 Though like a wanderer,
   Daylight all gone,
Darkness be over me,
   My rest a stone,
Yet in my dreams I'd be
Nearer, my God, to thee,
Nearer to thee.

3 There let the way appear
   Steps up to heaven;
All that thou sendest me
   In mercy given,
Angels to beckon me
Nearer, my God, to thee,
Nearer to thee.

4 Then with my waking thoughts,
   Bright with thy praise,
Out of my stony griefs,
   Bethel I'll raise;
So by my woes to be
Nearer, my God, to thee,
Nearer to thee.

5 Or if on joyful wing,
   Cleaving the sky,
Sun, moon, and stars forgot,
   Upward I fly,
Still all my song shall be,
Nearer, my God, to thee,
Nearer to thee.

492.

1 SAVIOUR! thy gentle voice
   Gladly we hear;
Author of all our joys,
   Ever be near;
Our souls would cling to thee,
Let us thy fullness see,
Our life to cheer.

2 Fountain of life divine!
   Thee we adore;
We would be wholly thine
   Forevermore;
Freely forgive our sin,
Grant heavenly peace within,
Thy light restore.

3 Though to our faith unseen,
   While darkness reigns,
On thee alone we lean
   While life remains;
By thy free grace restored,
Our souls shall bless the Lord
In joyful strains!

493.

1 GOD leads me—and I go!
   He takes the care;
I need not wish to know,
   Or question where;
The goal is drawing near,
My way will all be clear,
   When I am there.

2 God leads me—so my heart
   In faith shall rest;
No fear my soul shall part
   From Jesus' breast;
What path my life doth go,
Since he permitteth so,
   That must be best.

160   CHRISTIAN.
DUKE STREET. L. M.   J. Hatton.

1. 'Tis by the faith of joys to come, We walk thro' deserts dark as night; Till we arrive at heaven, our home, Faith is our guide, and faith our light.

494.
Faith.

2 The want of sight she well supplies,
   She makes the pearly gates appear;
   Far into distant worlds she pries,
   And brings eternal glories near.

3 Cheerful we tread the desert through,
   While faith inspires a heavenly ray,
   Though lions roar, and tempests blow,
   And rocks and dangers fill the way.

4 So Abra'm by divine command,
   Left his own house to walk with God;
   His faith beheld the promised land,
   And fired his zeal along the road.

495.
Self-Denial.

1 If on our daily course our mind
   Be set, to hallow all we find,
   New treasures still, of countless price,
   God will provide for sacrifice.

2 Old friends, old scenes, will lovelier be,
   As more of heaven in each we see;
   Some softening gleam of love and prayer
   Shall dawn on every cross and care.

3 Oh! could we learn that sacrifice,
   What light would all around us rise!
   How would our hearts with wisdom talk,
   Along life's dullest, dreariest walk!

4 The trivial round, the common task,
   Will furnish all we ought to ask;—
   Room to deny ourselves, a road
   To bring us daily nearer God.

496.
Love.

1 Had I the tongues of Greeks and Jews,
   And nobler speech than angels use,
   If love be absent, I am found
   Like tinkling brass, an empty sound.

2 Were I inspired to preach and tell
   All that is done in heaven and hell—
   Or could my faith the world remove,
   Still I am nothing without love.

3 Should I distribute all my store
   To feed the hungry, clothe the poor;
   Or give my body to the flame,
   To gain a martyr's glorious name:

4 If love to God and love to men
   Be absent, all my hopes are vain;
   Nor tongues, nor gifts, nor fiery zeal,
   The work of love can e'er fulfill.

497.
Consistency.

1 So let our lips and lives express
   The holy gospel, we profess;
   So let our works and virtues shine,
   To prove the doctrine all-divine.

2 Thus shall we best proclaim abroad
   The honors of our Saviour God;
   When his salvation reigns within,
   And grace subdues the power of sin.

3 Religion bears our spirits up,
   While we expect that blessed hope,—
   The bright appearance of the Lord:
   And faith stands leaning on his word.

GRACES.

GRATITUDE. L. M. Bost.

1. My God, how end-less is thy love! Thy gifts are ev-ery eve-ning new;
And morn-ing mer-cies from a-bove, Gen-tly dis-till like ear-ly dew.

498.
Gratitude.

2 Thou spread'st the curtains of the night,
Great Guardian of my sleeping hours!
Thy sovereign word restores the light,
And quickens all my drowsy powers.

3 I yield my powers to thy command;
To thee I consecrate my days;
Perpetual blessings, from thy hand,
Demand perpetual songs of praise.

499.
Completeness.

1 COMPLETE in thee, no work of mine
May take, dear Lord, the place of thine;
Thy blood has pardon bought for me,
And I am now complete in thee.

2 Complete in thee—no more shall sin
Thy grace has conquered, reign within;
Thy voice will bid the tempter flee,
And I shall stand complete in thee.

3 Complete in thee—each want supplied,
And no good thing to me denied,
Since thou my portion, Lord, wilt be,
I ask no more—complete in thee.

4 Dear Saviour! when, before thy bar
All tribes and tongues assembled are,
Among thy chosen may I be
At thy right hand—complete in thee.

5 Complete in thee, forever blest,
Of all thy fullness, Lord, possessed,
Thy praise throughout eternity—
Thy love I 'll sing, complete in thee.

500.
Contentment.

1 O LORD, how full of sweet content
Our years of pilgrimage are spent!
Where'er we dwell, we dwell with thee,
In heaven, in earth, or on the sea.

2 To us remains nor place nor time;
Our country is in every clime:
We can be calm and free from care
On any shore, since God is there.

3 While place we seek, or place we shun,
The soul finds happiness in none;
But with our God to guide our way,
'T is equal joy to go or stay.

4 Could we be cast where thou art not,
That were indeed a dreadful lot;
But regions none remote we call,
Secure of finding God in all.

501.
Meekness.

1 HAPPY the meek whose gentle breast,
Clear as the summer's evening ray,
Calm as the regions of the blest,
Enjoys on earth celestial day.

2 His heart no broken friendships sting,
No storms his peaceful tent invade;
He rests beneath th' Almighty's wing,
Hostile to none, of none afraid.

3 Spirit of grace, all meek and mild!
Inspire our breasts, our souls possess:
Repel each passion rude and wild,
And bless us as we aim to bless.

162 CHRISTIAN.

VALENTIA. C. M. — Eberwein.

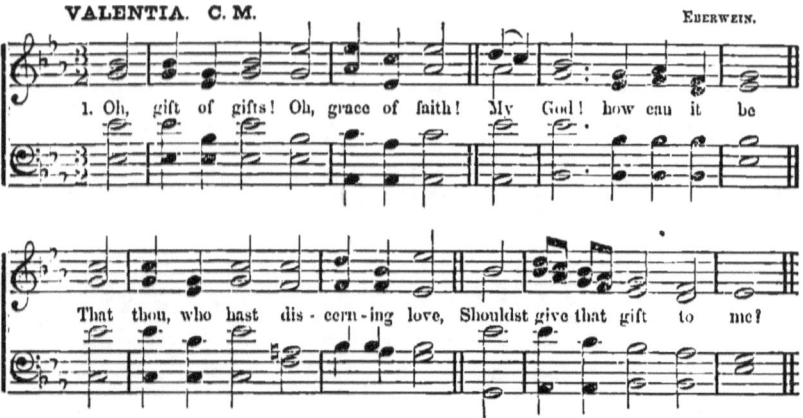

1. Oh, gift of gifts! Oh, grace of faith! My God! how can it be
That thou, who hast discerning love, Shouldst give that gift to me?

502.
Faith.

2 How many hearts thou mightst have had
More innocent than mine!
How many souls more worthy far
Of that sweet touch of thine!

3 Ah, grace! into unlikeliest hearts
It is thy boast to come,
The glory of thy light to find
In darkest spots a home.

4 The crowd of cares, the weightiest cross,
Seem trifles less than light—
Earth looks so little and so low
When faith shines full and bright.

5 Oh, happy, happy that I am!
If thou canst be, O faith,
The treasure that thou art in life,
What wilt thou be in death?

503.
Gentleness.

1 SPEAK gently—it is better far
To rule by love than fear;
Speak gently—let no harsh word mar
The good we may do here.

2 Speak gently to the young—for they
Will have enough to bear;
Pass through this life as best they may,
'T is full of anxious care.

3 Speak gently to the aged one,
Grieve not the careworn heart;
The sands of life are nearly run,
Let them in peace depart.

4 Speak gently to the erring ones—
They must have toiled in vain;
Perchance unkindness made them so;
Oh, win them back again!

5 Speak gently—'t is a little thing,
Dropped in the heart's deep well;
The good, the joy, that it may bring,
Eternity shall tell.

504.
Godly Sincerity.

1 WALK in the light! so shalt thou know
That fellowship of love,
His Spirit only can bestow,
Who reigns in light above.

2 Walk in the light! and thou shalt find
Thy heart made truly his,
Who dwells in cloudless light enshrined,
In whom no darkness is.

3 Walk in the light! and sin abhorred
Shall ne'er defile again;
The blood of Jesus Christ the Lord
Shall cleanse from every sin.

4 Walk in the light! and ev'n the tomb
No fearful shade shall wear;
Glory shall chase away its gloom,
For Christ hath conquered there.

5 Walk in the light! and thou shalt see
Thy path, though thorny, bright,
For God by grace shall dwell in thee,
And God himself is light.

GRACES. 163

NAOMI. C. M. — Dr. L. Mason.

1. Fa-ther! what-e'er of earth-ly bliss Thy sovereign will de-nies, Ac-cept-ed at thy throne of grace, Let this pe-ti-tion rise:—

505.
Devotion.

2 "Give me a calm, a thankful heart,
From every murmur free;
The blessings of thy grace impart,
And make me live to thee.

3 "Let the sweet hope that thou art mine
My life and death attend;
Thy presence through my journey shine,
And crown my journey's end."

506.
Calmness.

1 Calm me, my God, and keep me calm:
Let thine outstretched wing
Be like the shade of Elim's palm,
Beside her desert spring.

2 Yes, keep me calm, though loud and rude
The sounds my ear that greet,—
Calm in the closet's solitude,
Calm in the bustling street,—

3 Calm in the hour of buoyant health,
Calm in the hour of pain,
Calm in my poverty or wealth,
Calm in my loss or gain,—

4 Calm in the sufferance of wrong,
Like him who bore my shame,
Calm 'mid the threatening, taunting throng,
Who hate thy holy name.

5 Calm me, my God, and keep me calm,
Soft resting on thy breast;
Soothe me with holy hymn and psalm,
And bid my spirit rest.

507.
Charitableness.

1 Think gently of the erring one!
And let us not forget,
However darkly stained by sin,
He is our brother yet.

2 Heir of the same inheritance,
Child of the self-same God;
He hath but stumbled in the path,
We have in weakness trod.

3 Speak gently to the erring one:
Thou yet may'st lead him back,
With holy words, and tones of love,
From misery's thorny track.

4 Forget not thou hast often sinned,
And sinful yet must be:
Deal gently with the erring one,
As God has dealt with thee.

508.
Humility.

1 Is there ambition in my heart?
Search, gracious God, and see;
Or do I act a haughty part?
Lord, I appeal to thee.

2 I charge my thoughts, be humble still,
And all my carriage mild;
Content, my Father, with thy will,
And quiet as a child.

3 The patient soul, the lowly mind,
Shall have a large reward;
Let saints in sorrow lie resigned,
And trust a faithful Lord.

CHRISTIAN.

164

CAMBRIDGE. C. M.   Dr. Randall.

1. Glo-ry to God! whose witness-train, Those heroes bold in faith, Could smile on pov-er-ty and pain, And triumph ev'n in death, And triumph ev'n in death, And triumph ev'n in death.

509.
Martyr-Faith.

2 Oh! may that faith our hearts sustain,
  Wherein they fearless stood,
When, in the power of cruel men,
  They poured their willing blood.

3 God, whom we serve, our God, can save,
  Can damp the scorching flame,
Can build an ark, can smooth the wave,
  For such as love his name.

4 Lord! if thine arm support us still
  With its eternal strength,
We shall o'ercome the mightiest ill,
  And conquerors prove at length.

510.
Trust.

1 What though no flowers the fig-tree
    clothe,
  Though vines their fruit deny,
The labor of the olive fail,
  And fields no food supply;—

2 Though from the fold with sad surprise,
  My flock cut off I see;
Though famine pine in empty stalls,
  Where herds were wont to be;—

3 Yet in the Lord will I be glad,
  And glory in his love;
In him rejoice, who will the God
  Of my salvation prove.

4 God is the treasure of my soul,
  The source of lasting joy;
A joy, which want shall not impair,
  Nor death itself destroy.

511.
Submission.

1 O Lord! my best desires fulfil,
  And help me to resign
Life, health, and comfort to thy will,
  And make thy pleasure mine.

2 Why should I shrink at thy command,
  Thy love forbids my fears;
Why tremble at the gracious hand,
  That wipes away my tears?

3 No,—let me rather freely yield
  What most I prize, to thee;
Thou never hast a good withheld,
  Nor wilt withhold from me.

4 Thy favor, all my journey through,
  Shall be my rich supply;
What more I want, or think I do,
  Let wisdom still deny.

512.
Humility.

1 Thy home is with the humble, Lord!
  The simple are the best;
Thy lodging is in child-like hearts;
  Thou makest there thy rest.

2 Dear Comforter! eternal Love!
  If thou wilt stay with me,
Of lowly thoughts and simple ways
  I'll build a house for thee.

3 Who made this breathing heart of mine
  But thou, my heavenly Guest?
Let no one have it, then, but thee,
  And let it be thy rest!

GRACES.

MOUNT AUBURN. C. M. — Kingsley. — **165**

1. Happy the heart where graces reign, Where love inspires the breast; Love is the brightest of the train, And strengthens all the rest.

513.
Love.

2 Knowledge, alas! 't is all in vain,
And all in vain our fear;
Our stubborn sins will fight and reign,
If love be absent there.

3 This is the grace that lives and sings,
When faith and hope shall cease;
'T is this shall strike our joyful strings,
In the sweet realms of bliss.

4 Before we quite forsake our clay,
Or leave this dark abode,
The wings of love bear us away,
To see our smiling God.

514.
Faith.

1 Lord, I believe; thy power I own;
Thy word I would obey;
I wander comfortless and lone,
When from thy truth I stray.

2 Lord, I believe; but gloomy fears
Sometimes bedim my sight;
I look to thee with prayers and tears,
And cry for strength and light.

3 Lord, I believe; but oft, I know,
My faith is cold and weak:
My weakness strengthen, and bestow
The confidence I seek.

4 Yes! I believe; and only thou
Canst give my soul relief:
Lord, to thy truth my spirit bow;
"Help thou mine unbelief!"

515.
Sensibility.

1 And can mine eyes, without a tear,
A weeping Saviour see?
Shall I not weep his groans to hear
Who groaned and died for me?

2 Blest Jesus! let those tears of thine
Subdue each stubborn foe;
Come, fill my heart with love divine,
And bid my sorrows flow.

516.
Faith.

1 Faith adds new charms to earthly bliss,
And saves me from its snares;
Its aid, in every duty, brings,
And softens all my cares.

2 The wounded conscience knows its power
The healing balm to give;
That balm the saddest heart can cheer,
And make the dying live.

3 Wide it unvails celestial worlds,
Where deathless pleasures reign;
And bids me seek my portion there,
Nor bids me seek in vain.

4 It shows the precious promise sealed
With the Redeemer's blood;
And helps my feeble hope to rest
Upon a faithful God.

5 There—there unshaken would I rest,
Till this vile body dies;
And then, on faith's triumphant wings,
To endless glory rise.

CHRISTIAN.

TUCKER. S. M.   ABBEY.

1. Re-joice in God al-way; When earth looks heaven-ly bright, When joy makes glad the live-long day, And peace shuts in the night.

517.
Joy.

2 Rejoice when care and woe
   The fainting soul oppress;
When tears at wakeful midnight flow,
   And morn brings heaviness.

3 Rejoice in hope and fear;
   Rejoice in life and death;
Rejoice when threatening storms are near,
   And comfort languisheth.

4 When should not they rejoice,
   Whom Christ his brethren calls;
Who hear and know his guiding voice,
   When on their hearts it falls?

5 So, though our path is steep,
   And many a tempest lowers,
Shall his own peace our spirits keep,
   And Christ's dear love be ours.

518.
Self-Renunciation.

1 Man's wisdom is to seek
   His strength in God alone;
And ev'n an angel would be weak,
   Who trusted in his own.

2 Retreat beneath his wings,
   And in his grace confide;
This more exalts the King of kings,
   Than all your works beside.

3 In Jesus is our store;
   Grace issues from his throne;
Whoever says,—"I want no more,"
   Confesses he has none.

519.
Resignation.

1 Be tranquil, O my soul,
   Be quiet every fear!
Thy Father hath supreme control,
   And he is ever near.

2 Ne'er of thy lot complain,
   Whatever may befall;
Sickness or sorrow, care or pain,
   'T is well appointed all.

3 A Father's chastening hand
   Is leading thee along;
Nor distant is the promised land,
   Where swells th' immortal song.

4 Oh! then, my soul, be still!
   Await heaven's high decree;
Seek but to do thy Father's will,
   It shall be well with thee.

520.
Confidence.

1 In true and patient hope,
   My soul, on God attend;
And calmly, confidently look
   Till he salvation send.

2 I shall his goodness see,
   While on his name I call;
He will defend and strengthen me,
   And I shall never fall.

3 Jesus, to thee I fly,
   My refuge, and my tower;
Upon thy faithful love rely,
   And find thy saving power.

GRACES. 167

DENNIS. S. M. NAGELI.

1. If, through unruffled seas, Toward heaven we calmly sail, With grateful hearts, O God, to thee, We'll own the favoring gale.

521.
Faith in Trouble.

1 IF, through unruffled seas,
  Toward heaven we calmly sail,
  With grateful hearts, O God, to thee,
  We'll own the favoring gale.

2 But should the surges rise,
  And rest delay to come,
  Blest be the sorrow—kind the storm,
  Which drives us nearer home.

3 Soon shall our doubts and fears
  All yield to thy control:
  Thy tender mercies shall illume
  The midnight of the soul.

4 Teach us, in every state,
  To make thy will our own;
  And when the joys of sense depart,
  To live by faith alone.

522.
Devotion.

1 JESUS, my strength, my hope,
  On thee I cast my care,
  With humble confidence look up,
  And know thou hear'st my prayer.

2 Give me on thee to wait,
  Till I can all things do;
  On thee, almighty, to create,
  Almighty to renew.

3 I want a sober mind,
  A self-renouncing will,
  That tramples down, and casts behind
  The baits of pleasing ill;

4 A soul inured to pain,
  To hardship, grief and loss,
  Bold to take up, firm to sustain
  The consecrated cross;

5 I want a godly fear,
  A quick-discerning eye,
  That looks to thee when sin is near,
  And sees the tempter fly;

6 A spirit still prepared,
  And armed with jealous care,
  Forever standing on its guard,
  And watching unto prayer.

523.
Trust in God.

1 WHERE wilt thou put thy trust?
  In a frail form of clay,
  That to its element of dust
  Must soon resolve away?

2 Where wilt thou cast thy care?
  Upon an erring heart,
  Which hath its own sore ills to bear,
  And shrinks from sorrow's dart?

3 No,—place thy trust above
  This shadowy realm of night,
  In him, whose boundless power and love
  Thy confidence invite.

4 His mercies still endure
  When skies and stars grow dim,
  His changeless promise standeth sure,—
  Go,—cast thy care on him.

168 CHRISTIAN.

HENDON. 7s. Dr. Malan.

1. Christ, of all my hopes the Ground, Christ, the Spring of all my joy, Still in thee let me be found, Still for thee my powers em-ploy, Still for thee my powers employ.

524.
Living to Christ.

1 Christ, of all my hopes the Ground,
  Christ, the Spring of all my joy,
Still in thee let me be found,
  Still for thee my powers employ.

2 Fountain of o'erflowing grace!
  Freely from thy fullness give;
Till I close my earthly race,
  Be it "Christ for me to live!"

3 Firmly trusting in thy blood,
  Nothing shall my heart confound;
Safely I shall pass the flood,
  Safely reach Immanuel's ground.

4 When I touch the blessed shore,
  Back the closing waves shall roll!
Death's dark stream shall nevermore
  Part from thee my ravished soul.

5 Thus,—oh, thus an entrance give
  To the land of cloudless sky;
Having known it, "Christ to live,"
  Let me know it "gain to die."

525.
Likeness to Christ.

1 Father of eternal grace!
  Glorify thyself in me;
Meekly beaming in my face,
  May the world thine image see.

2 Happy only in thy love,
  Poor, unfriended, or unknown;
Fix my thoughts on things above,—
  Stay my heart on thee alone.

3 Humble, holy, all-resigned
  To thy will:—thy will be done!
Give me, Lord! the perfect mind
  Of thy well-beloved Son.

4 Counting gain and glory loss,
  May I tread the path he trod;
Die with Jesus on the cross,—
  Rise with him, to thee, my God!

526.
Rejoicing.

1 Joyful be the hours to-day;
  Joyful let the season be;
Let us sing, for well we may:
  Jesus! we will sing of thee.

2 Should thy people silent be,
  Then the very stones would sing:
What a debt we owe to thee,
  Thee, our Saviour, thee, our King!

3 Joyful are we now to own,
  Rapture thrills us as we trace
All the deeds thy love hath done,
  All the riches of thy grace.

4 'Tis thy grace alone can save;
  Every blessing comes from thee—
All we have and hope to have,
  All we are and hope to be.

5 Thine the name to sinners dear!
  Thine the Name all names before!
Blessèd here and everywhere;
  Blessèd now and evermore!

GRACES. 169

KARL. 7s, or 8s & 7s. WEBB.

1. Lord, for-ev-er at thy side Let my place and por-tion be;
Strip me of the robe of pride, Clothe me with hu-mil-i-ty.

527.
Humility.

1 Lord, forever at thy side
  Let my place and portion be;
  Strip me of the robe of pride;
  Clothe me with humility.

2 Meekly may my soul receive
  All thy Spirit hath revealed;
  Thou hast spoken; I believe,
  Though the oracle be sealed.

3 Humble as a little child,
  Weaned from the mother's breast,
  By no subtleties beguiled,
  On thy faithful word I rest.

4 Israel, now and evermore
  In the Lord Jehovah trust;
  Him in all his ways adore,
  Wise, and powerful, and just.

528.
Consistency.

1 Jesus, Lord, we look to thee;
  Let us in thy name agree;
  Show thyself the Prince of Peace;
  Bid our jars forever cease.

2 By thy reconciling love,
  Every stumbling-block remove:
  Each to each unite, endear;
  Come, and spread thy banner here.

3 Make us of one heart and mind—
  Courteous, pitiful, and kind;
  Lowly, meek, in thought and word—
  Altogether like our Lord.

4 Let us for each other care;
  Each the other's burden bear;
  To thy church the pattern give;
  Show how true believers live.

5 Free from anger and from pride,
  Let us thus in God abide;
  All the depths of love express—
  All the heights of holiness.

6 Let us then with joy remove
  To the family above;
  On the wings of angels fly;
  Show how true believers die.

529.
Humility.

1 Lord, if thou thy grace impart,
  Poor in spirit, meek in heart,
  I shall as my Master be,
  Rooted in humility;

2 Simple, teachable, and mild,
  Changed into a little child;
  Pleased with all the Lord provides,
  Weaned from all the world besides.

3 Father, fix my soul on thee;
  Every evil let me flee;
  Nothing want, beneath, above,
  Happy in thy precious love.

4 Oh, that all may seek and find
  Every good in Jesus joined!
  Him let Israel still adore,
  Trust him, praise him evermore.

CHRISTIAN.

BLENDON. L. M.   GIARDINI.

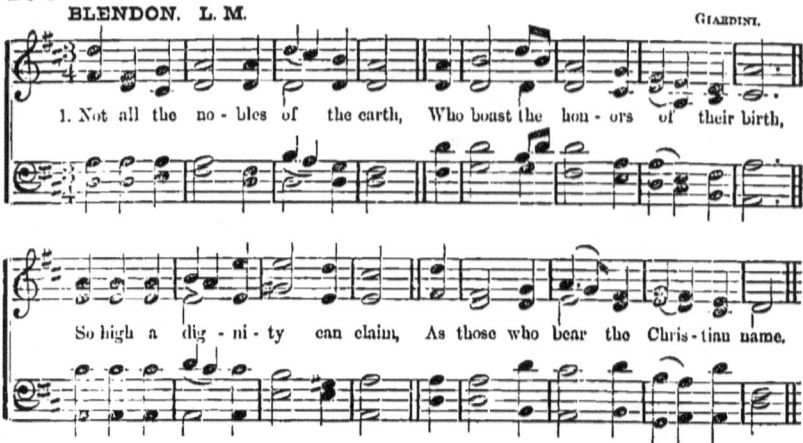

1. Not all the nobles of the earth, Who boast the honors of their birth, So high a dignity can claim, As those who bear the Christian name.

530.
Adoption.

1 Not all the nobles of the earth,
Who boast the honors of their birth,
So high a dignity can claim,
As those who bear the Christian name.

2 To them the privilege is given
To be the sons and heirs of heaven;
Sons of the God who reigns on high,
And heirs of joy beyond the sky.

3 His will he makes them early know,
And teaches their young feet to go;
Whispers instruction to their minds,
And on their hearts his precepts binds.

4 Their daily wants his hands supply,
Their steps he guards with watchful eye;
Leads them from earth to heaven above,
And crowns them with eternal love.

531.
Perseverance.

1 Who shall the Lord's elect condemn?
'T is God that justifies their souls;
And mercy, like a mighty stream,
O'er all their sins divinely rolls.

2 Who shall adjudge the saints to hell?
'T is Christ that suffered in their stead;
And their salvation to fulfill,
Behold him rising from the dead!

3 He lives, he lives, and sits above,
Forever interceding there:
Who shall divide us from his love,
Or what shall tempt us to despair?

4 Shall persecution, or distress,
Famine, or sword, or nakedness?
He who hath loved us bears us through,
And makes us more than conquerors too!

5 Not all that men on earth can do,
Nor powers on high, nor powers below,
Shall cause his mercy to remove,
Or wean our hearts from Christ, our love.

532.
Security.

1 Lord, how secure and blest are they,
Who feel the joys of pardoned sin!
Should storms of wrath shake earth and sea,
Their minds have heaven and peace within.

2 The day glides swiftly o'er their heads,
Made up of innocence and love;
And soft and silent as the shades,
Their nightly minutes gently move.

3 Quick as their thoughts their joys come on,
But fly not half so swift away;
Their souls are ever bright as noon,
And calm as summer evenings be.

4 How oft they look to heavenly hills,
Where streams of living pleasures flow;
And longing hopes and cheerful smiles
Sit undisturbed upon their brow!

5 They scorn to seek earth's golden toys,
But spend the day, and share the night,
In numbering o'er the richer joys
That heaven prepares for their delight.

PRIVILEGES. 171

SMITH. L. M. *Arranged by* KINGSLEY.

1. Now to the power of God supreme Be ev-er-last-ing hon-ors given; He saves from hell—we bless his name,— He calls our wandering feet to heaven.

533.
Grace.

2 Not for our duties or deserts,
But of his own abounding grace,
He works salvation in our hearts,
And forms a people for his praise.

3 'T was his own purpose that begun
To rescue rebels doomed to die :
He gave us grace in Christ, his Son,
Before he spread the starry sky.

4 Jesus, the Lord, appears at last,
And makes his Father's counsels known;
Declares the great transactions past,
And brings immortal blessings down.

5 He died; and in that dreadful night
Did all the powers of hell destroy;
Rising he brought our heaven to light,
And took possession of the joy.

534.
Grace sufficient.

1 Let me but hear my Saviour say,
"Strength shall be equal to thy day;"
Then I rejoice in deep distress,
Leaning on all-sufficient grace.

2 I can do all things—or can bear
All suffering, if my Lord be there ;
Sweet pleasures mingle with the pains,
While he my sinking head sustains.

3 I glory in infirmity,
That Christ's own power can rest on me ;
When I am weak, then am I strong;
Grace is my shield, and Christ my song.

535.
Grace.

1 No more, ye wise ! your wisdom boast;
No more, ye strong ! your valor trust ;
No more, ye rich ! survey your store,
Elate with heaps of shining ore.

2 Glory, ye saints, in this alone,—
That God, your God, to you is known ;
That you have owned his sovereign sway,—
That you have felt his cheering ray.

3 All else, which we our treasure call,
May in one fatal moment fall ;
But what their happiness can move,
Whom God, the blessed, deigns to love?

536.
Resort to Christ.

1 Away from earth my spirit turns,
Away from every transient good ;
With strong desire my bosom burns,
To feast on heaven's immortal food.

2 Thou, Saviour, art the living bread ;
Thou wilt my every want supply :
By thee sustained, and cheered, and led,
I 'll press through dangers to the sky.

3 What though temptations oft distress,
And sin assails and breaks my peace ;
Thou wilt uphold, and save, and bless,
And bid the storms of passion cease.

4 Then let me take thy gracious hand,
And walk beside thee onward still ;
Till my glad feet shall safely stand,
Forever firm on Zion's hill.

172 CHRISTIAN.

BROWN. C. M.   Wm. B. Bradbury.

1. Now let our cheer-ful eyes sur-vey Our great High Priest a-bove, And cel-e-brate his con-stant care, And sym-pa-thet-ic love.

537.
Perseverance.

2 Though raised to a superior throne,
  Where angels bow around,
And high o'er all the shining train,
  With matchless honors crowned;—

3 The names of all his saints he bears
  Engraven on his heart;
Nor shall a name once treasured there
  E'er from his care depart.

4 Those characters shall fair abide,
  Our everlasting trust,
When gems, and monuments, and crowns
  Are mouldered down to dust.

5 So, gracious Saviour! on my breast,
  May thy dear name be worn,
A sacred ornament and guard,
  To endless ages borne.

538.
God's Peace.

1 We bless thee for thy peace, O God!
  Deep as the soundless sea,
Which falls like sunshine on the road
  Of those who trust in thee.

2 We ask not, Father, for repose
  Which comes from outward rest,
If we may have through all life's woes
  Thy peace within our breast;—

3 That peace which suffers and is strong,
  Trusts where it cannot see,
Deems not the trial way too long,
  But leaves the end with thee;—

4 That peace which, though the billows surge,
  And angry tempests roar,
Rings forth no melancholy dirge,
  But joyeth evermore;—

5 That peace which flows serene and deep—
  A river in the soul,
Whose banks a living verdure keep:
  God's sunshine o'er the whole!—

6 Such, Father, give our hearts such peace,
  Whate'er the outward be,
Till all life's discipline shall cease,
  And we go home to thee.

539.
"All things are yours."

1 If God is mine, then present things
  And things to come are mine;
Yea, Christ, his word, and Spirit too,
  And glory all divine.

2 If he is mine, then from his love
  He every trouble sends;
All things are working for my good,
  And bliss his rod attends.

3 If he is mine, let friends forsake,
  Let wealth and honor flee;
Sure he who giveth me himself
  Is more than these to me.

4 Oh! tell me, Lord, that thou art mine;
  What can I wish beside?
My soul shall at the fountain live,
  When all the streams are dried.

PRIVILEGES. 173

BRIDGMAN. C. M.   *Arranged from* BEETHOVEN.

1. O God of Beth - el! by whose hand Thy peo - ple still are fed;
Who through this wea - ry pil - grim - age Hast all our fa - thers led;

540.
Divine Guidance.

2 Our vows, our prayers, we now present
Before thy throne of grace;
God of our fathers! be the God
Of their succeeding race.

3 Through each perplexing path of life
Our wandering footsteps guide;
Give us, each day, our daily bread,
And raiment fit provide.

4 Oh, spread thy covering wings around,
Till all our wanderings cease,
And at our Father's loved abode,
Our souls arrive in peace.

5 Such blessings from thy gracious hand
Our humble prayers implore;
And thou shalt be our chosen God,
Our portion evermore.

541.
Adoption.

1 My Father, God! how sweet the sound,
How tender and how dear!
Not all the melody of heaven
Could so delight the ear.

2 Come, sacred Spirit, seal the name
On my expanding heart;
And show, that in Jehovah's grace
I share a filial part.

3 Cheered by a signal so divine,
Unwavering I believe;
My spirit Abba, Father, cries,
Nor can the sign deceive.

542.
Perseverance.

1 Firm as the earth thy gospel stands,
My Lord, my hope, my trust;
If I am found in Jesus' hands,
My soul can ne'er be lost.

2 His honor is engaged to save
The meanest of his sheep;
All, whom his heavenly Father gave,
His hands securely keep.

3 Nor death nor hell shall e'er remove
His favorites from his breast;
In the dear bosom of his love
They must forever rest.

543.
Adoption.

1 My God, my Father, blissful name!
Oh, may I call thee mine?
May I with sweet assurance claim
A portion so divine?

2 Whate'er thy providence denies
I calmly would resign,
For thou art good and just and wise:
Oh, bend my will to thine!

3 Whate'er thy sacred will ordains,
Oh, give me strength to bear!
And let me know my Father reigns,
And trust his tender care.

4 Thy sovereign ways are all unknown
To my weak, erring sight;
Yet let my soul adoring own
That all thy ways are right.

174 CHRISTIAN.

THATCHER. S. M. HANDEL.

1. Thou very present aid In suffering and distress, The mind which still on thee is stayed, Is kept in perfect peace.

544.
Rest in God.

1 Thou very present aid
In suffering and distress,
The mind which still on thee is stayed,
Is kept in perfect peace.
2 The soul by faith reclined
On the Redeemer's breast;
'Mid raging storms, exults to find
An everlasting rest.
3 Sorrow and fear are gone,
Whene'er thy face appears;
It stills the sighing orphan's moan,
And dries the widow's tears.
4 It hallows every cross;
It sweetly comforts me;
Makes me forget my every loss,
And find my all in thee.
5 Jesus, to whom I fly,
Doth all my wishes fill;
What though created streams are dry?
I have the fountain still.
6 Stripped of each earthly friend,
I find them all in one,
And peace and joy which never end,
And heaven, in Christ, begun.

545.
Love of God.

1 In every trying hour
My soul to Jesus flies;
I trust in his almighty power,
When swelling billows rise.

2 His comforts bear me up;
I trust a faithful God;
The sure foundation of my hope
Is in my Saviour's blood.
3 Loud hallelujahs sing
To our Redeemer's name;
In joy or sorrow—life or death—
His love is still the same.

546.
Kept of God.

1 What cheering words are these;
Their sweetness who can tell?
In time and to eternal days,
"'T is with the righteous well."
2 In every state secure,
Kept as Jehovah's eye,
'T is well with them while life endures,
And well when called to die.
3 Well when they see his face,
Or sink amidst the flood;
Well in affliction's thorny maze,
Or on the mount with God.
4 'T is well when joys arise,
'T is well when sorrows flow,
'T is well when darkness vails the skies,
And strong temptations grow.
5 'T is well when Jesus calls,
"From earth and sin arise,
To join the hosts of ransomed souls,
Made to salvation wise!"

PRIVILEGES.

SILVER STREET. S. M.   I. SMITH.

1. Here I can firm-ly rest; I dare to boast of this,
That God, the high-est and the best, My Friend and Fa-ther is.

547.
Adoption.

2 Naught have I of my own,
  Naught in the life I lead;
  What Christ hath given, that alone
  Is worth all love indeed.

3 I rest upon the ground
  Of Jesus and his blood;
  It is through him that I have found
  My soul's eternal good.

4 At cost of all I have,
  At cost of life and limb,
  I cling to God who yet shall save;—
  I will not turn from him.

5 His Spirit in me dwells,
  O'er all my mind he reigns;
  My care and sadness he dispels,
  And soothes away my pains.

6 He prospers day by day
  His work within my heart,
  Till I have strength and faith to say,
  Thou, God, my Father art!

548.
Grace.

1 GRACE! 't is a charming sound!
  Harmonious to the ear!
  Heaven with the echo shall resound,
  And all the earth shall hear.

2 Grace first contrived a way
  To save rebellious man;
  And all the steps that grace display,
  Which drew the wondrous plan.

3 Grace led my roving feet
  To tread the heavenly road;
  And new supplies each hour I meet
  While pressing on to God.

4 Grace all the work shall crown,
  Through everlasting days;
  It lays in heaven the topmost stone,
  And well deserves the praise.

549.
Adoption.

1 BEHOLD what wondrous grace
  The Father has bestowed
  On sinners of a mortal race,
  To call them sons of God!

2 Nor doth it yet appear
  How great we must be made;
  But when we see our Saviour here,
  We shall be like our head.

3 A hope so much divine
  May trials well endure,
  May purge our souls from sense and sin,
  As Christ the Lord is pure.

4 If in my Father's love
  I share a filial part,
  Send down thy Spirit, like a dove,
  To rest upon my heart.

5 We would no longer lie
  Like slaves beneath the throne;
  Our faith shall Abba, Father! cry,
  And thou the kindred own.

176 CHRISTIAN.

BISHOP. L. M. Don José.

1. Go, labor on; spend and be spent.—Thy joy to do the Father's will:
It is the way the Master went; Should not the servant tread it still?

550.
Zeal.

2 Go, labor on; 't is not for naught;
Thine earthly loss is heavenly gain:
Men heed thee, love thee, praise thee not;
The Master praises,—what are men?

3 Go, labor on; enough, while here,
If he shall praise thee, if he deign
Thy willing heart to mark and cheer:
No toil for him shall be in vain.

4 Toil on, and in thy toil rejoice;
For toil comes rest, for exile home;
Soon shalt thou hear the Bridegroom's voice,
The midnight peal: " Behold, I come!"

551.
Liberality.

1 When Jesus dwelt in mortal clay,
What were his works from day to day,
But miracles of power and grace,
That spread salvation through our race?

2 Teach us, O Lord, to keep in view
Thy pattern, and thy steps pursue;
Let alms bestowed, let kindness done,
Be witnessed by each rolling sun.

3 That man may last, but never lives,
Who much receives, but nothing gives;
Whom none can love, whom none can thank,
Creation's blot, creation's blank!

4 But he who marks, from day to day,
In generous acts his radiant way,
Treads the same path his Saviour trod,
The path to glory and to God.

552.
Zeal.

1 Go, labor on, while it is day;
The world's dark night is hastening on:
Speed, speed thy work,—cast sloth away!
It is not thus that souls are won.

2 Men die in darkness at your side,
Without a hope to cheer the tomb:
Take up the torch and wave it wide—
The torch that lights time's thickest gloom.

3 Toil on,—faint not; keep watch and pray!
Be wise the erring soul to win;
Go forth into the world's highway;
Compel the wanderer to come in.

4 Go, labor on; your hands are weak;
Your knees are faint, your soul cast down;
Yet falter not; the prize you seek
Is near,—a kingdom and a crown!

553.
The Poor.

1 Thou God of hope, to thee we bow!
Thou art our refuge in distress;
The Husband of the widow thou,
The Father of the fatherless.

2 The poor are thy peculiar care;
To them thy promises are sure:
Thy gifts the poor in spirit share;
Oh! may we always thus be poor!

3 May we thy law of love fulfill,
To bear each other's burdens here,
Endure and do thy righteous will,
And walk in all thy faith and fear.

DUTIES. 177

REMSEN. C. M.   J. P. HOLBROOK.

1. Father of mercies, send thy grace, All powerful from above,
To form, in our obedient souls, The image of thy love.

554.
Brotherly Kindness.

1 Father of mercies! send thy grace,
All powerful from above,
To form, in our obedient souls,
The image of thy love.

2 Oh, may our sympathizing breasts
The generous pleasure know,
Kindly to share in others' joy,
And weep for others' woe!

3 When the most helpless sons of grief
In low distress are laid,
Soft be our hearts their pains to feel,
And swift our hands to aid.

4 So Jesus looked on dying men,
When throned above the skies;
And mid th' embraces of his God,
He felt compassion rise.

5 On wings of love the Saviour flew,
To raise us from the ground,
And made the richest of his blood,
A balm for every wound.

555.
Charity.

1 Blest is the man whose softening heart
Feels all another's pain;
To whom the supplicating eye
Was never raised in vain:—

2 Whose breast expands with generous warmth,
A stranger's woes to feel;
And bleeds in pity o'er the wound
He wants the power to heal.

3 He spreads his kind, supporting arms,
To every child of grief;
His secret bounty largely flows,
And brings unasked relief.

4 To gentle offices of love
His feet are never slow:
He views, through mercy's melting eye,
A brother in a foe.

5 Peace from the bosom of his God,
The Saviour's grace shall give;
And when he kneels before the throne,
His trembling soul shall live.

556.
Trivial Efforts.

1 Scorn not the slightest word or deed,
Nor deem it void of power;
There's fruit in each wind-wafted seed,
That waits its natal hour.

2 A whispered word may touch the heart,
And call it back to life;
A look of love bid sin depart,
And still unholy strife.

3 No act falls fruitless; none can tell
How vast its power may be,
Nor what results infolded dwell
Within it silently.

4 Work on, despair not, bring thy mite,
Nor care how small it be;
God is with all that serve the right,
The holy, true, and free.

CHRISTIAN.

557.
Watchfulness.

1 My soul, be on thy guard,
  Ten thousand foes arise;
  And hosts of sin are pressing hard
  To draw thee from the skies.

2 Oh, watch, and fight, and pray!
  The battle ne'er give o'er;
  Renew it boldly every day,
  And help divine implore.

3 Ne'er think the victory won,
  Nor once at ease sit down;
  Thy arduous work will not be done
  Till thou obtain thy crown.

4 Fight on, my soul, till death
  Shall bring thee to thy God!
  He'll take thee at thy parting breath,
  Up to his blest abode.

558.
Seed-Sowing.

1 Sow in the morn thy seed;
  At eve hold not thy hand;
  To doubt and fear give thou no heed;
  Broadcast it o'er the land!

2 Beside all waters sow,
  The highway furrows stock,
  Drop it where thorns and thistles grow,
  Scatter it on the rock.

3 The good, the fruitful ground
  Expect not here nor there;
  O'er hill and dale by plots 't is found;
  Go forth, then, everywhere.

4 And duly shall appear,
  In verdure, beauty, strength,
  The tender blade, the stalk, the ear,
  And the full corn at length.

5 Thou canst not toil in vain;
  Cold, heat and moist, and dry,
  Shall foster and mature the grain
  For garners in the sky.

6 Then, when the glorious end,
  The day of God shall come,
  The angel-reapers shall descend,
  And heaven cry, "Harvest home!"

559.
Energy of Zeal.

1 Make haste, O man, to live,
  For thou so soon must die;
  Time hurries past thee like the breeze;
  How swift its moments fly!

2 To breathe, and wake, and sleep,
  To smile, to sigh, to grieve,
  To move in idleness through earth—
  This, this is not to live.

3 Make haste, O man, to do
  Whatever must be done;
  Thou hast no time to lose in sloth,
  Thy day will soon be gone.

4 Up, then, with speed, and work;
  Fling ease and self away—
  This is no time for thee to sleep—
  Up, watch, and work and pray!

DUTIES.

LEIGHTON. S. M. GREATOREX COLL.

1. La-borers of Christ, a-rise, And gird you for the toil!
The dew of prom-ise from the skies Al-rea-dy cheers the soil.

560.
Active Effort.

1 LABORERS of Christ, arise,
  And gird you for the toil!
The dew of promise from the skies
  Already cheers the soil.

2 Go where the sick recline,
  Where mourning hearts deplore;
And where the sons of sorrow pine,
  Dispense your hallowed lore.

3 Be faith, which looks above,
  With prayer, your constant guest;
And wrap the Saviour's changeless love
  A mantle round your breast.

4 So shall you share the wealth
  That earth may ne'er despoil,
And the blest gospel's saving health
  Repay your arduous toil.

561.
Waiting.

1 MINE eyes and my desire
  Are ever to the Lord;
I love to plead his promises,
  And rest upon his word.

2 Lord, turn thee to my soul;
  Bring thy salvation near;
When will thy hand release my feet
  From sin's destructive snare?

3 When shall the sovereign grace
  Of my forgiving God
Restore me from those dangerous ways
  My wandering feet have trod?

4 Oh, keep my soul from death,
  Nor put my hope to shame!
For I have placed my only trust
  In my Redeemer's name.

5 With humble faith I wait
  To see thy face again;
Of Israel it shall ne'er be said,
  He sought the Lord in vain.

562.
Reform.

1 MOURN for the thousands slain,
  The youthful and the strong;
Mourn for the wine-cup's fearful reign,
  And the deluded throng.

2 Mourn for the tarnished gem—
  For reason's light divine,
Quenched from the soul's bright diadem,
  Where God had bid it shine.

3 Mourn for the ruined soul—
  Eternal life and light
Lost by the fiery, maddening bowl,
  And turned to helpless night.

4 Mourn for the lost—but call,
  Call to the strong, the free;
Rouse them to shun that dreadful fall;
  And to the refuge flee.

5 Mourn for the lost—but pray,
  Pray to our God above,
To break the fell destroyer's sway,
  And show his saving love.

180   CHRISTIAN.

STOCKWELL. 8s & 7s.   D. E. Jones.

1. He that goeth forth with weeping,
Bearing precious seed in love,
Never tiring, never sleeping,
Findeth mercy from above.

563.
Work Encouraged.

2 Soft descend the dews of heaven,
  Bright the rays celestial shine;
Precious fruits will thus be given,
  Through an influence all divine.

3 Sow thy seed, be never weary,
  Let no fears thy soul annoy;
Be the prospect ne'er so dreary,
  Thou shalt reap the fruits of joy.

4 Lo, the scene of verdure brightening!
  See the rising grain appear;
Look, again! the fields are whitening,
  For the harvest time is near.

564.
Success from God.

1 Vainly through night's weary hours,
  Keep we watch, lest foes alarm;—
Vain our bulwarks, and our towers,
  But for God's protecting arm.

2 Vain were all our toil and labor,
  Did not God that labor bless;
Vain, without his grace and favor,
  Every talent we possess.

3 Vainer still the hope of heaven,
  That on human strength relies;
But to him shall help be given,
  Who in humble faith applies.

4 Seek we, then, the Lord's Anointed;
  He shall grant us peace and rest:
Ne'er was suppliant disappointed,
  Who to Christ his prayer addressed.

565.
Self-Denial.

1 Pilgrims in this vale of sorrow,
  Pressing onward toward the prize,
Strength and comfort here we borrow
  From the Hand that rules the skies.

2 'Mid these scenes of self-denial,
  We are called the race to run;
We must meet full many a trial
  Ere the victor's crown is won.

3 Love shall every conflict lighten,
  Hope shall urge us swifter on,
Faith shall every prospect brighten,
  Till the morn of heaven shall dawn.

4 On th' Eternal arm reclining,
  We at length shall win the day;
All the powers of earth combining,
  Shall not snatch our crown away.

566.
Progress.

1 Like the eagle, upward, onward,
  Let my soul in faith be borne;
Calmly gazing, skyward, sunward,
  Let my eye unshrinking turn!

2 Where the cross, God's love revealing,
  Sets the fettered spirit free,
Where it sheds its wondrous healing,
  There, my soul, thy rest shall be!

3 Oh, may I no longer dreaming,
  Idly waste my golden day,
But, each precious hour redeeming,
  Upward, onward press my way!

DUTIES.   181

SOLNEY. 8s & 7s.   SHULZ.

1. Cast thy bread up-on the wa-ters, Think-ing not 'tis thrown a-way;
God him-self saith, thou shalt gath-er It a-gain some fu-ture day.

567.
Benevolent Efforts.

1 Cast thy bread upon the waters,
Thinking not 't is thrown away;
God himself saith, thou shalt gather
It again some future day.

2 Cast thy bread upon the waters;
Wildly though the billows roll,
They but aid thee as thou toilest
Truth to spread from pole to pole.

3 As the seed, by billows floated,
To some distant island lone,
So to human souls benighted,
That thou flingest may be borne.

4 Cast thy bread upon the waters;
Why wilt thou still doubting stand?
Bounteous shall God send the harvest,
If thou sow'st with liberal hand.

5 Give then freely of thy substance—
O'er this cause the Lord doth reign;
Cast thy bread, and toil with patience,
Thou shalt labor not in vain.

568.
" Brother's Keeper."

1 Blessed angels, high in heaven
O'er the penitent rejoice;
Hast thou for thy brother striven
With an importuning voice?

2 Art thou not thy brother's keeper?
Canst thou not his soul obtain?
He that wakes his brother sleeper
Double light himself shall gain.

3 Ah! how many may be given
To that during, fiery lake,
Who had found a place in heaven
Had'st thou toiled for Jesus' sake.

4 Think how words in season spoken,
In the sinful heart sink deep,
And the first link may have broken
Of the chains that round him creep.

5 Think of *that* day when each brother
To his brother shall be known:
If thy prayers have saved another,
God will then thy service own.

6 Then, when ends this life's short fever,
They, who many turn to God,
Like the stars shall shine for ever,
In th' eternal brotherhood!

569.
Contribution.

1 With my substance I will honor
My Redeemer and my Lord;
Were ten thousand worlds my manor,
All were nothing to his word.

2 While the heralds of salvation
His abounding grace proclaim,
Let his friends, of every station,
Gladly join to spread his fame.

3 Be his kingdom now promoted,
Let the earth her Monarch know;
Be my all to him devoted:
To my Lord my all I owe.

CHRISTIAN.

WOODWORTH. L. M.   Wm. B. Bradbury.

1. My God, my Father, while I stray Far from my home on life's rough way, Oh! teach me from my heart to say, "Thy will be done, thy will be done."

570.

1 My God, my Father, while I stray
Far from my home, on life's rough way,
Oh, teach me from my heart to say,
"Thy will be done, thy will be done!"

2 What though in lonely grief I sigh
For friends beloved no longer nigh;
Submissive still would I reply,
"Thy will be done, thy will be done!"

3 If thou should'st call me to resign
What most I prize,—it ne'er was mine;
I only yield thee what was thine:
"Thy will be done, thy will be done!"

4 If but my fainting heart be blest
With thy sweet Spirit for its guest,
My God, to thee I leave the rest;
"Thy will be done, thy will be done!"

5 Renew my will from day to day;
Blend it with thine, and take away
Whate'er now makes it hard to say,
"Thy will be done, thy will be done!"

6 Then when on earth I breathe no more,
The prayer oft mixed with tears before
I'll sing upon a happier shore:
"Thy will be done, thy will be done!"

571.

1 I bless thee, Lord, for sorrows sent
To break the dream of human power,
For now my shallow cistern's spent,
I find thy fount and thirst no more.

2 I take thy hand and fears grow still;
Behold thy face, and doubts remove:
Who would not yield his wavering will
To perfect truth and boundless love!

3 That truth gives promise of a dawn,
Beneath whose light I am to see,
When all these blinding vails are drawn,
This was the wisest path for me.

4 That love this restless soul doth teach
The strength of thy eternal calm;
And tune its sad and broken speech,
To sing ev'n now the angels' psalm.

572.

1 I cannot always trace the way
Where thou, Almighty One, dost move;
But I can always, always say,
That God is love, that God is love.

2 When fear her chilling mantle throws
O'er earth, my soul to heaven above,
As to her native home, upsprings,
For God is love, for God is love.

3 When mystery clouds my darkened path,
I'll check my dread, my doubts reprove,
In this my soul sweet comfort hath,
That God is love, that God is love.

4 Yes, God is love;—a thought like this
Can every gloomy thought remove,
And turn all tears, all woes, to bliss,
For God is love, for God is love.

AFFLICTIONS. 183

BEETHOVEN. L. M.   HAYDN.

1. Oh, deem not they are blest a-lone, Whose lives a peace-ful ten-or keep;
For God, who pit-ies man, hath shown A bless-ing for the eyes that weep.

573.

1 Oh, deem not they are blest alone,
Whose lives a peaceful tenor keep ;
For God, who pities man, hath shown
A blessing for the eyes that weep.

2 The light of smiles shall fill again
The lids that overflow with tears ;
And weary hours of woe and pain
Are promises of happier years.

3 There is a day of sunny rest
For every dark and troubled night ;
And grief may bide an evening guest,
But joy shall come with early light.

4 Nor let the good man's trust depart,
Though life its common gifts deny ;
Though with a pierced and broken heart,
And spurned of men, he goes to die.

5 For God has marked each sorrowing day,
And numbered every secret tear,
And heaven's long age of bliss shall pay
For all his children suffer here.

574.

1 Thy will be done ! I will not fear
The fate provided by thy love ;
Tho' clouds and darkness shroud me here,
I know that all is bright above.

2 The stars of heaven are shining on,
Tho' these frail eyes are dimmed with tears,
The hopes of earth indeed are gone,
But are not ours the immortal years ?

3 Father ! forgive the heart that clings,
Thus trembling, to the things of time ;
And bid my soul, on angel wings,
Ascend into a purer clime.

4 There shall no doubts disturb its trust,
No sorrows dim celestial love ;
But these afflictions of the dust,
Like shadows of the night, remove.

5 Ev'n now, above, there's radiant day,
While clouds and darkness brood below ;
Then, Father, joyful on my way
To drink the bitter cup I go.

575.

1 If life in sorrow must be spent,
So be it ; I am well content ;
And meekly wait my last remove,
Desiring only trustful love.

2 No bliss I'll seek, but to fulfill
In life, in death, thy perfect will ;
No succors in my woes I want,
But what my Lord is pleased to grant.

3 Our days are numbered : let us spare
Our anxious hearts a needless care ;
'T is thine to number out our days ;
'T is ours to give them to thy praise.

4 Faith is our only business here—
Faith simple, constant, and sincere ;
Oh, blessed days thy servants see !
Thus spent, O Lord ! in pleasing thee.

SILOAM. C. M.   I. B. Woodbury.

1. When musing sorrow weeps the past, And mourns the present pain, 'Tis sweet to think of peace at last, And feel that death is gain.

576.

2 'Tis not that murmuring thoughts arise,
  And dread a Father's will;
  'Tis not that meek submission flies,
  And would not suffer still.

3 It is that heaven-born faith surveys
  The path that leads to light,
  And longs her eagle plumes to raise,
  And lose herself in sight.

4 Oh! let me wing my hallowed flight
  From earth-born woe and care,
  And soar above these clouds of night,
  My Saviour's bliss to share.

577.

1 It is the Lord—enthroned in light,
  Whose claims are all divine,
  Who has an undisputed right
  To govern me and mine.

2 It is the Lord—who gives me all—
  My wealth, my friends, my ease;
  And of his bounties may recall
  Whatever part he please.

3 It is the Lord—my covenant God,
  Thrice blessed be his name;
  Whose gracious promise, sealed with blood,
  Must ever be the same.

4 Can I, with hopes so firmly built,
  Be sullen, or repine?
  No—gracious God—take what thou wilt,
  To thee I all resign.

578.

1 I cannot call affliction sweet;
  And yet 't was good to bear:
  Affliction brought me to thy feet,
  And I found comfort there.

2 My wearied soul was all resigned
  To thy most gracious will:
  Oh, had I kept that better mind,
  Or been afflicted still!

3 Where are the vows which then I vowed?
  The joys which then I knew?
  Those, vanished like the morning cloud;
  These, like the early dew.

4 Lord, grant me grace for every day,
  Whate'er my state may be
  Through life, in death, with truth to say,
  "My God is all to me."

579.

1 My times of sorrow and of joy,
  Great God! are in thy hand;
  My choicest comforts come from thee,
  And go at thy command.

2 If thou should'st take them all away,
  Yet would I not repine;
  Before they were possessed by me,
  They were entirely thine.

3 Nor would I drop a murmuring word,
  Though the whole world were gone,
  But seek enduring happiness,
  In thee, and thee alone.

AFFLICTIONS. 185

DOWNS. C. M. — Dr. L. Mason.

1. Be merciful to me, O God! Be merciful to me,
For tho' I sink beneath thy rod, Yet do I trust in thee.

580.

2 Thou art my refuge, and I know
My burden thou dost bear,
And I would seek, where'er I go,
To cast on thee my care.

3 Thou knowest, Lord, my flesh how frail,
Strong though my spirit be;
Oh! then assist when foes assail,
The soul that clings to thee.

4 And, gracious Lord, whate'er befall,
A thankful heart be mine—
A heart that answers to thy call,
One that is wholly thine.

5 And may I ne'er forget that thou
Wilt soon return again,
And those who love thy coming now
Shall shine in glory then.

581.

1 When waves of trouble round me swell,
My soul is not dismayed;
I hear a voice I know full well,—
"'T is I; be not afraid."

2 When black the threatening skies appear,
And storms my path invade,
Those accents tranquilize each fear,—
"'T is I; be not afraid."

3 There is a gulf that must be crossed;
Saviour, be near to aid!
Whisper, when my frail bark is tossed,—
"'T is I; be not afraid."

4 There is a dark and fearful vale,
Death hides within its shade;
Oh, say, when flesh and heart shall fail,—
"'T is I; be not afraid."

582.

1 I worship thee, sweet Will of God!
And all thy ways adore;
And every day I live, I long
To love thee more and more.

2 Man's weakness, waiting upon God,
Its end can never miss;
For man on earth no work can do
More angel-like than this.

3 He always wins who sides with God,
To him no chance is lost;
God's will is sweetest to him, when
It triumphs at his cost.

4 Ill, that God blesses, is our good,
And unblest good is ill;
And all is right that seems most wrong,
If it be his dear will!

5 When obstacles and trials seem
Like prison-walls to be,
I do the little I can do,
And leave the rest to thee.

6 I have no cares, O blessed Will!
For all my cares are thine;
I live in triumph, Lord! for thou
Hast made thy triumphs mine.

CHRISTIAN.

HELENA. C. M. — Wm. B. Bradbury.

1. O thou, who driest the mourn-er's tear, How dark this world would be, If, when by sor-rows wound-ed here, We could not fly to thee!

583.

2 But thou wilt heal the broken heart,
   Which, like the plants that throw
   Their fragrance from the wounded part,
   Breathes sweetness out of woe.

3 When joy no longer soothes or cheers,
   And ev'n the hope that threw
   A moment's sparkle o'er our tears
   Is dimmed and vanished too;

4 Oh, who would bear life's stormy doom,
   Did not thy wing of love
   Come, brightly wafting through the gloom
   Our peace-branch from above?

5 Then sorrow touched by thee grows bright,
   With more than rapture's ray;
   As darkness shows us worlds of light
   We never saw by day.

584.

1 One prayer I have—all prayers in one—
   When I am wholly thine;
   Thy will, my God, thy will be done,
   And let that will be mine.

2 All-wise, almighty, and all-good,
   In thee I firmly trust;
   Thy ways, unknown or understood,
   Are merciful and just.

3 May I remember that to thee
   Whate'er I have I owe;
   And back, in gratitude, from me
   May all thy bounties flow.

4 And though thy wisdom takes away,
   Shall I arraign thy will?
   No, let me bless thy name, and say,
   "The Lord is gracious still."

5 A pilgrim through the earth I roam,
   Of nothing long possessed;
   And all must fail when I go home,
   For this is not my rest.

585.

1 O thou whose gently chastening hand
   In mercy deals the blow!
   Make but thy servant understand
   Wherefore thou layest me low!

2 I ask thee not the rod to spare
   While thus thy love I see;
   But oh! let every suffering bear
   Some message, Lord, from thee!

3 Perhaps an erring wish I knew
   To read my future fate,
   And thou wouldst say: "Thy days are few,
   And vain thy best estate."

4 Perhaps thy glory seemed my choice,
   While I secured my own,
   And thus my kind Reprover's voice
   Tells me he works alone!

5 Oh! silence thou this murmuring will,
   Nor bid thy rough wind stay,
   Till with a furnace hotter still
   My dross is purged away!

AFFLICTIONS.

CROSS AND CROWN. C. M.

1. Must Jesus bear the cross alone, And all the world go free? No, there's a cross for every one, And there's a cross for me.

586.

1 Must Jesus bear the cross alone,
   And all the world go free?
 No, there's a cross for every one,
   And there's a cross for me.

2 The consecrated cross I'll bear,
   Till death shall set me free,
 And then go home my crown to wear,
   For there's a crown for me.

3 Upon the crystal pavement, down
   At Jesus' pierced feet,
 Joyful, I'll cast my golden crown,
   And his dear name repeat.

4 And palms shall wave, and harps shall ring,
   Beneath heaven's arches high;
 The Lord that lives, the ransomed sing,
   That lives no more to die.

5 Oh, precious cross! Oh, glorious crown!
   Oh, resurrection day!
 Ye angels, from the stars come down,
   And bear my soul away.

587.

1 Jesus, in sickness and in pain,
   Be near to succor me;
 My sinking spirit still sustain:
   To thee I turn, to thee.

2 When cares and sorrows thicken round,
   And nothing bright I see,
 In thee alone can help be found;
   To thee I turn, to thee.

3 Should strong temptations fierce assail,
   And Satan buffet me,
 Then in thy strength will I prevail,
   While still I turn to thee.

4 Through all my pilgrimage below,
   Whate'er my lot may be,
 In joy or sadness, weal or woe,
   Jesus, I'll turn to thee.

588.

1 When languor and disease invade
   This trembling house of clay,
 'Tis sweet to look beyond my pain,
   And long to fly away;

2 Sweet to look inward, and attend
   The whispers of his love;
 Sweet to look upward to the place
   Where Jesus pleads above;

3 Sweet on his faithfulness to rest,
   Whose love can never end;
 Sweet on his covenant of grace
   For all things to depend;

4 Sweet, in the confidence of faith,
   To trust his firm decrees;
 Sweet to lie passive in his hands,
   And know no will but his.

5 If such the sweetness of the streams,
   What must the fountain be,
 Where saints and angels draw their bliss
   Immediately from thee!

CHRISTIAN.

CAPELLO. S. M.   Cantica Laudis.

1. Oh, throw a-way thy rod! Oh, throw a-way thy wrath! My gra-cious Sa-viour and my God, Oh, take the gen-tle path!

589.

2 Thou seest my heart's desire
  Still unto thee is bent;
  Still does my longing soul aspire
  To an entire consent.

3 Although I fail, I weep;
  Although I halt in pace,
  Yet still with trembling steps I creep
  Unto the throne of grace.

4 Oh, then let wrath remove;
  For love will do the deed;
  Love will the conquest gain; with love
  Ev'n stony hearts will bleed.

5 Oh, throw away thy rod!
  What though man frailties hath?
  Thou art my Saviour and my God;
  Oh, throw away thy wrath!

590.

1 It is thy hand, my God;
  My sorrow comes from thee:
  I bow beneath thy chastening rod,
  'Tis love that bruises me.

2 I would not murmur, Lord;
  Before thee I am dumb:
  Lest I should breathe one murmuring word,
  To thee for help I come.

3 My God, thy name is Love;
  A Father's hand is thine;
  With tearful eyes I look above,
  And cry, "Thy will be mine!"

4 I know thy will is right,
  Though it may seem severe;
  Thy path is still unsullied light,
  Though dark it oft appear.

5 Jesus for me hath died;
  Thy Son thou didst not spare:
  His pierced hands, his bleeding side,
  Thy love for me declare.

6 Here my poor heart can rest;
  My God, it cleaves to thee:
  Thy will is love, thine end is blest,
  All work for good to me.

591.

1 Thy way, not mine, O Lord,
  However dark it be!
  Lead me by thy own faithful hand,
  Choose out the path for me.

2 Smooth let it be or rough,
  It will be still the best;
  Winding or straight, it matters not,
  It leads me to thy rest.

3 I dare not choose my lot:
  I would not if I might;
  Choose thou for me, my gracious God,
  So shall I walk aright.

4 The kingdom that I seek
  Is thine; so let the way
  That leads to it be truly thine,
  Else I must surely stray.

AFFLICTIONS.

DENNIS. S. M.   NAGELI.

1. How tender is thy hand, O thou be-lov-ed Lord! Af-flic-tions come at thy com-mand, And leave us at thy word.

592.

1 How tender is thy hand,
  O thou beloved Lord!
Afflictions come at thy command,
  And leave us at thy word.

2 How gentle was the rod
  That chastened us for sin!
How soon we found a smiling God,
  Where deep distress had been!

3 A Father's hand we felt,
  A Father's heart we knew;
With tears of penitence we knelt,
  And found his word was true.

4 We told him all our grief,
  We thought of Jesus' love;
A sense of pardon brought relief,
  And bade our pains remove.

5 Now we will bless the Lord,
  And in his strength confide;
Forever be his name adored;
  For there is none beside.

593.

1 "My times are in thy hand;"
  My God! I wish them there;
My life, my friends, my soul, I leave
  Entirely to thy care.

2 "My times are in thy hand,"
  Whatever they may be;
Pleasing or painful, dark or bright,
  As best may seem to thee.

3 "My times are in thy hand;"—
  Why should I doubt or fear?
My Father's hand will never cause
  His child a needless tear.

4 "My times are in thy hand,"—
  Jesus, the crucified!
The hand my cruel sins had pierced,
  Is now my guard and guide.

5 "My times are in thy hand;"
  I'll always trust in thee;
And, after death, at thy right hand
  I shall forever be.

594.

1 When overwhelmed with grief,
  My heart within me dies;
Helpless, and far from all relief,
  To heaven I lift mine eyes.

2 Oh, lead me to the Rock
  That's high above my head,
And make the covert of thy wings
  My shelter and my shade.

3 Within thy presence, Lord,
  Forever I'll abide;
Thou art the tower of my defense,
  The refuge where I hide.

4 Thou givest me the lot
  Of those that fear thy name;
If endless life be their reward,
  I shall possess the same.

190   CHRISTIAN.

PALESTINE. L. M. 6 lines.   Mazzinghi.

1. Peace, troubled soul, whose plaintive moan Hath taught each scene the notes of woe; Cease thy complaint, suppress thy groan, And let thy tears forget to flow; Behold, the precious balm is found, To lull thy pain, to heal thy wound.

595.

2 Come, freely come, by sin oppressed;
On Jesus cast thy weighty load;
In him thy refuge find, thy rest,
Safe in the mercy of thy God;
Thy God's thy Saviour—glorious word!
Forever love and praise the Lord.

596.

1 When gathering clouds around I view,
And days are dark, and friends are few,
On him I lean, who, not in vain,
Experienced every human pain;
He sees my wants, allays my fears,
And counts and treasures up my tears.

2 If aught should tempt my soul, to stray
From heavenly virtue's narrow way,—
To fly the good I would pursue,
Or do the sin I would not do,—
Still he, who felt temptation's power,
Shall guard me in that dangerous hour.

3 When sorrowing o'er some stone I bend,
Which covers all that was a friend,
And from his voice, his hand, his smile,
Divides me, for a little while,
My Saviour sees the tears I shed,
For Jesus wept o'er Lazarus dead.

4 And oh! when I have safely passed
Through every conflict, but the last,—
Still, still unchanging, watch beside
My painful bed,—for thou hast died;
Then point to realms of cloudless day,
And wipe my latest tear away.

597.

1 When adverse winds and waves arise,
And in my heart despondence sighs;
When life her throng of cares reveals,
And weakness o'er my spirit steals,
Grateful I hear the kind decree,
That "as my day, my strength shall be."

2 When, with sad footsteps, memory roves
'Mid smitten joys and buried loves,
When sleep my tearful pillow flies,
And dewy morning drinks my sighs,
Still to thy promise, Lord! I flee,
That "as my day, my strength shall be."

3 One trial more must yet be past,
One pang—the keenest and the last;
And when, with brow convulsed and pale,
My feeble, quivering heart-strings fail,
Redeemer! grant my soul to see
That "as her day, her strength shall be."

AFFLICTIONS.

MONTAGUE. 7s & 6s. J. P. Holbrook.

1. Why sinks my soul desponding, Why fill my eyes with tears,
When nature all surrounding The smile of beauty wears?
D. S. Each vision that I borrow With gloom and sadness fraught?
Why burdened still with sorrow Is every laboring thought?

598.

2 The pleasures that deceived me
My soul no more can charm;
Of rest they have bereaved me,
And filled me with alarm:
The objects I have cherished
Are empty as the wind;
My earthly joys have perished,—
What comfort shall I find?

3 If inward still inquiring
I turn my searching eye,
Or upward now aspiring,
I raise my feeble cry,
No heavenly light is beaming
To cheer my troubled breast;
No ray of comfort gleaming
To give my spirit rest.

4 Oh! from this dreadful anguish
Is there no refuge nigh?
'T is guilt that makes me languish,
And leaves me thus to die:
I will renounce my folly
Before the throne of grace;
And make the Lord most holy
My strength and righteousness.

599.

1 Lord God of my salvation,
To thee, to thee I cry;
Oh, let my supplication
Arrest thine ear on high!
Distresses round me thicken,
My life draws nigh the grave,
Descend, O Lord, to quicken,
Descend my soul to save.

2 Thy wrath lies hard upon me,
Thy billows o'er me roll;
My friends all seem to shun me,
And foes beset my soul.
Where'er on earth I turn me,
No comforter is near:
Wilt thou, my Father, spurn me,
Wilt thou refuse to hear?

3 No! banished and heart-broken,
My soul still clings to thee;
The promise thou hast spoken,
Still, still my refuge be;
To present ills and terrors,
My future joy increase,
And scourge me from my errors
To duty, hope, and peace.

192 CHURCH.

ALL SAINTS. L. M. — WM. KNAPP.

1. Fa-ther of mer-cies, bow thine ear, At-ten-tive to our ear-nest prayer;
We plead for those who plead for thee; Suc-cess-ful plead-ers may they be.

600.
Ministry.

2 Clothe thou with energy divine
Their words, and let those words be thine;
Teach them immortal souls to gain,
Nor let them labor, Lord, in vain.

3 Let thronging multitudes around
Hear from their lips the joyful sound;
And light thro' distant realms be spread,
Till Zion rears her drooping head.

601.
Dedication.

1 On, bow thine ear, Eternal One!
On thee our heart adoring calls;
To thee the followers of thy Son
Have raised, and now devote these walls.

2 Here let thy holy days be kept;
And be this place to worship given,
Like that bright spot where Jacob slept,
The house of God, the gate of heaven.

3 Here may thine honor dwell; and here,
As incense, let thy children's prayer,
From contrite hearts and lips sincere,
Rise on the still and holy air.

4 Here be thy praise devoutly sung;
Here let thy truth beam forth to save,
As when, of old, thy Spirit hung,
On wings of light, o'er Jordan's wave.

5 And when the lips, that with thy name
Are vocal now, to dust shall turn,
On others may devotion's flame
Be kindled here, and purely burn!

602.
Seeking a Pastor.

1 O LORD, thy pitying eye surveys
Our wandering paths, our trackless ways:
Send forth, in love, thy truth and light,
To guide our doubtful footsteps right.

2 In humble faith, behold we wait:
On thee we call at mercy's gate;
Our drooping hearts, O God! sustain,—
Shall Israel seek thy face in vain?

3 O Lord! in ways of peace return,
Nor let thy flock neglected mourn;
May our blest eyes a shepherd see,
Dear to our souls, and dear to thee.

603.
Welcoming a Pastor.

1 WE bid thee welcome in the name
Of Jesus, our exalted Head;
Come as a servant: so he came,
And we receive thee in his stead.

2 Come as a shepherd; guard and keep
This fold from hell, and earth, and sin;
Nourish the lambs, and feed the sheep,
The wounded heal, the lost bring in.

3 Come as a teacher, sent from God,
Charged his whole counsel to declare;
Lift o'er our ranks the prophet's rod,
While we uphold thy hands with prayer.

4 Come as a messenger of peace,
Filled with the Spirit, fired with love!
Live to behold our large increase,
And die to meet us all above.

INSTITUTIONS. 193

ASCENSION. L. M.   TEMPLI CARMINA.

1. How blest are those, how tru-ly wise, Who learn and keep the sa-cred road! How hap-py they whom heaven em-ploys To turn re-bel-lious hearts to God:—

604.
Ministry.

2 To win them from the fatal way
Where erring folly thoughtless roves,
And that blest righteousness display
Which Jesus wrought and God approves.

3 The shining firmament shall fade,
And sparkling stars resign their light;
But these shall know nor change nor shade,
Forever fair, forever bright.

605.
Convocation of Ministers.

1 Pour out thy Spirit from on high;
Lord! thine assembled servants bless;
Graces and gifts to each supply,
And clothe thy priests with righteousness.

2 Within thy temple where we stand,
To teach the truth as taught by thee,
Saviour! like stars in thy right hand,
The angels of the churches be!

3 Wisdom and zeal, and faith impart,
Firmness with meekness from above,
To bear thy people on our hearts,
And love the souls whom thou dost love:—

4 To watch and pray, and never faint;
By day and night strict guard to keep;
To warn the sinner, cheer the saint,
Nourish thy lambs, and feed thy sheep.

5 Then, when our work is finished here,
In humble hope, our charge resign:
When the chief Shepherd shall appear,
O God! may they and we be thine.

606.
Prayer for Pastor.

1 With heavenly power, O Lord, defend
Him whom we now to thee commend;
Thy faithful messenger secure,
And make him to the end endure.

2 Gird him with all-sufficient grace;
Direct his feet in paths of peace;
Thy truth and faithfulness fulfill,
And arm him to obey thy will.

607.
For Dedication.

1 The perfect world, by Adam trod,
Was the first temple built to God;
His fiat laid the corner-stone,
And heaved its pillars one by one.

2 He hung its starry roof on high—
The broad, illimitable sky;
He spread its pavement, green and bright,
And curtained it with morning light.

3 The mountains in their places stood,
The sea—the sky—and "all was good;"
And when its first few praises rang,
The "morning stars together sang."

4 Lord, 't is not ours to make the sea,
And earth, and sky, a house for thee;
But in thy sight our offering stands—
An humbler temple, "made with hands."

5 We cannot bid the morning star
To sing how bright thy glories are;
But, Lord, if thou wilt meet us here,
Thy praise shall be the Christian's tear.

194 CHURCH.

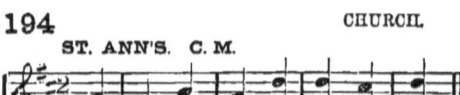

1. O thou, whose own vast temple stands, Built over earth and sea, Accept the walls that human hands Have raised to worship thee.

608.
For Dedication.

1 O THOU, whose own vast temple stands,
 Built over earth and sea,
 Accept the walls that human hands
 Have raised to worship thee.

2 Lord, from thine inmost glory send,
 Within these courts to bide,
 The peace that dwelleth without end,
 Serenely by thy side!

3 May erring minds that worship here
 Be taught the better way;
 And they who mourn, and they who fear,
 Be strengthened as they pray.

4 May faith grow firm, and love grow warm,
 And pure devotion rise,
 While round these hallowed walls the storm
 Of earth-born passion dies.

609.
For Organization.

1 CHURCH of the ever-living God,
 The Father's gracious choice,
 Amid the voices of this earth
 How feeble is thy voice!

2 A little flock!—so calls he thee
 Who bought thee with his blood;
 A little flock, disowned of men,
 But owned and loved of God.

3 Not many rich or noble called,
 Not many great or wise;
 They whom God makes his kings and priests
 Are poor in human eyes.

4 But the chief Shepherd comes at length;
 Their feeble days are o'er,
 No more a handful in the earth,
 A little flock no more.

5 No more a lily among thorns,
 Weary and faint and few;
 But countless as the stars of heaven,
 Or as the early dew.

6 Then entering th' eternal halls,
 In robes of victory,
 That mighty multitude shall keep
 The joyous jubilee.

610.
For Organization.

1 On, where are kings and empires now
 Of old that went and came?
 But, Lord, thy church is praying yet,
 A thousand years the same.

2 We mark her goodly battlements,
 And her foundations strong;
 We hear within the solemn voice
 Of her unending song.

3 For not like kingdoms of the world
 Thy holy church, O God!
 Though earthquake shocks are threatening her,
 And tempests are abroad;

4 Unshaken as eternal hills,
 Immovable she stands,
 A mountain that shall fill the earth,
 A house not made by hands.

BAPTISM. 195

SILOAM. C. M.   I. B. Woodbury.

1. By cool Si-lo-am's sha-dy rill How sweet the li-ly grows! How sweet the breath, be-neath the hill, Of Sha-ron's dew-y rose!

611.

2 Lo! such the child whose early feet
    The paths of peace have trod,
Whose secret heart, with influence sweet,
    Is upward drawn to God.

3 By cool Siloam's shady rill
    The lily must decay;
The rose, that blooms beneath the hill,
    Must shortly fade away.

4 O thou who givest life and breath,
    We seek thy grace alone,
In childhood, manhood, age, and death,
    To keep us still thine own.

612.*

1 Come, Holy Spirit, from on high;
    Baptizer of our spirits thou!
The sacramental seal apply,
    And witness with the water now.

2 Exert thy energy divine,
    And sprinkle the atoning blood;
May Father, Son, and Spirit, join
    To seal this child, a child of God.

613.

1 "Forbid them not," the Saviour cried,
    "But suffer them to come;"
Ah, then maternal tears were dried,
    And unbelief was dumb.

2 Lord, we believe, and we obey;
    We bring them at thy word;
Be thou our children's strength and stay,
    Their portion and reward.

* Sing Hebron, p. 28.

614.

1 See Israel's gentle Shepherd stand,
    With all-engaging charms;
Hark! how he calls the tender lambs,
    And folds them in his arms!

2 "Permit them to approach," he cries,
    "Nor scorn their humble name;
It was to bless such souls as these
    The Lord of angels came."

3 We bring them, Lord, with fervent prayer,
    And yield them up to thee;
Joyful that we ourselves are thine,
    Thine let our offspring be!

615.

1 How large the promise! how divine!
    To Abr'ham and his seed:
"I'll be a God to thee and thine,
    Supplying all their need."

2 The words of his extensive love
    From age to age endure:
The angel of the covenant proves,
    And seals the blessings sure.

3 Jesus the ancient faith confirms
    To our great fathers given;
He takes young children to his arms,
    And calls them heirs of heaven.

4 Our God!—how faithful are his ways!
    His love endures the same;
Nor from the promise of his grace
    Blots out the children's name.

196 CHURCH.

PORTUGAL. L. M.   Thorley.

1. This child we dedicate to thee, O God of grace and purity! Shield it from sin and threatening wrong, And let thy love its life prolong.

616.

1 This child we dedicate to thee,
O God of grace and purity!
Shield it from sin and threatening wrong,
And let thy love its life prolong.

2 Oh, may thy Spirit gently draw
Its willing soul to keep thy law;
May virtue, piety, and truth,
Dawn even with its dawning youth.

3 We, too, before thy gracious sight,
Once shared the blest baptismal rite,
And would renew its solemn vow
With love, and thanks, and praises, now.

4 Grant that, with true and faithful heart,
We still may act the Christian's part,
Cheered by each promise thou hast given,
And laboring for the prize in heaven.

617.

1 Obedient to our Zion's King,
We to his holy laver bring
These happy converts, who have known
And trusted in his grace alone.

2 Lord, in thy house they seek thy face;
Oh, bless them with peculiar grace;
Refresh their souls with love divine;
Let beams of glory round them shine.

3 Ye, who your native vileness mourn,
And to the great Redeemer turn,
Arise, his gracious call obey,
And be baptized without delay.

618.

1 O Lord! encouraged by thy grace,
We bring our infant to thy throne;
Give it within thy heart a place,
Let it be thine, and thine alone.

2 Wash it from every stain of guilt,
And let this child be sanctified;
Lord! thou canst cleanse it, if thou wilt,
And all its native evils hide.

3 We ask not, for it, earthly bliss,
Or earthly honors, wealth or fame:
The sum of our request is this—
That it may love and fear thy name.

619.

1 Dear Saviour, if these lambs should stray,
From thy secure inclosure's bound,
And, lured by worldly joys away,
Among the thoughtless crowd be found;

2 Remember still that they are thine,
That thy dear sacred name they bear;
Think that the seal of love divine,
The sign of covenant grace they wear.

3 In all their erring, sinful years,
Oh! let them ne'er forgotten be;
Remember all the prayers and tears
Which made them consecrate to thee.

4 And when these lips no more can pray,
These eyes can weep for them no more,
Turn thou their feet from folly's way;
The wanderers to thy fold restore.

LORD'S SUPPER. 197

HAMBURG. L. M. *Arranged by Dr. L. Mason.*

1. Oh! the sweet wonders of that cross Where my Redeemer loved and died! Her noblest life my spirit draws From his dear wounds, and bleeding side.

620.

1 Oh! the sweet wonders of that cross
Where my Redeemer loved and died!
Her noblest life my spirit draws
From his dear wounds, and bleeding side.

2 I would forever speak his name
In sounds to mortal ears unknown:
With angels join to praise the Lamb,
And worship at his Father's throne.

621.

1 Lord, I am thine, entirely thine,
Purchased and saved by blood divine!
With full consent thine I would be,
And own thy sovereign right in me.

2 Grant one poor sinner more a place,
Among the children of thy grace;
A wretched sinner, lost to God,
But ransomed by Immanuel's blood.

3 Thine would I live, thine would I die,
Be thine through all eternity;
The vow is passed beyond repeal;
Now will I set the solemn seal.

4 Here at that cross where flows the blood
That bought my guilty soul for God;
Thee, my new Master, now I call,
And consecrate to thee my all.

5 Do thou assist a feeble worm,
The great engagement to perform;
Thy grace can full assistance lend,
And on that grace I dare depend.

622.

1 We pray thee, wounded Lamb of God,
Cleanse us in thy atoning blood;
Grant us by faith to view thy cross,
Then life or death is gain to us.

2 Take our poor hearts and let them be
Forever closed to all but thee;
Seal thou our breasts, and let us wear
That pledge of love forever there.

623.

1 My gracious Lord, I own thy right
To every service I can pay,
And call it my supreme delight
To hear thy dictates and obey.

2 What is my being, but for thee,
Its sure support, its noblest end?
Thine ever smiling face to see,
And serve the cause of such a Friend.

3 I would not breathe for worldly joy,
Or to increase my worldly good;
Nor future days nor powers employ
To spread a sounding name abroad.

4 'T is to my Saviour I would live,
To him who for my ransom died;
Nor could the bowers of Eden give
Such bliss as blossoms at his side.

5 His work my hoary age shall bless,
When youthful vigor is no more;
And my last hour of life confess
His dying love, his saving power.

198   CHURCH.

DEDHAM. C. M.   Gardner.

1. According to thy gracious word, In meek humility, This will I do, my dying Lord! I will remember thee.

621.

1 According to thy gracious word,
  In meek humility,
  This will I do, my dying Lord!
  I will remember thee.

2 Thy body, broken for my sake,
  My bread from heaven shall be;
  Thy testamental cup I take,
  And thus remember thee.

3 Gethsemane can I forget?
  Or there thy conflict see,
  Thine agony and bloody sweat—
  And not remember thee?

4 When to the cross I turn my eyes,
  And rest on Calvary,
  O Lamb of God! my sacrifice,
  I must remember thee!

5 Remember thee and all thy pains,
  And all thy love to me;
  Yea, while I breathe, a pulse remains,
  Will I remember thee.

6 And when these failing lips grow dumb,
  And mind and memory flee,
  When in thy kingdom thou shalt come,
  Jesus, remember me!

625.

1 Jesus, at whose supreme command,
  We now approach to God,
  Before us in thy vesture stand,
  Thy vesture dipped in blood.

2 Now, Saviour, now thyself reveal,
  And make thy nature known;
  Affix thy blessed Spirit's seal,
  And stamp us for thine own.

3 Obedient to thy gracious word,
  We break the hallowed bread,
  Commemorate our dying Lord,
  And trust on thee to feed.

4 The cup of blessing, blest by thee,
  Let it thy blood impart;
  The broken bread thy body be,
  To cheer each languid heart.

626.

1 Oppressed with noon-day's scorching heat,
  To yonder cross I flee;
  Beneath its shelter take my seat:
  No shade like this for me!

2 Beneath that cross clear waters burst—
  A fountain sparkling free;
  And there I quench my desert thirst:
  No spring like this for me!

3 A stranger here, I pitch my tent
  Beneath this spreading tree;
  Here shall my pilgrim life be spent:
  No home like this for me!

4 For burdened ones a resting-place,
  Beside that cross I see;
  I here cast off my weariness:
  No rest like this for me!

LORD'S SUPPER. 199

DUNDEE. C. M. *Scottish.*

1. How sweet and aw-ful is the place, With Christ with-in the doors; While ev-er-last-ing love dis-plays The choi-cest of her stores!

627.

2 While all our hearts, and all our songs,
Join to admire the feast,
Each of us cries, with thankful tongue,—
"Lord, why was I a guest?"

3 "Why was I made to hear thy voice,
And enter while there's room,
When thousands make a wretched choice,
And rather starve than come?"

4 'Twas the same love that spread the feast,
That sweetly drew us in;
Else we had still refused to taste,
And perished in our sin.

5 Pity the nations, O our God!
Constrain the earth to come;
Send thy victorious word abroad,
And bring the strangers home.

6 We long to see thy churches full,
That all the chosen race
May, with one voice and heart and soul,
Sing thy redeeming grace.

628.

1 Prepare us, Lord, to view thy cross,
Who all our griefs hast borne;
To look on thee, whom we have pierced—
To look on thee, and mourn.

2 While thus we mourn, we would rejoice,
And, as thy cross we see,
Let each exclaim in faith and hope—
"The Saviour died for me!"

629.

1 Together with these symbols, Lord,
Thy blessèd self impart;
And let thy holy flesh and blood
Feed the believing heart.

2 Let us from all our sins be washed
In thy atoning blood:
And let thy Spirit be the seal
That we are born of God.

3 Come, Holy Ghost, with Jesus' love,
Prepare us for this feast;
Oh! let us banquet with our Lord,
And lean upon his breast.

630.

1 If human kindness meets return,
And owns the grateful tie;
If tender thoughts within us burn,
To feel a friend is nigh;—

2 Oh, shall not warmer accents tell
The gratitude we owe
To him, who died, our fears to quell—
Who bore our guilt and woe!

3 While yet in anguish he surveyed
Those pangs he would not flee,
What love his latest words displayed,—
"Meet and remember me!"

4 Remember thee—thy death, thy shame,
Our sinful hearts to share!—
O memory! leave no other name
But his recorded there.

CHURCH.

SICILIAN HYMN. 8s & 7s.

1. Cross, reproach, and tribulation! Ye to me are welcome guests, When I have this consolation, That my soul in Jesus rests.

631.

1 Cross, reproach, and tribulation!
  Ye to me are welcome guests,
  When I have this consolation,
  That my soul in Jesus rests.

2 The reproach of Christ is glorious!
  Those who here his burden bear,
  In the end shall prove victorious,
  And eternal gladness share.

3 Bear, then, the reproach of Jesus,
  Ye who live a life of faith!
  Lift triumphant songs and praises
  Ev'n in martyrdom and death.

4 Bonds and stripes, and evil story,
  Are our honorable crowns;
  Pain is peace, and shame is glory,
  Gloomy dungeons are as thrones.

632.

1 Jesus spreads his banner o'er us,
  Cheers our famished souls with food;
  He the banquet spreads before us,
  Of his mystic flesh and blood.

2 Precious banquet; bread of heaven;
  Wine of gladness, flowing free;
  May we taste it, kindly given,
  In remembrance, Lord, of thee!

3 In thy trial and rejection;
  In thy sufferings on the tree;
  In thy glorious resurrection;
  May we, Lord, remember thee.

633.

1 From the table now retiring,
  Which for us the Lord hath spread,
  May our souls, refreshment finding,
  Grow in all things like our Head!

2 His example by beholding,
  May our lives his image bear;
  Him our Lord and Master calling,
  His commands may we revere.

3 Love to God and man displaying,
  Walking steadfast in his way,
  Joy attend us in believing,
  Peace from God through endless day.

4 Praise and honor to the Father,
  Praise and honor to the Son,
  Praise and honor to the Spirit,
  Ever Three and ever One.

634.

1 While in sweet communion feeding
  On this earthly bread and wine,
  Saviour, may we see thee bleeding
  On the cross, to make us thine.

2 Though unseen, now be thou near us,
  With the still small voice of love;
  Whispering words of peace to cheer us—
  Every doubt and fear remove.

3 Bring before us all the story,
  Of thy life and death of woe;
  And with hopes of endless glory,
  Wean our hearts from all below.

LORD'S SUPPER. 201

PLEYEL'S HYMN. 7s. — PLEYEL.

1. Bread of heaven! on thee we feed, For thy flesh is meat indeed: Ever let our souls be fed With this true and living bread!

635.

1 BREAD of heaven! on thee we feed,
For thy flesh is meat indeed:
Ever let our souls be fed
With this true and living bread!

2 Vine of heaven! thy blood supplies
This blest cup of sacrifice:
Lord! thy wounds our healing give,
To thy cross we look and live.

3 Day by day with strength supplied,
Through the life of him who died:
Lord of life! oh, let us be
Rooted, grafted, built on thee!

636.

1 JESUS, Master! hear me now,
While I would renew my vow,
And record thy dying love;
Hear, and help me from above.

2 Feed me, Saviour, with this bread,
Broken in thy body's stead;
Cheer my spirit with this wine,
Streaming like that blood of thine.

3 And as now I eat and drink,
Let me truly, sweetly think,
Thou didst hang upon the tree,
Broken, bleeding, there—for me!

637.

1 HOLY Lamb, who thee receive,
Who in thee begin to live,
Day and night they cry to thee,
"As thou art, so let us be!"

2 Gladly would we now be clean;
Cleanse us, Lord, from every sin:
Fix, oh, fix our wavering mind!
To thy cross our spirit bind.

3 Dust and ashes though we be,
Full of sin and misery,
Thine we are, thou Son of God:
Take the purchase of thy blood!

638.

1 AT the Lamb's high feast we sing,
Praise to our victorious King,
Who hath washed us in the tide,
Flowing from his wounded side.

2 Praise we him, whose love divine
Gives his sacred blood for wine,
Gives his body for the feast,
Christ the victim, Christ the Priest.

3 Where the Paschal blood is poured,
Death's dark angel sheaths his sword;
Israel's hosts triumphant go
Through the wave that drowns the foe.

4 Christ, our Paschal Lamb, is slain,
Holy victim, without stain;
Death and hell defeated lie,
Heaven unfolds its gates on high.

5 Hymns of glory and of praise,
Father, unto thee we raise;
Risen Lord, all praise to thee,
With the Spirit ever be.

202 CHURCH.

ROCK OF AGES. 7s.   Dr. Hastings.

1. Rock of Ages, cleft for me! Let me hide myself in thee;
D. C. Be of sin the double cure; Cleanse me from its guilt and power.

Let the water and the blood, From thy wounded side that flowed,

639.

1 Rock of Ages, cleft for me!
Let me hide myself in thee;
Let the water and the blood,
From thy wounded side that flowed,
Be of sin the double cure;
Cleanse me from its guilt and power.

2 Not the labor of my hands
Can fulfill the law's demands;
Could my zeal no respite know,
Could my tears forever flow,
All for sin could not atone,
Thou must save, and thou alone.

3 Nothing in my hand I bring,
Simply to thy cross I cling;
Naked, come to thee for dress,
Helpless, look to thee for grace,
Vile, I to the fountain fly,
Wash me, Saviour, or I die!

4 While I draw this fleeting breath,
When my eyelids close in death,
When I soar to worlds unknown,
See thee on thy judgment-throne,
Rock of Ages, cleft for me!
Let me hide myself in thee.

640.

1 From the cross uplifted high,
Where the Saviour deigns to die,
What melodious sounds we hear,
Bursting on the ravished ear!—
"Love's redeeming work is done—
Come and welcome, sinner, come!

2 "Sprinkled now with blood the throne—
Why beneath thy burdens groan?
On my pierced body laid,
Justice owns the ransom paid—
Bow the knee, and kiss the Son—
Come and welcome, sinner, come!

3 "Spread for thee, the festal board
See with richest bounty stored;
To thy Father's bosom pressed,
Thou shalt be a child confessed,
Never from his house to roam;
Come and welcome, sinner, come!

4 "Soon the days of life shall end—
Lo, I come—your Saviour, Friend!
Safe your spirit to convey
To the realms of endless day,
Up to my eternal home—
Come and welcome, sinner, come!"

641.

1 Ye who in these courts are found,
Listening to the joyful sound,—
Lost and helpless, as ye are,
Sons of sorrow, sin, and care,—
Glorify the King of Kings,
Take the peace the gospel brings.

2 Turn to Christ your longing eyes,
View his bleeding sacrifice;
See, in him your sins forgiven,
Pardon, holiness, and heaven:
Glorify the King of kings,
Take the peace the gospel brings.

LORD'S SUPPER. 203

ZADOC. 7s. 6 lines. — Dr. Hastings.

1. Saviour of our ruined race, Fountain of redeeming grace,
D. C. Hearken to our ardent prayer— Let us all thy blessing share.

Let us now thy fullness see, While we here converse with thee;

612.

2 While we thus, with glad accord
Meet around thy table, Lord,
Bid us feast with joy divine,
On th' appointed bread and wine:
Emblems may they truly prove
Of the Saviour's bleeding love.

3 Weak, unworthy, sinful, vile,
Yet we seek thy heavenly smile:
Canst thou all our sins forgive?
Dost thou bid us look and live?
Lord, we wonder and adore!
Oh, for grace to love thee more!

613.

1 Son of God! to thee I cry:
By the holy mystery
Of thy dwelling here on earth,
By thy pure and holy birth,
Hear, oh, hear my lowly plea,
Manifest thyself to me!

2 Lamb of God! to thee I cry:
By thy bitter agony,
By thy pangs to us unknown,
By thy spirit's parting groan,
Hear, oh, hear my lowly plea:
Manifest thyself to me!

3 Prince of Life! to thee I cry:
By thy glorious majesty,
By thy triumph o'er the grave,
Meek to suffer, strong to save,
Hear, oh, hear my fervid plea:
Manifest thyself to me!

4 Lord of glory, God most high!
Man exalted to the sky,
With thy love my bosom fill;
Prompt me to perform thy will:
Then thy glory I shall see—
Thou wilt bring me home to thee.

614.

1 Blessèd Saviour! thee I love,
All my other joys above;
All my hopes in thee abide,
Thou my hope, and naught beside:
Ever let my glory be,
Only, only, only thee.

2 Once again beside the cross,
All my gain I count but loss;
Earthly pleasures fade away,—
Clouds they are that hide my day:
Hence, vain shadows! let me see
Jesus crucified for me.

3 From beneath that thorny crown
Trickle drops of cleansing down;
Pardon from thy pierced hand
Now I take, while here I stand:
Only then I live to thee,
When thy wounded side I see.

4 Blessèd Saviour! thine am I,
Thine to live, and thine to die;
Height or depth, or earthly power
Ne'er shall hide my Saviour more:
Ever shall my glory be,
Only, only, only thee!

WINDHAM. L. M. READ.

1. 'Twas on that dark, that doleful night,
When powers of earth and hell arose
Against the Son of God's delight,
And friends betrayed him to his foes.

645.

2 Before the mournful scene began,
He took the bread, and blessed and brake;
What love through all his actions ran!
What wondrous words of grace he spake!

3 "This is my body broke for sin :
Receive and eat the living food;"
Then took the cup and blessed the wine;
"'T is the new covenant in my blood."

4 "Do this, (he cried,) 'till time shall end,
In memory of your dying Friend;
Meet at my table, and record
The love of your departed Lord."

5 Jesus, thy feast we celebrate,
We show thy death, we sing thy name,
'Till thou return, and we shall eat
The marriage supper of the Lamb.

646.

1 Here we have seen thy face, O Lord,
And viewed salvation with our eyes,
Tasted and felt the living Word,
The Bread descending from the skies.

2 Thou hast prepared this dying Lamb,
Hast set his blood before our face,
To teach the terrors of thy name,
And show the wonders of thy grace.

3 He is our Light; our Morning-star
Shall shine on nations yet unknown;
The glory of thine Israel here,
And joy of spirits near thy throne.

647.

1 Dear Lord, amid the throng that pressed
Around thee on the cursed tree,
Some loyal, loving hearts were there,
Some pitying eyes that wept for thee.

2 Like them may we rejoice to own
Our dying Lord, though crowned with thorn;
Like thee, thy blessed self, endure
The cross with all its joy or scorn.

3 Thy cross, thy lonely path below,
Show what thy brethren all should be;
Pilgrims on earth, disowned by those
Who see no beauty, Lord, in thee.

648.

1 At thy command, O Lord, our hope,
We come around thy table here ;
We break the bread, we bless the cup,
That show thy death till thou appear.

2 Our faith adores thy bleeding love,
And trusts for life in One that died;
We hope for heavenly crowns above,
From a Redeemer crucified.

3 Let the vain world pronounce it shame,
And cast their scandals on thy cause!
We come to boast our Saviour's name,
And make our triumph in his cross.

4 With joy we tell the scoffing age,—
He that was dead hath left his tomb;
He lives above their utmost rage,
And we are waiting till he come.

LORD'S SUPPER.

FEDERAL STREET. L. M. H. K. Oliver.

1. I feed by faith on Christ, my bread, His body broken on the tree; I live in him, my living Head, Who died, and rose again, for me.

649.

2 This be my joy and comfort here,
This pledge of future glory mine;
Jesus, in spirit now appear,
And break the bread and pour the wine.

3 From thy dear hand may I receive
The tokens of thy dying love;
And, while I feast on earth, believe
That I shall feast with thee above.

650.

1 Oh, happy day that fixed my choice
On thee, my Saviour, and my God!
Well may this glowing heart rejoice,
And tell its raptures all abroad.

2 Oh, happy bond, that seals my vows
To him who merits all my love!
Let cheerful anthems fill his house,
While to that sacred shrine I move.

3 'T is done; the great transaction's done:
I am my Lord's, and he is mine;
He drew me, and I followed on,
Charmed to confess the voice divine.

4 Now rest, my long-divided heart!
Fixed on this blissful centre, rest;
Here have I found a nobler part,
Here heavenly pleasures fill my breast.

5 High Heaven, that hears the solemn vow,
That vow renewed, shall daily hear;
Till, in life's latest hour, I bow,
And bless in death a bond so dear.

651.

1 Draw near, O Holy Dove, draw near,
With peace and gladness on thy wing;
Reveal the Saviour's presence here,
And light, and life, and comfort bring.

2 "Eat, O my friends—drink, O beloved!"
We hear the Master's voice exclaim:
Our hearts with new desire are moved,
And kindled with a heavenly flame.

3 No room for doubt, no room for dread,
Nor tears, nor groans, nor anxious sighs;
We do not mourn a Saviour dead,
But hail him living in the skies!

4 While this we do, remembering thee,
Dear Saviour, let our graces prove
We have thy blessèd company,
Thy banner over us is love.

652.

1 While to thy table I repair,
And seal the sacred contract there,
Witness, O Lord! my solemn vow;
Angels and men! attest it too.

2 Here at that cross, where flows the blood
That bought my guilty soul for God,
Thee, Lord and Master, now I call,
I consecrate to thee my all.

3 Do thou assist a feeble worm
The great engagement to perform;
Thy grace can full assistance lend,
And on that grace I dare depend.

MISSIONARY HYMN. 7s & 6s. Dr. L. Mason.

1. From Greenland's icy mountains, From India's coral strand, Where Afric's sunny fountains Roll down their golden sand: From many an ancient river, From many a palmy plain, They call us to deliver Their land from error's chain.

653.

What though the spicy breezes
Blow soft o'er Ceylon's isle—
Though every prospect pleases,
And only man is vile?—
In vain with lavish kindness
The gifts of God are strown;
The heathen, in his blindness,
Bows down to wood and stone.

3 Shall we, whose souls are lighted
With wisdom from on high,—
Shall we to men benighted,
The lamp of life deny?
Salvation! Oh, Salvation!—
The joyful sound proclaim,
Till earth's remotest nation,
Has learned Messiah's name.

4 Waft—waft, ye winds! his story,
And you, ye waters, roll,—
Till, like a sea of glory,
It spreads from pole to pole!
Till o'er our ransomed nature,
The Lamb for sinners slain,
Redeemer, King, Creator,
In bliss returns to reign!

654.

1 Now be the gospel banner,
In every land, unfurled;
And be the shout,—"Hosanna!"
Re-echoed through the world;
Till every isle and nation,
Till every tribe and tongue,
Receive the great salvation,
And join the happy throng.

2 What, though th' embattled legions
Of earth and hell combine?
His arm, throughout their regions,
Shall soon resplendent shine:
Ride on, O Lord! victorious,
Immanuel, Prince of Peace!
Thy triumph shall be glorious,—
Thy empire still increase.

3 Yes,—thou shalt reign for ever,
O Jesus, King of kings!
Thy light, thy love, thy favor,
Each ransomed captive sings:
The isles for thee are waiting,
The deserts learn thy praise,
The hills and valleys greeting,
The song responsive raise.

PROGRESS AND MISSIONS.

WEBB. 7s & 6s. Geo. James Webb.

1. The morn-ing light is break-ing, The darkness dis-ap-pears; The sons of earth are wak-ing To pen-i-ten-tial tears: Each breeze that sweeps the ocean Brings ti-dings from a-far Of na-tions in com-mo-tion, Prepared for Zion's war.

655.

2 See heathen nations bending
   Before the God we love,
And thousand hearts ascending
   In gratitude above ;
While sinners, now confessing,
   The gospel call obey,
And seek the Saviour's blessing,—
   A nation in a day.

3 Blest river of salvation !
   Pursue thine onward way ;
Flow thou to every nation,
   Nor in thy richness stay :
Stay not till all the lowly
   Triumphant reach their home :
Stay not till all the holy
   Proclaim—"The Lord is come !"

656.

1 Hail to the Lord's Anointed,
   Great David's greater Son !
Hail in the time appointed,
   His reign on earth begun !
He comes to break oppression,
   To set the captive free,
To take away transgression,
   And rule in equity.

2 He comes with succor speedy,
   To those who suffer wrong ;
To help the poor and needy,
   And bid the weak be strong ;
To give them songs for sighing,
   Their darkness turn to light,
Whose souls condemned and dying,
   Were precious in his sight.

3 He shall come down, like showers
   Upon the fruitful earth,
And love, and joy, like flowers,
   Spring in his path to birth :
Before him on the mountains,
   Shall peace, the herald, go ;
And righteousness, in fountains,
   From hill to valley flow.

4 For him shall prayer unceasing
   And daily vows ascend ;
His kingdom still increasing,—
   A kingdom without end :
The tide of time shall never
   His covenant remove ;
His name shall stand forever,—
   That name to us is—Love.

208 CHURCH.
ELLICOTT. L. M. J. N. PATTISON.

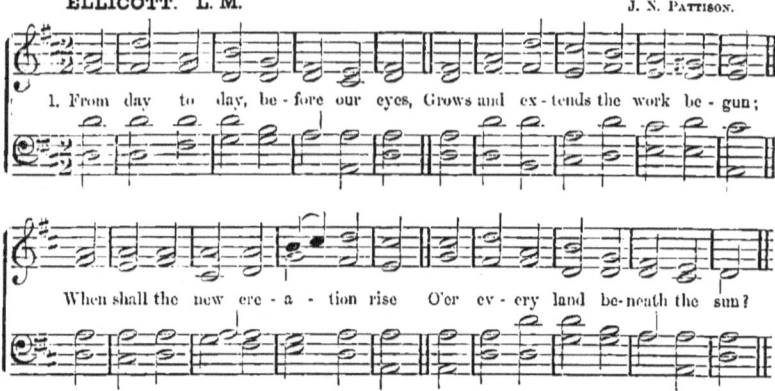

1. From day to day, before our eyes, Grows and extends the work begun; When shall the new creation rise O'er every land beneath the sun?

657.

2 When, in the sabbath of his love,
Shall God from all his labors rest;
And bending from his throne above,
Again pronounce his creatures blest?

3 As sang the morning stars of old,
Shouted the sons of God for joy;
His widening reign while we behold,
Let praise and prayers our tongues employ.

4 Till the redeemed in every clime,
Yea, all that breathe, and move, and live,
To Christ, through every age of time,
The kingdom, power, and glory give.

658.

1 INDULGENT Sovereign of the skies!
And wilt thou bow thy gracious ear?
While feeble mortals raise their cries,
Wilt thou, the great Jehovah, hear?

2 How shall thy servants give thee rest,
Till Zion's mouldering walls thou raise?
Till thine own power shall stand confessed,
And make Jerusalem a praise?

3 Look down, O God! with pitying eye,
And view the desolations round;
See, what wide realms in darkness lie,
What scenes of woe and crime abound!

4 Loud let the gospel trumpet blow,
And call the nations from afar;
Let all the isles their Saviour know,
And earth's remotest ends draw near.

659.

1 O SUN of righteousness, arise,
With gentle beams on Zion shine;
Dispel the darkness from our eyes,
And souls awake to life divine.

2 On all around, let grace descend,
Like heavenly dew, or copious showers;
That we may call our God our friend;
That we may hail salvation ours.

660.

1 GREAT God, whose universal sway
The known and unknown worlds obey,
Now give the kingdom to thy Son,
Extend his power, exalt his throne.

2 Thy sceptre well becomes his hands,
All heaven submits to his commands;
His justice shall avenge the poor,
And pride and rage prevail no more.

3 With power he vindicates the just,
And treads th' oppressor in the dust;
His worship and his fear shall last,
Till hours, and years, and time be past.

4 The heathen lands that lie beneath
The shades of overspreading death,
Revive at his first dawning light,
And deserts blossom at the sight.

5 The saints shall flourish in his days,
Dressed in the robes of joy and praise;
Peace, like a river from his throne,
Shall flow to nations yet unknown.

PROGRESS AND MISSIONS.

WARD. L. M. — Dr. L. Mason.

1. God is the ref-uge of his saints When storms of sharp dis-tress in-vade; Ere we can of-fer our com-plaints, Be-hold him pres-ent with his aid!

661.

2 Let mountains from their seats be hurled
Down to the deep, and buried there,
Convulsions shake the solid world—
Our faith shall never yield to fear.

3 Loud may the troubled ocean roar;
In sacred peace our souls abide;
While every nation, every shore,
Trembles and dreads the swelling tide.

4 There is a stream whose gentle flow
Supplies the city of our God,
Life, love, and joy, still gliding through,
And watering our divine abode.

5 That sacred stream, thine holy word,
Our grief allays, our fear controls;
Sweet peace thy promises afford,
And give new strength to fainting souls.

6 Zion enjoys her Monarch's love,
Secure against a threatening hour;
Nor can her firm foundation move,
Built on his truth and armed with power.

662.

1 Behold th' expected time draw near,
The shades disperse, the dawn appear!
Behold the wilderness assume
The beauteous tints of Eden's bloom!

2 Events with prophecies conspire,
To raise our faith, our zeal to fire:
The ripening fields, already white,
Present a harvest to the sight.

3 The untaught heathen waits to know
The joy the gospel will bestow;
The exiled captive, to receive
The freedom Jesus has to give.

4 Come, let us, with a grateful heart,
In the blest labor share a part;
Our prayers and offerings gladly bring,
To aid the triumphs of our King.

663.

1 O Spirit of the living God,
In all thy plenitude of grace,
Where'er the foot of man hath trod,
Descend on our apostate race.

2 Give tongues of fire, and hearts of love,
To preach the reconciling word;
Give power and unction from above,
Where'er the joyful sound is heard.

3 Be darkness, at thy coming, light;
Confusion—order, in thy path;
Souls without strength, inspire with might;
Bid mercy triumph over wrath.

4 Baptize the nations, far and nigh
The triumphs of the cross record;
The name of Jesus glorify,
Till every kindred call him Lord.

5 O Spirit of the Lord! prepare
All the round earth her God to meet,
Breathe thou abroad like morning air,
Till hearts of stone begin to beat.

CHURCH.

ASHWELL. L. M. — Dr. L. Mason.

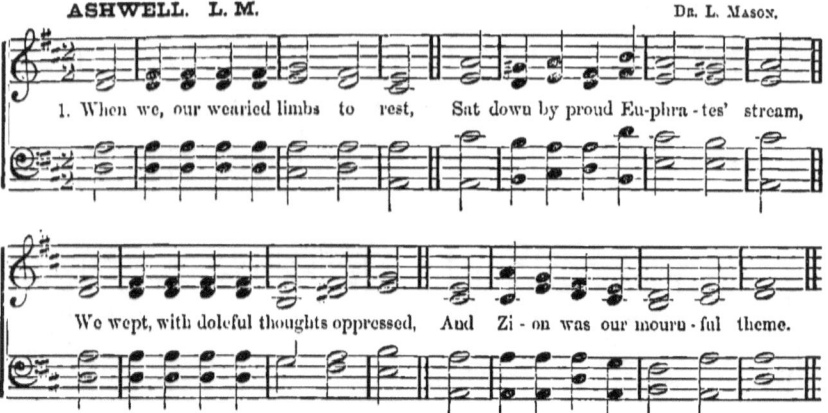

1. When we, our wearied limbs to rest, Sat down by proud Euphrates' stream, We wept, with doleful thoughts oppressed, And Zion was our mournful theme.

664.

1 When we, our wearied limbs to rest,
Sat down by proud Euphrates' stream,
We wept, with doleful thoughts oppressed,
And Zion was our mournful theme.

2 Our harps that, when with joy we sung,
Were wont their tuneful parts to bear,
With silent strings neglected hung
On willow trees that withered there.

3 How shall we tune our voice to sing,
Or touch our harps with skillful hands?
Shall hymns of joy, to God our King,
Be sung by slaves in foreign lands?

4 O Salem! our once happy seat,
When I of thee forgetful prove,
Let then my trembling hand forget
The tuneful strings with art to move.

665.

1 O Zion! when I think on thee,
I wish for pinions like the dove,
And mourn to think that I should be
So distant from the place I love.

2 A captive here, and far from home,
For Zion's sacred walls I sigh;
Thither the ransomed nations come,
And see the Saviour eye to eye.

3 While here I walk on hostile ground;
The few, that I can call my friends,
Are like myself with fetters bound,
And weariness our steps attends.

4 But we shall yet behold the day
When Zion's children shall return;
Our sorrows then shall flee away,
And we again shall never mourn.

5 The hope that such a day will come,
Makes ev'n the captive's portion sweet;
Though now we wander far from home,
In Zion soon we all shall meet.

666.

1 Why, on the bending willows hung,
Israel! still sleeps thy tuneful string?—
Still mute remains thy sullen tongue,
And Zion's song denies to sing?

2 Awake! thy sweetest raptures raise;
Let harp and voice unite their strains:
Thy promised King his sceptre sways;
Jesus, thine own Messiah, reigns!

3 No taunting foes the song require;
No strangers mock thy captive chain;
But friends provoke the silent lyre,
And brethren ask the holy strain.

4 Nor fear thy Salem's hills to wrong,
If other lands thy triumph share:
A heavenly city claims thy song;
A brighter Salem rises there.

5 By foreign streams no longer roam;
Nor, weeping, think of Jordan's flood:
In every clime behold a home,
In every temple see thy God.

PROGRESS AND MISSIONS.

PARK STREET. L. M. Vesta.

1. Hark! how the choral song of heaven Swells full of peace and joy a-bove; Hark! how they strike their golden harps, And raise the tuneful notes of love, And raise the tuneful notes of love.

667.

2 No anxious care nor thrilling grief,
No deep despair, nor gloomy woe
They feel, when high their lofty strains
In noblest, sweetest concord flow.

3 When shall we join the heavenly host,
Who sing Immanuel's praise on high,
And leave behind our doubts and fears,
To swell the chorus of the sky?

4 Oh! come, thou rapture-bringing morn,
And usher in the joyful day;
We long to see thy rising sun
Drive all these clouds of grief away.

668.

1 ETERNAL Father! thou hast said,
That Christ all glory shall obtain;
That he who once a sufferer bled,
Shall o'er the world, a conqueror, reign.

2 We wait thy triumph, Saviour King!
Long ages have prepared thy way;
Now all abroad thy banner fling,
Set Time's great battle in array.

3 Thy hosts are mustered to the field;
"The Cross! The Cross!" the battle-call;
The old grim towers of darkness yield,
And soon shall totter to their fall.

4 On mountain tops the watch-fires glow,
Where scattered wide the watchmen stand;
Voice echoes voice, and onward flow
The joyous shouts, from land to land.

5 Oh, fill thy church with faith and power!
Bid her long night of weeping cease;
To groaning nations haste the hour,
Of life and freedom, light and peace.

6 Come, Spirit, make thy wonders known!
Fulfill the Father's high decree;
Then earth, the might of hell o'erthrown,
Shall keep her last great jubilee.

669.

1 JESUS shall reign where'er the sun
Does his successive journeys run;
His kingdom stretch from shore to shore,
Till moons shall wax and wane no more.

2 For him shall endless prayer be made,
And praises throng to crown his head;
His name, like sweet perfume, shall rise
With every morning sacrifice.

3 People and realms of every tongue
Dwell on his love with sweetest song;
And infant voices shall proclaim
Their early blessings on his name.

4 Blessings abound where'er he reigns,
The prisoner leaps to lose his chains;
The weary find eternal rest,
And all the sons of want are blest.

5 Let every creature rise, and bring
Peculiar honors to their King;
Angels descend with songs again,
And earth repeat the long amen.

CHURCH.

ANVERN. L. M.   *Arranged by* Dr. L. Mason.

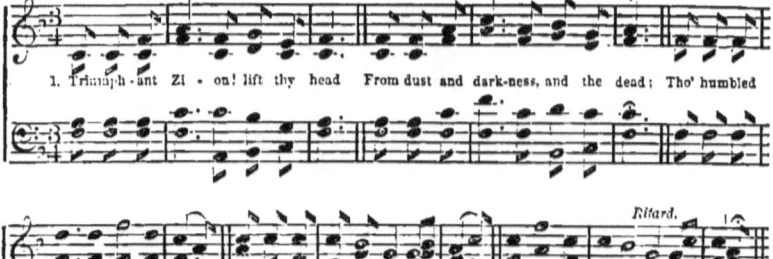

1. Triumphant Zion! lift thy head From dust and darkness, and the dead; Tho' humbled

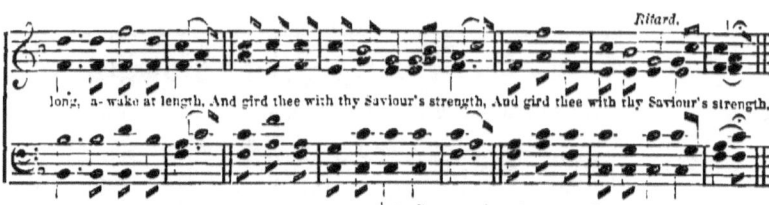

long, awake at length, And gird thee with thy Saviour's strength, And gird thee with thy Saviour's strength.

670.

2 Put all thy beauteous garments on,
And let thy various charms be known;
Then decked in robes of righteousness,
The world thy glories shall confess.

3 No more shall foes unclean invade,
And fill thy hallowed walls with dread:
No more shall hell's insulting host
Their victory and thy sorrows boast.

4 God, from on high, thy groans will hear;
His hands thy ruins shall repair:
Nor will thy watchful Monarch cease
To guard thee in eternal peace.

671.

1 Ye Christian heralds! go, proclaim
Salvation through Immanuel's name;
To distant climes the tidings bear,
And plant the rose of Sharon there.

2 He'll shield you with a wall of fire,
With flaming zeal your breast inspire,
Bid raging winds their fury cease,
And hush the tempest into peace.

3 And when our labors all are o'er,
Then we shall meet to part no more,—
Meet with the blood-bought throng, to fall,
And crown our Jesus—Lord of all!

672.

1 Sovereign of worlds! display thy power;
Be this thy Zion's favored hour;
Bid the bright morning Star arise,
And point the nations to the skies.

2 Set up thy throne where Satan reigns,—
On Afric's shore, on India's plains,
On wilds and continents unknown,—
And make the nations all thine own.

3 Speak! and the world shall hear thy voice;
Speak! and the desert shall rejoice;
Scatter the gloom of heathen night,
And bid all nations hail the light.

673.

1 Ascend thy throne, almighty King,
And spread thy glories all abroad;
Let thine own arm salvation bring,
And be thou known the gracious God.

2 Let millions bow before thy seat,
Let humble mourners seek thy face,
Bring daring rebels to thy feet,
Subdued by thy victorious grace.

3 Oh, let the kingdoms of the world
Become the kingdoms of the Lord!
Let saints and angels praise thy name;
Be thou thro' heaven and earth adored.

674.

1 Worthy the Lamb of boundless sway—
In earth and heaven the Lord of all!
Let all the powers of earth obey,
And low before his footstool fall.

2 Higher—still higher, swell the strain,
Creation's voice the note prolong!
Jesus, the Lamb, shall ever reign:—
Let hallelujahs crown the song.

PROGRESS AND MISSIONS. 213

MISSIONARY CHANT. L. M.   Ch. Zeuner.

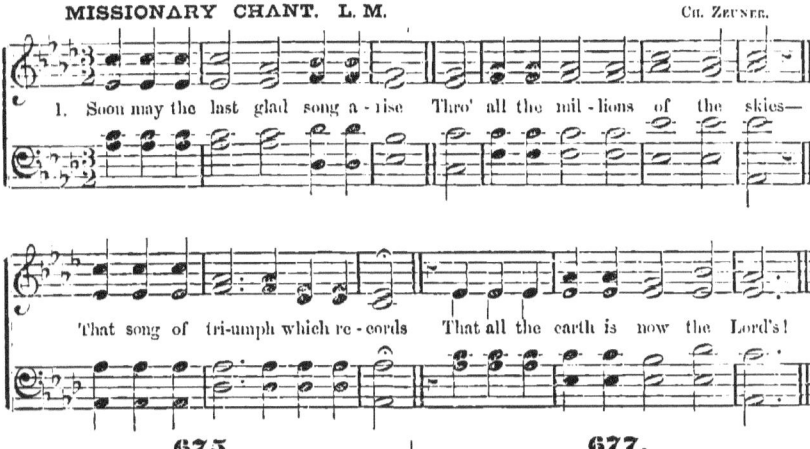

1. Soon may the last glad song a-rise
Thro' all the mil-lions of the skies—
That song of tri-umph which re-cords
That all the earth is now the Lord's!

675.

1 Soon may the last glad song arise
Through all the millions of the skies—
That song of triumph which records
That all the earth is now the Lord's!

2 Let thrones and powers and kingdoms be
Obedient, mighty God, to thee!
And, over land and stream and main,
Wave thou the sceptre of thy reign!

3 Oh, let that glorious anthem swell,
Let host to host the triumph tell,
That not one rebel heart remains,
But over all the Saviour reigns!

676.

1 Assembled at thy great command,
Before thy face, dread King, we stand;
The voice that marshaled every star,
Has called thy people from afar.

2 We meet, thro' distant lands to spread
The truth for which the martyrs bled;
Along the line, to either pole,
The thunder of thy praise to roll.

3 Our prayers assist, accept our praise,
Our hopes revive, our courage raise;
Our counsels aid, to each impart
The single eye, the faithful heart.

4 Forth with thy chosen heralds come,
Recall the wandering spirits home;
From Zion's mount send forth the sound,
To spread the spacious earth around.

677.

1 Marked as the purpose of the skies,
This promise meets our anxious eyes,
That heathen lands the Lord shall know,
And warm with faith each bosom glow.

2 Ev'n now the hallowed scenes appear;
Ev'n now unfolds the promised year;
Lo! distant shores thy heralds trace,
And bear the tidings of thy grace.

3 'Mid burning climes and frozen plains,
Where pagan darkness brooding reigns,
Lord! mark their steps, their fears subdue,
And nerve their arm, and clear their view.

4 When, worn by toil, their spirits fail,
Bid them the glorious future hail;
Bid them the crown of life survey,
And onward urge their conquering way.

678.

1 Though now the nations sit beneath
The darkness of o'erspreading death,
God will arise with light divine,
On Zion's holy towers to shine.

2 That light shall glance on distant lands,
And heathen tribes, in joyful bands,
Come with exulting haste to prove
The power and greatness of his love.

3 Lord, spread the triumphs of thy grace;
Let truth and righteousness and peace,
In mild and lovely forms, display
The glories of the latter day.

214 CHURCH.

HAIL TO THE BRIGHTNESS. 11s & 10s. Dr. L. Mason.

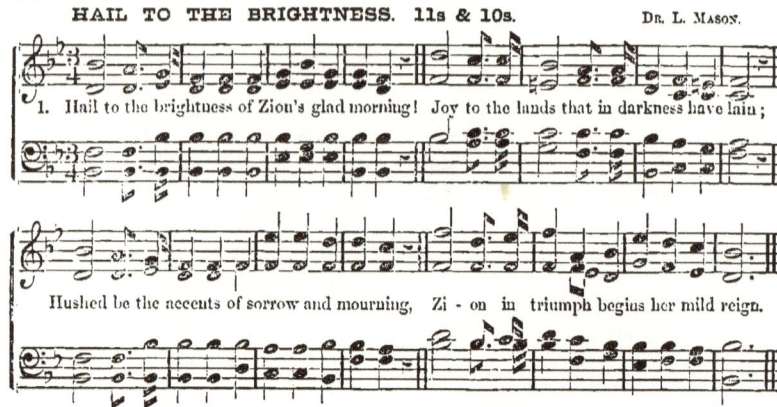

1. Hail to the brightness of Zion's glad morning! Joy to the lands that in darkness have lain; Hushed be the accents of sorrow and mourning, Zi-on in triumph begins her mild reign.

679.

2 Hail to the brightness of Zion's glad morning,
Long by the prophets of Israel foretold;
Hail to the millions from bondage returning,
Gentiles and Jews the blest vision behold.

3 Lo! in the desert rich flowers are springing,
Streams ever copious are gliding along:
Loud from the mountain-tops echoes are ringing,
Wastes rise in verdure and mingle in song.

4 See, from all lands—from the isles of the ocean,
Praise to Jehovah ascending on high;
Fallen are the engines of war and commotion,
Shouts of salvation are rending the sky.

680.

1 DAUGHTER of Zion, awake from thy sadness;
Awake, for thy foes shall oppress thee no more:
Bright o'er thy hills dawns the day-star of gladness;
Arise, for the night of thy sorrow is o'er.

2 Strong were thy foes; but the arm that subdued them,
And scattered their legions, was mightier far;
They fled like the chaff from the scourge that pursued them;
Vain were their steeds and their chariots of war.

3 Daughter of Zion, the power that hath saved thee
Extolled with the harp and the timbrel should be;
Shout, for the foe is destroyed that enslaved thee;
Th' oppressor is vanquished, and Zion is free.

681.

1 WAKE thee, O Zion—thy mourning is ended;
God—thine own God, hath regarded thy prayer:
Wake thee—and hail him, in glory descended,
Thy darkness to scatter—thy wastes to repair.

2 Wake thee, O Zion—his Spirit of power
To newness of life is awaking the dead;
Array thee in beauty, and greet the glad hour,
That brings thee salvation, through Jesus who bled.

3 Saviour—we gladly with voices resounding,
Loud as the thunder—our chorus would swell;
Till from rock, wood and mountain its echoes rebounding,
To all the wide world of salvation shall tell.

PROGRESS AND MISSIONS. 215

ZION. 8s, 7s & 4s. Dr. Hastings.

1. On the moun-tain's top ap-pear-ing, Lo! the sa-cred her-ald stands, Welcome news to Zi-on bear-ing, Zi-on long in hos-tile lands. Mourning captive, God himself shall loose thy bands, Mourning captive, God himself shall loose thy bands.

682.

2 Has thy night been long and mournful?
Have thy friends unfaithful proved?
Have thy foes been proud and scornful,
By thy sighs and tears unmoved?
Cease thy mourning;
Zion still is well beloved.

3 God, thy God, will now restore thee;
He himself appears thy Friend;
All thy foes shall flee before thee;
Here their boasts and triumphs end;
Great deliverance
Zion's King will surely send.

4 Peace and joy shall now attend thee;
All thy warfare now is past;
God thy Saviour will defend thee;
Victory is thine at last;
All thy conflicts
End in everlasting rest.

683.

1 O'er the realms of pagan darkness
Let the eye of pity gaze;
See the kindreds of the people,
Lost in sin's bewildering maze;—
Darkness brooding
On the face of all the earth!

2 Light of them who sit in error!
Rise and shine—thy blessings bring;
Light—to lighten all the Gentiles!
Rise with healing in thy wing:
To thy brightness,
Let all kings and nations come.

3 Let the heathen, now adoring
Idol gods of wood and stone,
Come, and, worshiping before him,
Serve the living God alone:
Let thy glory
Fill the earth, as floods the sea.

4 Thou! to whom all power is given,
Speak the word; at thy command,
Let the company of heralds
Spread thy name from land to land:
Lord! be with them,
Always till time's latest end.

684.

1 O'er the gloomy hills of darkness,
Cheered by no celestial ray,
Sun of righteousness! arising,
Bring the bright, the glorious day;
Send the gospel
To the earth's remotest bound.

2 Kingdoms wide that sit in darkness,—
Grant them, Lord! the glorious light
And, from eastern coast to western,
May the morning chase the night;
And redemption,
Freely purchased, win the day.

3 Fly abroad, thou mighty gospel!
Win and conquer, never cease;
May thy lasting, wide dominions,
Multiply and still increase;
Sway thy sceptre,
Saviour! all the world around.

216

PERRY. 7s. Double. CHURCH. *Arranged by* J. P. HOLBROOK.

1. Hark, the song of Jubilee, Loud as mighty thunders roar; Or the fullness of the sea, When it breaks upon the shore! Hallelujah, for the Lord God Omnipotent shall reign! Hallelujah! let the word Echo thro' the earth and main.

685.

2 Hallelujah! hark, the sound,
 From the depths unto the skies,
 Wakes above, beneath, around,
 All creation's harmonies!
 See Jehovah's banners furled,
 Sheathed his sword, he speaks—'t is done!
 And the kingdoms of this world
 Are the kingdoms of his Son.

3 He shall reign from pole to pole,
 With illimitable sway;
 He shall reign, when like a scroll
 Yonder heavens are passed away;
 Then the end: beneath his rod
 Man's last enemy shall fall:
 Hallelujah! Christ in God,
 God in Christ, is all in all!

686.

1 HASTEN, Lord, the glorious time,
 When, beneath Messiah's sway,
 Every nation, every clime,
 Shall the gospel call obey.

2 Mightiest kings his power shall own,
 Heathen tribes his name adore;
 Satan and his host, o'erthrown,
 Bound in chains, shall hurt no more.

3 Then shall wars and tumults cease,
 Then be banished grief and pain;
 Righteousness, and joy, and peace,
 Undisturbed shall ever reign.

4 Bless we, then, our gracious Lord,
 Ever praise his glorious name;
 All his mighty acts record,
 All his wondrous love proclaim.

687.

1 SEE the ransomed millions stand,—
 Palms of conquest in their hands!
 This before the throne their strain,—
 "Hell is vanquished—death is slain!—

2 "Blessing, honor, glory, might,
 Are the Conqueror's native right;
 Thrones and powers before him fall,—
 Lamb of God, and Lord of all!"

3 Hasten, Lord! the promised hour;
 Come in glory and in power;
 Still thy foes are unsubdued—
 Nature sighs to be renewed:

4 Time has nearly reached its sun;
 All things with the bride, say, "Come!"
 Jesus! whom all worlds adore,
 Come,—and reign forevermore.

PROGRESS AND MISSIONS. 217

NUREMBURG. 7s. *German.*

1. Sons of men, behold from far, Hail the long-expected star! Star of truth that gilds the night, Guides bewildered men aright.

688.

2 Mild it shines on all beneath,
Piercing through the shades of death;
Scattering error's wide-spread night;
Kindling darkness into light.

3 Nations all, remote and near,
Haste to see your Lord appear;
Haste, for him your hearts prepare,
Meet him manifested there!

4 There behold the day-spring rise,
Pouring light on mortal eyes;
See it chase the shades away,
Shining to the perfect day.

689.

1 COME, Desire of nations, come!
Hasten, Lord, the general doom!
Hear the Spirit and the Bride;
Come, and take us to thy side.

2 Thou, who hast our place prepared,
Make us meet for our reward;
Then with all thy saints descend:
Then our earthly trials end.

3 Mindful of thy chosen race,
Shorten these vindictive days;
Hear us now, and save thine own,
Who for full redemption groan.

4 Now destroy the man of sin,
Now thine ancient flock bring in!
Filled with righteousness divine,
Claim a ransomed world for thine.

5 Plant thy heavenly kingdom here;
Glorious in thy saints appear:
Speak the sacred number sealed;
Speak the mystery revealed.

6 Take to thee thy royal power:
Reign! when sin shall be no more;
Reign! when death no more shall be;
Reign to all eternity!

690.

1 SAW ye not the cloud arise,
Little as the human hand?
Now it spreads along the skies,
Hangs o'er all the thirsty land.

2 Lo, the promise of a shower
Drops already from above;
But the Lord will shortly pour
All the blessings of his love.

3 When he first the work begun,
Small and feeble was the day;
Now the word doth swiftly run,
Now it wins its widening way.

4 More and more it spreads and grows,
Ever mighty to prevail;
Sin's strongholds it now o'erthrows,
Shakes the trembling gates of hell.

5 Sons of God! your Saviour praise;
He the door hath opened wide;
He hath given the word of grace;
Jesus' word is glorified.

218 CHURCH.

ORIOLA. C. M. Double.   Wm. B. Bradbury.

1. Dear Saviour, ev-er at my side, How lov-ing thou must be, To leave thy home in heaven, to guard A lit-tle child like me. Thy beau-ti-ful and shin-ing face I see not, tho' so near; The sweetness of thy soft low voice I am too deaf to hear.

691.

2 I cannot feel thee touch my hand
  With pressure light and mild,
To cheek me, as my mother did,
  When I was but a child;
But I have felt thee in my thoughts
  Fighting with sin for me;
And when my heart loves God, I know
  The sweetness is from thee.

3 And when, dear Saviour! I kneel down
  Morning and night to prayer,
Something there is within my heart
  Which tells me thou art there;
Yes! when I pray, thou prayest too—
  Thy prayer is all for me;
But when I sleep, thou sleepest not,
  But watchest patiently.

692.

1 Remember thy Creator now,
  In these thy youthful days;
He will accept thine earliest vow,
  And listen to thy praise.

2 Remember thy Creator now,
  Seek him while he is near;
For evil days will come, when thou
  Shalt find no comfort here.

3 Remember thy Creator now;
  His willing servant be:
Then, when thy head in death shall bow,
  He will remember thee.

4 Almighty God! our hearts incline
  Thy heavenly voice to hear;
Let all our future days be thine,
  Devoted to thy fear.

693.

1 Dear Jesus, let thy pitying eye
  Look kindly down on me:
A sinful, weak, and helpless child,
  I come thy child to be.

2 O blessèd Saviour! take my heart,
  This sinful heart of mine,
And wash it clean in every part;
  Make me a child of thine.

3 My sins, though great, thou canst forgive,
  For thou hast died for me;
Amazing love! Help me, O God,
  Thine own dear child to be.

4 For thou hast said, "Forbid them not:
  Let children come to me:"
I hear thy voice, and now, dear Lord,
  I come thy child to be.

SABBATH SCHOOL. 219

BROWN. C. M.   Wm. B. Bradbury.

1. How glorious is our heavenly King, Who reigns above the sky! How shall a child presume to sing His dreadful majesty!

694.

2 How great his power, none can tell,
   Nor think how large his grace ;
   Not men below, nor saints that dwell
   On high before his face ;

3 Not angels that stand round the Lord
   Can search his secret will ;
   But they perform his holy word,
   And sing his praises still.

4 Then let me join this heavenly train,
   And my first offerings bring ;
   Th' eternal God will not disdain
   To hear an infant sing.

5 My heart resolves, my tongue obeys,
   And angels shall rejoice,
   To hear their mighty Maker's praise
   Sound from a feeble voice.

695.

1 There is a fold whence none can stray,
   And pastures ever green,
   Where sultry sun, or stormy day,
   Or night, is never seen.

2 Far up the everlasting hills,
   In God's own light it lies ;
   His smile its vast dimension fills
   With joy that never dies.

3 One narrow vale, one darksome wave,
   Divides that land from this ;
   I have a Shepherd pledged to save,
   And bear me home to bliss.

4 Soon at his feet my soul will lie,
   In life's last struggling breath ;
   But I shall only seem to die,
   I shall not taste of death.

5 Far from this guilty world, to be
   Exempt from toil and strife ;
   To spend eternity with thee,
   My Saviour, this is life !

696.

1 There is a glorious world of light,
   Above the starry sky,
   Where saints departed, clothed in white,
   Adore the Lord most high.

2 And hark ! amid the sacred songs
   Those heavenly voices raise,
   Ten thousand thousand infant tongues
   Unite in perfect praise.

3 Those are the hymns that we shall know,
   If Jesus we obey :
   That is the place where we shall go,
   If found in wisdom's way.

4 Soon will our earthly race be run,
   Our mortal frame decay ;
   Parents and children, one by one,
   Must die and pass away.

5 Great God, impress the serious thought,
   This day, on every breast,
   That both the teachers and the taught,
   May enter to thy rest.

220   CHURCH.

DUANE. L. M. Double.   Rev. G. Coles.

697.

1 A poor, wayfaring man of grief
   Hath often crossed me on my way,
Who sued so humbly for relief,
   That I could never answer nay.
I had not power to ask his name,
   Whither he went, or whence he came;
Yet there was something in his eye,
   That won my love, I knew not why.

2 Once when my scanty meal was spread,
   He entered; not a word he spake;
Just perishing for want of bread,
   I gave him all; he blessed it, brake,
And ate, but gave me part again;
   Mine was an angel's portion then;
And while I fed with eager haste,
   The crust was manna to my taste.

3 I spied him where a fountain burst
   Clear from the rock; his strength was gone;
The heedless water mocked his thirst;
   He heard it, saw it hurrying on:
I ran and raised the sufferer up;
   Thrice from the stream he drained my cup;
Dipped, and returned it running o'er—
   I drank and never thirsted more.

4 Then, in a moment, to my view
   The stranger started from disguise;
The tokens in his hands I knew;
   My Saviour stood before my eyes!
He spake, and my poor name he named:
   "Of me, thou hast not been ashamed;
These deeds shall thy memorial be;
   Fear not! thou didst it unto me."

698.

1 What are those soul-reviving strains,
   Which echo thus from Salem's plains?
What anthems loud, and louder still,
   Sweetly resound from Zion's hill?
2 Lo! 't is an infant chorus sings,
   Hosanna to the King of kings:
The Saviour comes! and babes proclaim
   Salvation, sent in Jesus' name.

3 Nor these alone their voice shall raise,
   For we will join this song of praise;
Still Israel's children forward press
   To hail the Lord their Righteousness.
4 Proclaim hosannas loud and clear;
   See David's son and Lord appear!
Glory and praise on earth be given;
   Hosanna in the highest heaven!

SABBATH SCHOOL. 221

FULTON. 7s. Wm. B. Bradbury.

1. Chil-dren! lis-ten to the Lord, And o-bey his gra-cious word;
Seek his face with heart and mind— Ear-ly seek, and you shall find.

699.

2 Sorrowful, your sins confess;
Plead his perfect righteousness;
See the Saviour's bleeding side;—
Come—you will not be denied.

3 For his worship now prepare;
Kneel to him in fervent prayer;
Serve him with a perfect heart;
Never from his ways depart.

700.

1 Saviour! teach me, day by day,
Love's sweet lesson to obey;
Sweeter lesson cannot be,
Loving him who first loved me.

2 With a child-like heart of love,
At thy bidding may I move;
Prompt to serve and follow thee,
Loving him who first loved me.

3 Teach me all thy steps to trace,
Strong to follow in thy grace;
Learning how to love from thee,
Loving him who first loved me.

4 Love in loving finds employ—
In obedience all her joy;
Ever new that joy will be,
Loving him who first loved me.

5 Thus may I rejoice to show
That I feel the love I owe;
Singing, till thy face I see,
Of his love who first loved me.

701.

1 Glory to the Father give,
God in whom we move and live;
Children's prayers he deigns to hear,
Children's songs delight his ear.

2 Glory to the Son we bring,
Christ our Prophet, Priest, and King;
Children, raise your sweetest strain
To the Lamb, for he was slain.

3 Glory to the Holy Ghost;
Be this day a Pentecost;
Children's minds may he inspire,
Give them tongues of holy fire.

4 Glory in the highest be
To the blessèd Trinity,
For the gospel from above,
For the word, that "God is love."

702.

1 God of mercy! throned on high,
Listen from thy lofty seat;
Hear, oh, hear our feeble cry;
Guide, oh, guide our wandering feet.

2 Young and erring travelers, we
All our dangers do not know;
Scarcely fear the stormy sea,
Hardly feel the tempest blow.

3 Jesus, lover of the young,
Cleanse us with thy love divine;
Ere the tide of sin grow strong,
Save us, keep us, make us thine.

BRIGHT CROWN. C. M.

Wm. B. Bradbury.

1. Ye val-iant sol-diers of the cross, Ye hap-py, pray-ing band;
Tho' in this world you suf-fer loss, You'll reach fair Ca-naan's land;
Let us nev-er mind the scoffs nor the frowns of the world, For we've all got the cross to bear;
It will on-ly make the crown the bright-er to shine, When we have the crown to wear.

703.

2 All earthly pleasures we'll forsake,
When heaven appears in view;
In Jesus' strength we'll undertake
To fight our passage through.
Chorus.—Let us never, etc.

3 Oh, what a glorious shout there'll be,
When we arrive at home!
Our friends and Jesus we shall see,
And God shall say, "Well done!"
Chorus.—Let us never, etc.

GOLDEN SHORE. 8s & 7s.

Wm. B. Bradbury.

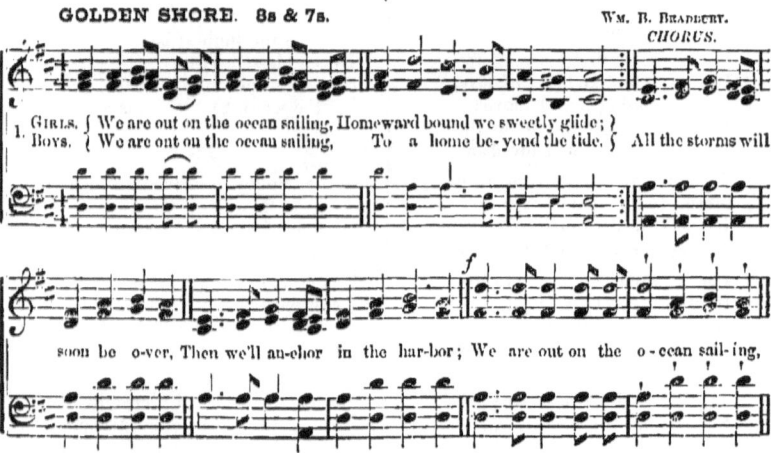

1. Girls. We are out on the ocean sailing, Homeward bound we sweetly glide;
Boys. We are out on the ocean sailing, To a home be-yond the tide.
All the storms will soon be o-ver, Then we'll an-chor in the har-bor; We are out on the o-cean sail-ing,

GOLDEN SHORE. (Concluded.)

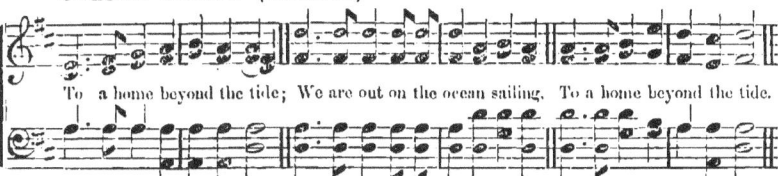

704.

2 Millions now are safely landed
  Over on the golden shore;
  Millions now are on their journey,
  Yet there's room for millions more.—
  Chorus.

3 Spread your sails, while heavenly breezes
  Gently waft our vessel on;
  All on board are sweetly singing—
  Free salvation is the song.—*Chorus.*

4 When we all are safely anchored,
  We will shout—our trials o'er;
  We will walk about the city,
  And we'll sing forevermore.—*Chorus.*

Hymn **705.**

PRAISE. 8s & 7s.   Sabb. School Pearl.

1. High we raise our hal-le-lu-jahs To our dear Redeemer's name, Who, to seek the lost and wandering, And to save the sinner, came. 2. Praise him for his blest example, For his life of peace and truth, Fold-ing chil-dren to his bo-som, Gent-ly guid-ing age and youth, till we die.

3. Praise him for the great sal-va-tion He to young and old extends, Bids them strive for heavenly mansions, Calls believing souls his friends. 4. We would better learn to praise him, Love and serve him till our joy-ful hal-le-lu-jahs Join the an-thems of the sky.

CHURCH.

SING OF JESUS. 7s & 6s. SAB. SCHOOL BELL.

1. Come, let us sing of Jesus, While hearts and accents blend; Come, let us sing of Jesus, The sinner's on-ly Friend; His ho-ly soul re-joic-es, Amid the choirs a--bove, To hear our youth-ful voic-es Ex-ult-ing in his love.

706.

2 We love to sing of Jesus,
   Who wept our path along;
   We love to sing of Jesus,
   The tempted and the strong;
   None who besought his healing,
   He passed unheeded by:
   And still retains his feeling
   For us above the sky.

3 We love to sing of Jesus,
   Who died our souls to save;
   We love to sing of Jesus,
   Triumphant o'er the grave;

And in our hour of danger,
   We'll trust his love alone,
   Who once slept in a manger,
   And now sits on the throne.

4 Then let us sing of Jesus,
   While yet on earth we stay,
   And hope to sing of Jesus
   Throughout eternal day;
   For those who here confess him,
   He will in heaven confess;
   And faithful hearts that bless him,
   He will forever bless.

GOLDEN CHAIN. 8s & 7s. Double. WM. B. BRADBURY.

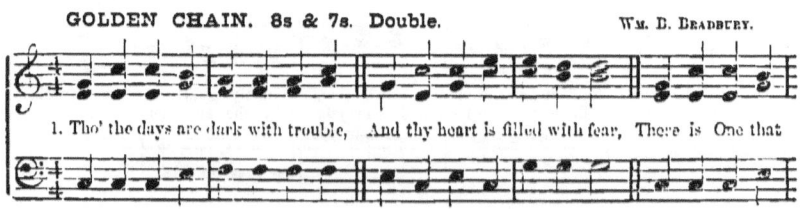

1. Tho' the days are dark with trouble, And thy heart is filled with fear, There is One that

GOLDEN CHAIN. (Concluded.)

707.

2 All thy prospects will seem brighter
When the shadow leaves the heart,
And the steps of time beat lighter,
When the gloomy clouds depart.
Many days have dawned serenely,
While the birds sang with delight,
But the skies were dark and gloomy
Ere the sun had reached its height.—
Ref.

3 Soon will dawn a brighter morning
On a blesséd, tranquil shore ;
Sighs will then give place to singing,
Tears to bliss forevermore.
Thou shalt see a world of glory,
And eternal joy and bliss ;
Let not then thy soul be moaning
O'er the woes and cares of this.—*Ref.*

708.

1 Jesus, on thy throne of glory!
Higher than the angels are ;
Stoop to hear the children's story,
Deign to grant the children's prayer :
Thou so great, and we so feeble,
Thou so full, and we in need,
Jesus, listen to our pleading,
Be to us a friend indeed.—*Ref.*

2 When temptations spread around us,
And in snares our feet are twined,
In the hour when we forget thee,
Jesus, bear us still in mind :
Through the years thy love may grant us,
When we sleep at life's last end,
In the morning of our waking,
Jesus, Saviour, be our friend.—*Ref.*

226 CHURCH.

PARTING HYMN. C. M.

1. How pleasant thus to dwell below, In fellowship of love;
And tho' we part, 'tis bliss to know The good shall meet above.
The good shall meet above, To meet to part no more,
The good shall meet a-bove; And tho' we part, 'tis bliss to know The good shall meet a-bove.
Oh, that will be joy-ful, joy-ful, joy-ful! Oh, that will be joy-ful, To meet to part no more.

709.

2 Yes, happy thought! when we are free
From earthly grief and pain,
In heaven we shall each other see,
And never part again.
    Oh, that will be joyful! &c.

3 Then let us each, in strength divine,
Still walk in wisdom's ways;
That we, with those we love, may join
In never ending praise.
    Oh, that will be joyful! &c.

710.

1 On, haste away, my brethren dear!
And come to Canaan's shore;
We'll meet and sing forever there,
When all our toils are o'er.
    Oh, that will be joyful! &c.

2 How sweet to hear the hallowed theme
That saints shall ever sing;
To hear their voices all proclaim
"Salvation to the King!"
    Oh, that will be joyful! &c.

3 Around his throne, all clothed in white
Will all his saints appear;
And, shining in his glory bright,
We'll see our Saviour there.
    Oh, that will be joyful! &c.

4 Thro' heaven the shouts of angels ring,
When sons to God are born:
Oh, what a company will sing
On the millennial morn!
    Oh, that will be joyful! &c.

5 Through one eternal day we'll sing,
And bless his sacred name,
With hallelujah to the King,
And "Worthy is the Lamb!"
    Oh, that will be joyful! &c.

SOCIAL MEETINGS. 227

GRATITUDE. L. M. Dost.

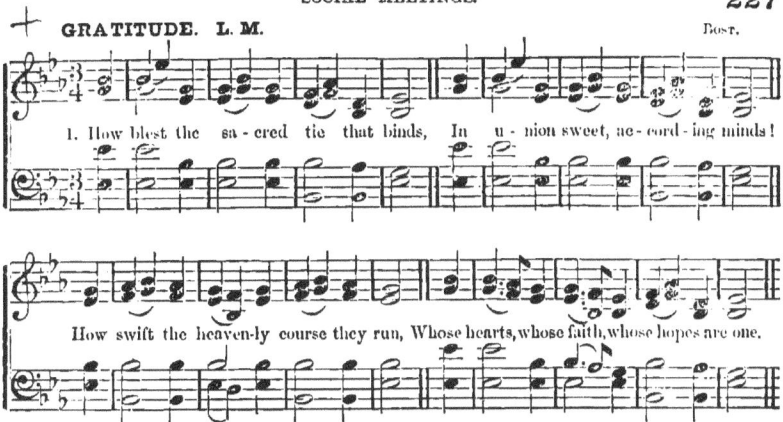

1. How blest the sa-cred tie that binds, In u-nion sweet, ac-cord-ing minds! How swift the heaven-ly course they run, Whose hearts, whose faith, whose hopes are one.

711.

2 To each, the soul of each how dear!
What watchful love, what holy fear!
How doth the generous flame within
Refine from earth, and cleanse from sin!

3 Their streaming eyes together flow
For human guilt and mortal woe;
Their ardent prayers together rise,
Like mingling flames in sacrifice.

4 Together oft they seek the place
Where God reveals his awful face;
How high, how strong their raptures swell,
There's none but kindred souls can tell.

5 Nor shall the glowing flame expire
'Midst nature's drooping, sickening fire:
Soon shall they meet in realms above,
A heaven of joy, because of love.

712.

1 KINDRED in Christ! for his dear sake
A hearty welcome here receive;
May we together now partake
The joys which only he can give.

2 May he, by whose kind care we meet,
Send his good Spirit from above;
Make our communications sweet,
And cause our hearts to burn with love.

3 Forgotten be each worldly theme,
When Christians meet together thus;
We only wish to speak of him,
Who lived, and died, and reigns, for us.

4 We'll talk of all he did and said,
And suffered for us here below;—
The path he marked for us to tread,
And what he's doing for us now.

5 Thus,—as the moments pass away,—
We'll love, and wonder, and adore;
And hasten on the glorious day,
When we shall meet to part no more.

713.

1 GREAT God! to thee my evening song
With humble gratitude I raise;
Oh, let thy mercy tune my tongue,
And fill my heart with lively praise.

2 My days unclouded as they pass,
And every gentle, rolling hour,
Are monuments of wondrous grace,
And witness to thy love and power.

3 And yet this thoughtless, wretched heart,
Too oft regardless of thy love,
Ungrateful, can from thee depart,
And, fond of trifles, vainly rove.

4 Seal my forgiveness in the blood
Of Jesus; his dear name alone
I plead for pardon, gracious God!
And kind acceptance at thy throne.

5 Let this blest hope mine eyelids close,
With sleep refresh my feeble frame;
Safe in thy care may I repose,
And wake with praises to thy name.

CHURCH.

BOARDMAN. C. M.   TEMPLI CARMINA.

1. Oh, it is joy in one to meet Whom one com-mu-nion blends, Coun-cil to hold in con-verse sweet, And talk as Chris-tian friends.

714.

1 Oh, it is joy in one to meet
   Whom one communion blends,
Council to hold in converse sweet,
   And talk as Christian friends.

2 'T is joy to think the angel train,
   Who 'mid heaven's temple shine,
To seek our earthly temples deign,
   And in our anthems join.

3 But chief 't is joy to think that He,
   To whom his church is dear,
Delights her gathered flock to see,
   Her joint devotions hear.

4 Then who would choose to walk abroad,
   While here such joys are given?
" This is indeed the house of God,
   And this the gate of heaven!"

715.

1 BLEST be the dear, uniting love,
   That will not let us part:
Our bodies may far off remove;
   We still are one in heart.

2 Joined in one spirit to our Head,
   Where he appoints we go;
We still in Jesus' footsteps tread,
   And show his praise below.

3 Oh, may we ever walk in him,
   And nothing know beside!
Nothing desire, nothing esteem,
   But Jesus crucified!

4 Partakers of the Saviour's grace,
   The same in mind and heart,
Not joy nor grief nor time nor place
   Nor life nor death can part.

716.

1 LET saints below in concert sing
   With those to glory gone:
For all the servants of our King,
   In earth and heaven, are one.

2 One family—we dwell in him—
   One church above, beneath,
Though now divided by the stream,—
   The narrow stream of death;

3 One army of the living God,
   To his command we bow;
Part of the host have crossed the flood,
   And part are crossing now.

4 Ev'n now to their eternal home
   Some happy spirits fly;
And we are to the margin come,
   And soon expect to die.

5 Ev'n now, by faith, we join our hands
   With those that went before,
And greet the ransomed blessed bands
   Upon th' eternal shore.

6 Lord Jesus! be our constant guide:
   And, when the word is given,
Bid death's cold flood its waves divide,
   And land us safe in heaven.

SOCIAL MEETINGS. 229

HEBER. C. M. GEO. KINGSLEY.

1. Hail, sweetest, dearest tie that binds
Our glowing hearts in one;
Hail, sacred hope, that tunes our minds
To harmony divine.

717.

2 What though the northern wintry blast
Shall howl around our cot;
What though beneath an eastern sun
Be cast our distant lot;—

3 No lingering look, no parting sigh,
Our future meeting knows;
There friendship beams from every eye,
And love immortal glows.

4 Oh, sacred hope! Oh, blissful hope!
Which Jesus' grace has given—
The hope, when days and years are past,
We all shall meet in heaven!

718.

1 Our souls, by love together knit,
Cemented, mixed in one,
One hope, one heart, one mind, one voice,
'T is heaven on earth begun.

2 Our hearts have often burned within,
And glowed with sacred fire,
While Jesus spoke, and fed, and blessed,
And filled the enlarged desire.

3 The little cloud increases still,
The heavens are big with rain;
We haste to catch the teeming shower,
And all its moisture drain.

4 A rill, a stream, a torrent flows!
But pour a mighty flood;
Oh, sweep the nations, shake the earth,
'Till all proclaim thee, God!

5 And when thou mak'st thy jewels up,
And sett'st thy starry crown;
When all thy sparkling gems shall shine,
Proclaimed by thee thine own;—

6 May we, a little band of love,
We sinners, saved by grace,
From glory unto glory changed,
Behold thee face to face.

719.

1 How sweet, how heavenly is the sight,
When those who love the Lord
In one another's peace delight,
And so fulfill his word!

2 When each can feel his brother's sigh,
And with him bear a part!
When sorrow flows from eye to eye,
And joy from heart to heart!

3 When, free from envy, scorn and pride,
Our wishes all above,
Each can his brother's failings hide,
And show a brother's love!

4 Let love, in one delightful stream,
Through every bosom flow,
And union sweet, and dear esteem,
In every action glow.

5 Love is the golden chain that binds
The happy souls above;
And he's an heir of heaven who finds
His bosom glow with love.

CHURCH.

STATE STREET. S. M. — Woodman.

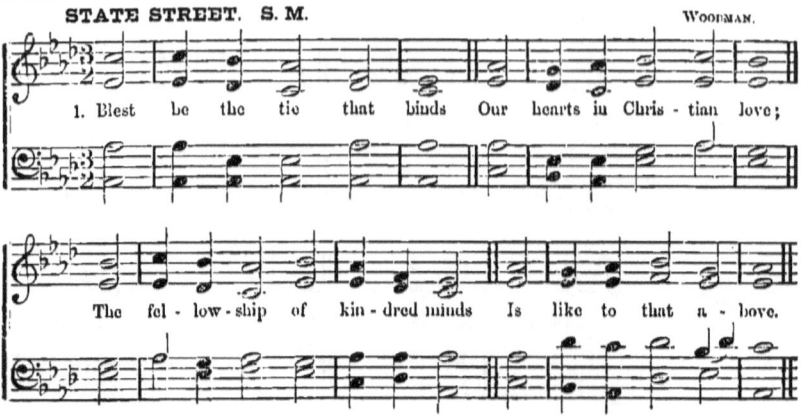

1. Blest be the tie that binds
Our hearts in Christian love;
The fellowship of kindred minds
Is like to that above.

720.

2 Before our Father's throne
We pour our ardent prayers;
Our fears, our hopes, our aims are one,
Our comforts and our cares.

3 We share our mutual woes,
Our mutual burdens bear;
And often for each other flows
The sympathizing tear.

4 When we asunder part,
It gives us inward pain;
But we shall still be joined in heart,
And hope to meet again.

5 This glorious hope revives
Our courage by the way;
While each in expectation lives,
And longs to see the day.

6 From sorrow, toil, and pain,
And sin, we shall be free,
And perfect love and friendship reign
Through all eternity.

721.

1 I LOVE thy kingdom, Lord,
The house of thine abode,
The Church, our blest Redeemer saved
With his own precious blood.

2 I love thy church, O God!
Her walls before thee stand,
Dear as the apple of thine eye,
And graven on thy hand.

3 For her my tears shall fall,
For her my prayers ascend;
To her my cares and toils be given,
Till toils and cares shall end.

4 Beyond my highest joy
I prize her heavenly ways,
Her sweet communion, solemn vows,
Her hymns of love and praise.

5 Jesus, thou Friend divine,
Our Saviour, and our King!
Thy hand from every snare and foe,
Shall great deliverance bring.

6 Sure as thy truth shall last,
To Zion shall be given
The brightest glories earth can yield,
And brighter bliss of heaven.

722.

1 LET party names no more
The Christian world o'erspread;
Gentile and Jew, and bond and free,
Are one in Christ their head.

2 Among the saints on earth,
Let mutual love be found;
Heirs of the same inheritance,
With mutual blessings crowned.

3 Thus will the church below
Resemble that above;
Where streams of pleasure ever flow,
And every heart is love.

SOCIAL MEETINGS.

SHIRLAND. S. M.   Stanley.

1. Our heaven-ly Fa-ther calls, And Christ in-vites us near;
With both, our friend-ship shall be sweet, And our com-mu-nion dear.

723.

1 Our heavenly Father calls,
   And Christ invites us near;
   With both, our friendship shall be sweet,
   And our communion dear.

2 God pities all our griefs:
   He pardons every day;
   Almighty to protect our souls,
   And wise to guide our way.

3 How large his bounties are!
   What various stores of good,
   Diffused from our Redeemer's hand,
   And purchased with his blood!

4 Jesus, our living head,
   We bless thy faithful care;
   Our advocate before the throne,
   And our forerunner there.

5 Here fix, my roving heart!
   Here wait, my warmest love!
   Till the communion be complete,
   In nobler scenes above.

724.

1 Behold the throne of grace!
   The promise calls me near;
   There Jesus shows a smiling face,
   And waits to answer prayer.

2 That rich atoning blood,
   Which sprinkled round I see,
   Provides for those who come to God
   An all-prevailing plea.

3 My soul! ask what thou wilt;
   Thou canst not be too bold:
   Since his own blood for thee he spilt,
   What else can he withhold?

4 Thine image, Lord, bestow,
   Thy presence and thy love;
   I ask to serve thee here below,
   And reign with thee above.

5 Teach me to live by faith;
   Conform my will to thine;
   Let me victorious be in death,
   And then in glory shine.

725.

1 Jesus, who knows full well
   The heart of every saint,
   Invites us, all our grief to tell,
   To pray and never faint.

2 He bows his gracious ear,—
   We never plead in vain;
   Then let us wait till he appear,
   And pray, and pray again.

3 Jesus, the Lord, will hear
   His chosen when they cry;
   Yes, though he may a while forbear,
   He'll help them from on high.

4 Then let us earnest cry,
   And never faint in prayer;
   He sees, he hears, and, from on high,
   Will make our cause his care.

232 CHURCH

RETREAT. L. M.   Dr. Hastings.

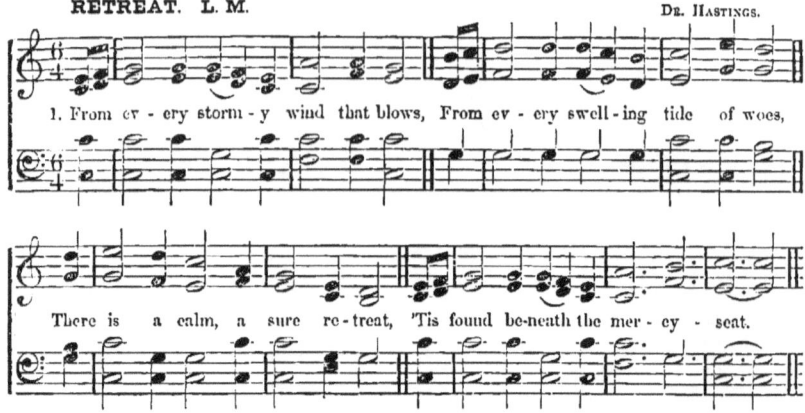

1. From ev-ery storm-y wind that blows, From ev-ery swell-ing tide of woes, There is a calm, a sure re-treat, 'Tis found be-neath the mer-cy-seat.

726.

2 There is a place where Jesus sheds
The oil of gladness on our heads,—
A place, than all besides, more sweet;
It is the blood-bought mercy-seat.

3 There is a scene where spirits blend,
Where friend holds fellowship with friend;
Though sundered far, by faith they meet
Around one common mercy-seat!

4 There, there, on eagle wings we soar,
And sense and sin molest no more,
And heaven comes down our souls to greet,
And glory crowns the mercy-seat.

5 Oh! let my hand forget her skill,
My tongue be silent, cold, and still,
This throbbing heart forget to beat,
If I forget the mercy-seat.

727.

1 Where high the heavenly temple stands,
The house of God not made with hands,
A great High Priest our nature wears,—
The Guardian of mankind appears.

2 Though now ascended up on high,
He bends on earth a brother's eye;
Partaker of the human name,
He knows the frailty of our frame.

3 Our Fellow-sufferer yet retains
A fellow-feeling of our pains;
And still remembers, in the skies,
His tears, his agonies, and cries.

4 In every pang that rends the heart,
The Man of Sorrows had a part;
He sympathizes with our grief,
And to the sufferer sends relief.

5 With boldness, therefore, at the throne,
Let us make all our sorrows known;
And ask the aid of heavenly power,
To help us in the evil hour.

728.

1 Forth from the dark and stormy sky,
Lord, to thine altar's shade we fly;
Forth from the world, its hope and fear,
Saviour, we seek thy shelter here.

2 Long have we roamed in want and pain,
Long have we sought thy rest in vain;
Weary and weak, thy grace we pray;
Turn not, O Lord! thy guests away.

729.

1 Where two or three, with sweet accord,
Obedient to their sovereign Lord,
Meet to recount his acts of grace,
And offer solemn prayer and praise;—

2 There will the gracious Saviour be,
To bless the little company;—
There, to unvail his smiling face,
And bid his glories fill the place.

3 We meet at thy command, O Lord!
Relying on thy faithful word;
Now send the Spirit from above,
And fill our hearts with heavenly love.

SOCIAL MEETINGS.

SOMERVILLE. L. M. — Templi Carmina.

1. Jesus, where'er thy people meet, There they behold thy mercy-seat; Where'er they seek thee thou art found, And every place is hallowed ground.

730.

2 For thou, within no walls confined,
Inhabitest the humble mind;
Such ever bring thee where they come,
And going, take thee to their home.

3 Great Shepherd of thy chosen few!
Thy former mercies here renew;
Here to our waiting hearts proclaim
The sweetness of thy saving name.

731.

1 And dost thou say, "Ask what thou wilt?"
Lord, I would seize the golden hour:
I pray to be released from guilt,
And freed from sin and Satan's power.

2 More of thy presence, Lord, impart;
More of thine image let me bear:
Erect thy throne within my heart,
And reign without a rival there.

3 Give me to read my pardon sealed,
And from thy joy to draw my strength;
Oh, be thy boundless love revealed
In all its height and breadth and length!

4 Grant these requests—I ask no more,
But to thy care the rest resign:
Sick, or in health, or rich, or poor,
All shall be well, if thou art mine.

732.

1 How sweet to leave the world awhile,
And seek the presence of our Lord!
Dear Saviour! on thy people smile,
And come, according to thy word.

2 From busy scenes we now retreat,
That we may here converse with thee:
Ah! Lord! behold us at thy feet;—
Let this the "gate of heaven" be.

3 "Chief of ten thousand!" now appear,
That we by faith may see thy face:
Oh! speak, that we thy voice may hear,
And let thy presence fill this place.

733.

1 What various hindrances we meet
In coming to a mercy-seat!
Yet who that knows the worth of prayer
But wishes to be often there?

2 Prayer makes the darkened clouds withdraw;
Prayer climbs the ladder Jacob saw,
Gives exercise to faith and love,
Brings every blessing from above.

3 Restraining prayer, we cease to fight;
Prayer makes the Christian's armor bright;
And Satan trembles when he sees
The weakest saint upon his knees.

4 Have you no words? ah! think again;
Words flow apace when you complain,
And fill a fellow-creature's ear
With the sad tale of all your care.

5 Were half the breath thus vainly spent
To heaven in supplication sent,
Our cheerful song would oftener be,
"Hear what the Lord hath done for me!"

234   CHURCH.

BYEFIELD. C. M.   Dr. Hastings.

1. Prayer is the soul's sincere desire, Uttered or unexpressed; The motion of a hidden fire, That trembles in the breast.

734.

2 Prayer is the burden of a sigh,
  The falling of a tear,
The upward glancing of an eye,
  When none but God is near.

3 Prayer is the simplest form of speech
  That infant lips can try;
Prayer the sublimest strains that reach
  The Majesty on high.

4 Prayer is the Christian's vital breath,
  The Christian's native air:
His watchword at the gates of death,—
  He enters heaven with prayer.

5 Prayer is the contrite sinner's voice,
  Returning from his ways;
While angels in their songs rejoice,
  And cry—"Behold he prays!"

6 O thou, by whom we come to God—
  The Life, the Truth, the Way;
The path of prayer thyself hast trod;
  Lord! teach us how to pray.

735.

1 The Saviour bids thee watch and pray
  Through life's momentous hour;
And grants the Spirit's quickening ray
  To those who seek his power.

2 The Saviour bids thee watch and pray,
  Maintain a warrior's strife;
O Christian! hear his voice to-day:
  Obedience is thy life.

3 The Saviour bids thee watch and pray,
  For soon the hour will come
That calls thee from the earth away
  To thy eternal home.

4 The Saviour bids thee watch and pray,
  Oh, hearken to his voice,
And follow where he leads the way,
  To heaven's eternal joys!

736.

1 Hail, tranquil hour of closing day!
  Begone, disturbing care!
And look, my soul, from earth away,
  To him who heareth prayer.

2 How sweet the tear of penitence,
  Before his throne of grace,
While, to the contrite spirit's sense,
  He shows his smiling face.

3 How sweet, thro' long-remembered years,
  His mercies to recall;
And, pressed with wants, and griefs, and
    fears,
  To trust his love for all.

4 How sweet to look, in thoughtful hope,
  Beyond this fading sky,
And hear him call his children up
  To his fair home on high.

5 Calmly the day forsakes our heaven
  To dawn beyond the west;
So let my soul, in life's last even,
  Retire to glorious rest.

SOCIAL MEETINGS.   235

WOODSTOCK. C. M.   D. DUTTON.

1. I love to steal awhile away From every cumbering care, And spend the hours of setting day In humble, grateful prayer.

737.

1 I LOVE to steal awhile away
   From every cumbering care,
   And spend the hours of setting day
   In humble, grateful prayer.

2 I love in solitude to shed
   The penitential tear,
   And all his promises to plead,
   Where none but God can hear.

3 I love to think on mercies past,
   And future good implore,
   And all my cares and sorrows cast
   On him whom I adore.

4 I love by faith to take a view
   Of brighter scenes in heaven;
   The prospect doth my strength renew,
   While here by tempests driven.

5 Thus, when life's toilsome day is o'er,
   May its departing ray
   Be calm as this impressive hour,
   And lead to endless day.

738.

1 THERE is an eye that never sleeps
   Beneath the wing of night;
   There is an ear that never shuts,
   When sink the beams of light.

2 There is an arm that never tires,
   When human strength gives way;
   There is a love that never fails,
   When earthly loves decay.

3 That eye is fixed on seraph throngs;
   That arm upholds the sky;
   That ear is filled with angel songs;
   That love is throned on high.

4 But there's a power which man can wield
   When mortal aid is vain,
   That eye, that arm, that love to reach,
   That listening ear to gain.

5 That power is prayer, which soars on high,
   Through Jesus, to the throne;
   And moves the hand which moves the world,
   To bring salvation down!

739.

1 DEAR Father, to thy mercy-seat
   My soul for shelter flies:
   'T is here I find a safe retreat
   When storms and tempests rise.

2 My cheerful hope can never die,
   If thou, my God, art near;
   Thy grace can raise my comforts high,
   And banish every fear.

3 My great Protector, and my Lord!
   Thy constant aid impart;
   Oh! let thy kind, thy gracious word
   Sustain my trembling heart.

4 Oh! never let my soul remove
   From this divine retreat;
   Still let me trust thy power and love,
   And dwell beneath thy feet.

HORTON. 7s.   German.

1. Come, my soul, thy suit prepare, Jesus loves to answer prayer; He himself has bid thee pray, Therefore will not say thee nay.

740.

2 With my burden I begin;—
Lord! remove this load of sin;
Let thy blood, for sinners spilt,
Set my conscience free from guilt.

3 Lord! I come to thee for rest,
Take possession of my breast;
There, thy sovereign right maintain,
And, without a rival, reign.

4 While I am a pilgrim here,
Let thy love my spirit cheer;
Be my guide, my guard, my friend,
Lead me to my journey's end.

5 Show me what I have to do,
Every hour my strength renew;
Let me live a life of faith,
Let me die thy people's death.

741.

1 Lord! I cannot let thee go,
Till a blessing thou bestow;
Do not turn away thy face,
Mine's an urgent, pressing case.

2 Once, a sinner, near despair,
Sought thy mercy-seat by prayer;
Mercy heard and set him free—
Lord! that mercy came to me.

3 Many days have passed since then,
Many changes I have seen;
Yet have been upheld till now;
Who could hold me up but thou?

4 Thou hast helped in every need—
This emboldens me to plead;
After so much mercy past,
Canst thou let me sink at last?

5 No—I must maintain my hold;
'Tis thy goodness makes me bold;
I can no denial take,
Since I plead for Jesus' sake.

742.

1 Lord, we come before thee now,
At thy feet we humbly bow;
Oh, do not our suit disdain!
Shall we seek thee, Lord, in vain?

2 Lord, on thee our souls depend,
In compassion now descend;
Fill our hearts with thy rich grace,
Tune our lips to sing thy praise.

3 In thine own appointed way,
Now we seek thee; here we stay;
Lord, we know not how to go,
Till a blessing thou bestow.

4 Comfort those who weep and mourn;
Let the time of joy return;
Those that are cast down lift up;
Make them strong in faith and hope.

5 Grant that all may seek and find
Thee a God supremely kind;
Heal the sick; the captive free;
Let us all rejoice in thee.

SOCIAL MEETINGS. 237

ALETTA. 7s.   Wm. B. Bradbury.

1. Soft and ho-ly is the place, Where the light that beams from heaven Shows the Sa-viour's smil-ing face, With the joy of sin for-given.

743.

2 There, with one accord we meet,
All the words of life to hear;
Bending low at Jesus' feet,
Worshiping with godly fear.

3 Let the world and all its cares
Now retire from every breast;
Let the tempter and his snares
Cease to hinder or molest.

4 Precious Sabbath of the Lord,
Fairest type of heaven above!
Purest joy thy scenes afford
To the heart that's tuned to love.

744.

1 Stealing from the world away,
We are come to seek thy face;
Kindly meet us, Lord, we pray,
Grant us thy reviving grace.

2 Yonder stars that gild the sky
Shine but with a borrowed light;
We, unless thy light be nigh,
Wander, wrapt in gloomy night.

3 Sun of Righteousness! dispel
All our darkness, doubts, and fears;
May thy light within us dwell,
Till eternal day appears.

4 Warm our hearts in prayer and praise,
Lift our every thought above;
Hear the grateful songs we raise,
Fill us with thy perfect love.

745.

1 Thou, from whom we never part,
Thou, whose love is everywhere,
Thou, who seest every heart,
Listen to our evening prayer.

2 Father, fill our hearts with love,
Love unfailing, full and free;
Love no injury can move,
Love that ever rests on thee.

3 Heavenly Father! through the night
Keep us safe from every ill,
Cheerful as the morning light
May we wake to do thy will.

746.

1 They who seek the throne of grace
Find that throne in every place;
If we live a life of prayer,
God is present everywhere.

2 In our sickness and our health,
In our want, or in our wealth,
If we look to God in prayer,
God is present everywhere.

3 When our earthly comforts fail,
When the woes of life prevail,
'T is the time for earnest prayer;
God is present everywhere.

4 Then, my soul, in every strait,
To thy Father come, and wait;
He will answer every prayer:
God is present everywhere.

SOCIAL MEETINGS. 239

HEAVENLY HOME. 11s. *English.*

1. My home is in heaven, my rest is not here; Then why should I murmur when trials are near? Be hushed, my dark spirit, the worst that can come, But shortens my journey, and hastens me home.

749.

2 It is not for me to be seeking my bliss,
And building my hopes in a region like this;
I look for a city which hands have not piled,
I pant for a country by sin undefiled.

3 The thorn and the thistle around me may grow,
I would not recline upon roses below,
I ask not my portion, I seek not my rest,
Till ever with Jesus, I lie on his breast.

750.

1 Oh, had I, my Saviour, the wings of a dove,
How soon would I soar to thy presence above;
How soon would I flee where the weary have rest,
And hide all my cares in thy sheltering breast.

2 I flutter, I struggle, I long to be free,
I feel me a captive while banished from thee;
A pilgrim and stranger, the desert I roam;
And look on to heaven, and fain would be home.

3 Ah, there the wild tempest forever shall cease,
No billow shall ruffle that haven of peace;

Temptation and trouble alike shall depart,
All tears from the eye, and all sin from the heart.

4 Soon, soon may this Eden of promise be mine;
Rise, bright sun of glory, no more to decline!
Thy light, yet unrisen, the wilderness cheers—
Oh, what will it be when the fullness appears!

751.

1 'Mid scenes of confusion, and creature complaints,
How sweet to my soul is communion with saints;
To find at the banquet of mercy there's room,
And feel in the presence of Jesus at home.

2 Sweet bonds that unite all the children of peace!
And thrice precious Jesus, whose love cannot cease!
Though oft from thy presence in sadness I roam,
I long to behold thee in glory at home.

3 I sigh from this body of sin to be free,
Which hinders my joy and communion with thee;
Though now my temptation like billows may foam,
All, all will be peace, when I'm with thee at home.

240 CHURCH

MT. BLANC. 7s & 6s. PLYMOUTH COLL.

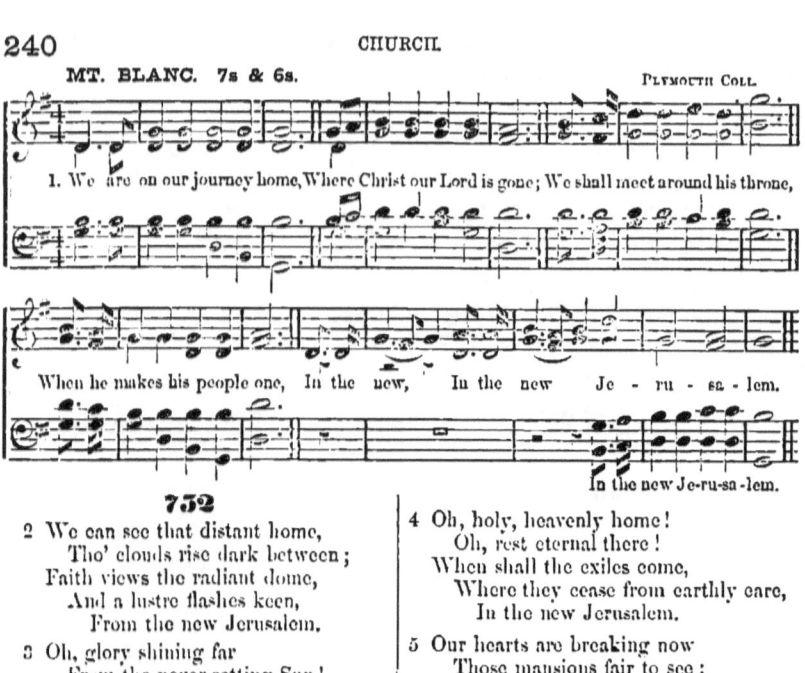

1. We are on our journey home, Where Christ our Lord is gone; We shall meet around his throne, When he makes his people one, In the new, In the new Jerusalem.
In the new Jerusalem.

752

2 We can see that distant home,
Tho' clouds rise dark between;
Faith views the radiant dome,
And a lustre flashes keen,
From the new Jerusalem.

3 Oh, glory shining far
From the never setting Sun!
Oh, trembling morning star!
Our journey's almost done,
To the new Jerusalem.

4 Oh, holy, heavenly home!
Oh, rest eternal there!
When shall the exiles come,
Where they cease from earthly care,
In the new Jerusalem.

5 Our hearts are breaking now
Those mansions fair to see;
O Lord! thy heavens bow,
And raise us up with thee
To the new Jerusalem.

I'M A PILGRIM.

1. I'm a pilgrim, and I'm a stranger; I can tarry, I can tarry but a night;
Do not detain me, for I am going To where the fountains are ever flowing.

753.

2 There the glory is ever shining!
Oh, my longing heart, my longing heart is there!
Here in this country so dark and dreary,
I long have wandered forlorn and weary.

3 There's the city to which I journey;
My Redeemer, my Redeemer is its light!
There is no sorrow, nor any sighing,
Nor any tears there, nor any dying!

REST FOR THE WEARY. 8s & 7s.

Rev. J. W. Dadmun.

1. In the Christian's home in glory There remains a land of rest, There my Saviour's gone before me To ful-fill my soul's request; There is rest for the wea-ry, There is rest for the wea-ry, There is rest for the wea-ry, There is rest for you— On the oth-er side of Jor-dan, In the sweet fields of E-den, Where the tree of life is blooming, There is rest for you!

754.

2 He is fitting up my mansion,
　Which eternally shall stand,
For my stay shall not be transient
　In that holy, happy land.
　　There is rest, etc.

3 Pain nor sickness ne'er shall enter,
　Grief nor woe my lot shall share;
But in that celestial centre
　I a crown of life shall wear.
　　There is rest, etc.

4 Death itself shall then be vanquished,
　And his sting shall be withdrawn;
Shout for gladness, O ye ransomed!
　Hail with joy the rising morn.
　　There is rest, etc.

5 Sing, oh, sing, ye heirs of glory!
　Shout your triumph as you go;
Zion's gates will open for you,
　You shall find an entrance through.
　　There is rest, etc.

CHURCH.

242. BEAUTIFUL ZION. 8s.
WM. B. BRADBURY.

1. Beau-ti-ful Zi-on, built a-bove, Beau-ti-ful cit-y that I love;
Beau-ti-ful gates of pearl-y white, Beau-ti-ful tem-ple—God its light;
He who was slain on Cal-va-ry, Opens those pearl-y gates to me.

755.

2 Beautiful heaven, where all is light,
Beautiful angels, clothed in white,
Beautiful strains, that never tire,
Beautiful harps through all the choir;
There shall I join the chorus sweet,
Worshiping at the Saviour's feet.

3 Beautiful crowns on every brow,
Beautiful palms the conquerors show,
Beautiful robes the ransomed wear,
Beautiful all who enter there;
Thither I press with eager feet,
There shall my rest be long and sweet.

4 Beautiful throne of Christ our King,
Beautiful songs the angels sing,
Beautiful rest, all wanderings cease,
Beautiful home of perfect peace;
There shall my eyes the Saviour see;
Haste to this heavenly home with me!

LOOKING HOME.
WM. B. BRADBURY.

1. Ah! this heart is void and chill, 'Mid earth's noisy throng-ing; For my Father's

SOCIAL MEETINGS. 243

LOOKING HOME. (Concluded.)

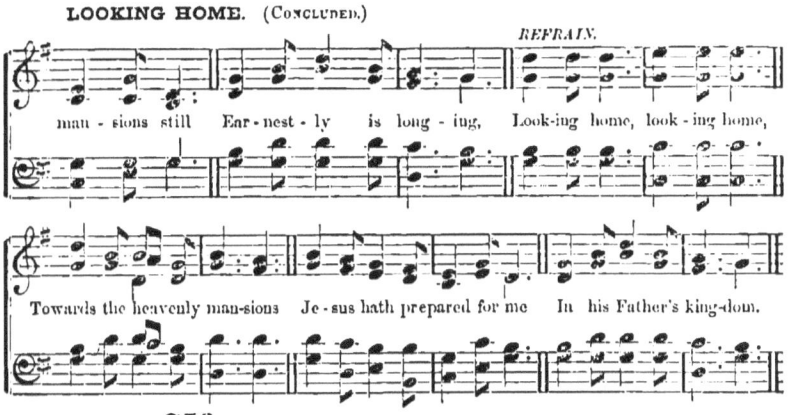

756.

2 Soon the glorious day will dawn,
  Heavenly pleasures bringing;
  Night will be exchanged for morn,
  Sighs give place to singing.—*Refrain.*

3 Oh! to be at home again,
  All for which we're sighing,
  From all earthly want and pain
  To be swiftly flying.—*Refrain.*

4 With this load of sin and care,
  Then no longer bending,
  But with waiting angels there
  On our soul attending.—

Refrain. Blesséd home, blesséd home,
  All for which we're sighing,
  Soon our Lord will bid us come
  To our Father's kingdom.—

SWEET LAND OF REST. C. M.   Wm. B. Bradbury.

757.

3 To Jesus Christ I sought for rest,
  He bade me cease to roam,
  But fly for succor to his breast,
  And he'd conduct me home.
  Home, home, etc.

4 Weary of wandering round and round,
  This vale of sin and gloom,
  I long to leave the unhallowed ground,
  And dwell with Christ at home.
  Home, home, etc.

244 DEATH AND JUDGMENT.

ZEPHYR. L. M.   Wm. B. Bradbury.

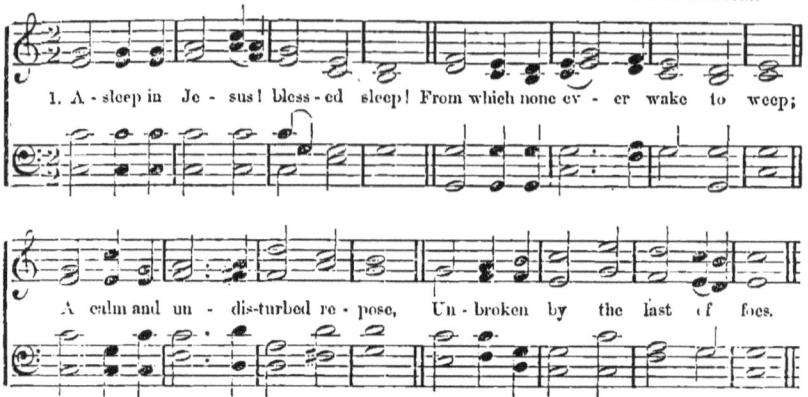

1. A-sleep in Je-sus! bless-ed sleep! From which none ev-er wake to weep;
A calm and un-dis-turbed re-pose, Un-broken by the last of foes.

758.

1 Asleep in Jesus! blessèd sleep!
From which none ever wake to weep;
A calm and undisturbed repose,
Unbroken by the last of foes.

2 Asleep in Jesus! oh, how sweet
To be for such a slumber meet!
With holy confidence to sing
That death hath lost its venomed sting!

3 Asleep in Jesus! peaceful rest!
Whose waking is supremely blest;
No fear—no woe, shall dim the hour
That manifests the Saviour's power.

4 Asleep in Jesus! oh, for me
May such a blissful refuge be:
Securely shall my ashes lie,
And wait the summons from on high.

5 Asleep in Jesus! far from thee
Thy kindred and their graves may be:
But there is still a blessèd sleep
From which none ever wake to weep.

759.

1 Why should we start, and fear to die!
What timorous worms we mortals are!
Death is the gate of endless joy,
And yet we dread to enter there.

2 The pains, the groans, and dying strife
Fright our approaching souls away;
We still shrink back again to life,
Fond of our prison and our clay.

3 Oh, if my Lord would come and meet,
My soul should stretch her wings in haste,
Fly fearless through death's iron gate,
Nor feel the terrors as she passed!

4 Jesus can make a dying bed
Feel soft as downy pillows are,
While on his breast I lean my head,
And breathe my life out sweetly there!

760.

1 How blest the righteous when he dies!
When sinks a weary soul to rest!
How mildly beam the closing eyes!
How gently heaves th' expiring breast!

2 So fades a summer cloud away;
So sinks the gale when storms are o'er;
So gently shuts the eye of day;
So dies a wave along the shore.

3 A holy quiet reigns around,
A calm which life nor death destroys;
And naught disturbs that peace profound
Which his unfettered soul enjoys.

4 Farewell, conflicting hopes and fears,
Where lights and shades alternate dwell;
How bright th' unchanging morn appears!
Farewell, inconstant world, farewell!

5 Life's labor done, as sinks the clay,
Light from its load the spirit flies,
While heaven and earth combine to say,
"How blest the righteous when he dies!"

DEATH AND JUDGMENT. 245

DODGE. L. M. — J. P. Holbrook.

1. Let me be with thee where thou art, My Saviour, my e-ter-nal Rest; Then on-ly will this long-ing heart Be ful-ly and for-ev-er blest.

761.

1 Let me be with thee where thou art,
My Saviour, my eternal Rest;
Then only will this longing heart
Be fully and forever blest.

2 Let me be with thee where thou art,
Thine unvailed glory to behold;
Then only will this wandering heart
Cease to be false to thee and cold.

3 Let me be with thee where thou art,
Where spotless saints thy name adore;
Then only will this sinful heart
Be evil and defiled no more.

4 Let me be with thee where thou art,
Where none can die, where none remove;
There neither death nor life will part
Me from thy presence and thy love.

762.

1 The hour of my departure's come,
I hear the voice that calls me home;
At last, O Lord! let trouble cease,
And let thy servant die in peace.

2 Not in mine innocence I trust;
I bow before thee in the dust;
And thro' my Saviour's blood alone,
I look for mercy at thy throne.

3 I leave the world without a tear,
Save for the friends I held so dear;
To heal their sorrows, Lord, descend,
And to the friendless prove a friend.

4 I come, I come at thy command,
I give my spirit to thy hand;
Stretch forth thine everlasting arms,
And shield me in the last alarms.

5 The hour of my departure's come,
I hear the voice that calls me home;
Now, oh! my God, let trouble cease,
Now let thy servant die in peace.

763.

1 Gently, my Saviour, let me down,
To slumber in the arms of death;
I rest my soul on thee alone,
Ev'n till my last, expiring breath.

2 Soon will the storm of life be o'er,
And I shall enter endless rest;
There I shall live to sin no more,
And bless thy name, forever blest.

3 Bid me possess sweet peace within;
Let child-like patience keep my heart;
Then shall I feel my heaven begin,
Before my spirit hence depart.

4 Oh, speed thy chariot, God of love,
And take me from this world of woe;
I long to reach those joys above,
And bid farewell to all below.

5 There shall my raptured spirit raise
Still louder notes than angels sing,—
High glories to Immanuel's grace,
My God, my Saviour, and my King!

246 DEATH AND JUDGMENT.

FEDERAL STREET. L. M.   H. K. Oliver.

1. So fades the love-ly, bloom-ing flower, Frail smil-ing sol-ace of an hour;
So soon our tran-sient com-forts fly, And pleasure on-ly blooms to die.

764.

2 Is there no kind, no healing art,
 To soothe the anguish of the heart?
 Divine Redeemer, be thou nigh:
 Thy comforts were not made to die.

3 Then gentle patience smiles on pain;
 And dying hope revives again;
 Hope wipes the tear from sorrow's eye,
 And faith points upward to the sky.

765.

1 Unvail thy bosom, faithful tomb;
 Take this new treasure to thy trust,
 And give these sacred relics room
 To slumber in the silent dust.

2 Nor pain, nor grief, nor anxious fear,
 Invade thy bounds; no mortal woes
 Can reach the peaceful sleeper here,
 While angels watch the soft repose.

3 So Jesus slept; God's dying Son
 Passed thro' the grave, and blessed the bed:
 Rest here, blest saint, till from his throne
 The morning break, and pierce the shade.

4 Break from his throne, illustrious morn!
 Attend, O earth! his sovereign word:
 Restore thy trust: a glorious form
 Shall then ascend to meet the Lord!

766.

1 What sinners value I resign;
 Lord! 't is enough that thou art mine;
 I shall behold thy blissful face,
 And stand complete in righteousness.

2 This life 's a dream—an empty show;
 But the bright world, to which I go,
 Hath joys substantial and sincere;
 When shall I wake, and find me there?

3 Oh! glorious hour!—oh! blest abode!
 I shall be near, and like my God;
 And flesh and sin no more control
 The sacred pleasures of the soul.

4 My flesh shall slumber in the ground,
 Till the last trumpet's joyful sound;
 Then burst the chains, with sweet surprise,
 And in my Saviour's image rise.

767.

1 "We've no abiding city here:"
 Sad truth, were this to be our home;
 But let this thought our spirits cheer,
 "We seek a city yet to come."

2 "We've no abiding city here;"
 We seek a city out of sight:
 Zion its name—the Lord is there,
 It shines with everlasting light.

3 O sweet abode of peace and love,
 Where pilgrims freed from toil are blest!
 Had I the pinions of a dove,
 I'd fly to thee, and be at rest.

4 But hush, my soul! nor dare repine;
 The time my God appoints is best:
 While here, to do his will be mine,
 And his to fix my time of rest.

JUDGMENT HYMN. L. M.

M. Luther.

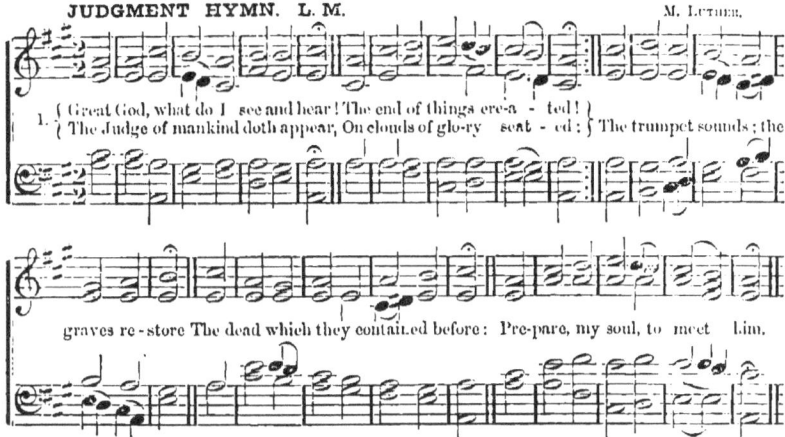

1. Great God, what do I see and hear! The end of things crea-ted! The Judge of mankind doth appear, On clouds of glory seat-ed; The trumpet sounds; the graves re-store The dead which they contained before: Pre-pare, my soul, to meet him.

768.

2 The dead in Christ shall first arise,
At the last trumpet's sounding,
Caught up to meet him in the skies,
With joy their Lord surrounding;
No gloomy fears their souls dismay,
His presence sheds eternal day
On those prepared to meet him.

3 But sinners, filled with guilty fears,
Behold his wrath prevailing;
For they shall rise, and find their tears
And sighs are unavailing:
The day of grace is past and gone;
Trembling they stand before the throne,
All unprepared to meet him.

4 Great God! what do I see and hear!
The end of things created!
The Judge of man I see appear,
On clouds of glory seated:
Beneath his cross I view the day
When heaven and earth shall pass away,
And thus prepare to meet him.

769.

1 THE day of wrath! that dreadful day,
When heaven and earth shall pass away!—
What power shall be the sinner's stay?
How shall he meet that dreadful day?—

2 When, shriveling like a parchéd scroll,
The flaming heavens together roll,
And louder yet, and yet more dread,
Swells the high trump that wakes the dead!

3 Oh, on that day, that wrathful day,
When man to judgment wakes from clay,
Be thou, O Christ, the sinner's stay,
Tho' heaven and earth shall pass away.

770.

1 THE Lord shall come! the earth shall quake;
The mountains to their centre shake:
And withering from the vault of night,
The stars withdraw their feeble light.

2 The Lord shall come! but not the same
As once in lowly form he came,—
A silent Lamb before his foes,
A weary man, and full of woes.

3 The Lord shall come! a dreadful form,
With wreath of flame, and robe of storm,
On cherub-wings, and wings of wind,
Anointed Judge of human kind!

4 Can this be he, who went to stray
A pilgrim on the world's highway,
By power oppressed, and mocked by pride,—
The Nazarene, the Crucified?

5 While sinners in despair shall call,
"Rocks, hide us! mountains, on us fall!"
The saints, ascending from the tomb,
Shall sing for joy, "The Lord is come!"

DEATH AND JUDGMENT.

CHINA. C. M. — SWAN.

1. Why do we mourn departing friends, Or shake at death's alarms? 'Tis but the voice that Jesus sends, To call them to his arms.

771.

1 Why do we mourn departing friends,
    Or shake at death's alarms?
  'Tis but the voice that Jesus sends,
    To call them to his arms.

2 Are we not tending upward, too,
    As fast as time can move?
  Nor would we wish the hours more slow,
    To keep us from our love.

3 Why should we tremble to convey
    Their bodies to the tomb?
  There the dear flesh of Jesus lay,
    And scattered all the gloom.

4 The graves of all his saints he blessed,
    And softened every bed;
  Where should the dying members rest,
    But with the dying Head?

5 Thence he arose, ascending high,
    And showed our feet the way;
  Up to the Lord we, too, shall fly,
    At the great rising day.

6 Then let the last loud trumpet sound,
    And bid our kindred rise;
  Awake! ye nations under ground;
    Ye saints! ascend the skies.

772.

1 Why should our tears in sorrow flow,
    When God recalls his own;
  And bids them leave a world of wo
    For an immortal crown?

2 Is not ev'n death a gain to those
    Whose life to God was given?
  Gladly to earth their eyes they close,
    To open them in heaven.

3 Their toils are past, their work is done,
    And they are fully blest:
  They fought the fight, the victory won,
    And entered into rest.

4 Then let our sorrows cease to flow,—
    God has recalled his own;
  And let our hearts in every woe,
    Still say,—"Thy will be done!"

773.

1 How still and peaceful is the grave!
    Where, life's vain tumults past,
  Th' appointed house, by heaven's decree,
    Receives us all at last.

2 The wicked there from troubling cease;
    Their passions rage no more;
  And there the weary pilgrim rests
    From all the toils he bore.

3 There servants, masters, small and great,
    Partake the same repose;
  And there, in peace, the ashes mix
    Of those who once were foes.

4 All, leveled by the hand of death,
    Lie sleeping in the tomb,
  Till God in judgment calls them forth,
    To meet their final doom.

DEATH AND JUDGMENT. 249

BARBY. C. M. TANSUR.

1. Oh, for an o-ver-com-ing faith To cheer my dy-ing hours! To tri-umph o'er the mon-ster, death, And all his fright-ful powers.

774.

1 Oh, for an overcoming faith
  To cheer my dying hours!
  To triumph o'er the monster, death,
  And all his frightful powers.

2 Joyful, with all the strength I have,
  My quivering lips should sing,
  "Where is thy boasted victory, grave?
  And where the monster's sting?"

3 If sin be pardoned, I'm secure;
  Death has no sting beside:
  The law gives sin its damning power,
  But Christ, my ransom, died.

4 Now to the God of victory
  Immortal thanks be paid,
  Who makes us conquerors while we die,
  Through Christ our living Head.

775.

1 Thro' sorrow's night, and danger's path,
  Amid the deepening gloom,
  We, followers of our suffering Lord,
  Are marching to the tomb.

2 There, when the turmoil is no more,
  And all our powers decay,
  Our cold remains in solitude
  Shall sleep the years away.

3 Our labors done, securely laid
  In this our last retreat,
  Unheeded o'er our silent dust
  The storms of earth shall beat.

4 Yet not thus buried or extinct,
  The vital spark shall lie;
  For o'er life's wreck that spark shall rise
  To seek its kindred sky.

5 These ashes, too, this little dust,
  Our Father's care shall keep,
  Till the last angel rise and break
  The long and dreary sleep.

6 Then love's soft dew o'er every eye
  Shall shed its mildest rays,
  And the long-silent voice awake
  With shouts of endless praise.

776.

1 DEAR as thou wert, and justly dear,
  We will not weep for thee:
  One thought shall check the starting tear:
  It is, that thou art free.

2 And thus shall faith's consoling power
  The tears of love restrain:
  Oh, who that saw thy parting hour,
  Could wish thee back again!

3 Triumphant in thy closing eye
  The hope of glory shone;
  Joy breathed in thy expiring sigh,
  To think the fight was won.

4 Gently the passing spirit fled,
  Sustained by grace divine:
  Oh, may such grace on me be shed,
  And make my end like thine!

250   DEATH AND JUDGMENT.

MORNINGTON. S. M.   Lord Mornington.

1. How swift the tor-rent rolls, That bears us to the sea! The tide that hur-ries thoughtless souls To vast e-ter-ni-ty.

777.

2 Our fathers, where are they,
   With all they called their own?
Their joys and griefs, and hopes and cares,
   And wealth and honor gone!

3 And where the fathers lie,
   Must all the children dwell;
Nor other heritage possess,
   But such a gloomy cell.

4 God of our fathers hear,
   Thou everlasting Friend!
While we, as on life's utmost verge,
   Our souls to thee commend.

5 Of all the pious dead
   May we the footsteps trace,
Till with them, in the land of light,
   We dwell before thy face.

778.

1 And must this body die?—
   This mortal frame decay?
And must these active limbs of mine
   Lie mouldering in the clay?

2 God, my Redeemer, lives,
   And, often from the skies,
Looks down and watches all my dust,
   Till he shall bid it rise.

3 Arrayed in glorious grace,
   Shall these vile bodies shine;
And every shape, and every face,
   Look heavenly and divine.

4 These lively hopes we owe
   To Jesus' dying love;
We would adore his grace below,
   And sing his power above.

5 Dear Lord! accept the praise
   Of these our humble songs;
Till tunes of nobler sound we raise,
   With our immortal tongues.

779.

1 Come, Lord, and tarry not!
   Bring the long-looked-for day;
Oh, why these years of waiting here,
   These ages of delay?

2 Come, for thy saints still wait;
   Daily ascends their sigh;
The Spirit and the Bride say, Come!
   Dost thou not hear the cry?

3 Come, for creation groans,
   Impatient of thy stay,
Worn out with these long years of ill,
   These ages of delay.

4 Come, and make all things new,
   Build up this ruined earth,
Restore our faded paradise,
   Creation's second birth.

5 Come and begin thy reign
   Of everlasting peace,
Come, take the kingdom to thyself,
   Great King of Righteousness!

DEATH AND JUDGMENT. 251

GREENWOOD. S. M.   Root & Sweetser's Coll.

1. It is not death to die— To leave this wea-ry road, And, 'mid the broth-er-hood on high, To be at home with God.

780.

2 It is not death to close
The eye long dimmed by tears,
And wake, in glorious repose
To spend eternal years.

3 It is not death to bear
The wrench that sets us free
From dungeon chain,—to breathe the air
Of boundless liberty.

4 It is not death to fling
Aside this sinful dust,
And rise, on strong exulting wing,
To live among the just.

5 Jesus, thou Prince of life!
Thy chosen cannot die;
Like thee, they conquer in the strife,
To reign with thee on high.

781.

1 "Servant of God, well done,
Rest from thy loved employ:
The battle fought, the victory won,
Enter thy Master's joy."

2 The voice at midnight came,
He started up to hear;
A mortal arrow pierced his frame,
He fell—but felt no fear.

3 Tranquil amidst alarms,
It found him on the field,
A veteran slumbering on his arms,
Beneath his red-cross shield.

4 His spirit, with a bound,
Left its encumbering clay;
His tent, at sunrise, on the ground,
A darkened ruin lay.

5 The pains of death are past,
Labor and sorrow cease;
And, life's long warfare closed at last,
His soul is found in peace.

6 Soldier of Christ, well done!
Praise be thy new employ;
And while eternal ages run,
Rest in thy Saviour's joy.

782.

1 Alas the brittle clay,
That built our body first!
And, every month, and every day,
'T is mouldering back to dust.

2 Our moments fly apace,
Nor will our minutes stay;
Just like a flood, our hasty days
Are sweeping us away.

3 Well, if our days must fly,
We'll keep their end in sight;
We'll spend them all in wisdom's way,
And let them speed their flight.

4 They'll waft us sooner o'er
This life's tempestuous sea:
Soon we shall reach the peaceful shore
Of blest eternity.

252   DEATH AND JUDGMENT.

OLMUTZ. S. M.   *Arranged by* Dr. L. Mason.

1. "For-ev-er with the Lord!" So, Je-sus! let it be;
Life from the dead is in that word; 'Tis im-mor-tal-i-ty.

783.

1 "Forever with the Lord!"
   So, Jesus! let it be;
Life from the dead is in that word;
   'T is immortality.

2 Here, in the body pent,
   Absent from thee I roam:
Yet nightly pitch my moving tent
   A day's march nearer home.

3 My Father's house on high,
   Home of my soul! how near,
At times, to faith's aspiring eye,
   Thy golden gates appear!

4 "Forever with the Lord!"
   Father, if 't is thy will,
The promise of thy gracious word,
   Ev'n here to me fulfill.

5 So, when my latest breath
   Shall rend the vail in twain,
By death I shall escape from death,
   And life eternal gain.

6 Knowing "as I am known,"
   How shall I love that word,
And oft repeat before the throne,
   "Forever with the Lord!"

784.

1 Oh, for the death of those
   Who slumber in the Lord!
Oh, be like theirs my last repose,
   Like theirs my last reward!

2 Their bodies in the ground,
   In silent hope may lie,
Till the last trumpet's joyful sound
   Shall call them to the sky.

3 Their ransomed spirits soar
   On wings of faith and love,
To meet the Saviour they adore,
   And reign with him above.

4 With us their names shall live
   Through long succeeding years,
Embalmed with all our hearts can give,
   Our praises and our tears.

5 Oh, for the death of those
   Who slumber in the Lord!
Oh, be like theirs my last repose,
   Like theirs my last reward!

785.

1 Behold, the day is come;
   The righteous Judge is near;
And sinners, trembling at their doom,
   Shall soon their sentence hear.

2 How awful is the sight!
   How loud the thunders roar!
The sun forbears to give his light,
   And stars are seen no more.

3 The whole creation groans;
   But saints arise and sing:
They are the ransomed of the Lord,
   And he their God and King.

DEATH AND JUDGMENT. 253

BOYLSTON. S. M.   Dr. L. Mason.

1. My soul, re-peat his praise, Whose mer-cies are so great; Whose an-ger is so slow to rise, So rea-dy to a-bate.

786.

2 The pity of the Lord,
   To those that fear his name,
Is such as tender parents feel;
   He knows our feeble frame.

3 Our days are as the grass,
   Or like the morning flower:
If one sharp blast sweep o'er the field,
   It withers in an hour.

4 But thy compassions, Lord,
   To endless years endure;
And children's children ever find
   Thy words of promise sure.

787.

1 LORD, let me know mine end,
   My days, how brief their date,
That I may timely comprehend
   How frail my best estate.

2 My life is but a span,
   Mine age is nought with thee;
Sure, in his highest honor, man
   Is dust and vanity.

3 Dumb at thy feet I lie,
   For thou hast brought me low;
Remove thy judgments, lest I die;
   I faint beneath thy blow.

4 At thy rebuke, the bloom
   Of man's vain beauty flies;
And grief shall like a moth consume
   All that delights our eyes.

5 Have pity on my fears,
   Hearken to my request;
Turn not in silence from my tears,
   But give the mourner rest.

6 Oh, spare me yet, I pray,
   Awhile my strength restore,
Ere I am summoned hence away,
   And seen on earth no more.

788.

1 REST for the toiling hand,
   Rest for the anxious brow,
Rest for the weary, way-worn feet,
   Rest from all labor now;—

2 Rest for the fevered brain,
   Rest for the throbbing eye;
Through these parched lips of thine no more
   Shall pass the moan or sigh.

3 Soon shall the trump of God
   Give out the welcome sound,
That shakes thy silent chamber-walls,
   And breaks the turf-sealed ground.

4 Ye dwellers in the dust,
   Awake! come forth and sing;
Sharp has your frost of winter been,
   But bright shall be your spring.

5 'T was sown in weakness here;
   'T will then be raised in power:
That which was sown an earthly seed,
   Shall rise a heavenly flower!

DEATH AND JUDGMENT.

FULTON. 7s. — Wm. B. Bradbury.

1. Brother, though from yonder sky Cometh neither voice nor cry, Yet we know for thee to-day, Every pain hath passed away.

789.

1 Brother, though from yonder sky
Cometh neither voice nor cry;
Yet we know for thee to-day,
Every pain hath passed away.

2 Not for thee shall tears be given,
Child of God, and heir of heaven!
For he gave thee sweet release;
Thine the Christian's death of peace.

3 Well we know thy living faith
Had the power to conquer death;
As a living rose may bloom
By the border of the tomb.

4 Brother, in that solemn trust
We commend thee, dust to dust!
In that faith we wait, till, risen,
Thou shalt meet us all in heaven.

5 While we weep as Jesus wept,
Thou shalt sleep as Jesus slept:
With thy Saviour thou shalt rest,
Crowned, and glorified, and blest.

790.

1 Hark! that shout of rapturous joy,
Bursting forth from yonder cloud!
Jesus comes, and through the sky
Angels tell their joy aloud!

2 Hark! the trumpet's awful voice
Sounds abroad, through sea and land;
Lo! his people now rejoice!
Their redemption is at hand.

3 See! the Lord appears in view;
Heaven and earth before him fly!
Rise, ye saints, he comes for you—
Rise to meet him in the sky.

4 Go, and dwell with him above,
Where no foe can e'er molest:
Happy in the Saviour's love!
Ever blessing, ever blest.

791.

1 Hark! a voice divides the sky!
Happy are the faithful dead
In the Lord who sweetly die!
They from all their toils are freed.

2 Ready for their glorious crown,
Sorrows past and sins forgiven,—
Here they lay their burden down,
Hallowed and made meet for heaven.

3 Yes! the Christian's course is run!
Ended is the glorious strife;
Fought the fight, the work is done;
Death is swallowed up in life!

4 Lo! the prisoner is released—
Lightened of his heavy load;
Where the weary are at rest,
He is gathered unto God!

5 When from flesh the spirit freed,
Hastens homeward to return,
Mortals cry, "A man is dead!"
Angels sing, "A child is born!"

DEATH AND JUDGMENT. 255

FREDERICK. 11s. — Geo. Kingsley.

1. I would not live alway; I ask not to stay Where storm after storm rises dark o'er the way; The few lurid mornings that dawn on us here, Are enough for life's woes, full enough for its cheer.

792.

2 I would not live alway; no,—welcome the tomb;
Since Jesus hath lain there, I dread not its gloom;
There, sweet be my rest, till he bid me arise,
To hail him in triumph descending the skies.
Who—who would live alway, away from his God;
Away from yon heaven, that blissful abode,

Where the rivers of pleasure flow o'er the bright plains,
And the noontide of glory eternally reigns?
4 There saints of all ages in harmony meet,
Their Saviour and brethren transported to greet;
While anthems of rapture unceasingly roll,
And the smile of the Lord is the feast of the soul.

BAXTER. 10s. — Frank Slye.

1. Go to the grave in all thy glorious prime, In full activity of zeal and power; Thou art not called away before thy time— The Lord's appointment is the servant's hour.

793.

2 Go to the grave: at noon from labor cease;
Rest on thy sheaves, thy harvest task is done;
Come from the heat of battle, and in peace,
Soldier, go home; with thee the fight is won.
3 Go to the grave; for there thy Saviour lay
In death's embraces, ere he rose on high;

And all the ransomed, by that narrow way,
Passed to eternal life beyond the sky.
4 Go to the grave:—no; take thy seat above;
Be thy pure spirit present with the Lord,
Where thou for faith and hope hast perfect love,
And open vision for the written word.

DEATH AND JUDGMENT.

REQUIEM. S. H. M. — Dr. Hastings.

1. This place is ho-ly ground; World, with its cares, a-way! A ho-ly, sol-emn still-ness round This life-less, mouldering clay; Nor pain, nor grief, nor anx-ious fear Can reach the peace-ful sleep-er here.

794.

2 Behold the bed of death—
  The pale and mortal clay;
  Heard ye the sob of parting breath?
  Marked ye the eye's last ray?
  No; life so sweetly ceased to be,
  It lapsed in immortality.

3 Why mourn the pious dead?
  Why sorrows swell our eyes?
  Can sighs recall the spirit fled?
  Shall vain regrets arise?
  Tho' death has caused this altered mien,
  In heaven the ransomed soul is seen.

4 Bury the dead and weep
  In stillness o'er the loss;
  Bury the dead! in Christ they sleep,
  Who bore on earth his cross;
  And from the grave their dust shall rise,
  In his own image to the skies.

795.

1 Friend after friend departs:
  Who hath not lost a friend?
  There is no union here of hearts
  That finds not here an end;
  Were this frail world our only rest,
  Living or dying, none were blest.

2 Beyond the flight of time,
  Beyond this vale of death,
  There surely is some blessed clime
  Where life is not a breath,
  Nor life's affections transient fire,
  Whose sparks fly upward to expire.

3 There is a world above,
  Where parting is unknown;
  A whole eternity of love,
  Formed for the good alone;
  And faith beholds the dying here
  Translated to that happier sphere.

4 Thus star by star declines,
  Till all are passed away,
  As morning high and higher shines,
  To pure and perfect day;
  Nor sink those stars in empty night—
  They hide themselves in heaven's own light.

DEATH AND JUDGMENT. 257

SCOTLAND. 12s. Dr. Clarke.

1. The voice of free grace cries, Escape to the mountain, For Adam's lost race Christ hath opened a fountain; { For sin and uncleanness, and ev-ery transgression, His { Halle-lu-jah to the Lamb, who hath purchased our pardon, We'll blood flows most freely in streams of salvation, His blood flows most freely in streams of salvation. praise him again, when we pass over Jordan, We'll praise him again, when we pass over Jordan.

796.

2 Ye souls that are wounded! oh, flee to the Saviour;
He calls you in mercy,—'t is infinite favor;
Your sins are increasing,—escape to the mountain,—
His blood can remove them,—it flows from the fountain.

3 O Jesus! ride onward, triumphantly glorious,
O'er sin, death, and hell, thou art more than victorious;
Thy name is the theme of the great congregation,
While angels and men raise the shout of salvation.

4 With joy shall we stand, when escaped to the shore;
With harps in our hands, we'll praise him the more;
We'll range the sweet plains on the bank of the river,
And sing of salvation forever and ever!

797.

1 Thou art gone to the grave! but we will not deplore thee,
Though sorrow and darkness encompass the tomb;
The Saviour hath passed through its portals before thee,
And the lamp of his love is thy guide through the gloom.

2 Thou art gone to the grave! we no longer behold thee,
Nor tread the rough paths of the world by thy side;
But the wide arms of mercy are spread to enfold thee,
And sinners may hope, for the Sinless hath died.

3 Thou art gone to the grave! and, its mansion forsaking,
What though thy weak spirit in fear lingered long:
The sunshine of Paradise beamed on thy waking,
And the sound which thou heard'st, was the seraphim's song.

4 Thou art gone to the grave! but we will not deplore thee,
For God was thy ransom, thy Guardian, and Guide
He gave thee, he took thee, and he will restore thee;
And death hath no sting, for the Saviour hath died.

DEATH AND JUDGMENT.

DORRNANCE. 8s & 7s. I. B. WOODBURY.

1. Jesus, while our hearts are bleeding
O'er the spoils that death has won,
We would, at this solemn meeting,
Calmly say,—thy will be done.

798.

1 JESUS, while our hearts are bleeding
O'er the spoils that death has won,
We would at this solemn meeting,
Calmly say,—thy will be done.

2 Though cast down, we 're not forsaken;
Though afflicted, not alone;
Thou didst give, and thou hast taken;
Blessèd Lord,—thy will be done.

3 Tho' to-day we 're filled with mourning,
Mercy still is on the throne;
With thy smiles of love returning,
We can sing—thy will be done.

4 By thy hands the boon was given,
Thou hast taken but thine own:
Lord of earth, and God of heaven,
Evermore,—thy will be done!

799.

1 TARRY with me, O my Saviour!
For the day is passing by;
See! the shades of evening gather,
And the night is drawing nigh.

2 Deeper, deeper grow the shadows,
Paler now the glowing west,
Swift the night of death advances;
Shall it be the night of rest?

3 Lonely seems the vale of shadow;
Sinks my heart with troubled fear;
Give me faith for clearer vision,
Speak thou, Lord, in words of cheer.

4 Let me hear thy voice behind me,
Calming all these wild alarms;
Let me, underneath my weakness,
Feel the everlasting arms.

5 Feeble, trembling, fainting, dying,
Lord, I cast myself on thee;
Tarry with me through the darkness;
While I sleep, still watch by me.

6 Tarry with me, O my Saviour!
Lay my head upon thy breast
Till the morning; then awake me—
Morning of eternal rest!

800.

1 CEASE, ye mourners, cease to languish
O'er the grave of those you love;
Pain and death and night and anguish
Enter not the world above.

2 While our silent steps are straying
Lonely thro' night's deepening shade,
Glory's brightest beams are playing
Round the happy Christian's head.

3 Light and peace at once deriving
From the hand of God most high,
In his glorious presence living,
They shall never, never die.

4 Now, ye mourners, cease to languish
O'er the grave of those you love;
Far removed from pain and anguish,
They are chanting hymns above.

DEATH AND JUDGMENT. 259

MT. VERNON. 8s & 7s. Dr. L. Mason.

1. Sister, thou wast mild and lovely,
Gentle as the summer breeze,
Pleasant as the air of evening,
When it floats among the trees.

801.

2 Peaceful be thy silent slumber—
Peaceful in the grave so low :
Thou no more wilt join our number;
Thou no more our songs shalt know.

3 Dearest sister, thou hast left us,
Here thy loss we deeply feel ;
But 't is God that hath bereft us,
He can all our sorrows heal.

4 Yet again we hope to meet thee,
When the day of life is fled ;
Then in heaven with joy to greet thee,
Where no farewell tear is shed.

802.

1 See the leaves around us falling,
Dry and withered to the ground ;
Thus to thoughtless mortals calling,
In a sad and solemn sound.

2 Sons of Adam, once in Eden,
When like him, ye blighted fell,
Hear the lesson we are reading,
'T is alas ! the truth we tell.

3 Youth, on length of days presuming,
Who the paths of pleasure tread,
View us, late in beauty blooming,
Numbered now among the dead.

4 Though as yet no losses grieve you,
Gay with health and many a grace,
Let no cloudless skies deceive you ;
Summer gives to autumn place.

5 Yearly in our course appearing,
Messengers of shortest stay,
Thus we preach in mortal hearing—
Ye, like us, shall pass away.

6 On the tree of life eternal,
Oh, let all our hopes be laid !
This alone, forever vernal,
Bears a leaf that shall not fade.

803.

1 Great Redeemer, Friend of sinners !
Thou hast wondrous power to save;
Grant me grace, and still protect me,
Over life's tempestuous wave.

2 May my soul, with sacred transport,
View the dawn while yet afar ;
And, until the sun arises,
Lead me by the Morning Star.

3 See the happy spirits waiting
On the banks beyond the stream ;
Sweet responses still repeating,
Jesus, Jesus is their theme.

4 Swiftly roll, ye lingering hours,
Seraphs lend your glittering wings ;
Love absorbs my ransomed powers,
Heavenly sounds around me ring.

5 Worlds of light ! and crowns of glory !
Far above yon azure sky ;
Though by faith I now behold you,
I 'll enjoy you soon on high.

DEATH AND JUDGMENT.

TAMWORTH. 8s, 7s & 4s.
LOCKHART.

1. See th' e-ter-nal Judge de-scend-ing, View him seat-ed on his throne!
   Now, poor sin-ner, now la-ment-ing, Stand and hear thine aw-ful doom!
   Trum-pets call thee, Trum-pets call thee; Stand and hear thine aw-ful doom!

804.

2 Hear the cries he now is venting,
　Filled with dread of fiercer pain;
　While in anguish thus lamenting,
　That he ne'er was born again:
　　Greatly mourning,
　That he ne'er was born again.

3 " Yonder sits the slighted Saviour,
　With the marks of dying love;
　Oh, that I had sought his favor,
　When I felt his Spirit move!
　　Golden moments,
　When I felt his Spirit move."

4 Now, despisers, look and wonder;
　Hope and sinners here must part:
　Louder than a peal of thunder,
　Hear the dreadful sound, " Depart!"
　　Lost forever,
　Hear the dreadful sound, " Depart!"

805.

1 Lo! he cometh,—countless trumpets
　Wake to life the slumbering dead;
　Mid ten thousand saints and angels,
　See their great exalted Head:
　　Hallelujah!—
　Welcome, welcome, Son of God!

2 Full of joyful expectation,
　Saints behold the Judge appear:
　Truth and justice go before him—
　Now the joyful sentence hear;
　　Hallelujah!—
　Welcome, welcome, Judge divine!

3 " Come, ye blessed of my Father!
　Enter into life and joy;
　Banish all your fears and sorrows;
　Endless praise be your employ:"
　　Hallelujah!—
　Welcome, welcome to the skies!

806.

1 Lo! he comes with clouds descending,
　Once for favored sinners slain!
　Thousand thousand saints attending,
　Swell the triumph of his train!
　　Hallelujah!
　Jesus comes, and comes to reign.

2 Every eye shall now behold him,
　Robed in dreadful majesty!
　Those who set at naught and sold him,
　Pierced and nailed him to the tree,
　　Deeply wailing,
　Shall the true Messiah see!

3 When the solemn trump has sounded,
　Heaven and earth shall flee away;
　All who hate him must, confounded,
　Hear the summons of that day—
　　Come to judgment!
　Come to judgment! come away!

4 Yea, Amen! let all adore thee,
　High on thine eternal throne!
　Saviour, take the power and glory;
　Make thy righteous sentence known!
　　Oh, come quickly,
　Claim the kingdom for thine own!

DEATH AND JUDGMENT. 261

BREST. 8s, 7s & 4s. *Carmina Sacra.*

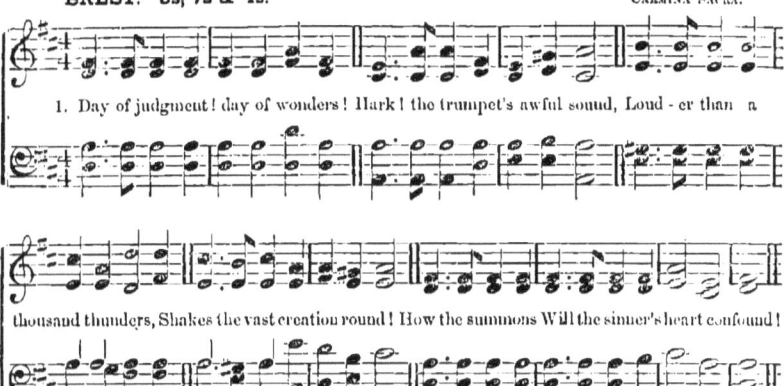

1. Day of judgment! day of wonders! Hark! the trumpet's awful sound, Loud-er than a thousand thunders, Shakes the vast creation round! How the summons Will the sinner's heart confound!

807.

1 Day of judgment! day of wonders!
Hark!—the trumpet's awful sound,
Louder than a thousand thunders,
Shakes the vast creation round :
How the summons
Will the sinner's heart confound!

2 See the Judge, our nature wearing,
Clothed in majesty divine!
You, who long for his appearing,
Then shall say, " This God is mine!"
Gracious Saviour!
Own me in that day for thine.

3 At his call, the dead awaken,
Rise to life from earth and sea;
All the powers of nature, shaken
By his looks, prepare to flee:
Careless sinner!
What will then become of thee?

4 But to those who have confessed,
Loved and served the Lord below,
He will say,—" Come near, ye blessed!
See the kingdom I bestow:
You forever
Shall my love and glory know."

808.

1 Lo! the mighty God appearing—
From on high Jehovah speaks!

Eastern lands the summons hearing,
O'er the west his thunder breaks:
Earth beholds him:
Universal nature shakes.

2 Zion all its light unfolding,
God in glory shall display:
Lo! he comes,—nor silence holding,
Fire and clouds prepare his way:
Tempests round him
Hasten on the dreadful day.

3 To the heavens his voice ascending,
To the earth beneath he cries—
" Souls immortal now descending,
Let the sleeping dust arise!
Rise to judgment;
Let my throne adorn the skies.

4 " Gather first my saints around me,
Those who to my covenant stood;
Those who humbly sought and found me,
Through the dying Saviour's blood:
Blest Redeemer!
Choicest sacrifice to God!"

5 Now the heavens on high adore him,
And his righteousness declare:
Sinners perish from before him,
But his saints his mercies share:
Just his judgment!
God, himself the Judge, is there.

HEAVEN.

LOWRY. L. M. Root & Sweetser's Coll.

1. Oh, for a sweet, in-spiring ray, To an-i-mate our fee-ble strains, From the bright realms of end-less day— The bliss-ful realms where Je-sus reigns.

809.

2 There, low before his glorious throne,
  Adoring saints and angels fall;
  And, with delightful worship, own
  His smile their bliss, their heaven, their all.

3 Immortal glories crown his head,
  While tuneful hallelujahs rise,
  And love and joy and triumph spread
  Through all th' assemblies of the skies.

4 He smiles,—and seraphs tune their songs
  To boundless rapture, while they gaze;
  Ten thousand thousand joyful tongues
  Resound his everlasting praise.

5 There all the followers of the Lamb
  Shall join at last the heavenly choir:
  Oh, may the joy-inspiring theme
  Awake our faith and warm desire!

810.

1 Now let our souls, on wings sublime,
  Rise from the vanities of time,
  Draw back the parting vail, and see
  The glories of eternity.

2 Born by a new celestial birth,
  Why should we grovel here on earth?
  Why grasp at transitory toys,
  So near to heaven's eternal joys?

3 Should aught beguile us on the road,
  When we are walking back to God?
  For strangers into life we come,
  And dying is but going home.

4 Welcome, sweet hour of full discharge!
  That sets our longing souls at large,
  Unbinds our chains, breaks up our cell,
  And gives us with our God to dwell.

5 To dwell with God—to feel his love,
  Is the full heaven enjoyed above;
  And the sweet expectation now
  Is the young dawn of heaven below.

811.

1 Descend from heaven, immortal Dove!
  Stoop down and take us on thy wings;
  And mount, and bear us far above
  The reach of these inferior things,—

2 Beyond, beyond this lower sky,
  Up where eternal ages roll,
  Where solid pleasures never die,
  And fruits immortal feast the soul.

3 Oh, for a sight, a pleasing sight,
  Of our almighty Father's throne!
  There sits our Saviour, crowned with light,
  Clothed in a body like our own.

4 Adoring saints around him stand,
  And thrones and powers before him fall:
  The God shines gracious through the Man,
  And sheds sweet glories on them all.

5 Oh! what amazing joys they feel,
  While to their golden harps they sing,
  And sit on every heavenly hill,
  And spread the triumph of their king!

HEAVEN. 263

PALMER. S. M. J. N. PATTISON.

1. I have a home above, From sin and sorrow free;
A mansion which eternal love Designed and formed for me.

812.

2 My Father's gracious hand
Has built this sweet abode;
From everlasting it was planned—
My dwelling-place with God.

3 My Saviour's precious blood
Has made my title sure;
He passed thro' death's dark raging flood
To make my rest secure.

4 The Comforter is come,
The earnest has been given;
He leads me onward to the home
Reserved for me in heaven.

5 Loved ones are gone before,
Whose pilgrim days are done;
I soon shall greet them on that shore
Where partings are unknown.

813.

1 AND is there, Lord, a rest
For weary souls designed,
Where not a care shall stir the breast,
Or sorrow entrance find?

2 Is there a blissful home,
Where kindred minds shall meet,
And live, and love, nor ever roam
From that serene retreat?

3 Are there bright, happy fields,
Where nought that blooms shall die;
Where each new scene fresh pleasure yields,
And healthful breezes sigh?

4 Are there celestial streams,
Where living waters glide,
With murmurs sweet as angel dreams,
And flowery banks beside?

5 Forever blessèd they,
Whose joyful feet shall stand,
While endless ages waste away,
Amid that glorious land!

6 My soul would thither tend,
While toilsome years are given;
Then let me, gracious God, ascend
To sweet repose in heaven!

814.

1 FAR from my heavenly home,
Far from my Father's breast,
Fainting, I cry, "Blest Spirit, come,
And speed me to my rest!"

2 Upon the willows long
My harp has silent hung;
How should I sing a cheerful song,
Till thou inspire my tongue?

3 My spirit homeward turns,
And fain would thither flee;
My heart, O Zion, droops and yearns,
When I remember thee.

4 To thee, to thee I press—
A dark and toilsome road:
When shall I pass the wilderness,
And reach the saints' abode?

HEAVEN.

VICTORY. 10s.

1. Joy-ful-ly, joy-ful-ly on-ward I move, Bound to the land of bright
 An-gel-ic chor-is-ters sing as I come, "Joy-ful-ly, joy-ful-ly

spi-rits a-bove; Soon, with my pil-grim-age end-ed be-low,
haste to thy home!" Home to the land of bright spi-rits I go;

Pilgrim and stranger no more shall I roam, Joy-ful-ly, joy-ful-ly rest-ing at home.

815.

2 Friends, fondly cherished, have passed on before;
Waiting, they watch me approaching the shore;
Singing to cheer me thro' death's chilling gloom:
"Joyfully, joyfully haste to thy home!"
Sounds of sweet melody fall on my ear;
Harps of the blessèd, your voices I hear!
Rings with the harmony heaven's high dome—
"Joyfully, joyfully haste to thy home!"

3 Death, with thy weapons of war lay me low,
Strike, king of terrors! I fear not the blow;
Jesus hath broken the bars of the tomb!
Joyfully, joyfully will I go home.
Bright will the morn of eternity dawn,
Death shall be banished, his sceptre be gone;
Joyfully, then shall I witness his doom,
Joyfully, joyfully, safely at home.

816.

1 Happy the spirit released from its clay;
Happy the soul that goes bounding away;
Singing, as upward it hastes to the skies,
Victory! victory! homeward I rise.
Many the toils it has passed through below,
Many the seasons of trial and woe;
Many the doubtings it never should sing,
Victory! victory! thus on the wing.

2 How can we wish them recalled from their home,
Longer in sorrowing exile to roam?
Safely they passed from their troubles beneath,
Victory! victory! shouting in death.
Thus let them slumber, till Christ from the skies,
Bids them in glorified body arise;
Singing, as upward they spring from the tomb,
Victory! victory! Jesus hath come.

HEAVEN.   265

BEULAH. 7s. Double.   E. IVES, JR.

1. Who are these in bright ar-ray, This in-nu-mer-a-ble throng,
Round the al-tar, night and day, Hymn-ing one tri-umph-ant song?—
D. S. Wis-dom, rich-es to ob-tain; New do-min-ion ev-ery hour."
"Wor-thy is the Lamb once slain, Bless-ing, hon-or, glo-ry, power,

817.

2 These through fiery trials trod,—
  These from great affliction came:
Now before the throne of God,
  Sealed with his almighty name,
Clad in raiment pure and white,
  Victor-palms in every hand,
Through their dear Redeemer's might
  More than conquerors they stand.

3 Hunger, thirst, disease unknown,
  On immortal fruits they feed:
Them, the Lamb, amidst the throne,
  Shall to living fountains lead:
Joy and gladness banish sighs,
  Perfect love dispel all fears,
And forever from their eyes
  God shall wipe away the tears.

818.

1 High in yonder realms of light,
  Dwell the raptured saints above;
Far beyond our feeble sight,
  Happy in Immanuel's love:
Once they knew, like us below,
  Pilgrims in this vale of tears,
Torturing pain and heavy woe,
  Gloomy doubts, distressing fears.

2 Oft the big, unbidden tear,
  Stealing down the furrowed cheek,
Told, in eloquence sincere,
  Tales of woe they could not speak.
But these days of weeping o'er,
  Passed this scene of toil and pain,
They shall feel distress no more—
  Never, never weep again.

3 'Mid the chorus of the skies,
  'Mid th' angelic lyres above,
Hark, their songs melodious rise,
  Songs of praise to Jesus' love!
Happy spirits, ye are fled
  Where no grief can entrance find;
Lulled to rest the aching head,
  Soothed the anguish of the mind.

4 All is tranquil and serene,
  Calm and undisturbed repose;
There no cloud can intervene,
  There no angry tempest blows;
Every tear is wiped away,
  Sighs no more shall heave the breast,
Night is lost in endless day,
  Sorrow—in eternal rest.

HEAVEN.

WOODLAND. C. M.   N. D. Gould.

1. There is an hour of peaceful rest, To mourning wanderers given; There is a joy for souls distressed, A balm for ev-ery wounded breast: 'Tis found a-bove—in heaven.

819.

1 There is an hour of peaceful rest,
   To mourning wanderers given;
  There is a joy for souls distressed,
   A balm for every wounded breast:
   'Tis found above—in heaven.

2 There is a home for weary souls,
   By sin and sorrow driven,—
  When tossed on life's tempestuous shoals,
  Where storms arise, and ocean rolls,
   And all is drear—but heaven.

3 There faith lifts up her cheerful eye
   To brighter prospects given;
  And views the tempest passing by,
  The evening shadows quickly fly,
   And all serene—in heaven.

4 There fragrant flowers immortal bloom,
   And joys supreme are given;
  There rays divine disperse the gloom;
  Beyond the confines of the tomb
   Appears the dawn of heaven!

820.

1 Give me the wings of faith, to rise
   Within the vail, and see
  The saints above,—how great their joys,—
   How bright their glories be.

2 I ask them,—whence their victory came?
   They, with united breath,
  Ascribe their conquest to the Lamb,—
   Their triumph to his death.

3 They marked the footsteps he had trod;
   His zeal inspired their breast;
  And following their incarnate God,
   Possess the promised rest.

4 Our glorious Leader claims our praise,
   For his own pattern given,—
  While the long cloud of witnesses
   Show the same path to heaven.

821.

1 Father! I long, I faint, to see
   The place of thine abode;
  I'd leave thine earthly courts, and flee
   Up to thy seat, my God!

2 Here I behold thy distant face,
   And 't is a pleasing sight;
  But, to abide in thine embrace
   Is infinite delight!

3 I'd part with all the joys of sense,
   To gaze upon thy throne;
  Pleasure springs fresh forever thence,
   Unspeakable, unknown.

4 There all the heavenly hosts are seen;
   In shining ranks they move;
  And drink immortal vigor in,
   With wonder and with love.

5 Father! I long, I faint to see
   The place of thine abode;
  I'd leave thine earthly courts to be
   Forever with my God.

HEAVEN.

TAPPAN. C. M.   Geo. Kingsley.

1. On Jordan's rugged banks I stand, And cast a wishful eye To Canaan's fair and happy land, To Canaan's fair and happy land, Where my possessions lie.

822.

2 Oh, the transporting, rapturous scene,
That rises to my sight!
Sweet fields arrayed in living green;
And rivers of delight!

3 O'er all those wide extended plains
Shines one eternal day;
There God, the Sun, forever reigns,
And scatters night away.

4 No chilling winds, or poisonous breath,
Can reach that healthful shore;
Sickness and sorrow, pain and death,
Are felt and feared no more.

5 When shall I reach that happy place,
And be forever blest?
When shall I see my Father's face,
And in his bosom rest?

6 Filled with delight, my raptured soul
Can here no longer stay;
Though Jordan's waves around me roll,
Fearless I'd launch away.

823.

1 There is a land of pure delight,
Where saints immortal reign,
Infinite day excludes the night,
And pleasures banish pain.

2 There everlasting spring abides,
And never-withering flowers:
Death, like a narrow sea, divides
This heavenly land from ours.

3 Sweet fields beyond the swelling flood
Stand dressed in living green;
So to the Jews old Canaan stood,
While Jordan rolled between.

4 But timorous mortals start and shrink
To cross this narrow sea,
And linger, shivering on the brink,
And fear to launch away.

5 Oh, could we make our doubts remove,
These gloomy doubts that rise,
And see the Canaan that we love,
With unbeclouded eyes:—

6 Could we but climb where Moses stood,
And view the landscape o'er,—
Not Jordan's stream, nor death's cold flood,
Should fright us from the shore.

824.

1 Seraphs, with elevated strains,
Circle the throne around,
And move and charm the starry plains
With an immortal sound.

2 Jesus, the Lord, their harps employs;
Jesus, my Love, they sing:
Jesus, the name of both our joys,
Sounds sweet from every string.

3 I would begin the music here,
And so my soul should rise;
Oh, for some heavenly notes to bear
My spirit to the skies!

HEAVEN.

RHINE. C. M.   German Melody.

1. O mother dear, Jerusalem, When shall I come to thee? When shall my sorrows have an end? Thy joys when shall I see? Thy joys when shall I see?

825.

2 O happy harbor of God's saints!
O sweet and pleasant soil!
In thee no sorrow can be found,
Nor grief, nor care, nor toil.

3 No dimly cloud o'ershadows thee,
Nor gloom, nor darksome night;
But every soul shines as the sun,
For God himself gives light.

4 Thy walls are made of precious stone,
Thy bulwarks diamond-square,
Thy gates are all of orient pearl—
O God! if I were there!

826.

1 O my sweet home, Jerusalem!
Thy joys when shall I see?—
The King that sitteth on thy throne
In his felicity!

2 Thy gardens and thy goodly walks
Continually are green,
Where grow such sweet and pleasant flowers
As nowhere else are seen.

3 Right thro' thy streets with pleasing sound
The flood of life doth flow;
And on the banks, on either side,
The trees of life do grow.

4 Those trees each month yield ripened fruit;
Forevermore they spring,
And all the nations of the earth
To thee their honors bring.

5 O mother dear, Jerusalem!
When shall I come to thee?
When shall my sorrows have an end?
Thy joys when shall I see?

827.

1 Arise, my soul, fly up and run
Through every heavenly street;
And say there's naught below the sun
That's worthy of thy feet.

2 There, on a high, majestic throne,
Th' Almighty Father reigns,
And sheds his glorious goodness down
On all the blissful plains.

3 Bright, like a sun, the Saviour sits,
And spreads eternal noon;
No evenings there, nor gloomy nights,
To want the feeble moon.

4 Amid those ever-shining skies
Behold the sacred Dove;
While banished sin and sorrow flies
From all the realms of love.

5 But oh, what beams of heavenly grace
Transport them all the while!
Ten thousand smiles from Jesus' face,
And love in every smile!

6 Jesus, and when shall that dear day,
That joyful hour appear,
When I shall leave this house of clay,
To dwell among them there?

HEAVEN. 269

MONSON. C. M. — Brown.

1. In vain our fancy strives to paint The moment after death,
The glories that surround a saint When yielding up his breath.

828.

1 In vain our fancy strives to paint
The moment after death,
The glories that surround a saint
When yielding up his breath.

2 One gentle sigh the bondage breaks;
We scarce can say—he's gone!
Before the willing spirit takes
Its mansion near the throne.

3 Faith strives, but all its efforts fail
To trace the spirit's flight;
No eye can pierce within the vail
Which hides the world of light.

4 Thus much, and 't is enough to know,
Saints are completely blest;
Have done with sin, and care, and woe,
And with their Saviour rest.

5 On harps of gold they praise his name,
And see him face to face;
Oh, let us catch the heavenly flame,
And live in his embrace!

829.

1 While thro' this changing world we roam
From infancy to age,
Heaven is the Christian pilgrim's home,
His rest at every stage.

2 Thither, his raptured thought ascends,
Eternal joys to share;
There, his adoring spirit bends,
While here, he kneels in prayer.

3 From earth his freed affections rise,
To fix on things above,
Where all his hope of glory lies—
Where all is perfect love.

4 There, too, may we our treasure place—
There let our hearts be found;
That still, where sin abounded, grace
May more and more abound.

5 Henceforth, our conversation be,
With Christ before the throne;
Ere long we, eye to eye, shall see,
And know as we are known.

830.

1 There is a house not made with hands,
Eternal, and on high;
And here my spirit waiting stands,
Till God shall bid it fly.

2 Shortly this prison of my clay
Must be dissolved and fall;
Then, O my soul, with joy obey
Thy heavenly Father's call.

3 We walk by faith of joys to come;
Faith lives upon his word;
But while the body is our home,
We're absent from the Lord.

4 'T is pleasant to believe thy grace,
But we had rather see;
We would be absent from the flesh,
And present, Lord, with thee.

270 HEAVEN.

AMSTERDAM. 7s & 6s.   Dr. Nares.

1. Rise, my soul, and stretch thy wings,
Thy better portion trace;
Rise from transitory things
Toward heaven, thy native place:
Sun, and moon, and stars decay,
Time shall soon this earth remove;
Rise, my soul, and haste away
To seats prepared above.

831.

2 Rivers to the ocean run,
  Nor stay in all their course;
Fire ascending, seeks the sun,
  Both speed them to their source:
So a soul that's born of God,
  Pants to view his glorious face,
Upward tends to his abode,
  To rest in his embrace.

3 Cease, ye pilgrims, cease to mourn,
  Press onward to the prize;
Soon our Saviour will return
  Triumphant in the skies:
There we'll join the heavenly train,
  Welcomed to partake the bliss;
Fly from sorrow and from pain
  To realms of endless peace.

832.

1 Tell me not of earthly toys
  The worldling may admire,
Tell me not of transient joys
  That sparkle and expire;
For there is a heavenly store,
  Earthly riches cannot buy,
Bliss supreme forevermore—
  A glorious home on high.

2 Tell me of my sin forgiven,
  Through Christ's atoning blood,
Point me to the rest of heaven,
  And bid me hope in God:
Tell me of the mansions blest
  By the Lord of life prepared,
Where the weary are at rest,
  No more by sin ensnared.

833.

1 Time is winging us away
  To our eternal home:
Life is but a winter's day,
  A journey to the tomb;
Youth and vigor soon will flee,
  Blooming beauty lose its charms;
All that's mortal soon will be
  Enclosed in death's cold arms.

2 Time is winging us away
  To our eternal home:
Life is but a winter's day,
  A journey to the tomb:
But the Christian shall enjoy
  Health and beauty soon above:
Far beyond the world's alloy,
  Secure in Jesus' love.

HEAVEN.

FROST. 7s & 6s. — J. P. HOLBROOK.

1. There is a holy city, A happy world above,
Beyond the starry regions, Built by the God of love;
An everlasting temple, And saints arrayed in white,
D.S. There serve their great Redeemer, And dwell with him in light.

834.

2 The meanest child of glory
  Outshines the radiant sun;
  But who can speak the splendor
  Of that eternal throne
  Where Jesus sits exalted,
  In godlike majesty?
  The elders fall before him,
  The angels bend the knee.

3 The hosts of saints around him
  Proclaim his work of grace;
  The patriarchs and prophets,
  And all the godly race,
  Who speak of fiery trials
  And tortures on their way—
  They came from tribulation
  To everlasting day.

4 And what shall be my journey,
  How long I'll stay below,
  Or what shall be my trials,
  Are not for me to know;
  In every day of trouble,
  I'll raise my thoughts on high;
  I'll think of the bright temple,
  And crowns above the sky.

835.

1 THERE is a land immortal,
  The beautiful of lands;
  Beside its ancient portal
  A silent sentry stands;
  He only can undo it,
  And open wide the door;
  And mortals who pass through it,
  Are mortals nevermore.

2 Though dark and drear the passage
  That leadeth to the gate,
  Yet grace comes with the message,
  To souls that watch and wait;
  And at the time appointed
  A messenger comes down,
  And leads the Lord's anointed
  From cross to glory's crown.

3 Their sighs are lost in singing,
  They're blessèd in their tears;
  Their journey heavenward winging,
  They leave on earth their fears:
  Death like an angel seemeth;
  "We welcome thee," they cry,
  Their face with glory beameth—
  'Tis life for them to die!

MISCELLANEOUS.

WINCHESTER. L. M.   Dr. Croft

1. Great God! we sing that might-y hand, By which support-ed still we stand; The opening year thy mer-cy shows,— Let mer-cy crown it till it close.

836.
New Year.

2 By day, by night—at home, abroad,
Still we are guarded by our God;
By his incessant bounty fed,
By his unerring counsel led.

3 With grateful hearts the past we own;
The future—all to us unknown—
We to thy guardian care commit,
And peaceful leave before thy feet.

4 In scenes exalted or depressed,
Be thou our joy, and thou our rest;
Thy goodness all our hopes shall raise,
Adored, through all our changing days.

5 When death shall close our earthly songs,
And seal, in silence, mortal tongues,
Our helper, God, in whom we trust,
Shall keep our souls and guard our dust.

837.
Thanksgiving.

1 ETERNAL source of every joy,
Well may thy praise our lips employ,
While in thy temple we appear,
To hail thee, Sovereign of the year!

2 Wide as the wheels of nature roll,
Thy hand supports and guides the whole,
The sun is taught by thee to rise,
And darkness when to vail the skies.

3 The flowery spring at thy command,
Perfumes the air, adorns the land;
The summer rays with vigor shine,
To raise the corn, and cheer the vine.

4 Thy hand, in autumn, richly pours,
Through all our coasts, redundant stores:
And winters, softened by thy care,
No more the face of horror wear.

5 Seasons and months, and weeks, and days,
Demand successive songs of praise;
And be the grateful homage paid,
With morning light and evening shade.

6 Here in thy house let incense rise,
And circling Sabbaths bless our eyes,
Till to those lofty heights we soar,
Where days and years revolve no more.

838.
New Year.

1 OUR Helper, God! we bless thy name,
Whose love forever is the same;
The tokens of thy gracious care
Open, and crown, and close the year.

2 Amid ten thousand snares we stand,
Supported by thy guardian hand;
And see, when we review our ways,
Ten thousand monuments of praise.

3 Thus far thine arm has led us on;
Thus far we make thy mercy known;
And, while we tread this desert land,
New mercies shall new songs demand.

4 Our grateful souls, on Jordan's shore,
Shall raise one sacred pillar more;
Then bear, in thy bright courts above,
Inscriptions of immortal love.

MISCELLANEOUS. 273

YOAKLEY. L. M.   Yoakley.

1. While o'er the deep thy ser-vants sail, Send thou, O Lord, the prosperous gale;
And on their hearts, where'er they go, Oh, let thy heavenly breez-es blow!

839.
Seamen.

2 When tempests rock the groaning bark,
Oh, hide them safe in Jesus' ark!
When in the tempting port they ride,
Oh, keep them safe at Jesus' side!

3 If life's wide ocean smile or roar,
Still guide them to the heavenly shore;
And grant their dust in Christ may sleep,
Abroad, at home, or in the deep.

840.
National.

1 O God, beneath thy guiding hand,
Our exiled fathers crossed the sea;
And when they trod the wintry strand,
With prayer and psalm they worshiped thee.

2 Thou heard'st, well pleased, the song, the prayer:
Thy blessing came; and still its power
Shall onward through all ages bear
The memory of that holy hour.

3 Laws, freedom, truth, and faith in God
Came with those exiles o'er the waves;
And where their pilgrim feet have trod,
The God they trusted guards their graves.

4 And here thy name, O God of love,
Their children's children shall adore,
Till these eternal hills remove,
And spring adorns the earth no more.

841.
Fast.

1 While o'er our guilty land, O Lord,
We view the terrors of thy sword;
Oh, whither shall the hopeless fly?
To whom but thee direct their cry?

2 On thee, our guardian God, we call,
Before thy throne of grace we fall;
And is there no deliverance there?
And must we perish in despair?

3 See, we repent, we weep, we mourn,
To our forsaken God we turn;
Oh, spare our guilty country, spare
The church, which thou hast planted here!

842.
Cemetery.

1 Dear is the spot where Christians sleep,
And sweet the strains their spirits pour;
Oh, why should we in anguish weep?—
They are not lost, but gone before.

2 Secure from every mortal care,
By sin and sorrow vexed no more
Eternal happiness they share
Who are not lost, but gone before.

3 To Zion's peaceful courts above
In faith triumphant may we soar,
Embracing in the arms of love,
The friends not lost, but gone before.

4 To Jordan's bank whene'er we come,
And hear the swelling waters roar;
Jesus! convey us safely home,
To friends not lost, but gone before.

274 MISCELLANEOUS.

GLASGOW. C. M.
Root & Sweetser's Coll.

1. Lord, while for all mankind we pray,
Of ev-ery clime and coast,
Oh, hear us for our na-tive land—
The land we love the most.

843.
National.

2 Oh, guard our shore from every foe,
With peace our borders bless,
With prosperous times our cities crown,
Our fields with plenteousness.

3 Unite us in the sacred love
Of knowledge, truth, and thee;
And let our hills and valleys shout
The songs of liberty.

4 Here may religion, pure and mild,
Smile on our Sabbath hours;
And piety and virtue bless
The home of us and ours.

5 Lord of the nations, thus to thee
Our country we commend;
Be thou her refuge and her trust,
Her everlasting friend.

844.
Seamen.

1 We come, O Lord, before thy throne,
And, with united plea,
We meet and pray for those who roam
Far off upon the sea.

2 Oh, may the Holy Spirit bow
The sailor's heart to thee,
Till tears of deep repentance flow,
Like rain-drops in the sea!

3 Then may a Saviour's dying love
Pour peace into his breast,
And waft him to the port above
Of everlasting rest.

845.
Fast.

1 See, gracious God, before thy throne,
Thy mourning people bend!
'Tis on thy sovereign grace alone,
Our humble hopes depend.

2 Alarming judgments from thy hand,
Thy dreadful power display;
Yet mercy spares this guilty land,
And yet we live to pray.

3 Oh, bid us turn, Almighty Lord,
By thy resistless grace;
Then shall our hearts obey thy word,
And humbly seek thy face.

846.
A Marriage Hymn.

1 Since Jesus freely did appear
To grace a marriage feast,
Dear Lord, we ask thy presence here,
To make a wedding guest.

2 Upon the bridal pair look down,
Who now have plighted hands;
Their union with thy favor crown,
And bless the nuptial bands.

3 In purest love their souls unite,
That they, with Christian care,
May make domestic burdens light,
By taking mutual share.

4 Oh, may each soul assembled here,
Be married, Lord, to thee!
Clad in thy robes, made white and fair,
To spend eternity.

MISCELLANEOUS.

MEAR. C. M.

1. Our Father! thro' the coming year We know not what shall be;
But we would leave without a fear Its ordering all to thee.

847.
New Year.

2 It may be we shall toil in vain
For what the world holds fair;
And all the good we thought to gain,
Deceive and prove but care.

3 It may be it shall darkly blend
Our love with anxious fears,
And snatch away the valued friend,
The tried of many years.

4 It may be it shall bring us days
And nights of lingering pain;
And bid us take a farewell gaze
Of these loved haunts of men.

5 But calmly, Lord, on thee we rest;
No fears our trust shall move;
Thou knowest what for each is best,
And thou art Perfect Love.

848.
Close of Year.

1 THEE we adore, eternal Name!
And humbly own to thee
How feeble is our mortal frame,
What dying worms are we!

2 The year rolls round, and steals away
The breath that first it gave;
Whate'er we do, whate'er we be,
We're traveling to the grave.

3 Great God! on what a slender thread
Hang everlasting things!
Th' eternal state of all the dead
Upon life's feeble strings!

4 Infinite joy, or endless woe,
Attends on every breath;
And yet, how unconcerned we go
Upon the brink of death!

5 Waken, O Lord, our drowsy sense,
To walk this dangerous road!
And if our souls are hurried hence,
May they be found with God.

849.
Those in Bonds.

1 FOR those in bonds as bound with them
To thee, O God! we pray,
That some celestial, radiant beam
May bring a brighter day.

2 Pity, O Lord! that injured race,
And thy deliverance send;
Grant them the treasures of thy grace,
And bid their bondage end.

3 They sit in darkness, slow to learn
The blessings that they need;
Nor can our anxious thought discern,
How best their cause to plead.

4 All helpless, and without a plan,
We come before thy throne;
We put no confidence in man,
But trust in thee alone.

5 The means of rescue, and the hour,
Thy mercy will reveal:
Thine is the wisdom, thine the power;
Teach us to do thy will.

276 MISCELLANEOUS.

CASEY. 7s. HARP OF DAVID.

1. Fount of ev-er-last-ing love! Rich thy streams of mer-cy are—
Flow-ing pure-ly from a-bove, Beau-ty marks their course a-far.

850.
Revival.

2 Lo! thy church, thy garden now
Blooms beneath the heavenly shower;
Sinners feel, and melt, and bow:
Mild, yet mighty, is thy power.

3 God of grace, before thy throne
Here our warmest thanks we bring;
Thine the glory, thine alone:
Loudest praise to thee we sing.

4 Hear, oh, hear, our grateful song;
Let thy Spirit still descend;
Roll the tide of grace along,
Widening, deepening, to the end.

851.
Thanksgiving.

1 Thank and praise Jehovah's name,
For his mercies, firm and sure,
From eternity the same,
To eternity endure.

2 Let the ransomed thus rejoice,
Gathered out of every land,
As the people of his choice,
Plucked from the destroyer's hand.

3 To a pleasant land he brings,
Where the vine and olive grow,
Where, from flowery hills, the springs
Through luxuriant valleys flow.

4 Oh, that men would praise the Lord
For his goodness to their race;
For the wonders of his word,
And the riches of his grace.

852.
Thanksgiving.

1 Praise to God, immortal praise,
For the love that crowns our days;
Bounteous source of every joy!
Let thy praise our tongues employ.

2 Flocks that whiten all the plain,
Yellow sheaves of ripened grain;
Clouds that drop their fattening dews,
Suns that temperate warmth diffuse;—

3 All that spring with bounteous hand
Scatters o'er the smiling land;
All that liberal autumn pours
From her rich o'erflowing stores;—

4 Lord, for these our souls shall raise
Grateful vows, and solemn praise:
And when every blessing's flown,
Love thee for thyself alone.

853.
Rain.

1 Praise on thee, in Zion's gates,
Daily, O Jehovah, waits;
Unto thee, O God, belong
Grateful words and holy song.

2 Thou dost visit earth, and rain
Blessings on the thirsty plain,
From the copious founts on high,
From the rivers of the sky.

3 Thus the clouds thy power confess,
And thy paths drop fruitfulness,
And the voice of song and mirth
Rises from the tribes of earth!

MISCELLANEOUS.

WESTMINSTER. 8s & 7s. J. P. Holbrook.

1. Zi-on, drear-y, and in an-guish, In the des-ert hast thou strayed?
O thou wea-ry, cease to lan-guish, Je-sus shall lift up thy head!

854.
Fast.

1 Zion, dreary, and in anguish,
    In the desert hast thou strayed?
  O thou weary, cease to languish,
    Jesus shall lift up thy head!

2 Still lamenting and bemoaning,
    'Mid thy follies and thy woes?
  Soon repenting and returning,
    All thy solitude shall close.

3 Though benighted and forsaken,
    Though afflicted and oppressed,
  His Almighty arm shall waken,
    Zion's King shall give thee rest.

4 Cease thy sadness, unbelieving,
    Soon his glory shalt thou see,
  Joy, and gladness, and thanksgiving,
    And the voice of melody.

855.
Seamen.

1 Tossed upon life's raging billow,
    Sweet it is, O Lord, to know,
  Thou did'st press a sailor's pillow,
    And canst feel a sailor's woe.

2 Never slumbering, never sleeping,
    Though the night be dark and drear,
  Thou the faithful watch art keeping,
    "All, all's well," thy constant cheer.

3 And though loud the wind is howling,
    Fierce though flash the lightnings red;
  Darkly though the storm-cloud's scowling
    O'er the sailor's anxious head;—

4 Thou canst calm the raging ocean,
    All its noise and tumult still,
  Hush the tempest's wild commotion,
    At the bidding of thy will.

5 Thus my heart the hope will cherish,
    While to thee I lift mine eye;
  Thou wilt save me ere I perish,
    Thou wilt hear the sailor's cry.

6 And though mast and sail be riven,
    Life's rough course will soon be o'er;
  Safely moored in heaven's wide haven,
    Storm and tempest vex no more.

856.
National Humiliation.

1 Dread Jehovah! God of nations!
    From thy temple in the skies,
  Hear thy people's supplications,
    Now for their deliverance rise.

2 Lo! with deep contrition turning,
    In thy holy place we bend;
  Hear us, fasting, praying, mourning,
    Hear us, spare us, and defend.

3 Though our sins, our hearts confounding,
    Long and loud for vengeance call,
  Thou hast mercy more abounding,
    Jesus' blood can cleanse them all.

4 Let that mercy vail transgression;
    Let that blood our guilt efface:
  Save thy people from oppression,
    Save from spoil thy holy place.

AMERICA. 6s & 4s.

1. My country, 'tis of thee, Sweet land of lib-er-ty, Of thee I sing: Land where my fathers died, Land of the pilgrim's pride, From every mountain side Let freedom ring!

857.
National.

2 My native country, thee—
Land of the noble free—
Thy name—I love;
I love thy rocks and rills,
Thy woods and templed hills:
My heart with rapture thrills
Like that above.

3 Let music swell the breeze,
And ring from all the trees
Sweet freedom's song:
Let mortal tongues awake;
Let all that breathe partake;
Let rocks their silence break,—
The sound prolong.

4 Our father's God! to thee,
Author of liberty,
To thee we sing:
Long may our land be bright
With freedom's holy light;
Protect us by thy might,
Great God, our King!

858.
Harvest.

1 THE God of harvest praise;
In loud thanksgiving raise
Hand, heart, and voice!
The valleys laugh and sing;
Forests and mountains ring;
The plains their tribute bring;
The streams rejoice.

2 Yea, bless his holy name,
And joyous thanks proclaim
Through all the earth;
To glory in your lot
Is comely; but be not
God's benefits forgot
Amid your mirth.

3 The God of harvest praise,
Hands, hearts, and voices raise,
With sweet accord;
From field to garner throng,
Bearing your sheaves along,
And in your harvest song
Bless ye the Lord.

859.
The Poor.

1 LORD, from thy blessèd throne
Sorrow look down upon!
God save the poor!
Teach them true liberty,
Make them from tyrants free,
Let their homes happy be!
God save the poor!

2 The arms of wicked men
Do thou with might restrain—
God save the poor!
Raise thou their lowliness,
Succor thou their distress,
Thou whom the meanest bless!
God save the poor!

3 Give them staunch honesty,
Let their pride manly be—
God save the poor!
Help them to hold the right,
Give them both truth and might,
Lord of all life and light!
God save the poor!

TUNES. 281

BEHRENS. (Concluded.)

MARIAN. C. M.   Ganzbach.

EDWARDS. S. M.   Beethoven.

TUNES.

BENJAMIN. S. M. *Arranged by* Wм. B. Bradbury.

"The Lord is risen in-deed!" Then is his work per-formed; The Might-y Cap-tive now is freed, And death, our foe, dis-armed, And death, our foe, dis-armed.

LEONARD. S. M. *Arranged from* Spohr.

Blest be the tie, that binds Our hearts in Chris-tian love; The fel-low-ship of kin-dred minds Is like to that a-bove.

KEITH. S. M. Ganzbach.

1. My spi-rit on thy care,..... Blest Sa-viour, I re-cline;
2. In thee I place my trust;.... On thee I calm-ly rest;

Thou wilt not leave me to de-spair, For thou art Love di-vine.
I know thee good, I know thee just, And count thy choice the best.

STANLEY. (Concluded.)

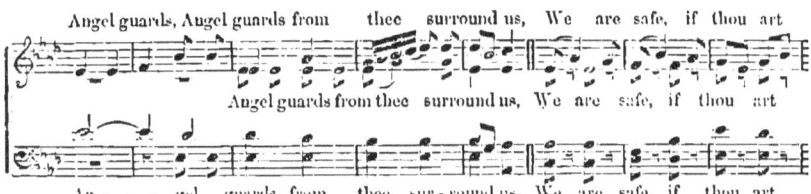

SEGUR. 8s, 7s & 4s.   J. P. Holbrook.

GENERAL INDEX OF TUNES.

It is to be understood that most of the Music, included in this Collection, is introduced "by permission," purchased or given. It must, therefore, not be used in any other without the consent of the authors, or of those who hold the copyright of the Tunes.

A.	PAGE
Adrian	98
Aletta	102, 237
All Saints	192
America	278
Amsterdam	275
Anvern	212
Ariel	114
Arlington	128
Ascension	193
Ashwell	210
Autumn	116
Ava	83
Avon	54, 97

B.	
Balerma	78
Barby	249
Baxter	235
Bayley	112
Beautiful Zion	212
Beethoven	54, 183
Behrens	280
Bemerton	9
Benevento	82
Benjamin	282
Bennington	55
Bera	80
Bethany	158
Beulah	205
Bishop	176
Blake	147
Blendon	170
Boardman	67, 248
Bonar	146
Boylston	254
Bradford	63
Brattle Street	40
Brayton	279
Brest	261
Bridgman	141, 173
Bright Crown	222
Brown	172, 219
Brownell	157
Byefield	234

C.	
Cambridge	164
Capello	75, 188
Carey	113
Carthage	59
Casey	276
Chesterfield	45, 111
China	248
Christmas	46, 127

	PAGE
Church	5, 135
Colman	7
Come, ye disconsolate	88
Cooling	108
Coronation	61
Cowper	70
Crawford	280
Cross and Crown	187
Crusaders' Hymn	145
Cyrus	288

D.	
Dedham	198
Denfield	112
Dennis	131, 167, 180
Desire	81
Detroit	112
Dodge	215
Dormance	101, 228
Downs	18, 185
Duane	221
Duke Street	57, 163
Dundee	44, 199

E.	
Easton	95
Edwards	281
Ellicott	138
Ely	155
Evan	109
Evening Hymn	13
Expostulation	86

F.	
Fatherland	273
Federal Street	205, 216
Ferguson	99
Frederick	255
Frost	12
Fulton	221, 254

G.	
Gaylord	117
Geer	113
Gerhardt	123
Glasgow	77, 274
Golden Chain	224
Golden Hill	153
Golden Shore	222
Goshen	57
Gratitude	161, 203
Greenville	30
Greenwood	152, 251
Griswold	285

H.	PAGE
Hail to the Brightness	214
Halle	151
Hamburg	52, 94, 197
Handy	285
Harwell	58
Haydn	68
Heavenly Home	239
Heber	139, 229
Hebron	28
Helena	10, 186
Hendon	168
Holley	118
Horton	60, 85, 236
Hummel	73
Huntington	280
Hymn	3

I.	
I'm a Pilgrim	240
Italian Hymn	27

J.	
Jewett	284
Judgment	36
Judgment Hymn	247

K.	
Karl	169
Keith	283
Knox	31
Koorbloh	279

L.	
Laban	178
Last Beam	31
Leighton	179
Lenox	55
Leonard	282
Lischer	12
Litchfield	110
Long	15
Looking Home	242
Louvan	39
Loving Kindness	145
Lowry	262
Lyons	24

M.	
Madison	143
Malvern	71
Manepy	149
Manoah	19, 96
Marian	281
Marlow	4

GENERAL INDEX OF TUNES.

	PAGE
Marth	283
Martyn	84, 114
Mear	275
Meribah	109
Messiah	115
Migdol	3
Milner	120
Missionary Chant	126, 213
Missionary Hymn	206
Monson	72, 269
Montague	191
Mornington	250
Mozart	60
Mt. Auburn	129, 165
Mt. Blanc	240
Mt. Vernon	259

N.

	PAGE
Naomi	163
Nelson	90
Nettleton	91
Newberry	284
Newbold	47
Nuremburg	217

O.

	PAGE
Octavius	17
Old Hundred	14
Olivet	121
Olmutz	82, 130, 252
Onido	23
Oriola	218
Ortonville	62

P.

	PAGE
Palestine	191
Palmer	263
Park Street	137, 211
Parting Hymn	226
Penitence	122
Perry	216
Pleading Saviour	80
Pleyel's Hymn	124, 201
Pomeroy	288
Portugal	196
Portuguese Hymn	134
Praise	223

R.

	PAGE
Rathbun	105
Refuge	286
Remsen	177
Rest for the Weary	241
Retreat	232
Return	79
Requiem	256
Rhine	268
Righini	26
Rockingham	38, 50
Rock of Ages	262
Rosefield	103
Rose Hill	106

S.

	PAGE
Sabbath	1
Say, Brothers	87
Scotland	257
Seasons	37
Sugur	257
Severance	283
Seymour	119
Shawmut	74
Shepherd	147
Shining Shore	238
Shirland	231
Sicilian Hymn	240
Siloam	184, 195
Silver Street	20, 175
Sing of Jesus	224
Smith	171
Solitude	58
Sidney	181
Somerville	286
Spohr	2
St. Ann's	42, 194
St. Petersburgh	156
St. Thomas	10
Stair	270
Stanley	286
State Street	21, 280
Stephens	66
Stockwell	181
Sweet Land of Rest	243

T.

	PAGE
Tamworth	260
Tappan	140, 267
Thatcher	174
Tuaxted	43
Tipstanley	283
To-day	58
Trent	48
Trust	150
Tucker	166
Tully	155

U.

	PAGE
Uxbridge	82

V.

	PAGE
Valentia	162
Victory	264

W.

	PAGE
Wanderer	83
Ward	209
Ware	13, 186
Warner	93
Warwick	6
Webb	207
Weber	29
Westminster	133, 277
Willington	83
Willis	125
Willkeith	283
Will you go	89
Wilmot	25
Wimborne	64
Winchester	272
Windham	70, 204
Woodland	266
Woodstock	285
Woolworth	92, 182
Wright	11

Y.

	PAGE
Yarmouth	154
Yoakley	273
York	35

Z.

	PAGE
Zadoc	203
Zephyr	65, 244
Zion	215

METRICAL INDEX.

L. M.	PAGE
All Saints	192
Anvern	212
Ascension	198
Ashwell	210
Beethoven	51, 183
Bennington	56
Bera	80
Bishop	176
Blake	107
Blendon	170
Brayton	279
Crawford	280
Desire	81
Dodge	245
Duane	220
Duke Street	57, 160
Easton	95
Ellicott	208
Evening Hymn	16
Federal Street	245, 246
Gratitude	161, 227
Hamburg	52, 94, 197
Hebron	28
Huntington	280
Judgment	86
Judgment Hymn	247
Koorbboh	279
Long	15
Louvan	89
Loving Kindness	145
Lowry	262
Malvern	71
Migdol	3
Missionary Chant	120, 243
Octavius	17
Old Hundred	18
Park Street	157, 214
Portugal	195
Retreat	233
Rockingham	58, 59
Rose Hill	166
Seasons	37
Smith	171
Solitude	53
Somerville	233
Spohr	2
Stair	279
Uxbridge	52
Ward	202
Ware	15, 133
Warner	93
Willington	55
Wimborne	64
Winchester	272
Windham	70, 244
Woodworth	94, 182
Yonkley	273
Zephyr	65, 244

C. M.	PAGE
Arlington	128
Avon	54, 97
Balerma	78
Barby	249
Behrens	280
Bemerton	9
Boardman	67, 228
Bradford	63
Brattle Street	40
Bridgman	141, 173
Brown	172, 219
Byefield	231
Cambridge	164
Chesterfield	45, 111
China	218
Christmas	46, 127
Church	5, 138
Colman	7
Cooling	108
Coronation	61
Cowper	76
Cross and Crown	187
Dedham	198
Denfield	142
Downs	18, 185
Dundee	44, 199
Evan	109
Geer	143
Glasgow	77, 274
Heber	139, 229
Helena	49, 186
Hummel	73
Hymn	8
Knox	34
Litchfield	110
Manoah	19, 96
Marian	281
Marlow	4
Mear	275
Monson	72, 269
Mt. Auburn	129, 135
Naomi	164
Newbold	47
Oriola	218
Ortonville	62
Parting Hymn	226
Remsen	177
Return	75
Rhine	265
Siloam	184, 195
St. Ann's	42, 134
Stephens	285
Tappan	146, 267
Thaxted	43
Trent	48
Valentia	182
Warwick	6
Woodland	266

	PAGE
Woodstock	235
York	35

S. M.

	PAGE
Adrian	98
Benjamin	282
Bonar	146
Boylston	253
Capello	75, 188
Carey	276
Dennis	131, 167, 189
Detroit	112
Edwards	281
Ferguson	99
Golden Hill	153
Greenwood	152, 251
Haydn	68
Keith	282
Laban	178
Leighton	179
Leonard	282
Mornington	250
Newberry	254
Olmutz	82, 130, 253
Palmer	253
Severance	283
Shawmut	74
Shirland	231
Silver Street	20, 175
St. Thomas	10
State Street	21, 280
Thatcher	174
Tipstanley	283
Tucker	166
Wanderer	53
Wright	11

L. M. 6 lines.

	PAGE
Beautiful Zion	243
Brownell	157
Handy	285
Palestine	191
St. Petersburgh	156

7s.

	PAGE
Aletta	102, 237
Benevento	22
Beulah	265
Casey	276
Cyrus	285
Fulton	221, 254
Griswold	285
Hendon	168
Holley	113
Horton	69, 85, 236
Karl	169
Martyn	84, 114

METRICAL INDEX.

	PAGE
Messiah	115
Mozart	60
Nuremburg	217
Onido	23
Perry	216
Pleyel's Hymn	124, 201
Refuge	286
Rosefield	108
Seymour	119
Weber	29
Willis	125
Willketh	288

7s. 6 lines.

Halle	151
Milner	120
Rock of Ages	202
Sabbath	1
Trust	150
Zadoc	203

L. C. M.

Ariel	114
Meribah	100

8s.

Madison	148
Manopy	149

8s & 7s.

Antuma	116
Bayley	132
Carthage	59
Dormance	104, 258
Gaylord	117
Greenville	30
Harwell	55
Mt. Vernon	250
Nettleton	91
Pleading Saviour	89
Praise	223
Ratubn	105
Refuge	256
Sicilian Hymn	200

	PAGE
Solney	181
Stanley	236
Stockwell	180
Westminster	133, 277
Winnot	25

8s, 7s & 4s.

Brest	261
Nelson	90
Segur	287
Tamworth	260
Zion	215

6s & 4s.

America	278
Bethany	158
Ely	159
Fatherland	238
Italian Hymn	27
Olivet	121
Rightni	26

7s, 6s & 8.

Penitence	192

7s & 6s.

Amsterdam	270
Frost	271
Gerhardt	123
Missionary Hymn	206
Montague	191
Pomeroy	288
Sing of Jesus	224
Tully	155
Webb	207
Yarmouth	154

7s & 5s.

Marth	283

10s.

Baxter	255
Victory	264

11s & 10s.

	PAGE
Come, ye Disconsolate	88
Hail to the Brightness	214

1s.

Expostulation	86
Frederick	255
Goshen	87
Heavenly Home	239
Portuguese Hymn	134

12s.

Scotland	257

H. M.

Lenox	55
Lischer	12

S. H. M.

Requiem	256

10s & 11s.

Lyons	24

6s.

Jewett	284

Peculiar.

Ava	66
Bright Crown	222
Crusaders' Hymn	145
Golden Chain	224
Golden Shore	222
I'm a Pilgrim	240
Last Beam	81
Looking Home	243
Mt. Blanc	240
Rest for the Weary	241
Say, Brothers	57
Shepherd	147
Shining Shore	233
To-day	83
Will you go	60

INDEX OF FIRST LINES.

	PAGE
A charge to keep I have................C. Wesley.	143
According to thy gracious word......Montgomery.	198
A glory gilds the sacred page.............Cowper.	35
Ah! how shall fallen man....................Watts.	74
Ah! this heart is void and chill..................	242
Ah! what avails my strife..............C. Wesley.	94
Alas! and did my Saviour bleed............Watts.	54
Alas! the brittle clay.........................Watts.	251
Alas! what hourly dangers rise........Mrs. Steele.	110
All hail the power of Jesus' name.......Duncan.	61
All people that on earth do....Sternhold—Hopkins.	14
Almighty God! thy word is cast..................	35
Always with us, always with us.............Nevin.	133
Amazing grace! how sweet the sound....Newton.	124
Am I a soldier of the cross....................Watts.	127
And can mine eyes without a tear..Heginbotham.	155
And canst thou, sinner, slight.................Hyde.	82
And dost thou say, "Ask what thou wilt".......	233
And is there, Lord, a rest..................Palmer.	283
And must this body die.......................Watts.	259
And shall I sit alone........................Beddome.	122
Angels rejoiced and sweetly sung...........Laura.	47
Angels, roll the rock away................Gibbons.	60
Another day has passed along.........E. Taylor.	2
Another six days' work is done...........Stenelt.	3
A poor wayfaring man of grief.......Montgomery.	229
Approach, my soul, the mercy-seat......Newton.	96
Arise, O King of grace, arise................Watts.	6
Arise, my soul, fly up and run..............Watts.	264
Ascend thy throne, almighty King....Beddome.	242
Asleep in Jesus, blessed sleep.......Mrs. Mackay.	244
As oft with worn and weary feet....Wilberforce.	156
As panting in the sultry beam....................	176
Assembled at thy great command.........Collyer.	21
As the hart, with eager looks........Montgomery.	15
Astonished and distressed................Toplady.	75
As when in silence vernal showers........Rippon.	65
At the Lamb's high feast we sing...............	204
At thy command, O Lord, our hope..... Watts.	204
Awake, and sing the song..............Hammond.	40
Awake, awake, the sacred song.......Mrs. Steele.	46
Awaked by Sinai's awful sound...........Occum.	101
Awake, my heart, arise, my tongue........Watts.	9
Awake, my soul, lift up thine eyes.Mrs. Barbauld.	123
Awake, my soul, stretch every nerve....Doddridge.	127
Awake, my soul, to joyful lays............Medley.	115
Awake, my tongue, thy tribute bring..Needham.	17
Awake, our souls! away, our fears..........Watts.	125
Awake, ye saints! awake...................Cotterill.	12
Away from earth my spirit turns.................	171
Beautiful Zion! built above.......................	212
Before Jehovah's awful throne..............Watts.	11
Begin, my tongue, some heavenly theme..Watts.	19
Behold a stranger at the door................Gregg.	81
Behold, the day is come..................Beddome.	252
Behold, th' expected time draws near.......Toke.	209
Behold the glories of the Lamb............Watts.	11
Behold the morning sun....................Watts.	11
Behold the Saviour of mankind............Wesley.	51
Behold the throne of grace..................Newton.	231
Behold, what wondrous grace................Watts.	115
Behold, where in a mortal form............Enfield.	48
Be merciful to me, O God........................	185

	PAGE
Be tranquil, O my soul!...................Hastings.	166
Blessed angels! high in heaven...................	181
Blessed Saviour! thee I love..............Doddrid.	203
Bless, O my soul! the living God...........Watts.	17
Blest are the souls that hear and know....Watts.	85
Blest be the dear uniting love..........C. Wesley.	248
Blest be the tie that binds..................Fawcett.	250
Blest be thou, O God of Israel...................	25
Blest Comforter divine...........................	63
Blest day of God, most calm, most bright......	8
Blest is the man, whose softening..Mrs. Barbauld.	177
Blest Jesus! when my soaring....Heginbotham.	142
Blest morning, whose young dawning rays..Watts.	4
Bread of heaven, on thee I feed............Conder.	201
Brethren, while we sojourn here...............	215
Bright King of glory! dreadful God........Watts.	57
Bread is the road that leads to death.....Watts.	70
Brother, hast thou wandered far............Clarke.	85
Brother, though from yonder sky......Benevert.	254
By cool Siloam's shady rill....................Heber.	105
Call Jehovah thy salvation...........Montgomery.	133
Calm me, my God, and keep me calm...Bonar.	163
Calm on the listening ear of night...............	47
Can sinners hope for heaven....................	74
Cast thy bread upon the waters...............	181
Cease, ye mourners, cease to languish..Collyer.	258
Child of sin and sorrow.....................Hastings.	72
Children, listen to the Lord..............Hastings.	221
Children of God, who faint and slow...Kanter.	215
Children of the heavenly King...........Cennick.	134
Christ, above all glory seated....................	59
Christ, of all my hopes the ground...Wardlaw.	198
Christ the Lord is risen to-day. Sons...Cudworth.	60
Chosen not for good in me................McCheyne.	159
Church of the ever-living God.............Cedar.	134
Come, blessed Spirit, source of light..Beddome.	2
Come, Desire of nations, come....................	217
Come, every pious heart...................Steuart.	55
Come, gracious Lord, descend and dwell..Watts.	2
Come, gracious Spirit, heavenly Dove...Browne.	65
Come, happy souls, approach your God...Watts.	76
Come hither, all ye weary souls.............Watts.	81
Come, Holy Ghost, Creator, come..............	66
Come, Holy Spirit, calm my mind.........Burder.	65
Come, Holy Spirit, come........................Hart.	68
Come, Holy Spirit, from on high................	66
Come, Holy Spirit, heavenly Dove..........Watts.	66
Come join, ye saints, with heart and voice......	112
Come, let us join our cheerful songs......Watts.	112
Come, let us join our songs of praise............	63
Come, let us sing of Jesus...................Bethune.	231
Come, let us sing the song of songs..Montgomery.	57
Come, Lord, and tarry not.................Bonar.	259
Come, my soul, thy suit prepare......Newton.	236
Come, O Creator! Spirit blest........Lyra Cath.	34
Come, O my soul, in sacred lays.......Blacklock.	34
Come, said Jesus' sacred voice.....................	85
Come, shout aloud the Father's grace Heginbotham.	19
Come, sound his praise abroad..............Watts.	20
Come, thou almighty King..................Madan.	23
Come, thou Desire of all my saints..Mrs. Steele.	8
Come, thou Fount of every blessing...Robinson.	105
Come, thou soul-transforming Spirit............	30

INDEX OF FIRST LINES.

First Line	Author	Page
Come to Calvary's holy mountain	Montgomery	91
Come to the ark, come to the ark		79
Come to the land of peace		83
Come, trembling sinner, lo whose	Jones	74
Come, weary souls, with sins distressed	Steele	81
Come, we who love the Lord	Watts	10
Come, ye disconsolate, where'er	Moore	88
Come, ye sinners, poor and wretched	Hart	60
Come, ye souls, by sin afflicted	Swain	91
Come, ye that know and fear the Lord	Burder	18
Come, ye that love the Saviour's name	Steele	7
Complete in thee—no work of mine	A. R. W.	151
Cross, reproach, and tribulation	Moravian	200
Daughter of Zion! awake from thy sadness		214
Day of judgment! day of wonders	Newton	251
Dear as thou wert, and justly dear	Dale	249
Dearest of all the names above	Watts	138
Dear Father! to thy mercy-seat	Mrs. Steele	235
Dear is the spot where Christians sleep		273
Dear Jesus! let thy pitying eye		219
Dear Lord, amid the throng that pressed		241
Dear Refuge of my weary soul	Steele	138
Dear Saviour! over at my side	Fuller	213
Dear Saviour! if these lambs should stray	Hyde	193
Dear Saviour! we are thine	Doddridge	132
Deep in our hearts let us record	Watts	53
Delay not, delay not, O sinner	Hastings	67
Depth of mercy! Can there be	C. Wesley	102
Descend from heaven, immortal Dove	Watts	262
Did Christ o'er sinners weep	Beddome	75
Dismiss us with Thy blessing, Lord	Hart	24
Does the gospel word proclaim	Newton	119
Do not I love thee, O my Lord	Doddridge	141
Draw near, O holy Dove, draw near	A. R. W.	205
Dread Jehovah, God of nations		277
Early, my God, without delay	Watts	4
Enthroned on high, almighty Lord	Humphries	67
Ere to the world again we go		24
Eternal Father, thou hast said	Palmer	211
Eternal God, celestial King	Wrangham	56
Eternal Source of every joy	Doddridge	272
Eternal Spirit, we confess	Watts	64
Eternal Wisdom! thee we praise	Watts	44
Fade, fade each earthly joy	Bonar	158
Fading, still fading		31
Faint not, Christian, though the road		121
Fairest Lord Jesus		143
Faith adds new charms to earthly	Watts	165
Far from my heavenly home	Lyte	263
Far from the world, O Lord, I flee	Cowper	5
Father, I long, I faint to see	Watts	266
Father of eternal grace	Montgomery	168
Father of heaven! whose love profound		83
Father of mercies! bow thine ear	Beddome	192
Father of mercies! God of love	Wimbotham	41
Father of mercies! in thy word	Mrs. Steele	35
Father of mercies! send thy grace	Doddridge	177
Father! what e'er of earthly bliss	Mrs. Steele	163
Firm as the earth thy gospel stands	Watts	173
For... son called to part	Newton	29
Forbid them not, the Saviour cried	Hastings	195
Forever with the Lord	Montgomery	252
For me to live is Christ		146
For the mercies of the day	Montgomery	29
Forth from the dark and stormy sky	Heber	232
For those in bonds, as bound with them	Hastings	275
Fountain of grace, rich, full and free		137
Fount of everlasting love	Palmer	276
Frequent the day of God returns	Browne	5
Friend after friend departs	Montgomery	256
From all that dwell below the skies	Watts	14
From Calvary a cry was heard	Cunningham	52
From day to day before our eyes	Montgomery	208
From every stormy wind that blows	Stowell	232
From Greenland's icy mountains	Heber	206
From the cross uplifted high	Haweis	202
From the table now retiring		200
Full of trembling expectation	C. Wesley	117
Gently, gently lay thy rod	Lyte	118
Gently, Lord, oh, gently lead us	Hastings	30
Gently, my Saviour, let me down	Hill	245
Give me the wings of faith to rise	Watts	266
Give to the Lord, ye sons of fame	Watts	15
Give to the winds thy fears	Gerhardt	130
Glory to God on high		27
Glory to God the Father be		18
Glory to God, whose witness-train		104
Glory to Thee, my God, this night	Ken	16
Glory to the Father give	Montgomery	221
Go, labor on; spend and be spent	Bonar	176
Go, labor on; while it is day	Bonar	176
Go to the grave in all thy glorious	Montgomery	255
Go, tune thy voice to sacred song		140
God, in the gospel of his Son	Beddome	32
God in the high and holy place	Montgomery	41
God is the refuge of his saints	Watts	209
God lends me—and I go		159
God moves in a mysterious way	Cowper	43
God of mercy, God of love	J. Taylor	119
God of mercy, throned on high		221
God of my life, thro' all my days	Doddridge	13
God of my life, thy boundless grace		92
God of my life, to thee belong		37
God of our salvation, hear us		80
God of the sunlight hours, how sad		9
Grace! 'tis a charming sound	Doddridge	175
Gracious Spirit! Love divine	Stocker	49
Great God, how Infinite art thou	Watts	44
Great God, to thee my evening song	Mrs. Steele	227
Great God, we sing that mighty hand	Doddridge	272
Great God, what do I see and hear	Luther	247
Great God, when I approach thy throne		77
Great God, whose universal sway	Watts	208
Great Redeemer, Friend of sinners		259
Great Ruler of all nature's frame	Doddridge	45
Had I the tongue of Greeks and Jews	Watts	160
Hail, my ever-blessed Jesus	Wingrove	58
Hail, sweetest, dearest tie that binds	Sutton	228
Hail, thou once despised Jesus	Bakewell	58
Hail to the brightness of Zion's	Hastings	214
Hail to the Lord's Anointed	Montgomery	207
Hail, tranquil hour of closing day	Bacon	234
Happy, Saviour! shall I be		150
Happy the heart where graces reign	Watts	165
Happy the meek, whose gentle breast	J. Scott	161
Happy the spirit released from its clay		264
Hark! a voice divides the sky	C. Wesley	254
Hark, how the choral song of heaven		211
Hark, my soul, it is the Lord	Cowper	125
Hark, ten thousand harps and voices	Kelly	58
Hark! that shout of rapturous joy	Kelly	254
Hark the glad sound ! the Saviour	Doddridge	47
Hark the herald angels sing	C. Wesley	60
Hark, the song of Jubilee	Montgomery	216
Hasten, Lord, the glorious time	Lyte	216
Hasten, sinner, to be wise	T. Scott	85
Hearken, Lord, to my complaints	Montgomery	120
Hear, O sinner ! mercy hails you	Reed	90
Hear what God the Lord hath spoken	Cowper	133
Here at thy cross, my dying Lord	Watts	93
Here I can firmly rest	Gerhardt	175
Here we have seen thy face, O Lord		204
He that goeth forth with weeping	Hastings	180
He who on earth as man was known	Newton	63
High in the heavens, eternal God	Watts	13
High in yonder realms of light	Raffles	265
Highly we raise our hallelujahs	Sigourney	223
Ho! every one that thirsts, draw nigh	C. Wesley	81
Holy and reverend is the name	Needham	11
Holy Ghost, with light divine	Reed	69
Holy, holy, holy Lord	Montgomery	22
Holy Lamb, who thee receive	J. Wesley	201
Holy Spirit, Lord of light	Lyra Cath.	48
Hosanna to the Prince of light	Watts	61
How are thy servants blest, O Lord	Addison	41
How beauteous were the marks divine	I. C. Cove	50
How blest are those, how truly wise	Mrs. Steele	193
How blest the righteous when he	Mrs. Barbauld	244
How blest the sacred tie that binds	Mrs. Barbauld	227

INDEX OF FIRST LINES. 295

	PAGE
How can I sink with such a prop............*Watts*.	128
How charming is the place................*S'enn. t.*	11
How did my heart rejoice to hear..........*Watts*.	7
How firm a foundation, ye saints........*Kirkham*.	134
How gentle God's commands..............*Doddridge*.	131
How glorious is our heavenly King........*W...*.	219
How heavy is the night....................*Beata*.	75
How hopeless guilty nature lies..........*Mrs. St...*	72
How large the promise, how divine........*Watts*.	175
How oft, alas! this wretched heart......*Mrs. ...*	109
How pleasant, how divinely fair..........*Watts*.	3
How ..... that to dwell below...............	225
How precious is the book divine..........*Faucett*.	34
How sad our state by nature is............*Watts*.	74
How shall the sons of men appear........*S'enn'l*.	71
How shall the young secure their heart...*Watts*.	31
How still and peaceful is the grave...............	218
How sweet and awful is the place..........*Watts*.	199
How sweet, how heavenly is the sight....*Swain*.	223
How sweetly flowed the gospel sound....*Bowring*.	50
How sweet the name of Jesus sounds....*Newton*.	173
How sweet to leave the world awhile......*Kelly*.	213
How swift the torrent rolls..............*Doddridge*.	253
How tedious and tasteless the hours....*Newton*.	113
How tender is thy hand..................*Hastings*.	183

I bless thee, Lord, for sorrows sent...............	182
I cannot always trace the way.....................	182
I cannot call affliction sweet............*Montgomery*.	184
I faint, my soul doth faint............*Mrs. Gilbert*.	113
I feed my faith on Christ; my bread...*Montgomery*.	205
If God is mine, then present things......*Beddome*.	174
If human kindness meets return..............*Nod*.	110
If life in sorrow must be spent............*Gulon*.	14
If on our daily course, our mind...................	161
If through unruffled seas.........................	157
I have a home above............................	283
I know that my Redeemer lives..........*C. Wesley*.	63
I lay my sins on Jesus..................*Bonar*.	155
I left the God of truth and light......*Montgomery*.	109
I lift my soul to God......................*Watts*.	113
I love the sacred Book of God..............*Kelly*.	33
I love thy kingdom, Lord..................*Dwight*.	20
I love to steal awhile away............*Mrs. Brown*.	215
I'm a pilgrim, and I'm a stranger................	210
I'm but a stranger here................*T. R. Taylor*.	233
I'm not ashamed to own my Lord..........*Watts*.	127
In all my vast concerns with thee........*Watts*.	43
Indulgent Sovereign of the skies......*Doddridge*.	208
In every trying hour.............................	171
In heavenly love abiding.........................	151
Inspirer and Hearer of prayer............*Toplady*.	113
In the Christian's home in glory................	211
In the cross of Christ I glory............*Bowring*.	105
In thy name, O Lord, assembling..........*Kelly*.	241
In true and patient hope................*C. Wesley*.	164
In vain our fancy strives to paint........*Newton*.	219
In vain we seek for peace with God........*Watts*.	72
I once was a stranger to grace and....*McCheyne*.	145
I saw One hanging on a tree..............*Newton*.	96
I send the joys of earth away............*Watts*.	95
I sing th' almighty power of God..........*Watts*.	44
I stand on Zion's mount..................*Swain*.	131
Is there ambition in my heart..............*Watts*.	103
Is this the kind return....................*Watts*.	75
It is not death to die....................*Bethune*.	251
It is the Lord, enthroned in light..........*Green*.	181
It is thy hand, my God....................*Darby*.	18
I was a wandering sheep..................*Bonar*.	118
I worship thee, sweet Will of God......*Lyra Cath*.	185
I would be thine, oh, take my heart...............	111
I would love thee, God and Father................	25
I would not live alway, I ask............*Muhlenberg*.	235

Jehovah reigns, his throne is high..........*Watts*.	11
Jesus, all-atoning Lamb....................*Wesley*.	163
Jesus, and didst thou leave the sky..........*Steele*.	77
Jesus, and shall it ever be..................*Gregg*.	137
Jesus, at whose supreme command......*C. Wesley*.	198
Jesus comes, his conflict over..............*Kelly*.	59
Jesus, engrave it on my heart..............*Medley*.	71
Jesus, full of all compassion..............*Turner*.	116

	PAGE
Jesus, full of truth and love.....................	102
Jesus, I come to thee....................*Bonar*.	99
Jesus, I love thy charming name......*Doddridge*.	139
Jesus, I my cross have taken............*Miss Grext*.	116
Jesus, in sickness and in pain............*Gallaudet*.	157
Jesus, let thy pitying eye.........................	122
Jesus, Lord, we look to thee............*C. Wesley*.	109
Jesus, lover of my soul..................*C. Wesley*.	114
Jesus, Master, hear me now.......................	201
Jesus, merciful and mild..................*Hastings*.	114
Jesus, my strength, my hope............*C. Wesley*.	167
Jesus, on thy throne of glory.....................	225
Jesus, save my dying soul................*Hastings*.	103
Jesus shall reign where'er the sun..........*Watts*.	211
Jesus spreads his banner o'er us.................	200
Jesus, the sinner's friend, to thee........*C. Wesley*.	95
Jesus, the very thought of thee..........*Bernard*.	139
Jesus, thou art the sinner's friend...............	111
Jesus, thou source of calm repose................	157
Jesus, thy love shall we forget...................	49
Jesus, where'er thy people meet..........*Cowper*.	238
Jesus, while our hearts are bleeding....*Hastings*.	258
Jesus, who knows full well................*Newton*.	231
Jesus, whom angel hosts adore............*Bonar*.	52
Jesus, who on Calvary's mountain................	105
Joyful be the hours to-day..................*Kelly*.	164
Joyfully, joyfully, onward I move................	254
Joy to the world! the Lord is come..........*Watts*.	46
Just as I am, without one plea..........*C. Elliott*.	92

Keep silence, all created things............*Watts*.	42
Kindred in Christ, for his dear sake......*Newton*.	227
Kingdoms and crowns to God belong........*Watts*.	38
Know, my soul, thy full salvation......*Miss Grant*.	139

Laborers of Christ, arise..................*Sigourney*.	170
Laboring and heavy-laden..................*Rankin*.	194
Let me be with thee where thou art...............	215
Let me but hear my Saviour say............*Watts*.	171
Let party names no more................*Beddome*.	230
Let saints below in concert sing............*C. Webb*.	195
Let us awake our joys..................*Kingsbury*.	26
Let us with a joyful mind..................*Milton*.	22
Light of the soul, O Saviour blest................	177
Like morning, when her early breeze......*Sicore*.	51
Like the eagle, upward, onward..................	189
Lo! he comes, with clouds descending....*Brigham*.	220
Lo! he cometh! countless trumpets...............	250
Lo! Jehovah, we adore thee.......................	39
Lo! on a narrow neck of land............*C. Wesley*.	161
Lord, as to thy dear cross we flee................	49
Lord, at thy feet we sinners lie............*Hastings*.	76
Lord, before thy throne we bend............*Watts*.	151
Lord, dismiss us with thy blessing..........*Barder*.	30
Lord, forever at thy side................*Montgomery*.	139
Lord, from thy blessed throne..............*Newton*.	274
Lord God of hosts! by all adored.................	13
Lord God of my salvation........................	154
Lord God, the Holy Ghost..............*Montgomery*.	68
Lord, how mysterious are thy ways......*Mrs. ...*	173
Lord, how secure and blest are they......*Watts*.	170
Lord, how secure my conscience was........*Watts*.	2
Lord, I am thine, entirely thine............*Davis*.	17
Lord, I am vile, conceived in sin............*Watts*.	74
Lord, I believe, thy power I own..........*Wreford*.	105
Lord, I cannot let thee go..................*Newton*.	235
Lord, if thou thy grace impart...................	169
Lord, I hear of showers of blessing...............	116
Lord, I look for all to thee..................*Lyte*.	120
Lord, in the morning thou shalt hear........*Watts*.	71
Lord, in this sacred hour.........................	21
Lord, let me know mine end............*Montgomery*.	28
Lord, may thy truth upon the heart...............	28
Lord, now we part in thy blest name.............	28
Lord, of all being! throned afar........*O. W. Holmes*.	39
Lord of earth! thy forming hand............*Grant*.	37
Lord of mercy, just and kind................*Good*.	102
Lord, thou hast searched and seen me......*Watts*.	37
Lord, thou hast won, at length I yield....*Newton*.	101
Lord, we come before thee now........*Hammond*.	235
Lord, when we bend before thy throne............	9
Lo! the mighty God appearing..............*Goode*.	261

INDEX OF FIRST LINES.

	PAGE
Loud hallelujahs to the Lord......*Watts.*	15
Love divine, all love excelling......*C. Wesley.*	132
Majestic sweetness sits enthroned......*Stennett.*	64
Make haste, O man, to live......	178
Man! wisdom is to seek......*Cowper.*	103
Marked as the purpose of the skies......*No. I.*	213
May not the sovereign Lord on high......*Watts.*	57
May the grace of God, our Saviour......*Newton.*	25
'Mid scenes of confusion and creature......	239
Mine eyes and my desire......*Watts.*	175
Mourn for the thousands slain......	149
Much in sorrow, oft in woe......*H. K. White.*	125
Must Jesus bear the cross alone......*Allen.*	187
My country! 'tis of thee......*S. F. Smith.*	253
My days are gliding swiftly by......	208
My dear Redeemer and my Lord......*Watts.*	50
M, faith looks up to thee......*Palmer.*	121
My Father bids me come......*Wesley.*	82
My Father God! how sweet the sound.*Doddridge.*	113
My former hopes are fled......*Cowper.*	74
My God, accept my heart this day......*Lyra Cath.*	97
My God, how endless is thy love......*Watts.*	161
My God, my Father! blissful name......*Mrs. Steele.*	173
My God, my Father, while I stray......*C. Elliott.*	132
My God, my Life, my Love......*Watts.*	153
My God, the spring of all my joys......*Watts.*	112
My gracious Lord! I own thy right......*Doddridge.*	197
My gracious Redeemer I love......*Francis.*	111
My home is in heaven, my rest is not here...*Lyte.*	235
My opening eyes with rapture see......	2
My Saviour, whom absent I love......*Cowper.*	118
My soul, be on thy guard......*H-th.*	175
My soul, how lovely is the place......*Watts.*	5
My soul, repeat his praise......*Watts.*	253
My spirit on thy care......*Lyte.*	152
My sufferings all to thee are known......*C. Wesley.*	93
My times are in thy hand......	180
My times of sorrow and of joy......*Beddome.*	184
Nearer, my God, to thee......*S. F. Adams.*	179
No more, my God, I boast no more......*Watts.*	91
No more, ye wise, your wisdom boast..*Doddridge.*	171
None loves me, Saviour, with thy love......	137
No room for mirth or trifling here......*C. Wesley.*	101
Not all the blood of beasts......*Watts.*	151
Not all the nobles of the earth......*Stennett.*	173
Not all the outward forms on earth......*Watts.*	73
Not to condemn the sons of men......*Watts.*	53
Not with our mortal eyes......*Watts.*	152
Now begin the heavenly theme......*Langford.*	125
Now be the gospel banner......*Hastings.*	206
Now is th' accepted time......*Dobell.*	87
Now let my soul, eternal King......*Higinbotham.*	35
Now let our cheerful eyes survey......*Doddridge.*	172
Now let our souls on wings sublime......*Gibbons.*	203
Now let our voices join......*Doddridge.*	21
Now may He, who from the dead......*Newton.*	29
Now the Saviour standeth pleading......	80
Now to the Lord a noble song......*Watts.*	16
Now to the Lord, who makes us know......*Watts.*	57
Now to the power of God supreme......*Watts.*	171
Obedient to our Zion's King......	106
O bless the Lord, my soul, His grace.*Montgomery.*	21
O bow thine ear, eternal One......	102
O cease, my wandering soul......*Muhlenberg.*	98
O could I find from day to day......	110
O could I speak the matchless worth......*Medley.*	144
O deem not they are blest alone......*Bryant.*	183
O'er the dark wave of Galilee......*Russell.*	51
O'er the gloomy hills of darkness......*Williams.*	215
O'er the realms of pagan darkness......*Cotterell.*	215
O eyes that are weary, and hearts......	135
O for a closer walk with God......*Cowper.*	109
O for a glance of heavenly day......*Hart.*	94
O for an overcoming faith......*Watts.*	249
O for a sweet, inspiring ray......*Mrs. Steele.*	202
O for a thousand tongues to sing......*C. Wesley.*	62
O for that tenderness of heart......*C. Wesley.*	108
O for the death of those......	252
O gift of gifts! oh, grace of faith......*Lyra Cath.*	102
O God, beneath thy guiding hand......*L. Bacon.*	273

	PAGE
O God, by whom the seed is given......*Heber.*	9
O God of Bethel, by whose hand......*Doddridge.*	173
O God of mercy, hear my call......*Watts.*	97
O God, thou art my God alone......*Montgomery.*	106
O God, we praise thee and confess......*Patrick.*	42
O had I, my Saviour, the wings of a dove......*Lyte.*	239
O happy day, that fixed my choice......*Doddridge.*	205
O haste away, my brethren dear......	226
O holy, holy, holy Lord......	26
O, if my soul was formed for woe......*Watts.*	54
O, it is joy in one to meet......	228
O Lord, encouraged by thy grace......*Mrs. Steele.*	196
O Lord, how full of sweet content......*Guion.*	161
O Lord, how infinite thy love......*Lyte.*	76
O Lord, my best desires fulfil......*Cowper.*	164
O Lord, thy pitying eye surveys......*Doddridge.*	192
O mother dear, Jerusalem......*Quarles.*	268
O my sweet home, Jerusalem......*Quarles.*	268
Once I thought my mountain strong......*Newton.*	120
Once more, my soul, the rising day......*Watts.*	7
One prayer I have, all prayers in one.*Montgomery.*	186
One there is above all others......*Newton.*	59
On Jordan's rugged banks I stand......*Stennett.*	267
On the mountain's top appearing......*Kelly.*	215
Onward, Christian! though the region......	133
Oppressed with noonday's scorching heat..*Doane.*	198
O praise ye the Lord! prepare your..*Tate—Brady.*	24
O sacred Head! now wounded......*Gerhardt.*	123
O Saviour! lend a listening ear......*Hastings.*	140
O see how Jesus trusts himself......	141
O sinner, bring not tears alone......	78
O speak that gracious word again......*Newton.*	143
O spirit of the living God......*Montgomery.*	209
O Sun of Righteousness, arise......	208
O sweetly breathe the lyres above......*Palmer.*	136
O tell me, thou Life and Delight......*Hastings.*	108
O that I could forever dwell......*Reed.*	136
O that I knew the secret place......*Watts.*	110
O that my load of sin were gone......*C. Wesley.*	85
O the sweet wonders of that cross......*Watts.*	107
O thou, above all praise......*Montgomery.*	44
O thou, above all praise......*Montgomery.*	44
O thou God, who hearest prayer......*Conder.*	131
O thou, to whose all-searching sight......*C. Wesley.*	107
O thou, who driest the mourner's tear......*Moore.*	185
O thou, who hear'st the prayer of faith..*Toplady.*	100
O thou, whose gently chastening hand......	186
O thou, whose own vast temple stands......*Bryant.*	194
O thou, whose tender mercy hears......*Mrs. Steele.*	97
O throw away thy rod......	188
O turn ye, oh, turn ye, for why will......	86
Our Father! through the coming year......	215
Our heavenly Father calls......*Doddridge.*	215
Our Helper, God, we bless thy name......*Doddridge.*	212
Our Lord is risen from the dead......*C. Wesley.*	38
Our souls by love together knit......	229
Out of the depths of woe......*Montgomery.*	112
O what amazing words of grace......*Medley.*	77
O where are kings and empires now......*A. C. Coxe.*	194
O where is now that glowing love......*Kelly.*	107
O where shall rest be found......*Montgomery.*	83
O worship the King, all-glorious above......*Grant.*	24
O Zion, afflicted with wave upon wave......	135
O Zion, when I think of thee......*Kelly.*	210
Palms of glory, raiment bright......*Montgomery.*	232
Peace, peace I leave with you......*Hastings.*	121
Peace, troubled soul! whose plaintive......	190
People of the living God......*Montgomery.*	103
"Perfect in love!" Lord, can it be......	157
Pilgrim, burdened with thy sin......	84
Pilgrims in this vale of sorrow......*Hastings.*	190
Pour out thy spirit from on high......*Montgomery.*	207
Press on thee in Zion's gates......*Conder.*	276
Praise the Lord, ye heavens, adore him......	25
Praise to God, immortal praise......*Mrs. Barbauld.*	216
Praise ye Jehovah's name......*Goode.*	27
Praise ye the Lord, let praise employ......*Mrs. Steele.*	17
Prayer is the soul's sincere desire......*Montgomery.*	234
Prepare us, Lord, to view thy cross......	199
Prince of Peace! control my will......	118
Raise your triumphant songs......*Watts.*	20

INDEX OF FIRST LINES.

First Line	Author	Page
Rejoice in God alway	Moultrie	166
Remember thy Creator now		218
Rest for the toiling hand	Bonar	251
Return, O wanderer, now return	Collyer	70
Return, O wanderer, to thy home	Hastings	79
Rise, my soul, and stretch thy wings	Seagrave	275
Rock of Ages! cleft for me	Toplady	232
Safely through another week	Newton	1
Salvation, oh, the joyful sound	Watts	77
Saviour, I follow on	C. S. R.	178
Saviour, I look to thee	Hastings	131
Saviour of our ruined race	Hastings	201
Saviour, teach me day by day		24
Saviour! thy gentle voice	Hastings	152
Saviour! visit thy plantation	Newton	117
Saviour, when in dust to thee	Grant	115
Saw ye not the cloud arise	C. Wesley	247
Say, brothers, will you meet us		87
Say, sinner, hath a voice within	Mrs. Hyde	83
Scorn not the slightest word or deed		177
Searcher of hearts! from mine erase	G. P. Morris	103
See a poor sinner, dearest Lord	Medley	166
See, gracious God, before thy throne	Mrs. Steele	271
See Israel's gentle Shepherd stand	Doddridge	135
See the eternal Judge descending		260
See the leaves around us falling	Horne	259
See the ransomed millions stand	Conder	215
Seraphs, with elevated strains	Watts	257
Servant of God, well done	Montgomery	251
Shall the vile race of flesh and blood	Watts	70
Shall we go on in sin	Watts	94
Show pity, Lord, O Lord forgive	Watts	94
Since Jesus freely did appear	Berridge	274
Since Jesus is my friend	Gerhardt	132
Sing, sing his lofty praise		24
Sinner, art thou still secure	Newton	84
Sinners, turn, why will ye die	C. Wesley	81
Sinners, will you scorn the message	Pen.	100
Sister, thou wast mild and lovely	S. F. Smith	253
So fades the lovely, blooming flower	Mrs. Steele	248
Soft and holy is the place	Hastings	237
Softly fades the twilight ray	S. F. Smith	2
Softly now the light of day	Doane	114
So let our lips and lives express	Watts	160
Son of God, to thee I cry		203
Sons of men, behold from far	Wesley	217
Soon may the last glad song arise		213
Sovereign of worlds, display thy power		212
Sovereign Ruler, Lord of all	Ryles	103
Sow in the morn thy seed	Montgomery	178
Speak gently; it is better far		163
Speak to me, Lord, thyself reveal	Wesley	138
Spirit divine! attend our prayer	Reed	66
Spirit of power and might, behold	Montgomery	67
Spirit of truth, on this thy day	H. ber.	9
Stand up, my soul, shake off thy fears	Watts	125
Stand up, stand up for Jesus	Duffield	154
Stay, thou insulted Spirit, stay	C. Wesley	65
Stealing from the world away	Palmer	237
Strait is the way, the door is strait	Watts	73
Stretched on the cross, the Saviour dies	Mrs. St. le	53
Sun of my soul! thou Saviour dear	Keble	136
Sure the blest Comforter is nigh	Mrs. Steele	65
Sweet is the work, my God, my King	Watts	3
Sweet is the work	Lyte	11
Sweet land of rest! for thee I sigh		243
Sweet the moments, rich in blessing		104
Sweet was the time when first I felt	Newton	108
Take my heart, O Father, take it		104
Tarry with me, O my Saviour		238
Tell me not of earthly toys	Hastings	270
Thank and praise Jehovah's name	Montgomery	276
The bird, let loose in eastern skies	Moore	8
The day of wrath, that dreadful day	W. Scott	205
Thee we adore, eternal name	Watts	273
The floods, O Lord, lift up their voice	Burgess	65
The God of harvest praise	Montgomery	278
The heavens declare thy glory, Lord	Watts	32
The hour of my departure's come	Logan	245
The King of saints, how fair his face	Watts	56
The Lord, how fearful is his name		45
The Lord, how wondrous are his ways	Watts	39
The Lord is King, lift up thy voice	Conder	16
The Lord is my Shepherd, he makes me	Keen	147
The Lord is my Shepherd, no want	Montgomery	134
The Lord my pasture shall prepare	Addison	157
The Lord my Shepherd is		221
The Lord our God is full of might	H. K. White	42
The Lord our God is Lord of all	H. K. White	43
The Lord shall come, the earth shall quake	Heber	217
The Lord will happiness divine	Cowper	111
The mighty was formed to mount		100
The morning dawns upon the place	Montgomery	51
The morning light is breaking	S. F. Smith	207
The perfect world, by Adam trod		163
There is a fold whence none can stray	Ent.	219
There is a fountain filled with blood	Cowper	76
There is a God, all nature speaks	Mrs. L.	26
There is a glorious world of light	J. Taylor	249
There is a holy city		271
There is a house, not made with hands	Watts	249
There is a land immortal		241
There is a land of pure delight	Watts	247
There is a line by us unseen	Alexander	78
There is an eye that never sleeps		235
There is an hour of peaceful rest	Tappan	236
The Saviour bids thee watch and pray	Hastings	224
The Saviour! oh! what endless charms	Mrs. St. le	63
The Saviour! what a noble flame	Cowper	48
The Spirit in our hearts		82
The starry firmament on high	Great	33
The sun himself shall fade	Gethsher	120
The voice of free grace cries, Escape	Thornby	257
They who seek the throne of grace		257
Thine earthly Sabbaths, Lord, we love	Doddridge	2
Think gently of the erring one	Mrs. Fletcher	163
This child we dedicate to thee		136
This is the day the Lord hath made		4
This place is holy ground	Montgomery	236
Thou art gone to the grave, but we will	Heber	257
Thou art the Way; to thee alone	Doane	40
Thou from whom we never part		207
Though faint yet pursuing, we go on		135
Though now the nations sit beneath		238
Though the days are dark with trouble		224
Thou God of hope, to thee we bow		176
Thou Judge of quick and dead	C. Wesley	83
Thou, Lord, who rear'st the mountain's	Sterling	38
Thou lovely Source of true delight	Mrs. Steele	54
Thou Lord of all above	Beddome	160
Thou, O my Jesus, thou didst me	Neander	143
Thou only Sovereign of my heart	Mrs. Steele	107
Thou seest my feebleness	C. Wesley	90
Thou very-present aid	C. Wesley	174
Thou, whose almighty word		207
Through sorrow's night and danger's	H. K. White	249
Thy home is with the humble, Lord		161
Thy name, almighty Lord	Watts	21
Thy way, not mine, O Lord	Bonar	188
Thy way, O Lord, is in the sea	Fawcett	45
Thy will be done, I will not fear	J. Roscoe	183
Time is winging us away	J. Burton	270
'Tis by the faith of joys to come	Watts	160
'Tis finished!" on the Saviour cried	Stennett	53
'Tis midnight—and on Olive's brow	Tappan	53
To-day the Saviour calls		88
Together with these symbols, Lord		199
To God, the only wise	Watts	20
To our Redeemer's glorious name	Mrs. Steele	112
Tossed upon life's raging billow		277
To thee, my God and Saviour	Burgess	56
To thy pastures, fair and large	Merrick	124
Triumphant Zion! lift thy head	Doddridge	212
'Twas on that dark, that doleful night	Watts	204
Unto thine altar, Lord		98
Unvail thy bosom, faithful tomb	Watts	246
Upon the Gospel's sacred page	Bowring	33
Upward I lift mine eyes	Watts	12
Vain are the hopes, the sons of men	Watts	73

INDEX OF FIRST LINES.

First Line	Author	Page
Vain, delusive world, adieu	C. Wesley	122
Vainly through night's weary hours	Lyte	180
Wait, my soul, upon the Lord		119
Wait, O my soul, thy Maker's will	Beddome	58
Wake thee, O Zion, thy mourning is		214
Walk in the light—so shalt thou know	Barton	162
We are on our journey home	C. Beecher	219
We are out on the ocean sailing		224
Wearied with earthly toils and cares	Mrs. Gilbert	8
Weary, Lord, of struggling here		154
Weary sinner, keep thine eyes		85
We bid thee welcome in the name	Montgomery	192
We bless thee for thy peace, O God		172
We come, O Lord, before thy throne		274
Welcome, delightful morn	Hayward	12
Welcome, O Saviour, to my heart		97
Welcome, sweet day of rest	Watts	10
We pray thee, wounded Lamb of God		197
We're traveling home to heaven above		80
We've no abiding city here	Kelly	246
What are those soul-reviving strains		220
What cheering words are these	Kent	171
What equal honors shall we bring	Watts	15
What finite power with ceaseless toil	E. Scott	57
What grace, O Lord, and beauty shone		48
What shall I render to my God	Watts	18
What shall the dying sinner do	Watts	71
What sinners value I resign	Watts	246
What though no flowers the fig-tree clothe	Logan	164
What various hindrances we meet	Cowper	233
When adverse winds and waves arise	Sigourney	190
When all thy mercies, O my God	Addison	40
Whence do our mournful thoughts arise	Watts	128
When gathering clouds around	Sir R. Grant	190
When human hopes all wither		123
When I can read my title clear	Watts	129
When I survey the wondrous cross	Watts	52
When I view my Saviour bleeding		91
When Jesus dwelt in mortal clay	Gibbons	176
When languor and disease invade	Toplady	187
When like a stranger on our sphere	Montgomery	51
When morning's first and hallowed ray		41
When musing sorrow weeps the past	Noel	184
When, my Saviour, shall I be	C. Wesley	118
When on Sinai's top I see	Montgomery	102
When overwhelmed with grief	Watts	189
When, rising from the bed of death	Addison	79
When thou, my righteous Judge, shalt come		100
When waves of trouble round me swell		185
When we, our wearied limbs to rest	Tate—Brady	210
Where high the heavenly temple stands	Logan	232
Where, O my soul, oh, where	T. Scott	113
Where two or three, with sweet accord	Stennett	232
Where wilt thou put thy trust	Sigourney	167
While in sweet communion feeding		230
While life prolongs its precious light	Dwight	80
While my Redeemer's near	Mrs. Steele	152
While now upon this Sabbath eve		28
While o'er our guilty land, O Lord	Davies	273
While o'er the deep thy servants sail	G. Burgess	273
While shepherds watched their flocks by	Tate	46
While thee I seek, protecting	Miss H. M. Williams	40
While through this changing world we roam		269
While to thy table I repair	Davies	205
While with ceaseless course the sun	Newton	22
Who are these in bright array	Montgomery	265
Who shall the Lord's elect condemn	Watts	170
Why do we mourn departing friends	Watts	248
Why is my heart so far from thee	Watts	111
Why on the bending willows hung		210
Why should I fear the darkest hour	Newton	156
Why should our tears in sorrow flow		248
Why should the children of a King	Watts	67
Why should we start and fear to die	Watts	244
Why sinks my soul desponding	Hastings	191
Why will ye waste on trifling cares	Doddridge	80
With broken heart and contrite sigh		93
With deepest reverence at thy throne		36
With glory clad, with strength	Tate—Brady	15
With heavenly power, O Lord, defend		193
With joy we hail the sacred day	Lyte	6
With my substance I will honor	Francis	181
With tearful eyes I look around		92
With tears of anguish I lament	Stennett	108
Worthy the Lamb of boundless sway	Shirley	212
Would'st thou eternal life obtain	Palmer	140
Ye angels, who stand round the throne	De Fleury	148
Ye Christian heralds! go, proclaim		212
Ye servants of God, your Master	C. Wesley	24
Yes, the Redeemer rose	Doddridge	55
Ye trembling souls, dismiss your fears	Beddome	129
Ye valiant soldiers of the cross		222
Ye, who in these courts are found		202
Your harps, ye trembling saints	Toplady	130
Zion, dreary, and in anguish	Hastings	277

INDEX OF SUBJECTS.

[The figures refer to the numbers of the Hymns.]

ABBA FATHER, 541, 549.
Abiding, Christ with Believers, 429, 799.
Abrahamic Covenant, 615, 619.
Absence from God, 72, 344, 352, 387.
Accepted Time, 272, 285.
Access to God, 723—725, 746.
Activity, 394—427, 550—569.
Adoption, 530, 541, 543, 547, 549.
Advent of Christ ;—
  At Birth, 148—153.
  To Judgment, 770, 779, 790.
Advocate, Christ our, 65, 203, 537, 446.
Afflictions, 284, 570—599.
Almost Christian, 226.
Angels ;—
  Attendants of Christ, 151, 178, 193, 194.
  Ministering Spirits, 419, 421, 464, 714.
  Sympathy in Redemption, 447.
Anniversaries ;—
  Church, 70, 711—720, 836—838, 847, 848.

  National, 840, 843, 857.
  Sabbath School, 707, 709, 710.
Ascension of Christ, 177, 179, 191.
Ashamed of Christ, 401, 402, 432, 536, 631.
Asleep in Jesus, 758.
Assurance ;—
  Expressed, 402, 403, 415, 417, 547.
  Prayed for, 215, 358, 384, 385.
  Urged, 397, 398, 406, 407, 410.
Atonement ;—
  Necessary, 224—244, 478.
  Completed, 245—251, 478, 167—176, 292, 639—641.

  Sufficient, 245—293, 639—641, 796.
Autumn, 802, 858.

Backsliding, 341—390, 457, 460, 470, 471.
Baptism, 611—619.
Benevolence, 550—556, 567—569.
Bible, 33, 101—113.
Brotherly Love, 496, 513, 554, 568, 709—722.
Burial of the Dead—See *Death, Heaven*.
  A Brother, 789, 793, 797.
  A Child, 764, 775, 802.
  A Sister, 776, 801.
  A Pastor, 781, 793.
  A Friend, 765, 795, 842.

Calmness, 475, 505, 506, 519.
Calvary, 167, 328.
Care—See *Conflict with Sin*.
  Experienced, 383, 385, 598, 599.
  Cast on Jesus, 414, 426, 471, 475, 481, 485, 488, 493, 595.

Charity—See *Brotherly Love* and *Liberality*.
Cheerfulness, 130, 473, 480, 482, 502, 517, 526.

Children ;—
  Baptism, 611—619.
  Sabbath School, 691—709.
Child-like Spirit, 508, 512, 527, 529.
Christ ;—
  Adoration as God, 47, 177—203, 430, 441, 451, 456, 461, 482.

Advent, 193, 148—153.
Advocate, 65, 203, 537, 446.
Ascension, 177, 179, 191.
Captain of Salvation, 396, 397, 479.
Character, 154—166.
Corner-stone, 610.
Death, 167—176, 640, 647.
Desire of Nations, 689.
Divinity, 47, 184, 189, 202.
Example, 154—166, 484, 524, 525.
Friend of Sinners, 190, 305, 336, 446. See *Friend*.
Hiding Place, 365.
Immanuel, 245, 449, 437.
King, 81, 82, 185, 186, 188, 195.
Lamb of God, 47, 85, 183, 196, 384.
Life, incidents, 154—166, 454.
Lord our Righteousness, 61.
Love, 157, 169, 190, 199, 247, 292, 323, 340, 395, 426, 434, 440, 453.
Mediator, 65, 203, 292, 537, 446.
Priest, 163, 182, 186, 203.
Prince of Glory, 47, 109, 179.
Prince of Peace, 152, 375.
Prophet, 161, 187, 438.
Refuge, 365, 379, 425, 435, 488.
Resurrection, 177, 178, 192, 194.
Rock of Ages, 639.
Shepherd, 392, 412, 423, 457, 459, 460, 474, 480, 436.

Sufferings, 167—176, 620, 621.
Sun of Righteousness, 102, 128, 193, 429.
Way, Truth, and Life, 159.
Word, 150.
Christians, 341—599.
  Afflictions, 570—599.
  Conflicts, 340—390.
  Duties, 550—569.
  Encouragements, 391—427.
  Fellowship, 709—722.
  Graces, 493—529.
  Love for the Saviour, 428—492.
  Privileges, 530—549.
Church, 600—757.
  Afflicted, 664—666.
  Beloved of God, 681, 682, 721.
  Institutions of, 600—610.
  Ordinances of, 611—652.
  Progress and Missions, 653—690.
  Revival of, 373, 658, 659, 690.
  Sabbath School, 691—710.
  Social Meetings, 709—757.
  Triumphant, 670, 679—682.
  Unity of, 716, 720—722.
  Uniting with, 169, 331, 621, 623, 650, 652.
Close of Worship, 79, 87—100.
Comforter—See *Holy Spirit*.
Communion of Christians ;—
  With each other, 709—722.
  With Christ at the Lord's Supper, 620—652.
  With God in devotion, 436, 473, 491, 561, 723—746.

Communion of Saints, 716. See *Heaven*.
Completeness in Christ, 454, 499.
Confession—See *Repentance* and *Conflict with Sin*.

INDEX OF SUBJECTS.

Confidence, 480, 485, 493, 510, 520.
Conflict with Sin, 341—396, 469—471.
Conformity to Christ, 154—160, 162, 458, 524, 525.

Conscience, 215, 233, 478.
Consecration ;—
　Of Possessions, 169, 569.
　Of Self to God, 5s, 169, 174, 199, 296, 312, 620—623, 644.
Consistency, 458, 497, 524, 523.
Consolation—See *Afflictions*.
Constancy, 544, 547, 561.
Contentment, 475, 480, 500, 505, 575, 582.
Conversion—See *Repentance*.
Conviction of Sin, 324, 308, 314, 823. See *Repentance*.
Corner-stone ;—
　Laying of Sanctuary, 610.
Courage, 391—427, 479.
Covenant, 58, 291, 422, 425, 577.
Creation, 68, 71, 73, 86, 128, 142, 143.
Cross ;—
　Bearing, 158, 293, 370, 390, 556.
　Glorying in, 336, 33s, 3s9, 620, 626, 631, 644,
　Salvation by, 169, 174, 277, 298, 299, 302, 306, 311, 442, 621, 640, 644.
Crucifixion of Christ, 173—176.

Death, 758—803, 842. See *Burial*.
Decrees of God, 121, 124. See *Sovereignty*.
Dedication of Sanctuary, 13, 601, 607, 60s.
Dedication of Self to God—See *Consecration*.
Delay of Repentance, 258, 255, 265, 272, 275, 281, 282.

Dependence ;—
　On God's Providence, 128, 12s, 129, 130, 134, 140, 564, 830.
　On the Saviour's Grace, 204, 305, 519, 344, 365, 366, 384, 385, 431, 459, 639.

Depravity, 224—244.
Despondency—See *Conflict with Sin* and *Encouragements*.
Devotion, 436, 473, 491, 561, 723—746.
Diligence—See *Activity*.
Doubt—See *Conflict with Sin* and *Encouragements*.
Doxologies, 34, 44, 6s, 79, 620, 674; pages 356, 357.

Early Piety, 691—702, 802.
Earnestness—See *Activity*.
Election—See *Decrees* and *Sovereignty*.
Encouragements, 391—427.
Energy—See *Activity*.
Eternity, 7s2, 7s9, 834, 835,
Evening, 14, 27, 50, 94, 92, 100, 713, 736, 737, 744, 745.

Exaltation of Christ, 177—203.
Example ;—
　Of Christ, 154—166, 484, 524, 525, 551.
　Of Christians, 497, 52s, 56s.

Faint-heartedness, 354, 361, 381, 353—386, 893, 425.
Faith—See *Confidence* and *Trust*.
　Gift of God, 502, 514.
　Instrument in Justification, 235, 302, 478, 516.
　Power of, 494, 500, 516, 521.
　Prayer for, 14, 509, 514.
Faithfulness of God—See *God*.
Fall of Man, 236, 239. See *Lost State of Man*.
Family, 611, 615, 691—709, 717—719, 728, 734—739, 745—757.
Fasting, 841, 845, 854, 856. See *Repentance*.
Father, God our—See *God*.
Fearfulness—See *Conflict with Sin* and *Encouragements*.
Fellowship of Christians, 709—722, 528.

Fidelity, Christian, 311, 363, 458, 495, 497, 504, 509, 524.

Forbearance ;—
　Divine, 66, 120, 243, 259, 315, 323, 350, 452, 457.

　Christian, 154, 156, 158, 162, 507, 528.
Forgiveness ;—
　Of Sin, 55, 301, 317.
　See *Atonement*, and *Repentance*.
　Of Injury, 156, 15s, 162, 507, 528.
Formality, 25, 212, 232, 234, 254, 351, 358, 504.
Funeral—See *Burial*.
Friend, Christ our, 190, 321, 367, 389, 458, 473, 706—708.

Friends in heaven—See *Heaven*.
Future Punishment, 253, 260, 270, 275, 804.

Gentleness, 156, 568, 567.
Gethsemane, 157, 168, 170.
Glory of God, 40, 41, 43, 50, 75, 83, 102, 122, 128, 144.

Glorying in Cross—See *Cross*.
God ;—
　All in All, 72, 102, 115, 128, 128, 140.
　Attributes, 39—86, 114—147.
　Being, 40, 41, 102, 117, 137.
　Benevolence, 40, 52, 55, 57, 58, 62, 66, 122, 127, 131.

　Compassion, 66, 169, 251, 786.
　Condescension, 43, 62, 549.
　Eternity, 41, 44, 141.
　Faithfulness, 60, 71, 395, 402, 405, 411, 415, 422, 424.

　Father, 62, 80, 132, 136, 519, 541, 543, 547, 549, 706.
　Forbearance, 66, 120, 243, 259, 315, 323, 350, 452, 457.

　Goodness, 71. See *Benevolence of God*.
　Holiness, 34, 73, 145.
　Immensity, 115, 11s, 123.
　Incomprehensibleness, 124, 126, 147.
　Infinity, 115, 11s, 128.
　Jehovah, 46, 114, 115.
　Justice, 40, 43, 124, 224, 232, 236, 269.
　King of Kings, 50, 482.
　See *Majesty of God*.
　Love, 34, 52, 57, 62, 144, 572.
　Majesty, 43, 51, 75, 76, 83, 125, 136.
　Mercy, 64, 127, 146, 163, 260, 262, 289, 295, 327, 407.
　Omnipotence, 122, 134, 135, 142, 144.
　Omnipresence, 115, 123, 128, 140.
　Omniscience, 54, 119, 138.
　Patience—See *Forbearance of God*.
　Pity—See *Compassion of God*.
　Providence, 124, 126, 129—134, 137, 139.
　Saviour, 13, 20, 65, 189, 482.
　Shepherd—See *Christ, a Shepherd*.
　Sovereignty, 43, 121, 124, 137, 139, 147, 502, 627.
　Supremacy, 34, 41, 42, 51, 56, 75, 83, 126, 144.
　Trinity, 83, 114, 116.
　Truth, 33, 44, 60, 68, 77, 103, 124, 127.
　Unchangeableness, 42, 6s, 77, 127, 141.

　Wisdom, 40, 43, 122, 124, 139, 143.
Gospel—See *Atonement* and *Way of Salvation*.
Grace, 52, 157, 240, 250, 403, 526, 533, 54s, 796.

Graces, Christian, 494—529.
Gratitude, 5s, 66, 49s, 551, 852.
Grave, 765, 771, 773, 794, 842.
Grieving the Holy Spirit—See *Holy Spirit*.
Growth in Grace, 156, 15s, 160, 206, 210, 216, 218, 419, 454, 491, 497, 504, 525, 529, 549, 566.
Guidance, Divine, 98, 109, 210, 345, 354, 366, 384, 392, 412, 425, 45s, 489, 493, 500, 540.

Happiness, 72, 322, 414, 426, 440, 465, 466, 473, 502, 526.

Harvest, 413, 837, 852, 858.
Hearing the Word, 86, 88, 97, 112, 113.
Heart ;—
　Change of—See *Regeneration*.
　Deceitfulness of, 340, 348, 350, 356, 352.
　Searching of, 254, 26s, 345, 351, 35s.
　Surrender of, 311, 316, 335, 35s, 357.

INDEX OF SUBJECTS. 301

Heaven, 809—835.
  Christ there, 72, 761, 766, 783, 830.

  Friends there. 771, 789, 795, 800, 812, 815, 842.
  Home there, 747—757. 812—816, 819.
  Rest there, 754, 757. 788, 791, 793.
Hell, 253, 269, 270, 282, 826, 804.
Heirship with Christ, 215. See *Adoption*.
Hiding-place, Christ, 865.
Holiness;—
  Of Saints—See *Conformity to Christ* and *Purity*.
  Of God—See *God*.
Holy Scriptures—See *Bible*.
Holy Spirit; 204—223.
  Divine, 213, 219, 220, 223.
  Grieved, 209, 261, 280, 282, 285.
  Striving, 209, 261, 273, 285.
  Witnessing, 208, 215, 216, 221, 547.
Home—See *Family* and *Heaven*.
Hope;—
  Under Affliction—See *Afflictions*.
  Under Conviction, 228, 229, 235, 238, 240, 248, 252, 295, 359.
  Under Despondency, 393, 402, 409, 417, 421.

  In Death—See *Death*.
Humiliation—See *Fasting*.
Humility, 508, 512, 527, 529.

Immanuel—See *Christ*.
Immortality, 747, 766, 778, 783, 792, 794, 795.

Imputation, 61, 165, 169, 174, 302, 306, 478, 689.
Incarnation—See *Advent*.
Importunity, 725, 741, 742.
Infants—See *Baptism*, and *Death*.
Ingratitude, 248, 300, 315, 332, 348.
Inspiration, 104, 107, 111.
Installation, 600, 603, 604, 606.
Intercession—See *Christ a Priest*, and *Prayer*.
Introduction to Worship, 1—38.
Invitations, 252—298, 442, 640, 641, 796.

Jehovah—See *God*.
Jews, 666.
Joining the Church, 169, 331, 621, 623, 650, 652.
Joy, 473, 480, 482, 502, 517, 526.
Jubilee, 668, 685.
Judgment-Day, 820, 825, 826, 768—770, 804—808.

Justice—See *God*.
Justification—See *Atonement* and *Faith*.

Kindness—See *Brotherly Love*.
Kingdom of Christ;—
  Prayer for, 185, 195, 654, 660, 663, 668, 672, 673, 686.

  Progress of, 655, 657, 669, 678, 680, 685, 690.
Knowledge, 104, 106, 111, 206, 513.

Labor—See *Activity*.
Lamb of God—See *Christ*.
Law;—
  And Gospel, 163, 225, 232, 233, 235, 328.
  Conviction under, 225, 229, 233, 238, 239, 324.

Liberality, 551, 553, 555, 567, 569.
Life;—
  Brevity, 141, 253, 325, 766, 777, 782.
  Object, 260, 270, 295, 322, 326, 388, 458, 559.
  Solemnity, 259, 260, 270, 326, 400, 401, 419, 559.

  Uncertainty, 273, 325, 767, 786, 795.
Little Things, 495, 555, 558.
Likeness to Christ—See *Conformity*.
Longing;—
  For God, 7, 11, 72, 303, 341, 352, 353, 383, 468, 483, 491.

  For Christ, 103, 343, 353, 365, 371, 384, 416, 761.
  See *Love*.
  For Heaven, 747—757, 761, 779, 783, 792, 814, 821, 829.

Long-suffering—See *Forbearance*.

Looking to Jesus, 277, 342, 383, 384, 385, 426.
Lord's Day—See *Sabbath*.
Lord's Prayer, 724, 725.
Lord's Supper, 620—652.
Lord our Righteousness, 61.
Lost State of Man, 224—244.
Love;—
  Of God—See *God*.
  Of Christ—See *Christ*.
  For God, 72, 80, 311, 341, 491, 493, 541, 547, 549.

  For the Saviour, 428—492.
  For the Saints, 528, 709—722.
  For Souls, 211, 545, 552, 563, 568.
  For the Church, 313, 331, 665, 716, 721.
Loving-Kindness, 455.
Lukewarmness—See *Formality*.

Majesty of God—See *God*.
Man, Fallen—See *Lost State*.
Marriage, 846.
Martyr-faith, 893, 896, 401, 405, 425, 509, 520.
Mediator—See *Christ*.
Mediatorial Reign—See *Kingdom*.
Meditation, 104, 108, 110, 732, 787.
Meekness, 501, 527, 529. See *Humility*.
Mercifulness, 503, 507, 528, 555, 568.
Mercy—See *God*.
Mercy-seat, 726, 733, 739. See *Prayer*.
Millennium, 610, 654, 656, 668, 669, 673, 678, 680, 685.

Ministry—See *Pastor*.
  Commission, 600, 603, 604.
  Convocation, 605, 676.
  Installation, 603, 606.
  Prayer for, 600, 602, 605, 606.
Miracles, 166, 551.
Missions, 653—670.
Missionaries, 600, 606, 671, 677.
Morning, 18, 33, 861, 913. See *Sabbath*.
Mortality—See *Death* and *Life*.
Mystery of Providence, 40, 115, 124, 126, 139, 147.

National, 840, 843, 856, 857.
Nature, Light of, 102, 117.
Nature, the Material Universe;—
  Beauties of, 3, 123.
  God seen in, 40, 48, 49, 54, 102, 117, 122, 128, 133, 140, 142, 143, 146.
Nearness to God, 352, 468, 491. See *Longing*.
Nearness to Heaven, 783, 810, 815, 853.
Needful, One Thing, 227, 259.
New Song in Heaven, 31, 183, 447, 667, 824.
New Year, 70, 836, 838, 847.
Night—See *Evening*.

Old Age, 422, 458, 792, 799.
Omnipotence—See *God*.
Omnipresence—See *God*.
Omniscience—See *God*.
Opening of Service, 1—38.
Oppressed, 849, 859.
Ordinances—See *Church*.
Ordination—See *Ministry*.
Orphans, 553.

Pardon—See *Forgiveness*.
Parting, 93, 98, 709.
Pastor;—
  Prayed for, 600, 606.
  Sought, 602.
  Welcomed, 603.
  Death of—See *Burial*.
Patience, 121, 124, 199, 380, 508, 509, 528, 534, 561.
Peace;—
  Christian, 375, 380, 528, 538, 641.
  National, 686, 841, 843.
Peace-makers, 501, 528, 555, 719, 722.
Penitence. See *Repentance*.
Pentecost, 213, 219.
Perseverance, 65, 395, 397, 402, 403, 405, 408, 424, 531, 537, 542.
Pestilence, 845, 856.

INDEX OF SUBJECTS.

"Pilgrim Fathers," 840.
Pilgrim-Spirit, 341, 367, 391, 409, 458, 747—753.
Pity of God—See *God's Compassion.*
Pleasures of Worldliness, 259, 271, 304, 313, 331, 388.

Poor, 551, 553, 554, 555, 697.
Praise :—
  Calls to, 20, 29, 31, 37, 57, 68, 74—76.
  Singing, 29, 31, 391, 441.
  To Trinity, 59, 73, 83, 114, 116.
  To Father, 34, 114—147.
  To Son, 47, 82, 85, 177—203.
  To Holy Spirit, 86, 204, 222.
Prayer, 723—746.
Preaching—See *Ministry.*
Predestination—See *Decrees.*
Pride—See *Humility.*
Procrastination—See *Delay.*
Prodigal Son, 252, 255, 256, 279, 294, 457.
Profession of Religion—See *Joining the Church.*
Progress—See *Growth in Grace.*
Promises, 60, 422, 424.
Providence—See *God.*
Purity, 61, 225, 245, 385, 504, 549, 639.
Punishment of Wicked—See *Future Punishment.*

Race, Christian, 398, 400.
Rain, 49, 853.
Receiving Christ, 294—340.
Redemption—See *Atonement.*
Refuge—See *Christ.*
Regeneration :—
  Necessary, 224—244, 324.
  Prayed for, 311, 335, 345, 356, 358, 387.
  Wrought by God, 204, 218, 223, 230, 231, 234.
Renunciation of the World, 304, 313, 351, 353.
Repentance, 174, 176, 294—339.
Resignation, 511, 519, 534. See *Affliction.*
Rest, 270, 276, 313, 544, 754, 757, 798, 791, 793.
Resurrection :—
  Of Saints, 765, 766, 775, 778, 784.
  Of Christ—See *Christ.*
Retirement—See *Meditation,* and *Devotion.*
Return to God, 255, 256, 278, 279, 281.
Revival, 212, 216, 217, 219, 371, 373, 416, 418, 463, 650.

Riches, 169, 569.
Righteousness, 61. See *Imputation.*
Rock of Ages, 639.

Sabbath, 1—37, 69, 90, 92, 95.
Sabbath-School, 691—709.
Sacraments, 611—652.
Sailors, 839, 844, 855.
Salvation—See *Grace.*
Sanctification—See *Growth in Grace.*
Sanctuary :—
  Attendance upon—See *Sabbath,* and *Worship.*
  Dedication, Corner-stone, 15, 601, 607, 608, 610.
  Love for, 7, 12, 16, 19, 30, 35, 721.
Saviour—See *Christ,* and *God.*
Science and Revelation, 106. See *Knowledge.*
Scriptures—See *Bible.*
Seamen—See *Sailors.*
Seasons, 847, 852.
  Spring, 837.
  Summer, 858.
  Autumn, 802, 837, 858.
  Winter, 848.
Self-deception, 340, 348, 350, 356, 382.
Self-dedication—See *Consecration* and *Heart.*
Self-denial, 226, 247, 401, 495, 584.
Self-examination, 254, 268, 345, 351, 358.
Self-renunciation, 174, 176, 518.   See *Consecration*
  See *Consecration* and *Heart.*

Self-righteousness, 169, 228, 236, 302, 305, 518.
Sensibility—See *Weeping.*
Shepherd—See *Christ.*
Sickness, 66, 467, 458, 575, 587, 588, 599.

Sin :—
  Indwelling—See *Heart* and *Conflict.*
  Original—See *Lost State of Man.*
  Conviction—See *Repentance.*
Sincerity, 25, 254, 351, 358, 504.
Sinners :—
  Warned—See *Invitation.*
  Penitent—See *Repentance.*
Slavery, 849.
Soldier, Christian, 20, 393, 396, 397, 401, 557.
Songs of Zion, 29, 31, 32, 391, 441.
Soul of Man—See *Immortality* and *Happiness.*
Souls, Love for—See *Love* and *Weeping.*
Sovereignty—See *God.*
Spirit—See *Holy Spirit.*
Spring, 456, 837.
Star of Bethlehem, 148.
Steadfastness—See *Constancy.*
Storm, 48, 49, 56, 140.
Strength, As our Day, 380, 584, 597.
Submission—See *Resignation.*
Summer, 858.   See *Seasons.*
Sun of Righteousness—See *Christ.*
Sympathy—See *Brotherly Love.*

Temperance, 562, 568.
Temptation—See *Conflict with Sin.*
Thanksgiving, 847, 851, 852, 858.   See *Praise.*
Time—See *Life.*
To-day, 261, 269, 272, 280, 282, 285.
To-morrow, 278, 280.
Trials—See *Conflict,* and *Afflictions,* and *Care.*
Trinity—See *God.*
Trust :—
  In Christ, 252, 277, 302, 388, 402, 466, 475, 489.
  In Providence, 124, 126, 139, 405, 407, 410, 424, 480, 485, 493, 510, 523.

Unbelief—See *Faith,* and *Conflict.*
Union of Saints :—
  To Christ, 454, 458, 476, 489, 499, 539, 542, 547, 639, 715.
  To each other—See *Fellowship.*
  In Heaven and on Earth, 709, 714, 716.
Unity—See *Church.*

Vows, 59.   See *Consecration,* and *Joining the Church.*

Waiting—See *Patience.*
Wandering—See *Conflict with Sin,* and *Backsliding.*
War—See *Peace.*
Warfare, Christian—See *Soldier.*
Warnings—See *Invitations.*
Watchfulness, 271, 497, 557, 735.
Way of Salvation, 224—340.
Way, Truth, and Life, 150.
Wealth—See *Riches.*
Weeping for Souls, 241, 413, 515, 563.
Winter, 837, 848.
Wisdom—See *God.*
Witness—See *Holy Spirit.*
Word of God—See *Bible.*
Worship—See *Opening* and *Close.*
  Family—See *Family.*
  Social, 709—757.
Wrath of God—See *Hell* and *Future Punishment.*

Zeal—See *Activity.*
Zion—See *Church.*

www.ingramcontent.com/pod-product-compliance
Lightning Source LLC
Chambersburg PA
CBHW022059230426
43672CB00008B/1221